Anonymous

Missions and Martyrs in Madagascar

Anonymous

Missions and Martyrs in Madagascar

ISBN/EAN: 9783337316907

Printed in Europe, USA, Canada, Australia, Japan

Cover: Foto ©ninafisch / pixelio.de

More available books at **www.hansebooks.com**

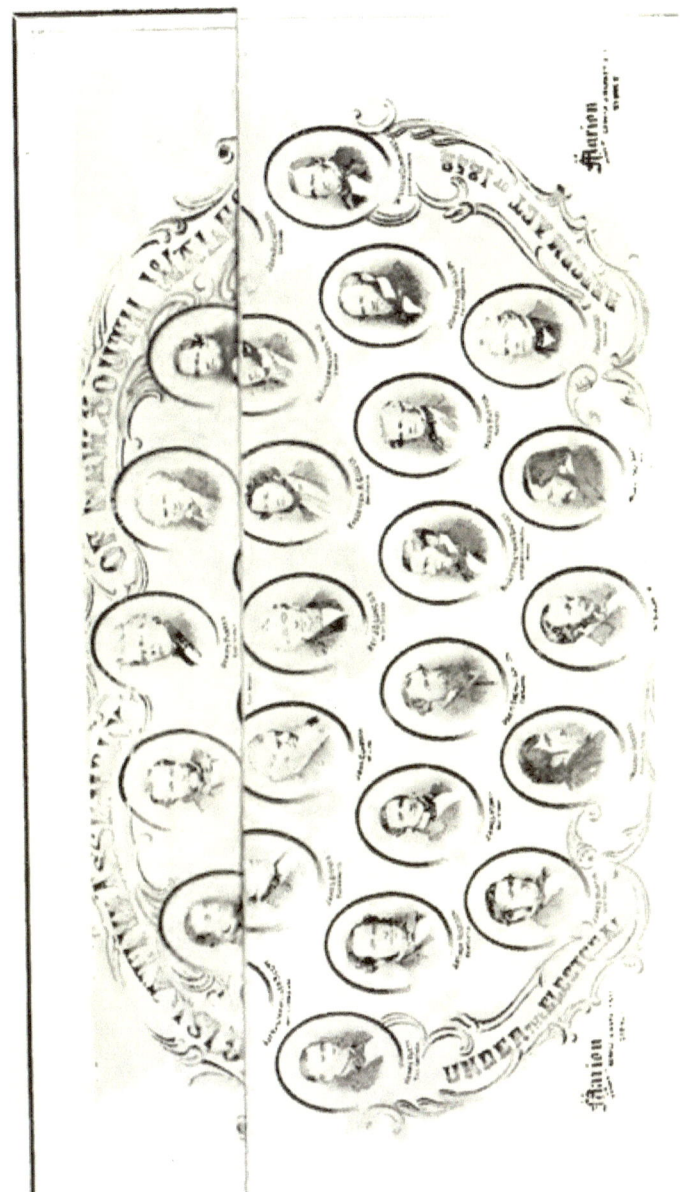

AUSTRALIAN PIONEERS AND REMINISCENCES

(ILLUSTRATED),

TOGETHER WITH PORTRAITS OF SOME OF THE

FOUNDERS OF AUSTRALIA.

BY THE LATE

NEHEMIAH BARTLEY.

EDITED BY J. J. KNIGHT.

PRICE TWELVE SHILLINGS AND SIXPENCE.

GORDON AND GOTCH,
PUBLISHING AGENTS
(For the Executrix and Children),
Brisbane.

PREFACE.

WERE it not for prescribed custom and the circumstances under which this volume has been published, "Australian Pioneers and Reminiscences" would probably have been ushered in without further introduction than that which its title page bears. These circumstances, while lending a melancholy interest to the book, appear to me to also make a preface necessary.

The work was started by Mr. Bartley with a laudable endeavour to add to the sparse Australian literature a few further facts concerning the pioneering period, and in fulfilment of a promise made, when he issued his earlier book, that at some future time he would record the reminiscences of forty years of that new and vivid life which came to Australia with the gold discovery. But man proposed; God disposed: and the hand which undertook this task was stilled by the levelling hand of Death, ere it could be completed.

Mr. Bartley himself requires no introduction. Added to his qualifications as a *litterateur*, he was a resident of the four colonies and possessed peculiar and remarkable advantages for the work in which he had embarked. Extensive travel enabled him to visit many scenes too far removed to permit of the ordinary eye viewing them.

On the very day on which Death overtook him with awful suddenness, he was engaged in furthering this publication. It was fortunate that he had collected his material; all that remained to be done was to arrange it. It was this duty which was allotted to me. This change has necessarily caused delay, but this notwithstanding, I feel confident that the old saw, "Better late than never" will be the verdict when subscribers shall have perused its pages.

It is, perhaps, necessary to emphasize the fact that, except in the matter of arrangement, and a few reminiscences contributed by friends and considered to be of such historical value to be worthy of inclusion, the work is wholly Mr. Bartley's. His style has been maintained, and only such photographs and pictures as were found among his papers and as were identifiable have been used.

It is to be hoped therefore, that, beyond the permanent value it may have, "Australian Pioneers and Reminiscences" will have the additional recommendation of personal interest.

As has been stated, works which enable us to look into the shadowy past—to realise the scenes and difficulties through which the pioneers of this great Continent lived and worked—and to learn the characteristics of Australian life generally, in its earlier stages, are not too plentiful ; and if this last effort of a patriotic and zealous colonist adds but one crumb to future's feast, any tardiness in its issue and any little shortcomings that may be detected ought to be easy of forgiveness.

J. J. KNIGHT.

Brisbane, 1896.

CONTENTS.

PAGE

CHAPTER I.—Half a Century Back—The First Australian "Inflation"—Men and Matters in Sydney—A Review—The Proud Forefathers of "Swell" Sydney—Old Camperdown—Memories of the Past—A Countrified Place—Sociability at Darling Point—Sunday Services at St. Mark's—The Interim Darkness Before the Dawn—"Caste" Superiority—Sydney's Quaint Suburbs ... ... 1 — 20

CHAPTER II.—New-born Luxury—Opening up "Way Back"—Pioneers on the Lower Murrumbidgee and Lachlan—Settlement on the Darling—Overlanding—Norbury, the Tracker—On the Murrumbidgee—A Martinet at Whist—Chess and Draughts—Navigation of the Murray—Phelps' of Canally—The Old Squatting Men—Captain Cadell—The "Lady Augusta"—Tyson Bros. on the Lachlan—A Risky Undertaking—Old Melbourne—Men and Matters—The Gold Era—New Melbourne .. .. 21 — 39

CHAPTER III—Early Settlers on the Clarence—Richard Craig's Discovery—Dr. Dobie's Days—Dr. Lang's Highland Immigrants—A Pathetic Incident—First Attempts at Sugar Making—Initial Difficulties—Crude Plants—The French Baron's Experiments—Scenes of Older Sydney—Memories of the Past—Sydney Banks and Banking—A Few Figures—The Crumbling of the Big Institutions—The Cobra and White Ant of Finance ... ... 40 — 66

CHAPTER IV.—The Curtain of Time drawn back—Early Men of Mark—Their Deeds of History—Major-General Macquarie—His Period of Governorship—William Forster—A Literary Legislator—A Marked Career—Edward Deas-Thomson—William Charles Wentworth—The Father of the Constitution ... 67 — 88

CONTENTS.

CHAPTER V. Early Men of Genius and Power—The List Continued—Sir Charles Cowper—The Anti-Transportation Battle—Sir Terence Aubrey Murray—The Struggle for Popular Rights—Sir James Martin—A Victim to Prejudice—A Pioneer of Protection—Captain Robert Johnston, R.N.—Hon. Robert Towns—Thomas Sutcliffe Mort—Earliest Meat Freezing Effort—"There shall be no more Waste!" 89–112

CHAPTER VI.—George Suttor—Early Sydney—Despotic Days—Suttor's Vain Appeal for Justice—Sir Francis Forbes—A Heavy Indictment—The Liberty of the Press Endangered—A Just Tribute—Sir John Robertson—Free Selection Before Survey—Sir John Hay—An Opponent to Sir John Robertson's Land Act 113–135

CHAPTER VII.—Early Men of Genius and Power—The List Continued—Dr. Lang—A Blow to Convictism—Dr. Lang as a Reformer—The Fight for Freedom—Dr. Richard L. Jenkins—The Education of the Masses—William Cox—The Track over the Blue Mountains—Hon Henry Dangar—Myall Creek—Hon. James White—Hon. David Jones—Alexander Berry—William H. Hovell—Hon. Henry Mort ... 136–165

CHAPTER VIII. The Youngest Colony—Early Days of Queensland—The Western Men—The First Squatters—The Leslies—The Condamine, McIntyre and Weir Rivers—The Incursions of the Blacks—A Western Notable—Paddy Macinnon—William Miles—The Dearth of Labour—Rough Times—An Early Election—A Risky Undertaking—Beck and Brown ... 166–187

CHAPTER IX.—North Queensland Legends and Myths—A Daring "Duffer"—The Gulf Country—A Run-Hunting Expedition—Breaking in a "Brombie"—A Terror to Drovers—An Abandoned Track—Back to the Early Forties—A Curious Mistake—Major Gorman—Patrick Leslie—D. C. McConnel—The First Squatter on the Brisbane—A Burnett Pioneer—"Blood for Blood" 188–208

CHAPTER X.—Early Queenslanders—The Surviving Few—Once More the Roll Call—Some of the Old Hands—John Petrie—George Thorne—Robert Little—Frederic Bigge—T. L. Murray-Prior—Sir Joshua P. Bell—Edwin Norris—James Warner—Robert Douglas—Simeon Lord—Captain Taylor Winship—James S. Mitchell 209–226

CHAPTER XI.—The Roll Call—Old Time Queenslanders—Additions to the List—Richard F. Phelan—Walter Scott—H. P. Fox—Richard S. Warry—George Harris—W. J. Munce—Thomas Lade—Robert Cribb—Henry Jordan—T. B. Stephens—A New Generation ... ... 227—239

CHAPTER XII.—The Capital of Queensland—Brisbane—Its Features and Characteristics—The First Survey—Sir George Gipps—Old Day Ocean Travelling—Amusing Incidents—McScotty's Triumph—Road Making Extraordinary—Philip D. Vigers—Jovial Evenings—Early Sugar Days—South Brisbane—Sea Sick Travellers—The Queensland Club—Its Founders—The Financial Crisis of '66—How it all Happened ... 240—261

CHAPTER XIII.—Life by the Sea Shore—Early Sandgate—My First Visit—What the Wild Waves were Saying—An Appreciable Soul—Good Company—Floods in the Brisbane—A Few Records—The Weather and the Seasons—Drought and Its Recurrence—Magnificent Queensland ... ... 262—277

CHAPTER XIV.—The Islands—At Tahiti—Eimeo—Papiete—A Mountain Climb—A Hearty Welcome—Ladrone Island Wonders—Among the Lonely Islets—Racatu—Hachin—Bora Bora—Gems of the South Pacific—The Marquesas—Female Types—The International Patrol—The Mountains of Raiatea—Fear Dispelled—Aripah's Farewell—A Story ... ... 278—302

STRAY PAPERS ... 303—418

INDEX ... ... 419—424

LIST OF ILLUSTRATIONS.

	PAGE
Portraits of the Members of the first Legislative Assembly of N.S. Wales under the Electoral Reform Act of 1858...	Frontispiece
Portraits of W. C. Wentworth, E. Deas-Thomson, Major-General L. Macquarie, Sir John Hay, Sir Charles Cowper	64
Portraits of Hon. Wm. Forster, Sir Francis Forbes, Sir James Martin, Sir John Robertson, Sir Terence A. Murray ...	96
Portraits of Thomas Sutcliffe Mort, Dr. John D. Lang, Capt. Robert Johnston, George Suttor, Dr. Richard L. Jenkins...	112
Portraits of Hon. David Jones, Hon. James White, Hon. John Fairfax, Hon. Henry Mort, Capt. O'Reilly	144
Portraits of Hon. Alex. Berry, J. Lansdale, W. H. Wiseman, N. V. Morrisset, W. H. Hovell	160
Portraits of T. B. Stephens, Hon. R. G. W. Herbert, Sir Maurice O'Connell, Samuel Brown, John Beck...	176
Portraits of Hon. Louis Hope, Judge Lutwyche, J. Turner, Colonel Sandeman, R. Little, Sir Joshua Peter Bell ...	192
Portraits of Robert Cribb, T. L. Murray-Prior, Colonel Gray, James Warner, John Petrie	208
Portraits of Hon. A. Macalister, Hon. John Douglas, Sir Charles Lilley, Hon. James Taylor, Sir A. Hodgson	224
Portraits of Christopher Rolleston, Sir A. H. Palmer, G. E. Dalrymple, Matthew Goggs, W. Bowman, Sir R. R. Mackenzie	240
Portraits of Capt. John Mackay, Dr. Dorsey, F. Bigge, T. de Lacy Moffat, Hon. R. Towns	256
Off the Islands ...	273
A Sheltered Bay	273
Women of Tahiti	288
Samoan Types	305
Interior of Chillagoe Cave, N. Queensland	320
On the Burdekin ...	336
A Bit of Old Brisbane...	352
A Queensland Squattage	368
The Glasshouse Mountains—Beerwah ...	384
„ „ Ngungun—Crook Neck—Tibbaroowoccum	400
A Marquesan Maiden ...	416

CHAPTER I.

Half-a-Century Back—The First Australian "Inflation"—Men and Matters in Sydney—A Review—The Proud Forefathers of "Swell" Sydney—Old Camperdown—Memories of the Past—A Countrified Place—Sociability at Darling Point—Sunday Services at St. Mark's—The Interim Darkness before the Dawn—"Caste" Superiority—Sydney's Quaint Suburbs.

AUSTRALIA was young in 1842. Even Sydney was juvenile; while, as for Port Phillip, New Zealand, and Moreton Bay, they were simply babies. It was the season of the first Australian "inflation," just before the first great Australian collapse. There have been many a "boom" and many a crisis since then, but '42 and '43 saw the first of the series. Let us take a glance at men and matters in Sydney at the date when London *Punch* and Charles Dickens were first coming into public notice, when the French were intriguing in Tahiti, and Pritchard was the much ill-used English consul there, when England and the United States had a "tiff" and the Prince of Wales was a baby in arms. No P. and O. steamers or Orient liners, then, in Port Jackson, but the gentle grandmothers of the pretty girls of the *haut ton*, who now "mash" the officers and male passengers on the street-like deck of the 7000-ton "boat," as they recline gracefully on the lounging chairs in the promenade bridge —endured all the martyrdom of seasickness (with the costumes and coquetry left out) on board the little Emma, the fashionable brig, of some 200 tons, which then traded to Adelaide and Hobart, under the command first of Captain Sproule and afterwards of Captain R. F. Pockley; and the "Waterlily" (in after days well known in the 'Frisco trade of '49 and '50) sailed, to the Derwent only, from Sydney. Moreton Bay was accommodated with the iron steamship "Shamrock," with her "powerful" (80-horse) engines ("powerful," that is, by the side of the old "Billy the Fourth" of Wollongong fame), and sent as a favour to Brisbane by the Hunter River Company, then under the management of Francis Clarke. The schooner "Edward," Captain Chambers, used, in 1842, to do her famous "ninety-hour" trips to the bar of the Brisbane River from Sydney.

The only ports in New Zealand which were, fifty years ago, favoured with the Sydney trade were Port Nicholson, Auckland, and the Bay of Islands, and for those places the schooner "Catherine," the brig "William Fulcher," and the barques "Amwell" and "Achilles" were regularly sent by Isaac Simmons, Ranulph Dacre, J. B. Metcalfe, or William Tucker. Sometimes the route included the Bay of Islands and Tahiti only; and sometimes Valparaiso was also included in the trip. The "Julia" and the "Jane Geordie," from R. Jones's wharf, were in the trade too. There must have been much settlement going on then in New Zealand, for the traders to that place were of the same tonnage as the London wool ships of 1842. Sydney used but little sugar then, and the "Charlotte," brig, of a modest 96 tons burden, was the Mauritius trader.

The Rev. Ralph Mansfield was then, and for many a long year afterwards, secretary to the Gas Company. The Rev. Robert Allwood used to lecture for Church of England purposes; and the legal firm which, in 1852, was Thurlow, Dick, and Brown was, ten years earlier, Chambers and

Thurlow. Wright's (the pioneer) brewery was running in opposition to Newnham and Tooth's before Robert and Edwin Tooth came from England in 1843 to assume command of affairs. Eldridge kept a chemist's shop in King-street; but was this the Ambrose Eldridge, of Brisbane, in after years? Binnie, the saddler, was then in Parramatta. T. and M. Woolley, of George-street and the Glebe, sold sheep-shears and chaff-cutters, while the fashionable drapers were Pite and Preston, Joseph Thompson, sen., David Jones, and Robert Bourne (father-in-law of George Raff, of Brisbane, and the erstwhile missionary for the Congregational Union to Raiatea and the Society Group in 1822). Most of them were in Pitt-street, where Sydney drapers and carpet men still do mostly congregate. In 1842 R. Campbell, jun., and Co. were general merchants in Bligh-street, Sydney; for R. Campbell, sen., was of the 1795 era in that town; they sold tea, rice, pickles, spirits, iron, and hemp goods. John Sands was a stationer in George-street; R. and T. Coveny sold V.D. land produce; MacHattie was then (even as ten years later) a very prominent name and household word in Bathurst; and J. T. Armitage and Co. bought wool at the salt-water end of King-street. Richard Rogers was the imperial ordnance storekeeper for New South Wales, and the Australian Club (in want of repairs and alterations even then) was situate in Bent-street even as it was fifty years later. The "boom" had not in 1842 ended in a crisis, for £30 a year was offered for a good female cook at "Linthorpe," Newtown, despite a plentiful supply of the convict article in the market. The Sydney and Calcutta firm, which was afterwards Thacker, Daniell, and Co., Thacker, Spink and Co., was, in 1842, Thacker, Mason, and Co. James Pye lived at Parramatta, and the firm of Cooper and Holt flourished. Old Walter Gray, of Ipswich, Moreton Bay, in 1854, was, in 1842, an accountant in George-street, opposite the Commercial Bank. The steamer "Maitland" traded to Port Macquarie, and, amongst other passengers, carried, in 1842, Mr. Tozer, an ancestor of the Queensland Colonial Secretary of fifty years later. Her cargo was maize and salt beef in tierces.

The Legislative Council of the period consisted of the Governor, Sir George Gipps, the Bishop, the Senior Military Officer, the Colonial Secretary, Attorney-General, Collector of Customs, Auditor-General, Mr. Campbell, Mr. Berry, Mr. R. Jones, Mr. Blaxland, Mr. Hannibal Macarthur, and Sir John Jamison, and they voted away the colony's money in this fashion:—The Governor, £5,000; private secretary, £300; aide-de-camp, 9s. 6d. per day and forage; Clerk of the Executive and Legislative Councils, £600; Colonial Secretary, £1500 a year, and his chief clerk £500; Colonial Treasurer, £1000; Auditor-General, £650; Collector of Customs, £1000; the rent of the Custom-house was £250; first-class clerks got £400, second-class £240 to £300; occasional clerks 6s. per day to make out deeds of grant, &c.; Postmaster-General, £650; Landing Surveyor, £400; Colonial Storekeeper, £200; Government Printer, £300; the museum got £200 a year; lighthouse-keeper, South Head, £80 per annum and £13 13s. for rations; five "prisoner" assistants got clothed and fed for 1s. a day each—£91 5s. a year for the lot; while the lighthouse horse and his shoes cost £60 a year!

The Law Courts sat as usual in Sydney in 1842, and Mr. Broadhurst pleaded before "the Chief" when Burdekin sued Lyons or Barker. Amongst the barristers in court were Darvall, Windeyer, Foster, and Fisher. The Mort and Co., the Richardson and Wrench, the L. E Threlkeld, the W. Dean and Co., the Purkiss and Lambert, the Frith and Payten of 1860 "were not" in 1842, but their places were anticipated by Foss. Was it he who bought the

chemist's business from Tawell, the Quaker murderer?
Foss and Lloyd used to sell wine, cheese, flannel, and pork
by auction, while Moore and Heydon were more in the
pastoral line. Stubbs, the elder, was the George Robins of
the earlier Sydney land booms; while Cornelius Prout (the
under sheriff in 1842, and many a year after that) did,
officially, a larger general auction business perhaps than any
of them. Samuel Hebblewhite was the importer of American
goods, ash oars, and rocking chairs in 1842 even as in 1860.
Thomas Agars (afterwards Agars and Stabler) was a stock
and station agent, and the Sydney Sugar Company had
their works at Canterbury under W. Knox Child, the
manager. Moffitt (the millionaire) had his modest book-
shop in Pitt-street then. Isaac Simmons and Sam Lyons
were also leading auctioneers in 1842, while Mr. Blackman
occupied the place in the real estate market which Richardson and Wrench now do. "Cap-a-Pie," the sire of so many
Australian racehorses, had just been advertised by Mr.
Scott, of Glendon, on the Hunter, imported two years before
by Mr. Kater, bred by Mr. Poyntz in 1837, and sired by
The Colonel out of sister to Cactus. Mr. Byrnes, the
auctioneer, of Parramatta, advertised the estate of Major
Wentworth at Toongabbee—fifty eligible lots of 30 acres
each, suitable for nurserymen, and away from the "noise
and bustle" of Sydney, in 1842.

At this very same time Sir Robert Peel was moving in
the Imperial Parliament for his "sliding scale" on imported
wheat, the duty to be 20s., when the market price was 50s.
per quarter and gradually decreasing to zero, when the
price (from scarcity) rose to 74s. The baronet's argument
was, that a great country like England should be self-
supporting in wheat and should not encourage foreign grain
unless from dire necessity. His speech was closely criticised
by Lord John Russell and Richard Cobden, the latter of

whom remarked, of Peel, that it was hopeless to expect "grapes from thorns or figs from thistles," and who converted Sir Robert, three years later, to his freetrade views.

People who nowadays are "squeamish" over the well-fed, well-treated kanaka labourer on Queensland plantations should have read Abram Polack's or Sam Lyons's advertisements of farms for sale fifty years ago near Sydney, where it was announced that so many convicts would remain on, and go with, the property to the new purchaser. It sounds a bit chattel and slave-like to our modern ears. Men, transported for murdering their wives, acted as nursemaids *(pour faute de mieux)* to tender little girls in arms, and were kinder than the female convict would have been. The Botany property of the then deceased Simeon Lord was up for sale in 1842. Imported wine was auctioned in pipes, and the bottled beer was by Dunbar, Byass, and Marzetti, for Foster and Guinness had not travelled to Australia then. The girls danced in Sydney fifty years ago, and wore "kid operas" and mock pearl coronets; and at an auction room next the (old) Bank of New South Wales eleven boxes of artificial flowers and wreaths were passed to the highest bidder on the 10th August, 1842.

Enterprise and settlement were setting in strongly then to New Zealand, and the Raphaels and the Nathans and the Barnetts helped to swell the passenger lists from Port Jackson to Port Nicholson. The larger ships which came out to Sydney in those days were unable to fill up with wool out of the season, and being too big even for the summer shipments were accustomed to go by the Barrier Reef and the Raines Island Passage to Java, there to load with rice, &c., for London. A ship of 700 or 800 tons could "make a big hole" in the entire wool clip of Sydney in 1840, or of Melbourne in 1850.

But the sheep have increased since then and (more's the

pity) so also have the rabbits. The curator of the Botanic
Gardens, Sydney, got £140 salary fifty years ago his
overseer 3s. per day, and thirty convicts, who did the work,
were all fed and clothed for £430 per annum. The harbour
master got £300 a year, and most of his subordinates were
convicts, rationed and clothed and foraged at the stereotyped
1s. a day each, and allowed 2d. a day extra in lieu of tea,
sugar, and tobacco for the thirty-two men on the staff. The
floating light at the "Sow and Pigs" was "run" by a
superintendent and four sailors at £191 12s. 6d. a year
for the lot (rations, fuel, and light extra), while oil for the
light alone absorbed £220 a year. Harbour-masters and
pilots were run cheaply then; the "screw" at Newcastle
was £100, with £40 allowed yearly for coals for the
"beacon"; Port Macquarie, £75; while at Wollongong
and Brisbane Water they were paid 5s. a day each.

Kemp and Fairfax published and owned the *Sydney
Morning Herald* then, and got 6d. a copy for their paper,
and I can, in my mind's eye, still see old Charles Kemp and
his wife in their carriage, but with no children, bowed to
and saluted as they drove about South-west Sydney; he,
short, stout, and with a peculiarity in one eye. They rest
now in the old Camperdown cemetery, where it looks out
on the distant Parramatta hills, and where also repose the
Macleays, the Dumaresqs, the O'Connells, and others of the
"upper ten" of bygone Sydney, a list far too numerous
here to catalogue, beyond making the remark that Camperdown shares, with St. Jude's at Randwick, the honour of
being the spot where

> The proud forefathers of "swell" Sydney sleep.

Let us stroll through this once favourite burying-place of
the old folk of Sydney; where lie some of Sydney's greatest.
A solitude in the heart of business, it is situated but a short

distance from the Newtown railway station, and a few minutes' walk down a lane-like street brings us to St. Stephen's Church, which though of a later date than the cemetery itself stands within its precincts. Unlatch the wicket gate and enter the field of graves. It is thickly sown. Flat stones and nameless mounds lie huddled with scarce a semblance of sectional order among the rank-growing grass. High and lowly lie side by side: for Death is the great leveller of all. Headstones, crosses, urns, uncouth attempts at sculptured figures, mossy blocks, hideous and shapeless; monuments of lighter and more elegant design and of every conceivable fashion crowd round on all sides. Noteworthy many of them—what memories they do recall!

Near the entrance a large white slab, rail-protected and carefully preserved, covers the remains of Sir Thomas Livingstone Mitchell, surveyor and explorer. Dying at Carthona, Darling Point, 4th October, 1855, he was buried here, with military honours, on the 9th. A stirring and a changeful life was his! The tumult of Badajos and Ciudad Rodrigo gave place to the stillness of Australian forests, and the abilities that had been employed in furthering the art of war, were diverted to the nobler work of assisting to open up the great south continent to settlement and civilisation. Higher up is the tomb of Sir Maurice Charles O'Connell, who, if his services to the country were less distinguished than those of Mitchell, was still a prominent personage in early colonial society. Known as an officer signalised in his profession, O'Connell arrived in Sydney with Macquarie in December, 1809, as Colonel of the 73rd, and Lieutenant Governor of the Territory, and in May following married Mrs. Putland, the widowed daughter of ex-Governor Bligh, and somewhat famous in connection with the episode of his arrest. Accompanying the 73rd, in 1814, to Ceylon, O'Connell returned to the colony in 1838, and was appointed Commander of

the Forces in New South Wales, a post he occupied until
1847. Military display on a small scale was a feature of
old Sydney, and women entering into years now, are fond
of recalling the school girl delight they took in watching the
martial figure of Sir Maurice at the reviews so frequently
held in the Domain. Relieved by General Wynyard, he
was preparing to return to England, when he died in May,
1848, at his house in Darlinghurst, on the day that had
been fixed for his sailing by the "Medway." He had taken
little part in politics, but the concern of the public for his
death showed how deep the sense of his private worth was
rooted in the heart of the community. His body, interred
elsewhere in 1848, was afterwards removed hither. The
inscription on the stone—cruciform, resting on a low plat-
form—is short and simple.

Cî GîT.
Lieutenant-General Sir Maurice O'Connell, H.M. 80th Regiment
of Foot, K.C.H.
Died May 25th, 1848.

No recording of his battles, no lauding of his virtues—only
underneath the words,

Until The Day Break And The
Shadows Flee Away.

So the old soldier rests. Hard by, "Two Sorrowing
Friends" commemorate Lieut.-Colonel Charles Lewis, also
of Her Majesty's 80th Regiment. From the Peninsula to
Sobraon he had "served his country gallantly and faithfully
for 40 years." Below O'Connell's monument is one to Sir
James Everard Howe, "captain of the "Calliope," and senior
officer of the Australian Squadron." (Died 1855, aged 55).
Beside it is a grave covered with an overgrowth of slovenly
herbage, through which a pale rose feebly struggles. The
stone is carved at top with anchor, trident, and other

nautical emblems, and, holding back the long coarse grass that has spread across the face, we read that William Ward Harvey, R.N., of the ship "Torch," and son of an English clergyman, was drowned off Sydney by the upsetting of the Torch's cutter on the 24th December, 1853, "aged nearly 20 years," "universally beloved," and "an officer of great promise." We know nothing of his friends save what the tombstone tells, yet one sadly thinks how loving thoughts of the absent lad may have gone out that Christmas season from the distant vicarage home, and no premonition of the calamity that had befallen have clouded its Christmas cheer. Not far off sleeps another sailor, Thomas Raine, captain of the "Surry," a merchant vessel of old colonial days. It was from the Surry's deck that Macquarie, in 1822, made his last farewells to the enthusiastic colonists who thronged to bid him God speed on his voyage. An ivy-wreathed stone cross is inscribed to Edward Broadhurst, father of the Bar of New South Wales; and there is a cenotaph to Dr. Woolley, who perished in the "London." Mrs. Broughton, wife of the first Australian Bishop, dying on Sunday, the 16th September, 1849, was carried to her burial here, four days later, amidst sincere and general mourning. Her death came with the shock of a painful surprise. While the serious nature of her own illness had been unsuspected, her husband was lying at the point of death; and when the muffled bells tolled on the night of the 16th from the steeple of St. James', no doubt of the event was felt, and men meeting each other in the morning spoke of the dead bishop, little dreaming that it was his devoted wife who had passed away. The bishop himself recovered for the time, and returned to England, where he subsequently died. The visitor may chance to stumble over a stone raised over two children of Sir William Denison, 11th Governor of New South Wales, and here, indeed, did time avail for the research, would be found the names of many intimately associated with the affairs and progress of the colony.

Funeral offerings testify to the remembrance of the living. A moment, parenthetically, we pause. It is strange, this decking of the tombs; and surely no age so "antithetically mixed" as ours is nothing more so than the tendency to break the fetters of old customs, and to forge new ones in their stead. We cast off "the scenes and the trappings of war" to replace them by the adjuncts of bridal festivity. Certain aspects of the innovation we can understand. "When I die," said Dickens' Little Nell, "put near me something that has loved the light and had the sky above it always." And so they laid green leaves and winter berries by her. We do not cavil at the garlanded barge of poor Elaine; and the poetess whose dreams had been of dying young, that she might lie strewn over "with rosemary and rue," was probably not singular in her sentimental fancy; but the prevailing practice of indiscriminately showering flowers upon the dead, strikes us at times with a curious sense of incongruity. Each to his liking.

Touch the topic gently, I fancy I hear somebody whisper. So I will; but methinks nothing can so become a bier as the "white flower of a blameless life." The signs of taste and care are but as specks in the surrounding waste. Note the carpet of tangled grass catching the feet as in a snare, which o'erspreads the ground and half conceals the spots where we would reverently forbear to tread; the yawning earth holes; the displaced and broken stones, the defaced inscriptions, the tall shrub we thrust aside to find perhaps an epitaph engraven to "a modest wife and tender mother;" the trees, planted at first in token of regard, which in numerous instances have reached to such a size as almost to destroy the grave, a glimpse of mouldering stone, corroding iron, or rotting paling discernible through the mass of foliage, alone declaring it is there. Verily the axe of the woodman, as well as the chisel of "Old Mortality" would be needed for the work of restoration here. Should this work of restoration be begun? "Does it really matter very much?" I hear somebody ask, "Why solicitous for that which is but dust?" Ah! apart from the belief in which the term "God's acre" has its root, care for that dust has been in all ages an inherent instinct in the race, and developed more or less according to the degree of civilisation attained. Close the wicket, leave the ruined tombs behind, pass again into the busy street, and, "letting the dead bury the dead," glance once more into the page of the living.

And what was doing in the world in 1832? Let's see. William IV. was king, and had for his queen the prim, pretty, small-featured Adelaide, who was only 27 years younger than her husband. Earl Grey was Premier, and Lord Brougham the High Chancellor, and Melbourne and Palmerston ruled the Home and Foreign Departments, while Sir James Pike was First Lord of the Admiralty. Judge Tindel presided at the Court of Pleas, and Lyndhurst at the Exchequer Court. And I may be excused for mentioning there was still reigning in 1832 the Emperor of Austria, born in 1768, who conjointly had been mixed up with the awful Napoleon Bonaparte business at the end of last and the beginning of this century. President Jackson held office in America. And now I pass me on to Sydney and New South Wales generally.

Sydney was a countrified sort of place in 1832, and you would have missed 75 per cent. of the present edifices then. No Union Bank, no Australasian; no bishop or cathedral; only the Bank of New South Wales and the Bank of Australia, the former far down the street and nearer to Davis's edifice than it now is. Two of the most prominent men of Sydney in 1832 were Richard Jones and James

Laidley, men of sound standing, well liked, and given to hospitality, and whose sons prospered, and their daughters married well. One of Mr. Jones' daughters married Robert R. Mackenzie, Bart, one time a squatter in New England, afterwards Colonial Treasurer of Queensland. Another married Captain Bligh O'Connell, son of Sir Maurice of that ilk, and afterwards of Mondure, Queensland. William Laidley's daughters married respectively, Thomas Mort, Henry Mort, John Sutherland Mitchell, and Judge Dowling. Richard Jones, in the early thirties, filled the offices of Chairman of the Bank of New South Wales, Chairman of the Sydney Chamber of Commerce, and Chairman of the only marine insurance company then in Australia. He was the inevitable president of all Sydney commercial institutions in King William's time. He afterwards became member for Moreton Bay *(alias* all Queensland), in the Sydney Parliament. At his garden on New Farm, near Brisbane, was raised the first stalk of sugar cane grown in Australia.

There was no Petty's Hotel, no Kent's Brewery, in Sydney in 1832. They came later on in 1834. St. John's Church was a dozen years old in King-street, and St. Phillip's had stood still longer on a spur of Flagstaff Hill. The Rev. R. Bourne still continued to preach to the natives of far-off Raiatea, in the Society Group, and had not come to cast his lot in Sydney, but the Rev. Ralph Mansfield run the official Sydney newspaper (the *Gazette*), tri-weekly, first born in 1803. The Sydney *Herald* was founded in 1832, a weekly paper, then under the auspices of Stephens and Stokes, and it was not a daily "morning" *Herald* till long after that. The *Australian* (weekly) started in 1824, and the *Monitor*, a bi-weekly, dating from 1826, were the only other Sydney journals in 1832.

Ah! who shall tell of the old ghosts and old interests,

old tales and histories of the lives and fates of Australian people from 1832 to 1852, locked up in those worn out and hoary old Sydney bank ledgers, nearly every page being the nucleus of a vivid three-volume novel if the whole surroundings were but tracked and delineated. Dost think there are no ghosts in Sydney? Beware it is not London. Has there been no time since 1788 for wrong to be done, for hearts to be broken, for mortgages to be foreclosed, fortunes to be made? Ruin here? Good luck there? Happiness and joy? Misery and despair? All told of indirectly in the ledger columns. Scrooge and Marley have lived in Sydney as well as in London.

The Domain changeth not, nor doth Macquarie's Chair. The odour of the gums and the sea, the pines and the fig tree is wafted across just as free, the same as it was in 1852 and 1832, when the demons now dead were alive and breathed it gladly and freely as we now do. For Sydney then, as now, was a place where there was a sense of "company" and companionship; the one spot in the lone South hemisphere where all was not wilderness, solitude, and the desolation of isolation.

There is a grand old fig tree in front of the Public Instruction Office in Sydney: and thereby hangs a tale. It was once officially proposed to cut that tree down and build public offices on its site. Plans and specifications were prepared and approved. The axes were sharpened to cut the tree down—by the way the grinding of axes is a great Australian institution, is it not?—everything was ready except one thing in the programme, namely, the projectors had omitted to take into their confidence a certain old gentleman (M. J. were his initials), who was a great friend of Sir John Robertson. Coming upon the scene unexpectedly he spoke as follows:—"Cut that blankety-blank tree down! I'll kill the man that lays a finger on it. Many a happy day I've spent under it," &c., &c. And it came to pass that the old tree stands and spreads to this day.

Good old early Sydney! What a place it was! There was always a halo of Captain Cook about it the same as at Tahiti, both of the classic and the poet. And how curious it was when the delegated authority of the far off King of England or Elector of Hanover met you at every turn; the lion and unicorn here; the lion and unicorn there; blue coat, cocked hat, epaulets—all strange and incongruous amongst the blacks and the gum trees of the great kangaroo land, to say nothing of the branded curiosity.

The old uniformed men of 1830 and their stout-waisted daughters of the same era have passed away from Sydney, and sleep peacefully now. And the little ball-room jealousies and questions of colonial procedure and official etiquette have all gone to rest as quietly as the folks who raised them.

It is difficult for us now to realise the Sydney of 1838 with the ladies all dressed as to hair and contour like Malibran, and before Tom Mort's beautiful garden was laid out at "Mrs. Darling's Point," when Captain Lamb stood proxy for the navy, and Laidley, dead only three years before, had represented the commissariat branch of the Imperial service; when R. R. Mackenzie and Stuart Donaldson were firm friends before the former's marriage with the daughter of Richard Jones caused him to espouse the latter's cause in the difference that afterwards arose with Stuart Donaldson. Who does not remember the neighbourly feeling that existed amongst the old residents of Darling Point? And Darling Point, be it understood by those who have never seen it, is not very greatly dissimilar to a little bit of the villa woodland of Jersey and Guernsey transported to the other hemisphere, due allowance being made for the difference of latitude and climate.

One proof of this neighbourly feeling was seen every Sunday after service at St. Mark's Church. Mr. T. S. Mort had his garden and grounds to the east of this church, and Mr. Thomas Ware Smart to the west of it, and each of them threw open his place as a thoroughfare and short cut to all those attending the service, so as to enable them to reach home without a long and roundabout walk by the public road. Mr. Smart was a wealthy miller, and one of whom Mr. Mort once said to me, "It's nice to have him on a board of directors with you, as he always took such common sense short cuts through any difficulty that arose."

What memories does a recollection of those who formed the congregation of St. Mark's at this date revive? There were Whistler Smiths of "Glenrock," the McCarthys of "Deepdene," the Skinners, Rotherys, S. H. Smythes, Robert Tooth of "Brooksby" or "Ecclesbourne," Croft of "Mt. Adelaide," Edye and William Manning, and Edwin Tooth of "Waratah."

Neither "Cranbrook" nor the mansions of Dalley and Holdsworth, near the lighthouse, were yet built. But "Potts's Point" was well "settled." There was "Tusculum," where Mr. Young, the wine merchant lived; the fine mansion of old Thomas Barker, the miller. The oldest residents of the "Point," perhaps, were the Macleays, who had for neighbours John Gilchrist and Challis (Flower, Salting, & Co.) Neither McQuade's house on the shores of Woolloomooloo Bay, nor J. D. McLean's "Quiraing" on the Edgecliffe-road had been brought into existence; but Mr. Henry Prince occupied a splendid house that looked on E. Tooth's "Waratah." I remember E. Tooth with Captain George Harrison, R.N. (a surveying shipmate of Captain Wickham, and afterwards of Castlemaine and Melbourne), and myself resolved, one Sunday, to walk to the lighthouse and back before dinner for an appetite. The Captain was

50, and 1 20, and as he put it he felt proud of a 10-mile spin with me.

And talking of dinners on Sundays reminds me that on one Sunday in 1853, at Edwin Tooth's, there were present his three brothers—Robert, Frederick, and Charles—when we were startled by the news that the Kent Brewery was ablaze. Off we all went post haste; found Donald Larnach and plenty of people there at rescue work. Malt and hops burned freely; and the rebuilding of the stone work, originally put up in 1834, was costly in 1853; with mason's wages verging on £1 a day, "all along of" the gold time. Such sympathy and assistance were shown by the neighbours that it became imperative to publicly advertise the firm's thanks therefor; and herein I made a proposal, namely, that each of the brothers and myself should write out a notice—expressive of gratitude—for publication; also that the form should be duly submitted to a committee of ladies (their wives), and the most aptly worded one of the four should be accepted. The ladies unanimously pronounced for mine, and it duly appeared; but it must be remembered that *I* had nothing at stake and wrote much more deliberately than they could be expected to in their flurry.

Business *was* brisk then. I remember that Robert Tooth, finding that the scarcity of copper change in Sydney seriously affected the consumption of the ale in the expansion of trade that took place between '51 and '53, offered £10,000 for £5,000 worth of copper if landed in Sydney by a certain date.

The convict system was at its full height in 1838. Never were class and caste distinctions more strongly drawn. A post-captain in the Royal Navy was as high and far removed above a "broad-arrow" prisoner as a Brahmin above a pariah or the King of England above the hangman. It was the interim darkness before the dawn.

It was absurd to note in the early convict days of Australia the airs assumed by some ladies related to the humbler grades of the army and navy officers: and the daughter of a half-pay lieutenant or petty officer in either branch scantily educated herself, in many cases, would be so inflated with pride at her "caste" superiority over the actual convicts and their people, as to deem any lady, even of the highest and free mercantile class, below her; also, there were tremendous attempts made in those early days to make the antipodean "aristocracy" consist entirely of the families of government officials of all grades, deeming, no doubt, that a government commission or post was the sole and only guarantee or diploma of absolute solvency on the one hand, and freedom from convict taint on the other. If Sir Francis Burdett had only been sent to Australia, in place of to the Tower, *he* would probably have encountered some colour-sergeant's daughter turning up her nose at him, had they met in a quadrille.

This was the era when James Paterson, of the A.S.N. Co., Sydney, and Captain Tilmouth J. Dye, of the Hunter River New Steam Co., used to smile at each other in the street, and (metaphorically), "cut each other's throats" with their opposition and reduced fares and freights; this was the time when the Howsons and Carandinis and Miss Hart delighted the gallery gods at the old "Vic." theatre in Sydney, when Torning danced his hornpipe and sang his "patter" songs; this was the era also when Mr. William Barton, the sharebroker, of Sydney, father of the subsequent Speaker and Attorney-General, did a flourishing business; arriving in Sydney in 1827, as secretary to the Australian Agricultural Company, at Port Stephens, he left their employ in 1830, and became the first "bull" and "bear" south of the equator; helped to float many of the early

Sydney banks and insurance companies, now towers of wealth, and *not* of the 1892 fungoid, mushroom, and liquidation type. He was on the London Stock Exchange in 1810, and served his time to old Mr. Barwise there, a venerable relic of the bygone, who, born in 1740, still wore in 1810 his hair powdered, pigtail, black knee breeches, and silver buckles of George II. days.

Yes, the old Sydney streets and stony walls, old nooks and corners of the young old city talk to me in a language that is all unheard by the present generation, and tell me tales to make me doubt whether to laugh or weep.

How that great dead metal clock, that towers high above the city life of restless Sydney does continue to ring its voice up; and with a semblance of living interest in all that transpires below it, warning every one that another "giant of time" has just skipped away for ever, and that there is only so much or so little time now left till that next little episode in one's daily work and life comes off, and which must be attended to or else ———.

And I have called it a dead clock, too. But is it? When we drowsily turn us over in the night there is that great sleepless giant still at his work the same as if it were high noon in George-street!

There are some quaint old suburbs in Sydney: not picturesque, but full of memories and associations. Their gum trees were cleared off about the time of the Battle of Waterloo, and the old mansions and villas (of 1838 or so), that followed later on and had fifty acres of "grounds" and paddocks round them passed into the hands of the Pitt-street trader, who built and lived there through the stages of schools and hotels; and streets sprang up all round the scene till at last the old houses had their bricks carted away and left no record except that the large suburbs took the name that the old family mansion once had. All this takes us back to the days when the wild flowers grew close up to where the post office tower now is; when the grandfathers of modern Sydney were young; when first Sydney found out that it could wield a cricket bat on the level swards of Port Jackson; and that fishing down the harbour was not the worst way of spending a day's or a week's holiday. But all this was long ago, and the then people, male and female, whose hair was not gray, and who were in their full prime in 1840, now only have a name in the cemeteries, or on old deed-boxes on lawyers' shelves, or in trust accounts, or, perchance, some street or square, embalms their name and memory for ever.

Yes, the town air was pure and fresh in early Sydney 1844 days, and one could travel overland from the top of the hill in William-street to Shepherd's nursery past the Kent Brewery and find what a native would call "good juberry and fine corn country," the whole way. For the benefit of the uninitiated English reader it may be explained that juberries are a wild nut fruit which do duty for blackberries, and grew in the suburbs of Sydney as do the blackberries over in the suburbs of London.

CHAPTER II.

NEW-BORN LUXURY—OPENING UP "WAY BACK"—PIONEERS ON THE LOWER MURRUMBIDGEE AND LACHLAN—SETTLEMENT ON THE DARLING—OVERLANDING—NORBURY, THE TRACKER—ON THE MURRUMBIDGEE—A MARTINET AT WHIST—CHESS AND DRAUGHTS—NAVIGATION OF THE MURRAY—PHELPS OF CANALLY—THE OLD SQUATTING MEN—CAPTAIN CADELL—THE "LADY AUGUSTA"—TYSON BROS. ON THE LACHLAN—A RISKY UNDERTAKING—OLD MELBOURNE—MEN AND MATTERS—THE GOLD ERA—NEW MELBOURNE.

WHAT new-born luxury flooded Sydney after 1852! The refinements of Regent-street and Bond-street appeared in the shop windows. New fabrics, new confectionery, gloves and shoes, velvets and plushes, brooches and necklets, furniture and pictures, *chef* wines and liqueurs, carriages and buggies of a class unknown in the forties, abounded, and, "never mind, we can afford it *now*," was the cry and the feeling all round.

Where now are the belles of 1852, the blondes and brunettes who blossomed at the time when the gold fruit budded in Australia, and who, with their lovers and husbands and children, partook of the newborn fatness and pleasures of the era of expansion and plenty? Where are they all now? Comely dames, most of them. A very few, in the sear and yellow leaf of life, have lived to see their grandchildren spring up under auspices and conditions greatly and sadly contrasted with those of the '52 era. Verily the folk who were born about 1830 had more to be thankful for than the babes of 1870 now have.

And where are the brave men who sacrificed what little "sociability" there was in Sydney and sought to open up the territory, even now sometimes spoken of as "way back?" Let us "review" a few of them.

The first to take up country on the Lower Murrumbidgee and Lachlan was Mr. Hobler, who, with his family, settled at Nap Nap. He it was who also took up Yanga and Paika. Then John Scott occupied Canally, which he afterwards sold to Phelps and Chadwick; while at the junction of the Murrumbidgee and the Murray the Jackson Bros. took up a cattle station. Next in order of time and below the Junction, William Ross formed Mailman Station, and at the same time (in May, 1846), Boomiaricool, or, as it is now known, Euston, was taken up by E. Morey. Plucky men both these latter selectors were, for neither of them was yet 20 years of age! Eight months later the country below Boomiaricool was taken up by John McKinlay, and then gradually Kilcool, Mildura, and other stations followed—Kilcool by Ebden and Keene, and Mildura by Jamison Bros. At this time the Fletcher family occupied Tapio, near the junction of the Darling with the Murray, and a number of thrifty Scots settled themselves on country on the Lower Darling.

During 1850, John McKinlay, John MacCallum, and the selector of Boomiaricool explored the country above the settlement on the Darling, and eventually stocked it—MacCallum at Menindee with sheep, McKinlay at Pooncaree and Pamameroo with cattle, and Morey at Tintanallogy and Lake Terawanea with cattle.

It was in 1853 that the influenza scourge passed over Sydney. I was one of the victims, and this, combined with the high pressure which characterised the work of a bank-teller in those days, caused me, on the advice of my medical man, to once more seek the fresh air. So I arranged with my kind uncle in Sydney the introduction which enabled me to travel overland with 10,000 sheep from Dubbo, on the Macquarie River, to Paika, on the Murrumbidgee. The two companions, who threw up their billets to come with me, were Felix Neeld Burne and G. V. James. We left Sydney in June, 1853. We met our "super," Mr. L., at Dubbo, and he of course travelled with us. This was a twelve-hundred mile trip. Burne, by the way, afterwards took up Lansdowne, on the Barcoo (Queensland). This trip with me was *his* introduction into squatting life, which he afterwards followed up in partnership with the master of the Sydney Mint and Captain Mayne. We had with us a blackboy, "Norbury," a tracker and a native of the Barwon and Namoi Rivers, in the McIntyre country. He and I used to go out on the dewy grass, at day dawn, to track, and bring in, the bullocks and horses which had strayed in the night. *I* could see a track in the soft ground, and so could any white fool; but, when it came to the stony ground, it was "Norbury, you bet." Often have I seen him (he had but one eye, and that was a "piercer") jump suddenly on one side, where the scent and track grew dim, and "spot" a place on the hard sandstone rock, and, when I asked him to show me what he saw, he would point to one grain, a mere speck, of sand, dislodged, by a horny hoof, from the main mass of rock, and, presto! we were full on the track again.

This was a great trip, full of adventure and incident for us all. I remember that before we got to Bendigo we heard from people we met, of a story, that certain American diggers, lately come from California, told of gold in immense quantities existing near some mountains on the other side of the

Lachlan, away from us; gold which, they said, would eclipse anything on Ballarat or the Turon, but for the one fact that there was no water anywhere near it. I have often wondered since whether the Lambing Flat, and other rich fields, which came to light many a year after our trip, were foreshadowed in the flying prospecting trips of solitary and scattered miners in those dim and early days of auriferous discovery. But none of us had wanted to cross the ditch-like Bogan, still less the muddy canal-looking Lachlan, both so contrasted with the clear waters of the Macquarie, Murrumbidgee, and Murray; our ideas were purely pastoral, and of the money to be made by stock-farming and the magnificent wild oats through which we travelled on August 19th, 1853, together with blue forget-me-nots and pleasant scented yellow and white flowers, were suggestive of good country, a good season, fat banking accounts, high profits, and gold diggings butchers purchasing fat stock and paying for it in "dust." One Saturday in August we camped by a large lake, which, somehow, in point of size at any rate, reminded me of Rose Bay in Port Jackson; it swarmed with ducks, teal, and wild geese then, and there were abundance of turkeys and emus handy.

Norbury, the black boy, captured a small opossum, and sold it to James for half-a-pound of tobacco. It was about this time, that I had a chance of witnessing this black boy's tracking powers. He was small and slim, and, as I have said, had but one eye, which glowed like a lamp. He and I went out after the bullocks early one morning on stony ground, where I could not perceive the ghost of a track, though now getting used to picking up a trail. But Norbury would jump from side to side as we journeyed on, and would "spot" a slight abrasion freshly made on a piece of sandstone by a hoof or horn, and that, too, ten or twelve feet aside from our straight line of march—abrasions and small scratches on the stone, that I, though with excellent sight for a white, should need a lens, and that at close quarters, in order to determine.

One day Mr. L. decided to push on in the afternoon by himself to try and find out Nicholas Chadwick's station, called Powpruck, which laid in the angle of the confluence of the Lachlan and Murrumbidgee. Chadwick was a partner of John Leckie Phelps, of Canally, on the Murrumbidgee, close to Wyndómel, its junction with the Murray. But L. got lost this time, and came back at 8 p.m., guided to us only by the light of our camp fire, and he did not find Chadwick's place that day. Next day we bore to the left through an opening, and made in towards the main river. Chadwick's storekeeper saw us, and made for us after dark. I lent my horse to Mr. L., who went on and found a shepherd lambing a flock. Chadwick's blacks, the lower Lachlan tribe, came up to us next morning in great numbers; one of them, Anthony, a huge fellow nearly seven feet in height, threw a reed spear with a "woomera" some four hundred feet into the air; it seemed to wriggle its way up right out of sight. Mr. Chadwick—or Shadwick, as they all called him—gave us a call this day, and piloted us safely along clear of his own flocks. Burne, James and I were asked up to his hut, where we found the almost-forgotten agrément of reading some newspapers. The walls were plastered with cuts from the *Illustrated News*, and we who felt like people off a sea voyage in having been shut out from the world for some weeks, read in the *Sydney Morning Herald*, and with some interest, about the heroic struggles of W. C. Wentworth and other citizens in the direction of securing Responsible Government and representative institutions for New South Wales. How the boon has worked, let those who read of the debates and deadlocks of 1877, declare.

When we left the lake, we travelled through a very dense and sandy scrub, and one of the shepherds and his flock got lost. We camped in the thick jungle, which we did not get quite through, as the horses were found very late in the morning. Norbury and I had our usual very wet early tramp after them. Burne and James set out next day after breakfast to find Paika. I got entangled in another thick scrub for two hours with a flock. Spied the clear plain at last, and picked up the dray tracks.

Mr. Kirby, the superintendent of Paika, came and met us with his trusty blackfellow, Martin, an eagle-eyed Australian chief. He camped with us that night, and discussed the Louisa Creek gold mania. I piloted a flock on to the Paika run next day, and we camped by the banks of Lake Tauri, a beautiful sheet of water, with grassy, flowery, well-wooded banks, and a high red sand ridge on one side of it. This was one of a series of lakes fed by the waters of the Murrumbidgee River; dry in some years, but generally full from the overflow of the stream through its ana branches.

On the following day Mr. L., Norbury, and a shepherd, went on to Paika head station, leaving me with the sheep by Tauri. I went through my usual round of washing and mending clothes whenever a spell offered. I cut out the sheep into two flocks. I took a few lessons in the noble art of cracking a stockwhip; explored the country round and found some very tolerable green substitute for cabbage. On the last day in August I set to work and made a brush fence and gateway for the purpose of counting the sheep. On the 1st September Mr. Kirby came and counted them, and found them to be 9,924, which, with six crawlers left on the road, and the skins on the dray of those killed for rations, just made up our tally.

We left two shepherds in charge at Lake Tauri, and rode

on to Lake Carandulke. Norbury and Mr. Kirby went thence to Paika. Mr. L. and James made for our Tauri camp, which I guessed better at the position of, than he did, for we differed as to the direction in which it lay, and my course proved to be the right one. On September 2nd we rode on to the Paika head station; distributed our four shepherds, each to an outstation, re-put the drayload over the ana branch of Paika Lake in a canoe; found Mr. Easton at the house and enjoyed a civilized game of chess in the evening.

And talking of chess calls to mind that towards the end of 1865 I was made an honorary member of the Victoria Club, in Castlereagh-street, and there met, at whist and pool, many whom I had not known before. George Thornton, Dan. Egan, Ted Lee, Fred. Cape, D. Melhado, Archie Thompson, Alec Dick, Cheeke, Grundy, and William Jolly; and there was the owner of Yattendon, too, whose name I forget, and a terrible old judge, whose name I also "disremember," but not so his prowess at whist. He was considered the greatest martinet in Sydney at that game. I was his partner one evening.

I was dealer, and turned up the nine of hearts; I also had the ten. In playing I put down the nine first, and afterwards the ten. His Honour cross-examined me: "Why did you not play the ten first in place of the nine!" "Because no other card could come between them, and it was immaterial which," I replied. "You are mistaken," retorted the judge, "it was anything but immaterial; it is a player's business to let his partner know all that he fairly can about the cards he holds. I knew you had the nine, the turn up, but not about the ten, therefore you missed a point by playing the nine first, and it might have made a difference both to me and to the game." I saw he was right, and that what seemed terribly high-class whist to me might be the mere alphabet of the game to such a Regius professor thereof as His Honour. But I never could give my mind, nor have the patience to bring intellect, to bear on any game where the competitors do not start on exactly equal terms, which they seldom or never do at cards.

It is only at chess and draughts that one starts level, and only here is it worth while to bring the brain to bear on the struggle; unfortunately, however, chess is so intricate as to be only fit for people who have nothing else to study if it is to be really played; and the games which amateurs contest in their recreation hours in the intervals of business are only chess strongly diluted, a mere parody on the real scientific game. Draughts is more to the purpose. Both these intellectual games originated in the strong brains of the eastern races, who first gave us arithmetic and algebra, only draughts is about 1,500 years the older of the two. And it has other advantages over chess. At the latter game, if you make a silly move, you can recall it next time, and so not *waste two moves* in place of *making one*. All this is impossible at draughts; you must bravely move on and on only, and take the consequences of all folly. "*Vestigia nulla retrorsum*" is the motto; move on and no liberty to retreat till you have "won your spurs" by piercing through to the enemy's back squares. Again at chess capture of a piece *en prise* is not compulsory, but it is so at draughts, and this opens the way to some of the subtlest strategy and brilliantly ingenious combinations of which the human intellect is capable. A skilful player can sacrifice his men and thereby "spread eagle" his adversary's more numerous ones into a helpless and losing position, past all power of retrievement. The startling development of a skilfully constructed combination in a draughts problem is one of the most engrossing and pleasurable fillips to a keen intellect that can be given to it.

But goodness me how diverting are these memories! I was far away at Paika when the thought of chess carried me back to the old Victoria Club. To resume.

I have elsewhere described, at greater length, this memorable journey to Paika. On reaching Paika, Burne, James, and I were summoned back to civilisation, all, however, on different errands. I shall never forget the times we had there. Among other things more vividly impressed upon me was the fact that we ran short of flour, and so serious did things become that we often were put on short allowance.

Tala, Yangar, and Paika, W. C. Wentworth's great stations, were near the junction of the Murray and Murrumbidgee. Up to 1851 all went well there. The supplies of flour and sugar, &c., were hauled overland 800 miles or 3,000 miles from Sydney or Melbourne, save as might be by bullock drays, and the wool travelled back the same road. To provide for contingencies, Wentworth kept 20 tons of flour *always* in stock, and other supplies in proportion; but, when the "gold broke out," no Melbourne teams would go beyond Bendigo, nor Sydney teams beyond Bathurst. They could get more per ton for the short trip, with loading for the gold fields, than any squatter could afford to pay them for the long trip; so, when I was at Paika, in 1853, no teams had been up, or down, for two years. There were two seasons' wool stored in the sheds; the remaining flour was awfully musty; boots, saddles, tinware, "slops," and the like, had, long since, "given out" in the store.

I remember we used to boil "fat hen" (a weed which resembles dandelion) for vegetables, and we bore the musty flour as best we could, when, presto! all the muddle came to an end. One fine day, as Mr. J. Lecky Phelps, of Canally, rode by the banks of the Murray, he espied an unwonted sight breaking in on the bush and watery solitude. Stranger and more wonderful than the fabled bunyip, there lay a steamer moored to the bank; the energetic explorer, Cadell, had brought up the "Lady Augusta," with Sir Henry Young, the Governor of South Australia, on board. Had pierced the shoals that beset the sea mouth of the river, and vanquished the inland wilderness of Australia by means of its waterway, till then only thought of as a drinking reservoir. And, what was best of all, there were 100 tons of goods tumbled out on the river bank. The two years' siege was raised. 50-lb bags of pure white flour, fresh from the mills of Adelaide; spick and span boxes of loaf sugar, and equally spick and span cases of Val Martell's brandy, and sperm candles, all so clean, and other goods "too numerous to mention." *Not* covered with the dust and mud of 800 miles and three months of weary bush travel; *not* doled out in occasional dray loads of 30 cwt. at a time, but fresh and clean only a week ago from the Adelaide stores and from the hold of the steamer and her roomy satellite barges. Here was a metamorphosis with a vengeance, and the congested wool stores soon afforded ample return loading for the steamer and her barges. And station property round those parts known as "Riverina" at once rose 100 per cent. in the market. Phelps and I went on board, and, in a glass of brandy "pawnee," drank success to the Murray River navigation, and its bold pioneer, Captain Cadell.

Mr. John Lecky Phelps, of Canally, was a man much in advance of his time. While other people for 150 miles round had no vegetables, he cultivated a half-acre on the river bank with potatoes, green peas, French beans, and cabbages, and he kept it irrigated by a very simple process, for rain was uncertain in that far inland spot. He had a Californian wooden pump, about 6 inches square, with its end fixed in the river, and about 150 feet of "osnaburgh" hose from it to the top of the garden, which was, perhaps, three feet higher than the lower end by the river, and half-an-hour of hand pumping every morning, sent the water flowing zig zag backwards and forwards and in and out through all the well-kept furrows and beds of the enclosure, and the vegetation was always fresh and green at Canally garden.

F. N. Burne returned to Sydney, via Wagga Wagga, to see after and sell some consignments sent out by an uncle, while I resolved to cut the land journey as short as possible by going home via Melbourne. To this end I made over to Lakes Tala and Yangar, a short distance from which I joined the party of Messrs. W. J. Buchanan and Hugh Harper, who had just delivered cattle from New England, on the Murrumbidgee, and were bound also to the metropolis of Victoria. It was December, 1853, and we had to face some hot, waterless plains, and mallee country, where we had to carry hogsheads of water on the dray for the bullocks and horses, and to travel by night in place of day over the burning hot shadeless levels ere we got clear of Poon Boon, the Wakool, and the Edwards rivers and sighted the reed-bed environs of Swan Hill, on the Murray, where a bottle of ale at 8s. was most welcome and tonic after the eternal relaxing tea of the preceding six months.

Here I noticed the difference between the Victorian and New South Wales squatting man of the period. The former usually dressed in a plaid "jumper," the latter in the fawn-coloured tweed of his native Parramatta. They looked as distinct as the denizens of two different countries, and the difference was apparent directly the border Murray River was passed. Our party made onwards past the Reedy Lake and Lake Boyd, and at last we saw mountains in the distance, the first to be seen since we left the Upper Lachlan River. These were Mount Pyramid and Mount Hope. Mount Korong (the golden) came in sight later on. We were now in Sir Thomas Mitchell's "Australia Felix." We recognised the fact, for anon we passed (with joy) the last solitary small lonely clump of the detested "mallee" scrub; the Loddon river, renowned for its pasture, and the "Durham Ox," a famous roadside inn of the golden era, were amongst our next experiences, and we passed on and drew nigh to Bullock Creek and Bendigo, and I now pushed ahead of the rest of the party, which travelled too slowly for me.

The story of how the navigation of the Murray was brought about is worth repeating.

There were really two staunch advocates of the navigation of the Murray—Mr. E. Morey and Mr. Samuel Macgregor. There were likewise two obstacles in the way, for Melbourne was jealous of the trade going to her southern neighbour, Adelaide, and it was difficult to find money with which to give effect to the venture.

The idea, like most other out-of-the-way propositions, was laughed at by business men. However, Morey saw Captain Stuart, the explorer, who had, on his last journey, pulled down the Murray, and had introduced him to Sir Henry Young, then Governor. The Governor requested Morey to furnish an estimate of the probable trade, a request which was speedily complied with; for Morey recognised that it was advisable to strike the iron while it was hot. Then Captain Cadell pulled down the Murray from Swan Hill to Lake Alexandria, and the impressions made on him are shown by the fact that shortly afterwards he took up what was the first steamer that ever traversed the waters of the great waterway. The craft was a rough-decked boat, with improvised engines, fitted by an enterprising miller from the Adelaide side. It took her a month to make Swan Hill, for her maximum speed was, stemming the current, but three or four miles an hour. After the vice-regal visit, for Governor Young travelled on the pioneer vessel—which, out of compliment for the efforts His Excellency had put forth, was named after his lady—trade quickly grew. Steamers and their satellite barges were multiplied, and the Murrumbidgee and the Darling, as well as their minor branches, suffered their fresh water shallows to be invaded, conquered, and explored by a flotilla of mercantile business-feeders of the flat-bottomed type.

The Tyson brothers were, in 1846, occupying the country at the extreme lower end of the Lachlan, where its muddy waters unite with the pellucid Murrumbidgee. They were keen business men, living in bark huts, of their own building, and always open to a "deal" in the way of cattle. The Lake Paika station was, afterwards, purchased by one of them, with 12,000 cattle, at £8 per head, the time and the proximity to a market being, alike, favourable to such a high price ruling. When the "Lady Young" first came up, and was tied to a tree below Euston, a drunken bushman came on board, and, pushing his head into the cabin where His Excellency was shaving, shouted "give us a passage up the river, Governor." Captain Cadell put him ashore *vi et armis*, when the fellow turned round and said to him, "Well! you are a hugly man." The crew laughed, but the bushman did not, for Cadell was a two-handed bruiser, and soon left the bushman nothing to complain of on the score of beauty, when once he had stepped on shore to him. The Murray explorer was brave to foolhardiness, whereof witnesseth the fact that he once drove up the Darling River, in a buggy, for 200 miles, with a view to learn its eligibility for navigation. Having done so, he, in place of coming back the same route, conceived the strange idea of cutting straight across country to the Murrumbidgee, overland, and away from the river!

Now, anyone who knows the "Old Man" plain, near

Hay, the dread of bushmen, can appreciate what a task it is to face a waterless prairie between two comparatively approximate rivers; and, still more, what it must be like to attempt to negotiate the third side of a triangle in waterless country, when the other two sides consist of two such widely divergent and lengthy streams as the Murrumbidgee and Darling are. Cadell's black boy tried, in vain, to dissuade him from the attempt, which was made, with the result that the two of them nearly perished from thirst and hunger. But what was so akin to a tragedy, had an element of comedy imported into it by the freely circulated, if not truthful, report, that, but for the abundant supply of hair pomade which the gallant explorer always carried with him, he and the black boy would have been unable to soften, and eat, the leather leggings, straps, valise, &c., which, it is coolly stated, alone saved them from starvation. How much "bush chaff," and what residuum of fact, there may be in this, I am unable to tell with certainty.

On the way back from Paika, I had as a companion Constable Lalor. I started on December 10th, 1853, walking, as I have said, from Canally to Yangan, there to pick up Buchanan's teams, for, though the steamer was up the Murray, I heard she wasn't to return to Goolwa until January. We arrived in Melbourne two days after Xmas, our yule tide festivities being partly spent at the Porcupine Inn. The traffic here was something tremendous. We met 200 drays, which was *so* strange after all the months of solitude. We camped at "Sawpit Gully" on Xmas night, and on the 27th made our destination, about which my diary says: "Arrived at Melbourne at half-past one; tents now all the way from Prince's Bridge to Liardet's boat shed."

I find on consulting my diary again that I *did* write Melbourne. At this date even I am led to wonder why I didn't call the place by its proper name; for Melbourne wasn't the name *most* people knew Sydney's great neighbour by. It was then, and for years afterwards, invariably spoken of as Port Phillip. But I said Melbourne in my jottings, and I suppose I had some special reason for so designating it, though for the life of me I cannot now conjure up the reason why. Falling across that little entry has revived memories of Melbourne, for Melbourne *has* a past, just as Sydney has.

> Oh! don't you remember old Melbourne, Ben Bolt,
>   When gold nuggets first were found out?
> When mid five feet of mud on the wharves and the streets
>   And all night "stickers-up" roamed about?
> Ah! those were the days, you just bet, Ben Bolt,
>   When dollars could quickly be made;
> You might buy what you liked, in both market and store,
>   For you "couldn't go wrong" in a trade.

Victoria and Van Diemen's Land were both a little like old England in climate; the elms and the hawthorn and the sweetbriar grew all about; and, in Tasmania, the swallows came back in the spring just as they do "at home." But the difference between the two colonies was in population and bustle, for Melbourne in 1853 was like a little London, while Tasmania was as dull as ever. Old mother Sydney began to wake up, rub her eyes, and note the strides that her eldest daughter was taking, under the stimulus of nine millions of gold per annum (increased to twelve millions in 1856), in a population of less than 300,000.

Miscamble, the veterinary surgeon, kept his place of business at the corner of Little Bourke and Elizabeth-streets. Melbourne proud to mimic London in everything and remembering her famous old inn yards whence country carriers used to start—places like Girard's Hall, in Basing-lane; the Swan with Two Necks, in Carter-lane; and all and sundry those square court yarded old inns with wooden galleries all round their inner sides, so famous in the pages of Chaucer and of Dickens; common alike to Southwark, Bishopsgate, and the lanes about Thames-street—Melbourne, I say, remembering all those old institutions, and their "neat wines," and ordinaries, and lemon nets, started one for herself named after the old "Blossoms" inn in London. In Elizabeth-street at the "Blossoms" yard one could, in the "early fifties," book luggage and parcels per carrier in the ante-railway days for Bendigo, Castlemaine, "Simpsons," Mount Blackwood, Ballarat, Creswick's Creek, and Beechworth, to say nothing of St. Kilda, Prahran, Richmond, and Emerald Hill. And, oh dear me, what a big, noisy, bustling, public house was Mat. Cantlon's, the Bull and Mouth, in Bourke-street, in those days.

What a job it was to get even a shakedown there; and how full the place was of fellows who appeared to have but two alternative missions in life since they returned gold-laden from Ballarat or Castlemaine; for they wanted to pay for everybody's liquor, or, in default of that, to fight everybody. They seldom ate, bathed still less frequently, and never seemed to go to bed at all, but passed their time over "sherry spiders," "sparkling 'ock," and similar money-melters. People dined with their hats on at Cantlon's, and with their pipes by the side of their plates. Outside in the streets the gold brokers outbid each other by 3d. or 6d. per ounce in the price for the heavy metal, as could be seen by reading the placards outside, and in the windows of each office; and the same could be seen in the windows at Ballarat and Castlemaine. Instead of "rags, bones, and bottles," as in England, or "wheat, wool, bark, barley, tallow, and hides," as in Hobart Town, it was, here, "highest price given for gold"; and over it all hung somehow an ever present and indefinable flavour of the Crimean War, that permeated the mental atmosphere, for it took away all the steamers of any size, and made public interest concentrate on the English mails brought by the "Black Ball" liners—"Red Jacket," "Blue Jacket," Donald McKay, and the rest of them; for the G.S.S. Co.'s boats were at Balaclava in place of Williamstown, and even the "Great Britain" herself was not a constant visitor after her first trip in 1852.

And though it was noisy and disorderly and unconventional at Cantlon's Bull and Mouth hotel, and all over Melbourne, too, for that matter, yet what absolute *"money"* there was in it all! None of your credit and inflation! How the money fed commerce and fertilized the avenues of trade! Never was the like before or since in the world, when native gold, fresh and rough from the earth, came pouring in at the rate of £40 a year for every man, woman, and baby in the colony of Victoria, and nearly £400 a year for every individual man, woman, child, and infant in the town of Melbourne. No wonder that matters were (more or less pleasantly) unhinged. It was all uncouth enough, no doubt, but it was good solid "financing" on one side, at any rate, and if there are any who doubt this—well, let them ask the millionaire, Cantlon, in his West End London villa, of later years, to say nothing of other retired plutocrats, who skimmed the cream of the teeming gold yield, and caught it in the vessels of trade.

Ah! those good old days of redundant Australian prosperity, when the gold of 1853 came teeming out of the earth, and no one knew its value, and everyone was afraid to touch it, and thought it would fall in price like silver in 1892. The days when there were no Australian mints, and but few assayers; and no one could tell properly whether the rough alluvial dirt-stained, ponderous yellow metal, lying in heaps in all directions, was worth £3 or £4 the ounce. The days when the Bank of New South Wales settled the matter (pro. tem.) by offering its paper notes at the rate of £2 10s. per ounce for all the £3 15s. gold it could secure far and wide, and when no other buyer was "game" even to give "that much." The glorious old days when Khull, of Melbourne, and John Godfrey Cohen, of Sydney (besides others) flourished as "gold brokers" (where is the need in 1892?) and skimmed the cream and shaved the edges of profit on this metal of then unknown assay and unknown value; the days when that notorious, rascally gold buyer at the Turon, held the powerful magnet perpetually sewn up in his coat sleeve, for the benefit of the steel beam of his scales as he poised them in air with the gold side of the beam just under his wrist; and whose troy weights, though often suspected, challenged, and tested, could never be found wanting by the keenest inspector, but who robbed the diggers none the less to a fearsome extent with the aid of the loadstone; the days when Australia did without "loans," and the digger could stand a lot of "robbing," and not feel it, as Dame Nature was his banker, and he got her gold by the pint and quart, and cared not whether it was 18 or 22-carat stuff; the days when the professional politician loafer had not come into play, nor sold his conscience to Satan for a few loaves of bread, and left Australia burdened with debt for uselessly duplicated political log-rolling railways.

Before I bid adieu to Melbourne, let me say a few more words about it. With the exception of a few hours spent there in passing through in 1853, I never saw Melbourne from early 1851 to late 1888, when I, of course, approached by the railway and Albury route, and *not* viâ Swan Hill. Heavens! what a metamorphosis was there in those thirty-eight years of gold-fostered development? Long ere I got to Spencer-street, and after I got out into Hobson's Bay also, there loomed the domes of the Supreme Court and the Exhibition Building. Heavenward pointed the tall steeples in Collins-street; towering buildings and factory chimneys marked the site of a city, indeed; where all was dull, tame, flat and empty, in 1851. St. James's Church, which stood out boldly across a grassy flat in 1851, was now stowed away somehow behind a mass of bewildering buildings, and I had to hunt for it. And I saw the glorious, garden-strewed, flower-decked, tram and train-served suburbs, where, in 1851, a punt and a dusty desolate road alone marked the site. St. Kilda, where some cottages, a gravel pit, and a waterhole did duty in 1851, was "some pumpkins" in 1888; but I cannot continue the list. Melbourne seen from the plains to the north, or from the lofty upper deck of a mail steamer in the bay, was a royal city then in every sense of the word. But then, the other changes, which do *not* appear on the surface, but which all bore their part! The Governors, from Latrobe and Hotham to Loch and Hopetoun; the premiers and cabinets, from the days of Ebden, Ireland, O'Shanassy, Michie, Fellows, Haines, Nicholson, through the times of Richard Heales, McCulloch, Francis, and Berry, down to the modern times of Gillies and Munro. What a chapter on or rather of Victorian history do they represent! The social growths, the "ups and downs" of fate, the constant onward progress since the good old days when Thomas Howard Fellows, and his colleagues of the Victorian Bar, took part in those glorious, witty, social circuit dinners and suppers of that by-gone time—well on in this same nineteenth century, perhaps, but still far back in the growth of the young giant known as the colony of Victoria.

CHAPTER III.

EARLY SETTLERS ON THE CLARENCE—RICHARD CRAIG'S DISCOVERY—
DR. DOBIE'S DAYS—DR. LANG'S HIGHLAND IMMIGRANTS—
A PATHETIC INCIDENT—FIRST ATTEMPTS AT SUGAR MAKING—
INITIAL DIFFICULTIES—CRUDE PLANTS—THE FRENCH BARON'S
EXPERIMENTS—SCENES OF OLDER SYDNEY—MEMORIES OF THE
PAST—SYDNEY BANKS AND BANKING—A FEW FIGURES—
THE CRUMBLING OF THE BIG INSTITUTIONS—THE COBRA AND
WHITE ANT OF FINANCE.

AT the time that Cook, in coasting the eastern shore of Australia, discovered and named Shoalwater Bay, he had no idea that it was the estuary of an important river, and it was not till the New England tableland was occupied by pioneer squatters that the coast country began to be explored. There were obstacles to be overcome. The country did not, at first sight, look inviting. The landing was, nearly everywhere, difficult and dangerous. The long stretches of sandy beach were lashed by the vast rollers of the Pacific. The few streams had their mouths more or less completely closed by sand-bars, on which the surf never ceased to beat, and it was neither safe to seek, nor easy to find, the few narrow and tortuous channels by which they could, when wind and tide served, be passed. Then, when the bar had been safely crossed, there was little to be seen but endless ranges of mangrove swamps—fetid mud below, and twisted roots and branches above. There was nothing to be got to compensate for the risk and trouble of such risky and troublesome navigation. Hence settlement progressed from the interior coastwards.

The first report of the existence of a great river flowing into the Pacific from the eastern mountain fringe of the New England tableland, was given by Richard Craig, an assigned servant of Dr. Dobie, of New England. Craig either took to the bush voluntarily, as many others did, or got lost in the ranges while out shepherding—the latter was his own story—and was carried down towards the coast by the blacks. He apparently got tired of such companionship, finding that he had even less liberty than as an assigned servant, and made his way back over the range, where he was forgiven in consideration of the information he had to give.

Just then a drought was raging in New England, and Dr. Dobie started him off with a flock of sheep to the low country, where he reported grass and water to be abundant. Craig said he had seen a river a mile wide, with its banks clothed with a dense cedar scrub, and good, sound, lightly timbered, and well-grassed ridges, with abundant well-filled creeks running between them. Such a pastoral paradise was not to be despised, and the Doctor followed with more stock. Others were not slow to imitate so good an example. Dr. Dobie took up country close to the present township of Grafton. The Ogilvies made their way through the ranges —almost impassable even now—from the Upper Hunter, and took up Yulgilbar. They endured almost incredible hardships on their journey; but the Hon. E. D. Ogilvie, now the only survivor of the party, has reaped a rich reward.

Eatanswill, which had its home station at a point overlooking the first crossing-place over the river above Grafton, was taken up soon after the "Pickwick Papers" reached

Australia, and the adventures of Mr. Pickwick at the Eatanswill election so tickled the original settlers, that they incontinently named their new station after the immortal rotten borough. It is now a thriving village, with numbers of farming settlers round it, but the inhabitants are ashamed of the old name, and have euphonised it into Eatonsville. What would Dickens think of the change?

It was not long before Sydney got news of the fine northern river, and of the apparently inexhaustible cedar scrub on its banks. The yield of cedar from the Shoalhaven brushes had, for some years, been falling off. The easily accessible timber had almost all been cut, and it was necessary for the sawyers to go long distances to find passable logs, and expend a great deal of time and labour in getting them out of the gullies where they had been cut. Mr. Small, of Kissing Point, determined to try what could be done on the newly-discovered river. He fitted out a schooner, the "Elizabeth," to look for a shipment of cedar, put on board a cargo of such supplies as he knew would be wanted, together with a party of timber-getters, and sent her to seek her fortune. The late Mr. Freeburn, for many years pilot at the Clarence Heads, was one of the schooner's crew. According to him, the entrance to Shoal Bay was then much wider than at present, and the schooner entered over what is now dry land, occupied by the township of Iluka, on the North Head.

The "Elizabeth" anchored near the little island that now bears her name, and the saws and axes went merrily to work. So plentiful was the cedar that there was little difficulty, as soon as she had discharged her cargo of supplies, in filling her up with cedar logs. It was necessary to do little more than fell the trees on the bank, bark them, crosscut them, roll the logs into the water, and float them alongside, to be hoisted on board by the schooner's tackle.

The timber trade was a most lucrative one, since the surplus supplies taken to the river by the schooners were eagerly bought up by the squatters of the upper river, who gladly availed themselves of the chance of replenishing their stocks of tea, sugar, flour, &c., by sea, rather than by the long land route round by New England, from the Hunter or Port Stephens.

It was not long before a farming population settled on the rich lands of the lower river. The first were station hands, who, having completed a term of service under indenture, had saved money enough to buy small farms. These men did not generally profit by the experience of the Illawarra and Hawkesbury settlers, who had learned the superior fertility of the brush lands. They dreaded the labour of clearing the heavy brush on the river bank, and settled on the less fertile forest lands at the back.

The first settler on the scrub lands on the river bank, was Mr. William Amos, who, after occupying a farm on the Williams River for several years, had migrated to the Manning, and, subsequently, at a land sale in Sydney, bought 80 acres at Ulmarra. There he made his home, and, long after, used to tell how he sold his first crop of maize, planted with the hoe among the logs and stumps, before the land was sufficiently cleared to get the plough through it, for £1 per bushel. Mr. Amos prospered exceedingly, and, subsequently, bought another and larger farm on Swan Creek, a few miles higher up the river, where he had, as a neighbour, Mr. William Small, one of the sons of the owner and builder of the historic schooner "Elizabeth." Another of Mr. Small's sons, John, settled on Woodford Island. Mr. Amos died a few years ago at a good old age, universally respected. He furnished a striking illustration of the truth that illiteracy is no bar to success in life. He could never do more than write his signature to a cheque, but was an excellent farmer, and a good clear-headed man of business.

In the fifties the lower river was settled by a number of Highlanders imported by Dr. Lang. They made excellent colonists, steady, shrewd, and industrious. A large proportion of the first generation never learned to speak English, and for years, even in the late seventies, Gaelic was the most prevalent language of many neighbourhoods, especially the islands of Shoal Bay. Many Germans, too, chiefly from the Rheinland and Bavaria, settled on the river. These also formed a most valuable element. They introduced the cultivation of the vine, and if the vineyards of the Clarence cannot pretend to vie in reputation with those of Albury, the Hunter, and Inverell, they are certainly neither less productive nor less profitable to their owners. The mixture of Celtic and Teutonic blood ought, combined with the warm East Australian climate, to produce a race-type which, in a century or so, will be worth the notice of ethnologists, and will reward their study by supplying some new facts and inferences.

Before the passing of Sir John Robertson's "Land Act of 1861," the settlement on the Clarence and adjacent river basins was sparse; but the district was one of those in which free selection did most good and least harm. There was no clashing between the interests of selectors and the pastoral tenants. The good lands were so heavily timbered as to be useless for grazing purposes. But the rich deep soil, when the timber is once cleared off, is just what the agricultural settler wants, and when the Act of '61 came into force, it was taken up freely, to the great profit of the selectors, and the immense gain of the country as a whole.

The basin of the Clarence is divided from that of the little river Bellinger, or "Bellingen," as the blacks call it, by a low volcanic range, which is clothed with a dense cedar scrub, the trees bound together by an almost inextricable tangle of vines and "lawyer canes." This formerly extended right across the Bellinger valley, and up into the mountains almost to the Guy Fawkes Mountain. It was, when first settled, a mine of wealth to the inhabitants of the many sawyers' camps which dotted the country, shipping their timber from the river by small vessels that regularly came for it when they could get into the river—which was not by any means always possible, for the bar was, and is now, as capricious as any fair lady. There is a story that a certain eminent politician and one time Premier of New South Wales, once at low water waded across the Bellinger bar from South Head to North Head. It will be readily believed that the river was then hermetically closed to navigation, and it has often been in the same condition both before and since. In such cases the population had no resource but to wait as patiently as they could for a flood to come down and sweep the obstructive sand into deep water. In times when the river was closed, the people were forced to live on boiled maize, beef, and kangaroo, with an occasional supply of tea, sugar, and flour brought on pack-horses from the Macleay.

The sawyers and timber-getters had a hard life on the Bellinger in the old times, and well into the sixties. It was alternately a feast and a famine.

When the small craft from Sydney got in with their cargoes of rations, drapery, tobacco, and rum, their arrival was celebrated with a wild orgie. Every man tapped his keg of fiery spirit, and men and women alike drowned their sorrows in the lethe of intoxication. Hard work and hard fare were alike forgotten for a time; but the saturnalia did not last more than a day or two. The schooner had to be loaded, and soon the hardy fellows braced themselves to their work. The logs from the upper river were generally rolled into the water, and left to float down without any further interference than was necessary, when they got aground, to roll or push them into deeper water. At the head of boat navigation, some five or six miles from the sea, the logs of each party would be formed into a "boom" (i.e., chained together end to end), or a "raft" (chained side by side), and anchored under the bank. Then, when the schooner has discharged her stores, the rafts and booms destined to form her cargo would be guided alongside, and the logs detached, and hoisted on board. There were cases in which, when the bar was bad, the vessels would lie to in the offing, and rafts and booms would be taken out to them by boats and shipped in the same way. This was a troublesome and dangerous operation requiring great skill and care, and particularly fine weather for its successful accomplishment. In some cases, however, considerable cargoes of timber have been shipped from open beaches; but in one of these instances, at least, the attempt resulted in the loss of the vessel, which was driven ashore and wrecked.

Just one episode to illustrate life in the cedar-country some five-and-twenty years ago. It was on the Richmond River. A sawyer named Jones, who was working in what was called the Big Scrub, had pulled down the river with his wife and their three-month's-old baby to meet the weekly steamer from Sydney at the heads. It was a long pull, and the heat of the day—it was in December—was made none the more tolerable by the scrub, which lined both banks of the river, excluding every breath of air. Jones did his business, and next morning they started for the long 20-miles' pull home against the stream.

Jones pulled away bravely, with an occasional spell for a rest and a drink. His wife sat in the stern-sheets with the baby sleeping quietly in her arms. Her parcels from the steamer were arranged around her. She heard the rippling murmur of the water on the boat's side, and the rattle of the sculls in the rowlocks. She felt the impulse of each stroke, and she knew the distance to the little slab and bark hut they called home was lessening. But it was hot! The shining water below seemed to reflect the heat of the pitiless blazing sky above. Suddenly the monotonous rattle of the sculls in the rowlocks stopped. The boat ceased to move. The current was slowly carrying her down the river. The woman in the stern-sheets looked up quickly, and saw her husband. He sat limply on the thwart. His hands still grasped the sculls. His eyes were open, but there was no light in them. There was foam on his bloodless lips. She sprang up and seized the sculls, while his body fell forward into the bottom of the boat. He was dead! The widow disposed the corpse as well as she could, closed the eyes, and then pulled the boat home with one hand, while she clasped her child to her breast with the other. There were no coroners or inquests in those days, and two or three compassionate neighbours buried the dead man.

It was not until 1864 that the idea of growing sugar-cane for profit was seriously entertained in New South Wales. It was found that cane would grow as far south as the Manning River, but the cost of machinery was a serious difficulty. In the year named, a French creole, from the Mauritius, made his appearance on the Manning, and induced some of the richer settlers to plant cane and put up a mill. He called himself a "Baron," and boasted of his experience and skill in sugar-making and distilling. The mill was a curiosity in its way. The "liquor" (cane juice) was pumped up from the rollers to the upper floor of the building, and was there clarified and boiled in deep copper pans holding some 300 gallons each. The result was that the syrup would not granulate, and, not having been properly clarified, had a most unpleasant taste. A very few trials sufficed to show that "the Baron" was a hopeless incompetent, if no worse. He had managed to get a good fat salary from his dupes for the twelve months or so that the delusion lasted; and, when the exposure came, he took himself off before worse came of it. The farmers ploughed out their cane, and disposed of their mill and its costly appliances for what they would fetch. Of course the whole thing was a transparent fraud from beginning to end.

The sugar-boom was louder, and lasted longer at Port Macquarie. The humid climate, and rich volcanic soil of that locality were evidently specially suited for sugar-cane, just as they also are for the production of a rich, full-bodied, coarse-flavoured red wine very like some of the vintages of the Ionian Islands and Southern Italy. Sugar was supposed to be a very profitable crop. It was well known what large returns the West Indian plantations once gave with really very primitive appliances, and there seemed really no reason why the same thing might not be done in Australia if skilled overseers and sugar-boilers could be got from the West Indies or elsewhere. At Port Macquarie a very considerable area was planted, chiefly with the rank-growing, juicy Bourbon cane. Some small mills were put up, and worked with horse-power. Sugar was made too, and it is quite possible that, if the enterprise had been persevered in under proper scientific direction, if experiments had been made to find a variety of cane really suited to the soil and climate, and proper appliances had been used for the extraction of the sugar, something might have come of it. As it turned out, the Bourbon cane was a dismal and unmitigated failure, as it afterwards proved in Queensland. It grew and flourished exceedingly, up to a certain point; but it proved extremely susceptible to the attacks of disease. Winter and wet weather were equally destructive, and it was financially ruinous.

The people of the Macleay River caught the sugar fever like the rest. Mr. Sydney Verge, a then wealthy landowner of the district, put up a large sugar-mill on the river, and the Colonial Sugar Refining Co. there erected their first Australian mill, which was subsequently removed to the Clarence. Nearly every one was bitten with the sugar mania, and all burned their fingers. It was not seen that the successful prosecution of that, or any other industry required knowledge and experience, and nobody had it. A few partial successes were achieved, but it was found that the cane suffered much from the winter frosts which stopped its growth, if they did not cut it down altogether. Perhaps, if the truth were known, the plants came in the first place from a diseased stock; but there was little room for selection. It was, in most cases, Hobson's choice, and anyone who wanted to grow cane had to take such plants as were offered to him or none, and in any case no one had the necessary knowledge and experience to guide him in making a selection.

It would not be easy to overrate the services rendered to the Colony by the Colonial Sugar Refining Company. When they erected their first mill on the Macleay, they were absolutely without experience in the treatment of cane and cane liquor. They began by trying to make "concrete"—boiling the syrup till it was a solid mass This was shipped to their Sydney works (then situated in Parramatta-street). It was soon found that the system did not pay, and it was abandoned. However, the Company was not discouraged. It persevered in its efforts, making new experiments when the old ones failed, and accumulating experience, the only source of real knowledge. The Macleay River mill, however, was soon removed to the Clarence, where, it was found, the cane would really thrive. All who had attempted growing cane on the Macleay soon came more or less heavily to grief; some, who had proceeded cautiously, only lost the produce of a year or two's work; but others, lured on by the hope of sudden wealth, and the idea that they would be able to play the part of the old-fashioned West India planters of the pre-emancipation days, had not only given time, labour, and land, but they had spent every penny at their command, and pledged their credit far beyond their means of repayment. Many were totally ruined beyond hope of redemption. It all resulted from the common folly of letting go the substance and grasping at the shadow. If the old West India planters had not had the advantage of slave labour with a monopoly of the English market for their sugar they would not have realised such splendid returns from their plantations, and the proof of this is to be found in the utter collapse of West India values when emancipation and free-trade came to take away slave labour and monopoly.

Further north the results were better. On the Bellinger, one small sugar-mill, owned by a farmer named Williams, survived till 1880. It was a curiosity in its way, made entirely by Williams himself, who was a blacksmith by trade, and a most ingenious man to boot. The rollers (a set of three, placed upright) had been cast and turned for him in Sydney: but he had himself made the strong iron frames in which they were set. The clarifiers and boiling-pans he made out of half tanks, and he built the furnace, flue, and chimney. He worked the farm and mill with the help of his numerous family, and it would have been very wonderful if, under such circumstances, with the most unremitting industry, the concern had not been made to pay. There was a similar example of industry and ingenuity combined on the Lower Clarence in John Bale, who lived on one of the islands of Shoal Bay. He was one of the first to plant cane, and as there was no mill to crush it for him, he resolved to make his own. As he had even less money than Williams, he could not buy iron rollers. He therefore turned them out of a bean-tree log (the hardest of Australian woods).

He even had to make his own lathe for the purpose. In fact, with the exception of a number of cog-wheels, and odds and ends, which he had bought as old iron, the whole mill was the work of John Bale's own hands.

The first sugar-mill on the Clarence was a co-operative affair at Ulmarra. It was opened by the Earl of Belmore, the then Governor, during his visit to the Clarence in 1868. The capital was subscribed by the farmers of the neighbourhood, but it was an utter and very costly failure. It never made a pound of sugar. It was designed by a local genius, and was of much the same type as "The Baron's" brilliant conception on the Manning. For many years it remained closed and useless; but in 1875, Mr. William Small, of Swan Creek, and his brother-in-law, Mr. Edward Creer, of Grafton, bought it from the co-operators, who were not sorry to get some of their money back. A manager from the Mauritius or West Indies was engaged, and the old building was newly equipped with rational appliances. The new manager was considered a failure. He could not make sugar, and the management was entrusted to Mr. Grey, who had just arrived as chief engineer of the new steamer "City of Grafton," from the Clyde. He worked the mill most successfully, till it was closed for want of cane to operate on. The C.S.R. Co.'s mill at Southgate, on the opposite side of the river, being also closed, and removed about the same time, and for the same reason—the persistent failure of the cane crops on the upper course of the stream.

There were others who entered on the business with various degrees of success. The farmers of Carr's Creek and Carr's Island, a few miles above Grafton, established a very well equipped little mill. But it shared the fate of almost all attempts at co-operation in Australia, and ultimately became the property of Mr. Thomas Bawden, of Grafton, who then represented the Clarence in the Legislative

Assembly. Mr. Martin, of Great Marlow, had a small mill worked by horse-power. These were the only two sugar-mills ever worked above Grafton, and they had to contend with that curious climatic influence which, in Australia, seems to forbid the sugar-cane to thrive anywhere beyond the influence of the sea breeze. At Southgate, Mr. William Leeson had a small mill, and did fairly well for many years till the cane crops began to fail in his neighbourhood, though he was heavily handicapped by the near neighbourhood of "The Company's" large mill. Mr. Alec. Meston had a sugar-mill at Ulmarra. He was a son of Archibald Meston, one of the earliest among the pioneers of the New England and Clarence districts. Alec. Meston has since removed to the Richmond River. One of his neighbours at Ulmarra was a Mr. Chowne, an old Plymouth shipwright, who had been in the West Indies, and had there seen enough to show him how sugar is made. His little mill was the nearest copy he could manage of a West India sugar-house, and he succeeded in making a very fair yellow sugar. There were many others who tempted fortune in the same way with varying success; but the recital would be wearisome. It is only interesting where the examples cited are typical of classes, or characterised by some special peculiarity.

One such case is that of Mr. Kinnear, of Chatsworth Island. Like Mr. Chowne, he was a shipwright. He hailed from Clydesdale. He was one of the earliest selectors on the Clarence, taking up the full area of 320 acres allowed under Sir John Robertson's Act. In those days timber was plentiful and good, and Mr. Kinnear made money by ship and boat building, and farming as a sort of recreation. When sugar promised to be a success, he planted cane and put up a mill. He soon found, however, that if his mill was to pay, he must have a great deal more cane to crush than he could grow, without employing more labour than he could profitably superintend or could well afford to pay for. He let most of his uncleared land on improving leases, paying for the timber when cut up and split for firewood. He bound the tenants to grow a certain area of cane, which he crushed for them "on the halves," and thus he killed several birds with one stone—got his land cleared and cultivated, firewood cut, and his mill supplied with cane on terms mutually advantageous to all concerned.

These instances prove the truth that West Indian experience is almost useless in dealing with Australian sugar. All the really good Australian managers, with perhaps two exceptions, have been men with exclusively Australian experience. Even the rare exceptions referred to, have had to unlearn all they knew, and begin afresh to learn an entirely new mode of manipulation. Australian bushmen, like the Mestons; shipwrights, like Messrs. Chowne and Kinnear, are examples in point. Then there is Mr. Grey, the newly-arrived engineer from the Clyde, and many another like example. There is also the example of the C.S.R. Co., which has always steadily set its face against the rule of thumb expert from over the sea, and has trusted to nothing but their own practical local experience and skill with genuine scientific knowledge, to guide them.

But, to return to the scenes of older Sydney! Why do they so persistently refuse to fade from my memory? Here I find myself once more in 1852, in the old Bank of New South Wales, in that dark, low and dismal building on the east side of George-street, with the dingy grass plot in front of it; how unlike a modern bank it is to look at! and yet they made money there. Once more do I pore over those ghostly old ledgers, rich in memories of embryo Australia —crammed with bygone names, each folio with its little story of surname, each one mingles somehow with the warp and weft of early Sydney family life. Trustees of Launcelott Iredale, William Ranken Scott, Rueben Uthar, George Swinnerton Yarnton, R. and E. Tooth, John Yates Ruther, R. A. A. Morehead, T. S. Mort, Herbert Salwey, W. C. Wentworth, R. R. C. Robertson, of Wellington Vale; John Smith, of Wallerawang; C. R. and W. D. G. Haly; and time would fail me to tell of the Paytons, the Tittertons, and of Tom Kite and of Elizabeth Beard, and of the times when the wild red and white epacris could be found growing two miles nearer to the General Post Office than they now can be.

Days when brave, manly, old family picknickers rowed heavy boats full of girls in the teeth of north easters and of southerly busters up and down the harbour, where steam launches now save all the work; brave old fellows who posted bank ledgers in the day-time, and made their wives and daughters happy with music in the evening, and who could pull an oar and sail a boat with the best; when they used to give concerts in the big room of the Royal Hotel, and when Tom Mort would be *the* funny man of his party there. When "Simon the Cellarer" was the latest sensation in bass songs, *vice* "The Standard Bearer" superseded *(pro tem.)* Where is this race and breed of the Sydney bank clerk now? It is extinct. You may search for it in vain in Parramatta-street or in Redfern, for it sleeps at Camperdown, looking out on the Ryde Hill; sleeps at Devonshire-street; sleeps at Waverley and Rookwood. 1852 has passed away. Forty odd years are not much, perhaps, in the history of a place like England, but in Sydney, ye heavens, what a tale they tell!

> Old Times, what sort of memories round them cling!
> Of hopes that blossom, warped, and died, in life's delightful spring;
> The time of my childhood, the land of my prime,
> All the passions and scenes of that rapturous time
> When the feelings were young and the world was new,
> Like the fresh bowers of Eden unopening to view.

1852 seems 500 years ago when one notes all the changes, the progress, improvements, births, deaths, and marriages, which have effaced so many old social and physical landmarks. Quaint, hut-like cottages, set solitary in the sand, snake-haunted scrub of Botany and North Shore, neatly furnished, and inhabited by faded ladies of the Bourke and Gipps era, have all been swept away to make room for modern terraces. How bright a Sydney Sunday was in 1852. The clear sun, the chiming bells, the streams of well-dressed, pretty girls, no matter whether it was winter at Christchurch, with Canon Walsh, or summer with the Rev. G. F. McArthur, at St. Mark's, Darling Point. The smell of flowers was in the air. The bank ledgers were closed for the day, and it was—Sydney! Sydney! that happy medium between the chills of Hobart and the heats of Brisbane. Sydney, with a remote touch of the tropics in its air at times, and yet able to grow lilac and apples, and be akin to the oak and elm-bearing lands of the earth.

To return to our dear old bank. The accountant, H. B. Cotton, was a tall, thin, mercurial gentleman, who in office hours wore a sort of long coat, and by way of relief to the tedium of eternal figures he would at times strike an attitude and quote Shakespeare, a proceeding which failed to meet the approval of John Hunter Bailey, our Scotch Secretary, a clever earnest man, a connection of Dr. Lang's, but foredoomed by the phthisis to a too brief career of usefulness. He checked his banking cough one day as he saw Cotton in a Shakespearian attitude, and uttered the words, "Is this sober earnestness in an accountant when there is a discrepancy in the balance?" alluding to some calling over that yet remained to be done over an undiscovered error, and which Bailey thought should take precedence even of Shakespeare.

Old John Black, the manager, lived on the premises,

which had not been constructed with that eye to the due separation of banking and domestic concerns which obtains now in the palatial banking houses. And it fell out one day that Mr. Bailey, while absorbed in writing letters of great importance to the London office, had his nerves shaken by feeling a something unknown and decidedly out of its place playing between his legs. The startled Secretary (who was childless himself), suspended his pen in mid air, dived under the office table, and beheld a half-clothed cherub (one of the junior Blacks) playing with the waste-paper basket. How it ever got there was a mystery, but it evoked this severe remark from the stern Scotch banking disciplinarian—"Ye little neckid savage! what are ye doing here?" Old Mr. Black at times took the counter himself if a teller were ill, and, as his eyesight was none too good, he generally on those rare occasions paid away some odd pounds too much to some dishonest cheque-cashers in the course of a day, which loss he balanced with a sigh and a dive into his own pocket for the sovereign; for he cared not to keep dinner waiting, had plenty of money and property, and was not one to cry over spilt milk. I can see his wry face, white hair and cravat, black dress suit and spectacles (he never *varied* his costume) before me now as vividly as in the earlier half of the century, a representative of the old Sydney school that we shall never see again.

In that dingy old den of a bank, there was actually a board room stowed away somewhere, and therein sat Richard Jones and Robert Firth; Donald Larnach and George Horne; William Rankin Scott and Joseph Scaif Willis; and they were men of "pluck," for they bought over four tons of gold for 50s. an ounce, well worth 75s.; and this, too, at a time when no one else in Australia would give even that for it, for Australian and Californian people lost their heads (outside of that board room) and felt sure that gold was going to be as plentiful as copper; and the Adelaide merchants packed up their wares, shut their warehouses, and took the contents to Melbourne, and came back laden with the yellow metal. At the dingy old den we kept a weird-looking foreigner down in the cellar, who melted the dust into bars for us. (I often played with the golden dumb-bells to stretch my arms after too much ledgers.)

It was then that John Godfrey Cohen, in Sydney, Edward Khull, in Melbourne, and a set of mining speculators blossomed out as "gold brokers" and "highest price given for rags, bones and bottles," or for "wool, wheat, tallow, hides, and wattle-bark" were superseded by notices of an extra 3d. here or 6d. there per ounce for gold from competing brokers so as to snap up parcels for shipment and save exchange on bank drafts.

What a lot of the "old" early original Sydney there was still left in 1852! And the faces that one then saw across the counter that are now missing! Richard Jones, of Moreton Bay, and Hovenden Hely; Bob Fitzgerald and F. B. Stephens; Rev. Ralph Mansfield, Irving and R. M. Roley; Father K. Mann; R. A. Hunt and Major Christie: E. Broadhurst, and E. Deas. Thomson—why go on? This is not a directory; and yet, primitive as the old Bank was in 1852, it had grown a bit since 1849; in the first quarter of which its modest record stood thus:—Notes circulated, £34,519; deposits, £225,767; coin, £157,564; land, etc., £12,579; debts due for bills discounted, etc., £225,793; and its assets were to its liabilities £401,528, to £260,286. The "Union" and the Australasia both more than doubled this record, and the "Commercial" was a good second to the New South. The Joint Stock was not born till 1852. The "New South" paid £50 to an 8 per cent. dividend. The Commercial, £3,237 to a 10 per cent. one, and the Union £25,317 to a 6 per cent. one; their reserve funds being—New South, £17,150; Commercial, £993 (how these two boys *have* grown since 31st March, 1849); Australasia, £53,451; and Union, £77,930. In the early days coin was kept more in the Colonial Treasury and the Military chest (as it was called) than in the banks, and up to 1837 the banks were in the minority for coin holding, for in that year the Colonial Treasury held £245,250 in coin, against a total of £182,182 held by *all* the banks.

Talking of banks, the Union of Australia started in 1837 (twenty years after the "New South,") and was so well supported in London that every share was taken up without even being publicly advertised. Its first essay was a junction with the Tamar Bank, at Launceston (V.D.L.), then a branch at Hobart. Then followed branches at Sydney, Melbourne, and New Zealand, in the order named. The Australasia started in 1835, but its early progress was marred by the insolvent Bank of Australia getting heavily into its debt in 1843; but by 1849 it was far ahead of all other banks in the magnitude of its transactions, though it still could pay no dividend owing to the cause just mentioned. As a proof of the "booms" and collapses that occurred even in the early days, I may mention that from 1834 to 1848 a duty of 30 per cent. was charged in Sydney on auction sales, which jumped from £513,388 in 1839 to £1,246,742 in 1840, and down to £310,831 in 1844. Liens on wool and mortgages on stock shewed equally curious fluctuations between '43 and '46.

Enough of statistics. Let us return to the old Bank. Abram Black and P. W. Plower banked there and elsewhere too, for they had plenty of spare money to lodge, albeit that one "strong room" was a mere iron box, or room with thin walls, and thieves would have found it without fire or thief-proof doors had it been attacked, and John Russell (brother of Peter Nicol R., iron-founder, of that ilk), often came over to it and fixed it up. He it was who went to a fancy ball in Sydney in a suit of armour of his own make. Our bank staff then included Robert Woodhouse, John Ponsford, Luke Clarence Garling, William Colley Lang, Samuel Nasmith, John Evans, and so on down to old Byron Drury, the night watchman, who had seen some bayonet charges in his young days, and feared no midnight burglars, though there were none in 1852, for money was too easily got then for people to want to thieve much.

Trade expanded enormously. One big firm who supplied most of the public houses in Sydney used to pay in £1000 a day in greasy bank notes, gold, silver, and copper, and they had another account at the Australasia as well, or (as we clerks used to call it in those days), the Goliath, and huge bank drafts for £30,000 and the like found their way from us to foreign parts, and came back in the shape of cargoes of tea and sugar from China and Manilla, sent for by people, too, who never before had been in that line, but who were not going to miss the golden chance of coining money at that busy season; all done on bills, too, which were punctually met at maturity later on. You could not go wrong then in buying anything, land, houses, merchandise, or what not, it all went up and up in price, the exception being station property, for there was no carriage for wool, all teams being taken up for the diggings, and all hands all clearing to the gold fields.

The crumbling of these big banks has been a matter of slow and sure growth. For many years the cobra and white ant of finance have been secretly at work where all looked sound and stout outside; in the days of the bygone, John Smith, squatter, of New South Wales (we will say), wanted to buy some 50,000 acres of his run, and it was managed by a stroke of the pen; no money passed, but a debit went in the bank ledger to John Smith, and a credit to the

Colonial Treasurer; and this sort of thing was repeated in the case of Thomas Brown, another " pastoral tenant of the Crown," and many more of them, but still no coin passed. It was all on paper, so to speak, till at last one day the Colonial Treasurer wanted some of his million sterling, and then, you see, John Smith's security was not quite so saleable as it might have been, and it became necessary to sell up some country storekeepers, who had sperm candles, galvanised iron, American axes, flour, and other articles that really *were* convertible into money. And then meetings of creditors and liquidators by arrangement swarmed in the land, and people said "times are bad, but we have touched bottom now." Yet it was not so. The rabbits, drought, and compound interest had a "cut in" at the game, but still the assets and advances looked well on paper, and then, by Jove, you know! the labour party took a hand in the deal, and foreign depositors at last began to " look askew" in real earnest. Another presto! something happened which made all hands, except, perhaps, bank shareholders, squirm. If the crash had come mercifully ten years earlier, when assets were more marketable, and when Baring Brothers and others were still " right side up," it would have been all right. Everyone wished that advances had been more "spread" and distributed, only on securities which came in from one to four times in each year. And now let us review matters a little.

In 1851 gold was discovered, and gazetted on May 10th, in Sydney. Capital and labour had worked together up to then, but labour cleared out at once and left his master's sheep and calves to the dingoes and eagle hawks. The sailor left his ship, the carpenter his bench and his contract, and capital was left lamenting without warning, consideration, or apology, and "capital" never forgot it. Afterwards —when the wheel of fortune had made another round—he, in turn, grew selfish; *he* was "on top" in 1853. On a population of some 200,000 Victoria raised £9,000,000 sterling in gold, and, in 1856, £12,000,000, or equal to £40 for every soul of her then population. This was more than she needed for currency, and it went home. But this did not last, and now N. S. Wales could barely find her own goldfield, or supply her own coin requirements; but Queensland raised £5 worth of gold yearly for every soul in her borders, and should certainly try to keep enough of it on hand to vary the monotony of too much paper and greenbacks in the near future. Trade is not what it was, and the English "rings" have "sat upon" Australia. Tin was worth £130 a ton till we found it here, and the "ring" dropped it permanently to £90; copper from £90 to £45. Bismuth and silver fell also, for fear that Australia should grow too rich, and wool travelled from 1s. 6d. down to 7d., flour from £50 to £11, and white sugar can now be got for the price we once paid for dark.

Everything that Australia produces except gold has shrunk terribly in value, and we *must* "face the music" and meet the altered times with some better weapons than strikes, phantom reserve funds, reconstruction, on the "family party system" and other modern-time blunders; and we must especially pray to be delivered from all reconstruction that only covers up old sores and that fails to use a surgical knife that would cut right off with heroic fortitude all bad debts, and start fair and square again. If not we shall break down and pull up lame before we are once round the course. Heaps of capital and confidence were both annihilated wholesale in years gone by through an idiotic anti-kanaka crusade.

And so it has come to pass at the close of the nineteenth century we witness the spectacle of men who have toiled

---

NOTE.—The above was penned at the time of the financial crisis of 1893.—EDITOR.

all their lives to amass a little current business money being asked to convert it into shares, and pay the impounders thereof interest for the use of it; the said impounders having now murdered all the confidence which once "greased the wheels" of commerce, and giving nothing whatever by way of substitute for it. They asked people to convert their current business cash into the shares of a new "bank" that has neither written off the bad debts, nor foresworn the sins of its parent and progenitor bank; and what is perhaps still worse, our Australian parliaments do not care to face the task of probing the piled up banking blunders of the past twenty-five years, the result being that the facilities which at one time helped trade along have disappeared, and without any removal of the old cancers to compensate the loss. How will it all end? We should pull through it all, terrible as the amount of dirt in the stable is, if people kept the ten commandments within the next twenty-five years, and refrained from coveting and stealing, and laboured for six days in the week, and so on. But—will they? We shall see.

I can understand bad times in a place like England, which cannot grow all its own meat and meal; or I could understand bad times in early Australian days, before the wilderness was subdued, and in the last century. But when I came to Australia in the "forties" a man with £100 a year was "passing rich," with bread and meat at 1d. a lb., eggs and butter 4d. the dozen and lb., and so forth, and plenty of good colonial tweed and leather to make clothing from. There were no "Boards of Health" or "zymotic diseases," or poison germs with long scientific names ending in "oid" floating around in those days. It was all gum trees and ozone. "Homespun" was the style both indoors and out, and as with Australia so with America. In the primitive days when men lived on pork and beans, there were no dreadful social and political problems to solve, no terrible suicides and embezzlements to report and shudder at. But when $100 broadcloth suits and $1000 diamond rings came into fashion, and whisky bars to boot, then the "trouble" began.

The gold discovery in California in 1849, and in Australia in 1851, sent the whole civilised world on a new track of luxury such as the fathers of that generation never dreamt of. I was one of the early rush to California from these colonies in 1849 with a cargo of produce, and of course all the sailors bolted on arrival, and I had to employ five American ship captains to unload my lot. They had all lost their own crews, and had nothing to do meantime, and so they worked like men for $10 a day in unloading boxes of Australian potatoes and planks of Australian timber into the steam scow. They were not proud. They were of the old American Connecticut stamp, and they wore jackets of green baize such as bakers' hot rolls are covered with at home. They belonged to the "pork and beans" section and era of the American community, and my money was as good to them as any other man's. We talk of bad times in Australia, yet the country grows all the food we eat and clothes we wear, or could do so, or ought to do so, or, if this be not the case *yet*, let us then learn to consume less *variety*, or else to make Australia grow it *all*. England never could do this for *herself*. We talk of bad times while the champagne and sardines class of luxuries figure so largely in our list of imports! It is clear we cannot afford to pay for these things, so let us leave off importing superfluities, and then see how soon the bad times would disappear.

There has been too much of the sudden "jump up" in Australia—the mother, for instance, at the wash-tub and the daughter at the piano, the father shouldering the hod

of bricks and the son driving a buggy and "putting on
side." *One* generation is not enough to carry over
such a metamorphosis; it would need to filter through three
or four of them in order to be a plant to take permanent
root. The very fact of our importing our domestic female
servants is a proof and outward sign of our unsoundness
in political economy; the daughters of the small yeoman
class, *born in the country*, should form its domestic servants
the same as they do in Great Britain, and are the only good
sort obtainable. As to the quality of the imported article,
you can search the pages of the various Australian
"Punches." But it is the old story with most of us; we
must have luxuries, and cannot be content with necessaries
only. Take the burglar who breaks into our house; does
he (in one case out of 500) do it to feed starving babies at
home? Not he, he does it in order to spend the proceeds
(heavily discounted beforehand by the receiving "fence")
in some wretched orgie in a den of infamy. Our very burglar *must* have his "luxuries." If people would but dispense
with all superfluities, be they ever so "good for trade;" if
men in bush and town would but take their wages home on
Saturday nights and not want to be pulled home by their
wives at 11 p.m.; if people would eschew imported luxuries
and fill their bellies and clothe their backs solely with the
rich and glorious abundance of colonial produce, we should
not need to care to know how the bullion stood in the bank,
or whether that terrible institution had any confidence in
us or did the other thing; whether the "balance of trade"
or "drain of bullion" were with us or against us. We
should laugh at "panics," knowing that we could not
possibly eat sovereigns and bank notes, but that with plenty
of Adelaide flour, Albury wine, Ipswich tweed, and so forth,
we were enjoying blessings which we should be a great deal
more grateful for, if those confounded phases of style con-

Hon. W. C. Wentworth.   Hon. E. Deas-Thomson.
Major-General L. Macquarie.
Sir John Hay.   Sir Charles Cowper.

sequent on the gold era had not so unsettled our brains that we don't know when we *are* well off, and sigh for all sorts of unattainable and needless luxuries; the dulness of our small colonial townships forms a much greater grievance for a man of intellect to contend with, than any sameness of food question does, and to it alone can be attributed the extent to which many a good man, who would hold his own in Sydney or London, or any other centre of intellect, and never fall, flies to the arms of Dr. Martell or Dr. James Hennessy for *consolation*, and learns, too late, what kind of an article in *that* line they dispense. And yet, a country town in Australia is no duller than one in England.

The gold discovery business is about played out now in America and Australia; we have derived some solid benefits from it in the shape of vested wealth, so let us hold on to them all we can, and not let them go; and the best way to do this, is to drop, at once and for ever, all the habits of luxury that came in with the zenith of the gold times, and return to the primitive days of 1849 as regards our *ideas* of style and expenditure. We should then soon think and see *how rich*, not how poor, we are.

Where is the enchantress so potent as Memory? Not Circe, nor Thalaba, nor Ormandine can weave so sweet a spell around us. In a moment, in a dream, a few music notes of an old sweet simple tune, unheard and forgotten since the dear dead mother or grandam sang us to sleep with it half-a-century before—come back unbidden, and lo! a veil is lifted. The shifted scene of old Father Time slides back again for a brief space, and the lump in our throat rises simultaneously with a delicious and reckless excitement and glamour as we are once more intoxicated, in sober old age, with one maddening glimpse of

> The home of our childhood, the haunts of our prime.

F

And then the young wife takes up the parable of music for us where the mother and grandam have dropped it, and, despite the baby, her skilled fingers, trained by constant "exercises," render us the masterpieces of the French and German school, with Italy and Hungary thrown in.

Why should Memory die? Why should the past glide from us and be forgotten? How dearer now it seems than it did when it was with us and was called "the present!" Long live Memory, say I, for nought else in heaven or earth can compare with its sweet litheness, its tender magic, with the music that comes to us again in dreams; music which in warm life played to us in the years that glowed and faded so long ago. Enough. Let me pass from the general to the particular—from the abstract to the concrete, and regard, with my mind's eye, the men whom Wentworth's genius decreed should form the first real Parliament of Australia, drawn from all the eastern half of the continent. How bright and young were Australia and ourselves then! Can it be that so many of them are now not here? Plunkett, Murray, Martin, Lang, Darvall, Arnold Holt, Henry Piddington, Nicholson, Cowper, Donaldson—not to mention the northern men: Macalister and Cribb. Ay, the inexorable scythe hath been mowing, and old Sydney suffereth a change; and the sepulchres are fuller and the living who sprang from the dead abound and are more and more with us. Above all Memory still lives, and they live with her. God bless Memory, say I, for what were life without her. But what of these early men whose genius and ability are in memory green spots of the past! Draw back the curtain of time, and let us see.

CHAPTER IV.

THE CURTAIN OF TIME DRAWN BACK—EARLY MEN OF MARK—
THEIR DEEDS OF HISTORY—MAJOR-GENERAL MACQUARIE—
HIS PERIOD OF GOVERNORSHIP—WILLIAM FORSTER—A
LITERARY LEGISLATOR—A MARKED CAREER—EDWARD DEAS-
THOMSON—WILLIAM CHARLES WENTWORTH—THE FATHER
OF THE CONSTITUTION.

MAJOR-GENERAL LACHLAN MACQUARIE, FIFTH GOVERNOR
OF NEW SOUTH WALES.

LACHLAN MACQUARIE was born in Scotland in 1768. He joined the army at the early age of eighteen; in course of time he became lieutenant-colonel in the 73rd regiment. When news reached the Secretary for the Colonies of the doings of the New South Wales Corps and the deposition of Governor Bligh, Lord Castlereagh looked about for a man possessed of firmness and decision to take up the reins of Government of New South Wales, then in a state approaching anarchy. His choice fell upon Lieutenant-Colonel Macquarie. Macquarie took up his new office on December 28th, 1809, and one of his first acts was to despatch the New South Wales Corps to India with a detachment of the 73rd regiment. After this he bent his energies to put the institutions of the country in fair working order. This proved no easy task, for he had to fight against vested interest, which had arisen under the rule of former governors. At this time the colony was in a sad state of poverty. Sydney practically consisted of a number of huts and tents, and, as might be expected from the class of people who then formed the population, vice of every kind was rampant. The population totalled 11,590 persons, nearly the whole of them being made up of officials and convicts. He declared null and void all the actions of the officers of the New South Wales Corps in connection with the deposition of Governor Bligh. Floods on the Hawkesbury had brought destitution on the farmers in that district. The Governor paid the district a visit and took active measures to relieve the distress, distributing relief where necessary, and, by his assistance and sympathy, revived the spirits of the settlers. He had marked out, sites for townships, and gave the settlers allotments for residences as well as for cultivation. He supplied them too with stock on the easiest terms. He then commenced the making of roads and the erection of bridges wherever they were likely to be of use, and might lead to settlement. At this time there existed a beaten track between Sydney and Parramatta, a portion of which is now George-street. This road was subsequently continued on to Windsor, and from being a miserable cart track was soon made into as fine a road as could be desired anywhere. He then commenced the road over the Blue Mountains from Sydney to Bathurst, a distance of one hundred and thirty miles—a stupendous work at that time, and, indeed, would be considered a work of considerable magnitude in the present day. It may be mentioned that it was not until 1813 that the feat of crossing the Blue Mountains was accomplished by William Charles Wentworth, Gregory Blaxland, and William Lawson, and the famous Bathurst plains thereby opened up for settlement. If Governor Macquarie was more remarkable for one thing than another, it was for the way in which he caused public buildings to be erected, not only in Sydney, but in all the towns of the colony. Courthouses, churches, hospitals, gaols, barracks—all were built under his direction. The present Parliament houses of New South Wales, the Sydney mint, Hyde Park barracks, now used for various court purposes, and the present Supreme Courthouse among the rest. In fact he erected no less than two hundred and three public buildings in the colony, in addition to forty-seven built in Van Diemen's Land.

Governor Macquarie's manner of dealing with the convict population was humane in comparison with his predecessors. He believed that punishment should be meted out to the convict with a view to deter him from crime as well as to punish him for the commission of it. A parliamentary committee appointed to inquire into transportation, in 1812, paid a high tribute to the efforts made by the Governor in this direction. He had to suffer, it is true, the enmity of the class who had resigned their posts in the New South Wales Corps when that body was ordered to India—a class who thought that the colony and the convicts were made for their special use, and abuse too. Before his departure from the colony, this section of the community preferred certain complaints against him. But his manly and straightforward defence was a complete refutation of the charges. He described the condition of the colony on his arrival, explained what he had done, and then set out the state in which he had left the colony. The population had increased more than threefold, and prosperity and progress existed everywhere. Property and stock had increased tenfold. The revenue increased nearly fourfold, and public buildings and roads were to be seen in all parts of the colony. These facts were plain and unanswerable.

Before his departure from the colony he became Major-General, and was presented with a gold cup by the inhabitants as a protest against the calumnies of a few of their number, and as evidence of the popularity and esteem in which he was held. Governor Macquarie's rule commenced 28th December, 1809, and ended 1st December, 1821. He left Sydney 15th February, 1822, and died in London 1st July, 1824.

The Honourable William Forster.

Among the men who, in the early days of responsible government, formed, and moulded the public life of the colony, none is more deserving of notice than that of the late William Forster.

William Forster was born at Madras in 1818; he arrived in Sydney when eleven years old. He was, like most of the leading men of his day, educated by Mr. W. T. Cape. After completing his education he went into the interior of the colony, and entered on squatting pursuits. While thus engaged he followed up his literary work, and supplied many contributions to the Sydney press dealing with the political questions which then agitated the public mind. He took the side of the squatters, and, in an able and most effective way, defended their rights. He strongly opposed the action of Sir George Gipps and his regulations respecting the pastoral interests. About this time Sir James Martin was editor of the *Atlas*, and Mr. Forster published a clever satire, entitled, "The Devil and the Governor." In it the following passage occurred:—

> "I grant you the praise you've fairly won
> By the deeds you do and the deeds you've done;
> I know that as causes corrupt the mind
> Like the chains by which tyrants have crushed mankind,
> That the blighting touch of a despot's rod
> Kills in man's spirit the breath of God.
> That the purpose he bade your race fulfil
> Is not for the meek slave's fettered will,

> That the cherishing light of the holy skies
> Falls barren and vain upon servile eyes,
> That the weeds of evil will thrive their best
> Where the fair shoots of nature are clipped and drest ;
> Yes, under those climes where the poisonous brood
> Of error is nursed by solitude—
> Where souls are bowed by the weight they bear,
> Where their moral sky looks dark, and their air
> Is thick with the filth that bondage breeds,
> I scatter my foul and fertile seeds—
> Where most I am bent on man's undoing
> The tyrant assists my work of ruin."

This at once brought him into prominence as a man possessed of no mean critical ability, and it bore testimony to a cultured and refined literary cast of mind. He wrote, among other poems, a sonnet on Russia :—

> " 'Twixt east and west a giant shape she grew,
>   To both akin, and making both afraid.
> Casting a lurid shadow on the new
>   And ancient world, her greedy eyes betrayed
> The tiger's heart, and ominously surveyed
>   The people destined for her future prey ;
> From Polar steppes and ice-encumbered seas
>   To where the warm and blue Symplegades
> Darken the splendour of a Grecian day,
>   She stretched her long grasp, conquering by degrees ;
> And, when at length the banded nations rose
>   In armed resistance, their combined array
> With equal arms she shrunk not to oppose,
>   But bravely stood, as still she stands, at bay."

On the attainment of Responsible Government, Mr. Forster sat in the House as member for the Murray electorate. At other times he represented East Sydney, St. Leonards, The Hastings, Queanbeyan, Illawarra, The Murrumbidgee, and Gundagai. He commenced as a supporter of the Cowper Ministry. He, however, opposed their education policy, being in favour of a purely secular system. Having ousted the Administration, he was called upon to form a Government. He succeeded in getting together a Ministry, in which Mr. Saul Samuel (now Sir Saul) became Colonial Treasurer, Mr. John Black, Minister for Lands; Mr. Geoffrey Eagar, Minister for Works, Mr. E. Wise (afterwards Judge of the Supreme Court) Attorney-General, and Mr. J. F. Hargrave (afterwards Judge of the Supreme Court) Solicitor-General. Mr. Forster's cabinet remained in power till March, 1860. It was then defeated on its Upper House Electoral Bill, and was succeeded by the Robertson-Cowper Ministry. When Sir James Martin formed his Ministry in 1863, Mr. Forster was offered and accepted the position of Colonial Secretary. The Ministry lasted until February, 1865, when they were defeated on their protectionist proposals. In October, 1868, he is found taking office as Minister for Lands under Sir John (then Mr.) Robertson, when he resigned in 1870. He again took office with Sir John Robertson in February, 1875. In October of that year he left for England as Agent-General, an office then held by Sir Charles Cowper, whose health, however, had incapacitated him from fully performing the duties. He was tendered a banquet, which took place at the Town Hall, a large number of his fellow colonists, of all shades of opinion, being present to do him honour.

Sir Charles Cowper having died in 1876, Mr. Forster received the appointment, which position he held till the end of 1880, when he was recalled by the Parkes Government. Sir Saul Samuel, the present Agent-General, was appointed to the post. Mr. Forster returned to Sydney in the early part of 1881. He found on his arrival that he had been elected to a seat in the Legislative Assembly for the electorate of Gundagai. He took his seat on the opposition side of the House, the Parkes Ministry being then in office. Some time before his return to the colony, the question of his removal from the office of Agent-General was debated in the House, as it was considered by a large section of the people and parliament that a great injustice had been done to him by his removal from the Agent-Generalship. It was said that the principal cause of his removal was a bold, if imprudent letter which he addressed to Sir Henry Parkes. It was at the same time acknowledged by even his political opponents that he filled the office in a most efficient manner. During the later years he attended to his parliamentary duties, and although recognised as the leader of the Opposition he never asserted the right to the position. The question of the opening of the museum and library on Sunday came up for discussion at this time. Mr. Forster took a prominent part in the debate, being a champion of secular education. In his speech on a motion affirming the desirability of opening these institutions on Sundays, he said, "I do not record the vote which I am about to give on any religious sanction. I do not say but that I respect them, or that I am without religious sanction for the votes which I am about to give; but it seems to me that in this particular case a view more consistent with public opinion, and the tendency of the colony may be taken. It appears to me that the main object of this resolution is that it proposes to make use of the Government and of our public institutions to enforce dogma—to enforce a particular view of a religious question. I am not one of those who, as it has been assumed, repudiate the institution of the Sabbath as a day of rest for the working man, but I do protest against a particular view of this day of rest being enforced by the authority of the Government or of Parliament; and it is upon this ground that I protest against this resolution. I object to the House or the Government being called upon to enforce, through the authority of public bodies, any doctrine so inconsistent with our previous tendency—with the course which we have taken in public affairs from the time responsible government was instituted. We have abolished State aid—we have announced to the world that we have no national religion—that religion is a thing to be left to the consciences of the people, and not to be controlled by the authority of the State. We have, I am told, adopted secularism in our national schools, though I do not think they are thoroughly secular. It seems to me that the teaching in the public schools embodies a good deal of dogmatic theology; and I hope the time will come when we shall go on in the path in which we have hitherto trodden, and that we shall make our public schools thoroughly secular. A country which has adopted this policy, which boasts that it has gone ahead of the mother country in liberal views, would be thoroughly disgraced by adopting a resolution of this kind. To carry this resolution would simply be a triumph of narrow sectarianism, of a spirit altogether opposed to that of our institutions, to the course which the colony has taken hitherto. I hope the House will not take this retrograde step, but if honourable members should assent to the motion, I have no doubt that their action will be reversed before long. Any Government which relies for support upon narrow sectarian feeling will rely on a broken reed; and however strong the present Government may be, they will put their strength to a very dangerous test if they venture to base it on any support like this." Although in favour of secular education, he strongly championed denominational independence, which he considered "the only bulwark we had against the very worst despotism—the despotism of democracy."

When the news of his death was announced to the House, regret for the event and admiration for his high character and great abilities were expressed from all sides of the House.

Sir Henry Parkes, who was Premier at the time, and a most uncompromising opponent of the deceased, spoke as follows:—"It is my painful duty to move what had become the practice of this House—that the House adjourn in respect to his memory. The name of Mr. William Forster had been before the public of the colony for over thirty years. I think it is thirty years since, sitting in that gallery, I heard Mr. Wentworth, in one of his great speeches, make a long quotation from one of Mr. Forster's satires. I became acquainted with Mr. Forster on the very first day of the meeting of the first Parliament, and though it might surprise younger and newer members of that House, for several years I lived on the most cordial terms of relationship with him as a member of the House together with my honourable friend behind me—Sir John Robertson. We worked together in the early years of responsible government, and our votes were recorded on the same side in almost every struggle. I therefore had opportunities of judging of the value of the late member equal to those of any other member of the House. I heard his first speech, I saw all his early struggles, I witnessed all his actions on both sides of the House from first to last. Mr. Forster had now passed away across that dividing line which effaces all personal dissensions, and in watching his figure retiring into the land of shadows, we can only remember the services he has rendered here. Not only was he a contributor to our public political literature of very considerable eminence, but when he first became a member of this House in 1856 he devoted himself to the movement for the extension of political privileges. It is not generally known in our day, but it is a fact known to many, that he was the originator of the Electoral Act. It was he who suggested nearly all the most essential provisions of the measure, which afterwards, under the auspices of Mr. Cowper and my honourable friend behind me—Sir

John Robertson—passed into law. We all of us know with what intimate acquaintance with the circumstances of the country, with what a fearless examination of the public business of parliament, with what fearless opposition to all abuses, with what steadiness of purpose, he supported every cause which he once espoused; with what sleepless vigour he opposed anything which he believed to be wrong. We all know those striking distinguishing qualities in the late member. We all of us see, I am quite sure, and acknowledge, that there cannot be higher qualities in a representative of the people in this or any other land. Mr. Forster has now passed for ever from our ranks, and neither this House nor any other Legislature can well afford to lose a member so distinguished in education, so distinguished in practical knowledge of this country, and so distinguished by ability to give effect to what he believed. We, therefore, not only deplore his sudden death, and offer our best consolation to his bereaved friends, but we mourn what is indeed a great public loss, and a loss to the representative quality of this House." This graceful tribute was well received by the House.

The leader of the Opposition, the late Sir Alexander Stuart, followed, and said:—"I rise with no ordinary feelfeelings of sorrow to second the motion of the Colonial Secretary. In the death of Mr. Forster we are called upon to mourn one who can be ill spared at this juncture. Even those who have most keenly felt his invective or his caustic sarcasm will acknowledge that in the loss of Mr. Forster we lose a man of great ability, a man of cultured intellect, and a man who could, and did make himself heard on every question affecting the public welfare of the colony since ever he took part in public life. If such are the feelings of his public foes, I can hardly express the feelings with which we, on this side of the House, learned of the departure of our friend. We feel that we have lost our brightest ornament. Our greatest champion is laid low ; his voice is no longer heard ; and we feel that our greatest debater has gone from us—one whom, not only we, but the whole country, can ill afford to lose."

Although Mr. Forster was a politician—indeed the title of statesman might be applied to him more than to most of the politicians of New South Wales—still it cannot be said that he was a *practical* politician. He was most difficult to deal with in a ministry. He was more a critic than an administrator.

Sir Edward Deas-Thomson, C.B., K.C.M.G.

Generally speaking, the old Imperial officials who practically governed the colony in its early days, proved themselves antagonistic to the inhabitants and threw obstacles in the way whenever the people endeavoured to obtain some of the popular privileges to which they considered themselves entitled. It is pleasing now to look back upon the work of Sir. E. Deas-Thomson, who could not by any means be included in this category. Whilst scrupulously fulfilling the duties imposed upon him by his high and responsible office, he never forgot that the people had rights. Sir Edward Deas-Thomson was born in Edinburgh June 1st, 1800, and was educated at the high school of that city ; he also spent some time at Harrow, and finished at Caen, in France. He was for a few years in a mercantile house, and at a later period he introduced the system of double entry into the book-keeping accounts in the office of the Accountant-General of the Navy, his father holding that position at the time. In 1828 he was appointed to the position of Clerk of the Council in New South Wales. He arrived in Sydney on the 24th December, 1828. Five years after, he married the second daughter of Sir Richard Bourke, who was then Governor of the colony. In 1837 he was appointed to the position of Colonial Secretary and Registrar of Records, at the same time he was made a member of the Legislative Council, also a member of the Executive Council. The first Council under the "Constitution Act of 1842-43" was inaugurated by Mr. Deas-Thomson. From this up to the time of the new constitution, he held the position of Colonial Secretary, giving the greatest satisfaction to all parties in the country.

Considering that Mr. Deas-Thomson held almost despotic power, being next to the Governor, it is evident that he filled the office which he held with the utmost impartiality. It can be said of him that he made no enemies throughout the whole course of his career. When the committee was appointed to draw up the draft of the New Constitution, Mr. Deas-Thomson's name was found alongside that of W. C. Wentworth, and throughout the whole of the agitation it is remarkable that he took the side of the people in their endeavours to obtain the privileges they sought. And on the passing of the "Constitution Act" by the Legislative Council, he was chosen, with Mr. Wentworth, to proceed to England and watch its passage through the British Parliament. At this time he obtained two years' leave of absence from the colony, and was appointed a commissioner to the Paris exhibition in 1855. He retired from office just after his arrival from the old country in 1856. At the first election under the "New Constitution Act," Mr. Deas-Thomson was one of the first requisitioned to come forward for one of the city constituencies. But his health not being good he declined the honour sought to be conferred. He however accepted a seat in the Upper House, and was appointed the representative of the Government in that chamber. Mr. Deas-Thomson took an active part in the passing of the Act founding the University of Sydney, and was one of its first senators. Those appointed to act with him in 1854 were A. J. Hamilton, E. Broadhurst, J. B. Darvall, Stuart A. Donaldson, A. Denison, J. Macarthur, F. L. S. Merewether, B. O'Brien, J. H. Plunkett, W. C. Wentworth, Justice Therry, Rev. W. B. Boyce, Right Rev. C. H. Davis, and Sir Charles Nicholson, the first Chancellor being Sir Charles Nicholson. The first degrees were conferred in 1857, A. Renwick, C. Sutling, and W. Sutling receiving the degree of B.A. In 1859 Messrs. M. Burdekin, W. C. Curtis, R. M. Fitzgerald, E. Lee, D. S. Mitchell, W. C. Windeyer, T. W. Johnson, and T. Kinloch had conferred upon them the degree of Master of Arts. In 1866 the LL.D. degree was conferred on Messrs. J. S. Patterson and G. H. Stanley; the LL.B. degree in 1867 on Mr. F. E. Rodgers; that of M.B. in 1867 on Mr. P Smith; and that of M.D. in 1868 on Mr. C. F. Goldsbrough. In 1865 Sir Edward Deas-Thomson was elected Chancellor of the University, which position he retained till April, 1878, retiring then owing to failing health. He received the honour of knighthood in 1874, having been made a Commander of the Bath in 1856. His death took place 16th July, 1879.

WILLIAM CHARLES WENTWORTH.

William Charles Wentworth has sometimes been alluded to, as incomparably the greatest man appearing in the annals of Australian politics, and one of the few men mentioned in New South Wales history worthy the title of "statesman." Certainly, considering the circumstances of his surroundings during his public career, the greatness of the man must be acknowledged. The immense amount of labour which he gave to the crowning work of his life—the founding of the Constitution—is striking testimony to this. William Charles Wentworth was born at Norfolk Island in 1791, his father being at the time the surgeon-superintendent of that Island. He was sent to England when seven years old to be educated. Young Wentworth's father left Norfolk Island in 1805—at the time of the breaking-up of the establishment there. He was appointed principal surgeon on his arrival in New South Wales, and afterwards held the position of Road Trustee, Treasurer and Superintendent of Police, and Magistrate of the Colony. When young Wentworth was twenty-two years of age he joined Messrs. Lawson and Blaxland in that exploring expedition which led to the discovery of the pass over the Blue Mountains and the Bathurst Plains. The young pioneers suffered considerable hardships while exploring the pass and the then unknown regions beyond. The great benefits bestowed on the colony by the opening up of the vast interior can scarcely be adequately gauged at the present day. He left the colony for England in 1817 with a view of reading for the Bar. He entered as a student at Cambridge, and whilst there he published his "Description of New South Wales," which drew the attention of the British public to the young colony. The book was well written, and ran through several editions in a few years. About four years later he competed for the Chancellor's Medal for the best English poem on Australasia. This production took only second place, W. Mackworth Praed, afterwards so well known in literary circles, taking first honours. On leaving Cambridge he was called to the Bar, and returned to Sydney, being admitted there in 1824. It may be well to mention in this connection that up to the time of Mr. Wentworth's admission to the Bar, both branches of the legal profession had right of audience in the Supreme Court, but, on his admission, he and Dr. Wardell moved for a division. Messrs. Norton, Allen, Chambers, Garling, Rowe, and Moore appeared for the other branch, and Chief Justice Forbes ruled in favour of the lower branch. In 1827 the division was made by the judges allowing all practising to choose which branch they preferred to follow. Mr. Wentworth brought out with him from England material for the printing of a newspaper, which he called the *Australian*, Dr. Wardell and himself being co-editors. The first number of this paper appeared on October 14th, 1824. At that time, it must be borne in mind, there were simply two classes in the colony —the Governor, with Crown-appointed officials who were practically responsible to nobody, and the convict class. The generous young Australian and future statesman on many occasions sided with the oppressed. In October, 1824, the first civil jury was empanelled at Liverpool by Chief Justice Forbes. In the month of February, 1825, the first jury was empanelled in the Supreme Court, when Mr. Wentworth and Dr. Wardell appealed for the Emancipasts against the compilation of the lists. The application was disallowed, being irregular. In 1827 a great meeting was held under the auspices of the Patriotic Association. Mr. Wentworth spoke strongly on the question, and moved the adoption of the petition in favour of the principle. The petition was entrusted to Sir James Macintosh, but he was unsuccessful. On the accession of William IV., an address of congratulation to the Throne was moved by public meeting. Mr. Wentworth moved an amendment that full participation in the benefits and privileges of the British Constitution should be asked for New South Wales. Mr. Lethbridge seconded the amendment, which was unanimously adopted by the meeting. The Full Court decided, three years later, that under the statute of 6th George IV., all free persons were entitled to all the privileges of freedom. This decision settled the question of the right of Emancipasts to sit on juries, and put an end to the military jury system, which up to that time obtained in the colony. Mr. Wentworth came into collision with Governor Gipps in con-

G

nection with the purchase of a large tract of land in New Zealand. In concert with the Consul there, Mr. Busby and others had acquired ten millions of acres in the Middle, and two hundred thousand in the North Island, paying £200 each, and life annuities of £100, to the chiefs who ceded. In 1840 a Bill was introduced to deal with these claims, which resulted in their disallowance, it being held that British subjects had no right to form colonies of themselves, and that the Maoris, as an uncivilised people, had no proprietary privileges or right of legal transfer. The Bill was passed, although Mr. Wentworth personally advocated his claims as well as his partner's in the transactions. Undoubtedly the principal work of Mr. Wentworth's public career was the working out of the Constitution, the great Act which handed his name for ever down to posterity. In October, 1825, the first public meeting held in New South Wales bearing on the popular privileges, the names of D'Arcy Wentworth and William Charles Wentworth are among the very first mentioned. The meeting was held to prepare an address to Governor Brisbane on his departure from New South Wales. Mr. Wentworth being one of the persons present appointed to present the address, took the opportunity of claiming for the colony the right of representation with taxation, and suggested the establishment of a House of Assembly of one hundred members. In 1827 another meeting was held, at which an address was adopted and sent home through Mr. Blaxland for presentation to both Houses of Parliament. Two years later a further fight was made for Constitutional privileges, at a meeting held in the Sydney Court House. A motion was moved by Mr. Wentworth, and seconded by Mr. Lawson, asking for a House of fifty members, and asserting the right of the colonies to dispose of their own revenue.

It was at this meeting that the first mention was made

of a paid Agent-General, the Governor being memorialised to appropriate £1,000 for the purpose. Another meeting under the auspices of the Patriotic Association was held in 1835 to discuss the proposed Constitution, and the qualifications of members and voters. A proposition was made to have an Upper and Lower House ; another proposal was that there should be one House of fifty members, forty to be elective. In 1841 still another meeting was held to petition the Queen to extend the constitutional privileges of representation to the colony, alleging that the existing legislature was neither capable nor desirous of representing the community. This meeting was presided over by Dr. Bland. Several other meetings were held throughout the colony, and similar resolutions carried. On January 5th, 1843, news was received in Sydney that, yielding to the demands of reason and justice, and the clearly-expressed desire of the people, the Imperial Parliament had passed an Act (July 29th, 1842) conferring a Constitution on New South Wales ; so that, after fifteen years' agitation on the part of the colonists, headed by Mr. Wentworth, a Representative Council was granted. The Council consisted of fifty-four members, thirty-six of whom were elective, and eighteen nominated by the Crown. Four of the elective members were to represent Port Phillip, and of the nominated members six were, by virtue of their offices— the Colonial Secretary, Colonial Treasurer, Auditor-General, Attorney-General, Commander of the Forces, and the Collector of Customs. A freeholder of £200, or a householder of £20, enjoyed the electoral privilege ; £2,000, or an annual income of £100, was the qualification of member of Council, the term of office being for five years. Seven years afterwards, Tasmania, South Australia, and West Australia were likewise allowed the elective rights, while Port Phillip was erected into a separate colony under the name of Victoria. The Act reduced the electoral qualification in New South Wales and Victoria. In 1843 the first election under the Constitution took place in Sydney, five candidates being nominated. On June 15th, Messrs. Wentworth and Bland were returned by a large majority over Messrs. O'Connell, Cooper, and Hustler, the other candidates. Open voting at elections was then in vogue, and great damage was done to both life and property owing to the rioting which resulted. In the month of August following, the first Parliament was convened, and was inaugurated by Mr. Deas-Thomson, Colonial Secretary. Mr. Macleay was chosen Speaker. Amongst legislation passed during this first session were an Act to inquire into the working of the Land Laws, a Debtors' Act, Liens on Wool, and one regulating mortgages of live stock. At this time it was evident that Mr. Wentworth's liberalism was on the wane; that he was slowly becoming more conservative. This was discernible towards the latter part of the movement for Responsible Government. Under the "Imperial Act of 1843" it will be seen that the members of the Ministry were nominees of the Crown, and virtually irresponsible to either Parliament or the electors. In 1851 Mr. Wentworth tabled a motion in the Council, in which a petition to the Queen was adopted, praying for a Constitution similar to that of Canada, and requesting the entire surrender of all revenues and legislative rights to the Colonial Legislature. And it was placed on the Minutes of the House that all offices of trust, except that of Governor, should be conferred by the colonists; that the public lands and all the departments should be subject only to the Colonial Legislature; that the Imperial Parliament had no right to tax the colonists; and that plenary powers should be conferred on the Colonial Legislature. A committee was appointed in 1852 to prepare a Constitution; the first name on that committee was that of W. C. Wentworth. Next year a despatch was received from the Secretary of State for the Colonies, ratifying the 1851 resolution of the Council, and conveying Her Majesty's wish that the Council should establish a new legislature on the basis of an elective Assembly, and a nominee Council. A second committee to frame a Constitution was then appointed, on the motion of Mr. Wentworth. It consisted of the mover, Messrs. E. Deas-Thomson, J. Macarthur, J. H. Plunkett, C. Cowper, J. Martin, C. S. Donaldson, Macleay, Thurlow, and Murray. On the report being brought up, it was found to contain a recommendation that the members of the Upper House should receive hereditary titles, and constitute a colonial nobility, whose descendants should have the privilege of electing members from among their own class. Large meetings of protest were held. The Bill was condemned as defective. The people appeared determined to have no constitution other than one based on popular suffrage. Mr. Wentworth, being the chief mover in the matter, brought in the Bill, making a powerful and statesmanlike speech in support of it, and carried it, peerage clause and all, by a large majority. The debate lasted seven days, the numbers being : for the Bill, thirty-four, and against it, eight. Three days after, a great meeting was held at the Circular Quay in condemnation of the measure, and to petition the Queen to refuse assent to the Bill. When the Bill got into committee in the Council, the peerage clause was eliminated, and the nomination of members for life was inserted. The measure passed its third reading on 21st December, amid great cheering, by twenty-seven to six. During the succeeding year, Mr. Wentworth and Mr. Deas-Thomson were commissioned to proceed to England to watch the passage of the Bill through the British Parliament. Before leaving for England, Mr. Wentworth was the recipient of a great public demonstration. A full length portrait of him was placed on the walls of the Legislative Assembly, and a service of plate was presented to him by the people.

A sketch, published in the *Australian Portrait Gallery*, speaking of Mr. Wentworth after the meeting of the first Parliament under Responsible Government, said:—"While the subject of this memoir was thus occupied in building up in the legislative records of this colony, a monument to himself, which should last beyond the dreams of prophecy, he was also engaged from time to time in other labours in the public interest. His life was a compact of these labours, and it may be justly said that his every thought and energy were expended in the service of his native land. In 1842 the great work of the establishment of the University of Sydney was conceived by his active and far-seeing mind, and with that ardour which he threw into all his undertakings, and the electric power which he possessed of influencing his contemporaries, he pushed that labour on to an ultimate success." On October 2nd, in the year named, he made an eloquent speech in his place in the Council in favour of the project, and saw the Bill passed in 1850. His services in this connection were worthily recognised by the wealth and culture of the colony, a splendid life-size statue of Mr. Wentworth being placed within the Great Hall of the University to mark the public appreciation of his efforts. The statue was unveiled in 1862, while the person thus unusually honoured was still alive. On that occasion Sir James Martin, who was then Premier, delivered an eulogistic address on the life and work of the recipient of the distinction, in the course of which he spoke as follows:—

"The next and the last of his public acts, I shall, on this occasion advert to, is the establishment of the Sydney University. With that noble institution, his name is for ever associated as its founder. Whatever may be the fate of our political institutions, how great soever may be their vicissitudes, here, at all events, is an institution likely to endure. Hitherward, in future times, will turn the steps of those who feel the promptings of a generous ambition. Conquerors in the realms of mind they will go forth into the world, vivifying the dull elements around them, and arousing, as by an electric shock, the sons of toil and trade and commerce to a conception of the true glories of the universe. To the man who, in this early stage of our history, placed these splendid opportunities within our reach, it cannot be thought remarkable, even if he had done nothing more, that the honour of a public statue should be offered. Accordingly, eight years ago, his friends, comprising not only those who had witnessed, but some who had aided him in his labours, met together on the eve of his departure from the colony for a time, and determined that, in acknowledgment of his many services, that the honour should be conferred upon him. The announcement was made at the moment of his embarkation amidst the cheers of his friends and the disapprobation of a few who regarded him as the enemy of his country. He who had done so much for the people, and had often been greeted with their loudest huzzas, had before that encountered their hootings and revilings; but no one knew better than he the inconstancy of popular favour. But although they break their idols as often as they make them, the people in the long run learn to do justice to their benefactors, and Mr. Wentworth has enjoyed the singular good fortune of living to see conferred on him an honour which is usually witnessed only by a man's posterity, and to see it conferred with the assent, not only of those who have ever been his friends, but of those who were the most bitter of his opponents. He has outlived the envy, hatred, and malignity which inevitably cross the path of every man who becomes eminent in public life; and now in his green old age, with his mind still clear, and his faculties still unclouded, he has been allowed a foretaste of the posthumous renown which awaits him." Mr. Wentworth returned in 1861. He was received with another popular demonstration, political opponents as well as friends meeting to do him honour. He remained until the latter part of 1862. During his stay he was appointed President of the Legislative Council. His family went to England with him in 1862. He died at Merleigh House, Wimbourne, Dorsetshire, March 30th, 1872. In accordance with his oft expressed wish during his lifetime, that he should be buried in Australian soil, his remains were brought to the colony, and a public funeral accorded him May 6th, 1873. An immense concourse of people attended the funeral. Sir James Martin delivered a burial oration, the remains being interred at Vaucluse, a few miles from the city of Sydney, on the shores of the harbour of Port Jackson.

CHAPTER V.

EARLY MEN OF GENIUS AND POWER—THE LIST CONTINUED—SIR CHARLES COWPER—THE ANTI-TRANSPORTATION BATTLE—SIR TERENCE AUBREY MURRAY—THE STRUGGLE FOR POPULAR RIGHTS—SIR JAMES MARTIN—A VICTIM TO PREJUDICE—A PIONEER OF PROTECTION—CAPTAIN ROBERT JOHNSTON, R.N.—HON. ROBERT TOWNS—THOMAS SUTCLIFFE MORT—EARLIEST MEAT FREEZING EFFORT—"THERE SHALL BE NO MORE WASTE!"

THE HON. SIR CHARLES COWPER, K.C.M.G.

SIR CHARLES COWPER, although born in England, may almost be claimed as a native of the colony, having come to Australia with his parents when only two years old. He was born at Drypool, Yorkshire, on April 26th, 1807. He was educated by private tutors. His first start in life was in the Commissariat Department, the Governor, Sir Thomas Brisbane, appointing him as a clerk, young Cowper being then only eighteen years of age. In the following year, Governor Darling appointed him Secretary to the Church and School Lands Corporation, which position he held until that body was done away with in 1833, the lands reverting to the Crown in accordance with the charter under which the corporation existed. He declined an appointment offered him by Sir Richard Bourke. He then entered on pastoral pursuits, taking up stations in the Argyle district, and others on the Murray. He followed this business for a considerable time. He had such a liking for political warfare that it somewhat distracted him from his squatting pursuits. He contested the electorate of Camden in 1843, being opposed by Mr. Roger Therry, who was then Attorney-General, the latter receiving the support of Mr. James Macarthur, a gentleman who wielded great influence in that electorate. Notwithstanding this, Mr. Cowper was only beaten by ten votes. Mr. Macarthur was nominated for Cumberland, his election being considered certain. Mr. Cowper's friends, being displeased with his opposition to his candidature, placed him in nomination against Mr. Macarthur, and secured Mr. Cowper's return by a large majority. For brilliancy of intellect and great political forethought, and oratorical ability, the men who composed our early parliaments and those who held the reins of power as ministers, would bear fair comparison with any legislative body in the world, not even excepting that "first assembly of gentlemen in the world"—the British House of Commons. Among this assemblage of talent, Mr. Cowper always held his own, as is abundantly shown, not only by the number of times he was Premier, but that he was called upon to form the second Ministry under Responsible Government. Mr. Cowper took a leading part in the anti-transportation agitation. He was a most uncompromising opponent of the revival of transportation to any of the colonies. Although the agitation lasted nearly twenty years, Mr. Cowper never departed from determined opposition to convictism. On 1st August, 1840, Governor Gipps announced to the Council that transportation to the colony had ceased. Two years afterwards a meeting was held to advocate the revival of transportation, and soon after a committee was appointed in the Council to consider the question. This committee reported in favour of the revival. The first meeting of the public, condemnatory of the committee's recommendation, was held in the old City Theatre, Sydney, in 1846. Mr. Cowper presided, and moved a resolution, "that the meeting had heard with the deepest feelings of alarm and regret that it was proposed to renew transportation to this colony," and that they "could not conceive any circumstances under which such a measure would be desirable or justifiable." The Venerable Archdeacon McEncroe, who always took the humane and popular side in the early struggles for the improvement of the colony, seconded the motion in an eloquent speech, and a petition for presentation to the Council was drawn up. The petition was presented on the last day of the session, and the motion that it be printed was negatived. In February, 1849, another monster meeting was held in the Victoria Theatre to protest against the revival of transportation. The Venerable Archdeacon McEncroe, and Mr. Robert Lowe (afterwards Lord Sherbrooke), addressed the meeting, as well as Mr. Cowper, and a petition was adopted stating that "they felt bound, humbly but firmly, to represent to Her Majesty, that it was their duty and their determination, by every legal and constitutional means, to oppose the revival of transportation in any shape." On the 9th March, another meeting was held in the Victoria Theatre, the Mayor presiding on this occasion, and, as at the previous meeting, the principal speakers were the Rev. John McEncroe, Mr. Cowper, and Mr. Lowe. In June, 1849, a large meeting was held at the Circular Quay, to protest against the misrepresentation of the Council in the matter of transportation. On June 8th, 1849, the "Hashemy," a convict vessel, arrived, being the first for ten years. There were some two hundred convicts on board. The meeting referred to was held on the 11th June, Mr. Robert Campbell being chairman. There was great excitement on the occasion, the guards at Government

House being doubled, and the guns of a man-of-warship made ready for firing on the crowded meeting. Mr. Lamb moved a resolution "that the people of the colony protested against the transportation of British criminals on the ground that the will of the majority was against it; that numbers had immigrated on the assurance of the British Government that the custom had ceased for ever; that it was unjust to sacrifice the social and political interests of the colony for the pecuniary profit of the few; and that the revival of the practice would tend to alienate the loyalty of the British subjects in Australia." Mr. Lowe seconded the resolution, and Messrs. Henry Parkes, G. A. Lloyd, J. R. Wilshire, Grant Peek, Flood, and Dr. Fullerton were among those who addressed the meeting. A deputation presented the petition to the Governor, and requested that the convict ship be sent back to England. This request was refused, and a meeting was held on the 18th June, at which a resolution was passed praying for the removal of Earl Grey from her counsels. The following day the convicts were landed, and were drafted to the different parts of the colony outside the County of Cumberland. At a meeting held at the old barrack square, 16th September, 1850, the Anti-Transportation Association was formed. Meetings also took place in various parts of the country, at which strong expressions of opinion were voiced on the question. On July 29th, 1851, yet another meeting was held, under the presidency of Mr. Cowper. A petition was adopted stating that "the petitioners felt compelled, humbly but firmly, to represent to Her Majesty in person, that the subterfuges, evasions, equivocations, and breaches of faith practised towards these colonies by Earl Grey, had unhappily destroyed all confidence in His Lordship's administration of colonial affairs." Messrs. Cowper, Parkes, Kemp, Archdeacon McEncroe, among others, spoke on the occasion.

THE ANTI-TRANSPORTATION BATTLE.

Transportation to Tasmania ceased February 10th, 1853, and on 26th January, 1865, the announcement was made that in three years, transportation to all the colonies would end. The last convict ship arrived in Western Australia on January 10th, 1868. On the defeat of the Donaldson Ministry, in 1856, Mr. Cowper was entrusted with the formation of a new Ministry. It was composed of the following gentlemen:—Mr. Robert Campbell, Colonial Treasurer; Terence Aubrey Murray, Minister for Lands and Works; Mr. James Martin, Attorney-General; and Mr. Lutwyche, Solicitor-General. The new Ministry were immediately met by a motion of censure, which was moved by Mr. John Hay, chiefly on account of the appointment of Mr. Martin to the Attorney-Generalship, he having been only admitted to the Bar a few days before. The vote of censure was carried, and the first Cowper Ministry resigned on October 2nd, 1856. Mr. Watson Parker formed the next Government, Mr. John Hay, the mover of the resolution which ousted the Ministry, taking the position of Minister for Lands and Works, and Mr. Donaldson that of Treasurer. In September, 1857, the Parker Ministry went out of office, Mr. Cowper coming in again as Premier and Colonial Secretary; Mr. Richard Jones was Colonial Treasurer; Mr. Murray, Lands and Works; Mr. Martin, Attorney-General; and Mr. Lutwyche Solicitor-General. Mr. Jones afterwards retired, and Mr. Robert Campbell again rose to the Treasurership. On Mr. Campbell's death, Mr. E. C. Weekes becoming Treasurer, Mr. Murray and Mr. John Robertson took the Lands, and Mr. Flood became Minister for Works. Mr. Martin also resigned the Attorney-Generalship, Mr. Lutwyche becoming Attorney-General; he, in turn, being succeeded by L. H. Bayley; Mr. W. B. Dalley and Mr. Hargrave as Solicitors-General. This Ministry passed the "Electoral Act of 1858," giving manhood suffrage, vote by ballot, and the division of the colony into electorates on a population basis. In October, 1859, the Ministry was defeated on a vote of censure moved by Mr. William Forster relative to the education question. Mr. Forster formed a Ministry, which was, however, defeated in March following, on its Upper House Electoral Bill. Mr. Robertson formed the next Ministry, Mr. Cowper being Colonial Secretary. In a short time Mr. Robertson handed over the Premiership to Mr. Cowper, whose Ministry remained in office from January 10, 1861, to October 15, 1863. This latter consisted of Elias Carpenter Weekes, Colonial Treasurer; John Robertson, Minister for Lands; Mr. W. M. Arnold, Secretary for Public Works; J. B. Darvall, Attorney-General; J. F. Hargrave, Solicitor-General; and Charles Cowper, Junior Clerk of the Executive Council. It was during their term of office that the "Free Selection before Survey Land Act" was passed. The "Abolition of State Aid to Religion" was another measure enacted by this Ministry, which when defeated in October, 1863, was succeeded by the Martin Ministry, it, in turn, being defeated on its Protectionist proposals in 1865. Mr. Cowper then again took up the reins of office, his colleagues being Messrs. Smart, Samuel, and Burdekin successively as Colonial Treasurers; Darvall and Plunkett successively as Attorneys-General; Robertson, Secretary for Lands, succeeded by W. M. Arnold; Arnold and Smart succeeding each other as Secretaries for Works, and J. A. Cunneen Postmaster-General. The Ministry lasted till January, 1866, when Mr. Henry Parkes defeated them on a question of the new duties. Mr. Cowper at this time retired from politics for some four years. Mr. Robertson then invited him to come forward and assume the position of Premier. Thus he was Premier from January 13th to December 15th, 1870; his colleagues were Messrs. Samuel and

Forster, succeeded by Messrs. Robertson, Sutherland, Manning, Salomons, Egan, and Robert Owen. He took the post of Agent-General for the Colony in December, 1870, starting for England immediately to enter on the duties of that office, which he held until 1875, when his health broke down. He died in England on October 20th, 1875. He married in 1831, Eliza, second daughter of Daniel Sutton, of Wivenhoe, near Colchester, England. He had six children, the present Sheriff of New South Wales being his eldest son. His brother is Dean Cowper, a leading figure among the members of the Church of England in Australia. Sir Charles Cowper was knighted in 1872, an honour which the recipient highly merited, and which, at that time, was rarely bestowed. Probably there has been no political leader in the colony of New South Wales who filled the position of Premier with such marked success at all times. He not only had the faculty of making friends, but also of keeping them.

Sir Terence Aubrey Murray, Kt. B.

Terence Aubrey Murray was born in Limerick, Ireland, in 1810. His father accepted an official appointment in New South Wales. After a residence of about seven years, he paid a visit to the old country, and, on his return to the colony, he brought with him his son, who, up to that time, had been educated at home. Soon after his arrival he went to Lake George, and started sheep-farming on his father's land. He returned to Sydney in 1833. He was gazetted a magistrate of the territory at the age of twenty-three, when he took an active part with Mr. Waddy in the efforts put forth against the bushrangers, who at that time were very active in various parts of the country. When the New Constitution was granted in 1843, Mr. Murray was elected to represent three counties—Murray, King, and

Georgiana. From this time up to his death he was closely connected with the political life of the colony. Amongst the names of those who were elected to the first Council were those of Wentworth, Bland, Cowper, Forster, Macleay, Nicholson, Lang, and Murray. On the motion of Mr. Murray, immediately after the Council met, a committee was appointed to inquire into the provisions of Lord Stanley's Land Act, as it related to New South Wales. Mr. Murray was appointed president of this committee. Sir Thomas Mitchell, the Surveyor-General, was examined, and his answer to a question as to how far the land policy tended to develop the resources of the colony, was, "In no way whatever, so far as the progress of colonisation goes. The colony is now available to temporary occupants only, and what they earn goes elsewhere, leaving nothing to make a colony with." Mr. Icely was also examined; he said "he had not known of anyone really settling on the land since the auction system commenced." After this the Orders-in-Council were passed leasing the land to those who wished to apply for it. An Act for the "Better Government of the Australian Colonies" received the Royal assent in 1850. This conferred legislative independence on Victoria, and introduced the elective principle into Tasmania, Western Australia, and South Australia. It reduced the franchise in New South Wales and Victoria to a £100 freehold or £10 household qualification, and gave Her Majesty power to erect other colonies. Mr. Murray's name appears prominently in all the struggles for popular rights; indeed it is found on the very first draft proposals to give free institutions to the colony. Mr. Murray was among the first members who were elected to the first parliament under Responsible Government, which met in Macquarie-street on May 22nd, 1856. He sat as member for the Southern Boroughs. When Sir Charles Cowper formed his second

HON WM. FORSTER.   SIR FRANCIS FORBES.
SIR JAMES MARTIN.
SIR JOHN ROBERTSON.   SIR TERENCE A. MURRAY.

Ministry, Mr. Murray accepted the position of Secretary for Lands and Works, and for a short period he acted as Auditor-General. The Ministries of the early days of Responsible Government were very short-lived, and this Ministry only lasted about two months. Mr. Murray held the office of Lands and Works from 7th September, 1857, to 12th January, 1858, when he resigned. In 1860 he was elected Speaker of the Legislative Assembly. Two years later he was appointed to a seat in the Upper House, and was elected President of the Council in 1862, in succession to W. C. Wentworth. He was created Knight Bachelor in 1869, and held office as President of the Legislative Council until his death (at the age of sixty-three), which occurred on the 22nd June, 1873.

THE HON. SIR JAMES MARTIN, KT. B., CHIEF JUSTICE.

The advent of Responsible Government in New South Wales drew out in a marked degree, not only the talent of those gentlemen who had the advantage of a high scholastic and sometimes university training in the old country, but also some young men natives of the soil, as well as those who were brought here by their parents at an early age, and who received their education in the colony. The latter, in brilliance and abilities, outshone the former class. Amongst all the names of our greatest men there is none which stands higher for intellectual power than that of Sir James Martin.

James Martin was born in the town of Middleton, County of Cork, Ireland, May 14, 1820. In 1821 his parents emigrated to Sydney, and immediately settled at Parramatta, where they remained till 1834. They then removed to Sydney. Young James went to a primary school at Parramatta, and on his removal to Sydney he studied under Mr. Cape. On leaving the Sydney Grammar School, where he spent some time, he was articled to Mr. G. R. Nichols, who was then the leading attorney in Sydney. Mr. Martin was himself admitted as an attorney in May, 1845. He commenced practising for himself. He also edited the *Atlas* some time after, and became a contributor to the *Empire* in 1851. In 1848 he was elected to represent the counties of Cook and Westmoreland under the old Council; he was, however, unseated on petition. A fresh election was held, when he was returned without opposition. He was re-elected in 1851. In 1852 he was appointed one of the committee to draft a Constitution for the colony. At the election in 1856 Mr. Martin was again taken on by his old constituents. He was then a liberal of the liberals, and at once joined the Opposition against Mr. Donaldson's Cabinet. On the defeat of the Ministry Mr. Martin became Attorney-General in the first Cowper Administration, having only been called to the Bar a day or two prior to his taking the portfolio. The Conservatives were at once up in arms against the young advocate, and so successfully did they wage their war that the Ministry was defeated in a little over a month from the time of taking office. On that occasion Mr. Martin made a splendid defence. He said he was surrounded by those who had raised themselves to high position by their own honorable exertions—true sons of the soil, not in the narrow sense in which the term is generally understood, but in the sense of the old Roman satirist, who applied the expression to those who owed their success in life neither to wealth, nor pedigree, nor fortune. Between them there were many things in common. He asked them, and he asked them confidently, not ungenerously and unjustly to desert him on that occasion. From his outset in life till that time, he had to achieve everything for himself, and from the humblest beginning he had fought his way almost to the highest point to which, in this colony, it was possible to attain. At every step he had been met with opposition, and had been compelled to make good his ground, and whatever he had achieved he owed not to the favour or affection of any man. He had never cringed, nor fawned, nor played the sycophant, and if his conduct was open to condemnation, it certainly was in a contrary direction. The lesson of self-reliance, of which, he trusted, he might be pardoned in regarding himself as an example, would not, he hoped, be shorn of its value by an unmerited reverse in the moment of triumph. As he had borne up against and overcome many obstacles of greater magnitude than the present, he trusted that he should successfully bear up against this one also, and that, in the stand which he then took, the generous and spontaneous sympathies of the House would go along with him, and that the only effect of the present storm would be, like those of the physical universe, to leave the atmosphere of public life purer than before." But his colleagues held to him, though, by doing so, they received defeat. The Ministry which succeeded the Cowper Administration, were, however, thrown out in September, 1857, and Mr. Martin again took office in the second Cowper Ministry. He resigned in November, 1858, and was again elected under the "New Electoral Act" in 1859 as one of the metropolitan members. After this he devoted most of his time to the practice of his profession until 1863, when he was found at the head of a Cabinet. This was the first Protectionist Government in the colony. The protectionist motion was passed by the Assembly, but was rejected by the Upper Chamber, a general election following. The greatest excitement prevailed all over the colony. But Mr. Martin was defeated. Speaking before the event, on Protection, he said:—"I think this most magnificent territory, teeming with the elements of every kind of wealth—mineral, pastoral, agricultural—was intended for other purposes than a sheep-walk, like a vast Asiatic steppe, or a mere commercial emporium, like some small city of the middle ages. With a territory larger than the greatest kingdom of Europe, and a population no greater than a sixth-rate European town, I thought there was an ample field, to which the starving thousands of the mother country might be removed—to the great relief of that country—to the great advantage of this. I knew that the skilled artizan of Britain could not be honestly asked to come to a country where the necessaries of life were dear, and the articles, in the manufacture of which he was an adept, were imported at a price with which he could not compete; and I felt that his position was not mended by the opportunity afforded of taking his wife to some remote gunyah on the Namoi or the Darling, or settling down on some alluvial patch, the fruits of which might, at any time, be reduced in price below the cost of their production by imports from foreign countries. There is a limit to the number of shepherds and bullock drivers, dock labourers, porters, warehousemen, and mercantile clerks required, and there are many other occupations equally desirable and equally ennobling. I knew that the greatness of England arose not from commerce, not from manufactures, not from agriculture alone—but from all combined. By the opportunities which a wise legislation afforded for every kind of industry and enterprise, those small islands became the habitation of the greatest and wealthiest people on the globe. The coal, the iron, the copper, the lead, the wool, the fertile soil, which constitute the foundation of England's greatness, are here as well as there, and in a larger measure; but while the British Islands supports thirty millions, this colony is unable to maintain in comfort four hundred thousand. I knew that such a state of things was most unnatural.

I knew that however lucrative it might be to supply cotton silks to the nobility of the Sandwich Islands, and shoddy cloth and Brummagem rubbish of all kinds to the simple savages of Oceania, but a very small number could participate in those advantages. We might, by trade of that kind, constitute a rude, barbaric, bastard sort of Antipodean Venice, with nothing of the greatness or grandeur of its prototype; but we could never by those means reproduce here a manly, vigorous, numerous British population. I wished to see this country largely peopled with such a population. And with that object I strove rather that everyone should be comfortable than that a few should be rich—that there should be fair scope for every man to elevate himself, or to bring up his children to, that pursuit to which his judgment or his fancy inclined him; and that no man should be found starving in a land of plenty, or begging and begging in vain —

> A brother of the earth
> To give him leave to toil."

But, with all the eloquence and force brought to bear on the question by Mr. Martin, the Ministry was defeated at the polls. Mr. Cowper again came into office. It was this Ministry which passed the *ad valorem* duties. Mr. Martin again came into power in 1866, coalescing with Sir Henry Parkes, who had strongly opposed him in 1863. Mr. Martin was Premier at the time the Duke of Edinburgh visited the colony in 1868; on that occasion he received the honour of knighthood. He retired from office consequent upon a vote of censure moved by Sir John Robertson in 1868. In December, 1870, he again became Premier, Mr. Robertson taking office under him. This Ministry remained in power till May, 1872. In November, 1873, Sir Henry Parkes being then Premier, appointed Sir James Martin Chief

Justice of the colony. Sir James Martin was three times Premier, five times Minister of the Crown, on each occasion holding the office of Attorney-General. It was he who established the Sydney branch of the Mint, which has proved of great advantage to the colony. As leader of the House he showed himself somewhat autocratic, and he always displayed great and almost overwhelming power in debate. As a lawyer, Sir James Martin in his day stood far above every man at the Bar in Australia.

He died after a brief illness on 4th November, 1886, at his residence, "Clarens," Potts' Point, Sydney, and was buried at St. Jude's, Randwick.

Captain Robert Johnston, R.N.

The name of Captain Johnston takes us back to stirring scenes in the early history of the colony. The family has indeed been identified with the interests of New South Wales since the foundation of the colony.

His father was the late Colonel Johnston, who landed with Governor Phillip, being then a lieutenant of marines. He afterwards took a leading part in deposing Governor Bligh.

Captain Robert Johnston was born in N.S. Wales on the 9th March, 1790. When seven years old he was taken to England by his father, and was educated at Newington Butts, Surrey, remaining there for six years. One day at school he was passing the Admiralty yard, when he saw a one-armed officer talking to a sailor with a wooden leg. When the officer had passed on, the boy asked the sailor who the officer was. "Lord Nelson," was the reply. At that time Lord Nelson was at the height of his fame, and the incident left an impression on the mind of the lad which during his life was never effaced. Not long after, he saw the funeral of the greatest naval commander England ever knew pass through the streets of London. On that occasion the boy narrowly escaped being crushed to death by the crowd. He was saved by taking refuge under the horse of one of the horse guards. On leaving school he entered the navy as a boy volunteer of the first class on board the 50-gun ship "Malabar." He served during the blockade of the French and Dutch fleets in the Texel; joined the "Namure" as a midshipman, being afterwards transferred to the 36-gun frigate "Semiramis," commissioned for active service off the coast of Spain and Portugal. He was present at the battle of Corunna, and afterwards joined the "Norge" as master's mate. He was present at the storming of Cadiz by the French under Marshal Soult, and took part in the attack on St. Mary's, where he was in command of a rocket boat. While so engaged the boat was struck by a round shot, and immediately sank, those who were not killed being rescued by the other boats. Some time after, he and another with 150 men took the captured 80-gun French ship "Neptune" to Majorca; later on he rejoined the "Norge," and returned in that ship to England. Subsequently he joined H.M.S. "Asia," the flagship of Vice-Admiral Sir Alexander Cochrane, bound for the American station. While at Bermuda he was promoted to a lieutenancy, and placed in command of a despatch boat, which procured him an introduction to the captain of Lord Nelson's ship "Victory," Sir Thomas Hardy. While still a lieutenant he was present at the capture of the City of Washington, and afterwards joined Sir Peter Parker, Bart., who was engaged blockading Baltimore with the "Menelaus" frigate. He also fought in the attack on Moorfields, in which engagement Sir Peter Parker was killed. At a later date we find him in the New Orleans expedition, and when peace was concluded he was appointed second lieutenant to the "Asia," under Captain

Alexander Skeene. When the "Asia" was paid off, Lieutenant Johnston applied to the Admiralty for active service, but this position not being available, he asked for and obtained leave of absence, in order to visit his family in Australia. He arrived in Sydney in October, 1816, being then twenty-six years of age, and his services were at once claimed by Governor Macquarie for purposes of navigation and exploration. It was he, may be remarked, who discovered the Clyde River, and the source of the Warragamba.

His leave of absence having expired, he was about returning to England, but, his elder brother having died, he found it necessary to remain to look after the family interests. He then went in for agricultural and pastoral pursuits with his brother, Mr. David Johnston. In 1831 he married the eldest daughter of Mr. Wellen, of Hammershaw, Bucks, England, by whom he had a family of seven sons and two daughters. Once, when returning to Sydney from the Cape of Good Hope, in command of the "Queen Charlotte," the vessel was saved from utter wreck at King's Island, Bass's Straits, by his (Captain Johnston's), presence of mind. In the night-time, during a heavy gale, a cry of "breakers ahead" was raised. The crew begged the captain to order the helm a-starboard. He, however, rushed to the helm himself, and sent it hard a-port. When daylight broke it was clearly seen that his action was the only one that could have saved the ship. On one occasion Captain Johnston went out alone to capture two bushrangers, who were reported to be asleep in the bush on George's Hill Estate. He was severely wounded on the face and thigh with a sheath-knife during the encounter. He, however, succeeded in capturing one of the men—the other fled. In 1822 he was "stuck up" by Tennant, a bushranger, who came to ask Captain Johnston to intercede for him with the authorities to obtain a mitigation of punishment if he gave himself

up. Captain Johnston succeeded in gaining the consent of
the authorities, and Tennant surrendered. In 1865 Captain
Johnston was promoted to the rank of Commander in
the Royal Navy. He preserved his strong vitality to the
end of his old age. Four years before his death, at the age
of eighty-eight, he made a voyage to New Zealand, and he
was to be seen driving about the city up to within a few
days of his death, which event took place at Annandale, on
the 8th September, 1882, at the ripe old age of ninety-two.
His funeral was attended by a large concourse of mourners,
and a party of sailors from H.M.S. "Nelson" fired a
farewell volley over the grave of the grand old sailor who
lived and took part in some of the most stirring events
of England's naval history.

THE HON. ROBERT TOWNS, M.L.C.

Among the men of large commercial influence in the
early days of N. S. Wales, none was more honoured by all
classes than Robert Towns, or, as he was more familiarly
called, "Bobby Towns." For fifty years he was closely
identified with the commercial life of Australia.

Robert Towns was born at Langhorsley, Northumberland,
on 10th November, 1794. What education he received was
at the village school of his native place. When quite young
he was placed on board a collier running between Shields
and London. While so employed he took every opportunity
to improve himself and gain knowledge, more particularly
about shipping matters. If his vessel were in port he would
attend a night-school kept by an old sailor, from whom he
learnt something about navigation. At the age of sixteen
he was appointed mate, and at eighteen he was placed in
command of a vessel. Soon after he was sent to the Mediterranean,
as commander of a brig. While in this trade, he
managed to save enough money to build a vessel for himself,

which he named "The Brothers." With this vessel he commenced the colonial passenger trade, and, although the traffic at that time was not very heavy, Captain Towns got the lion's share of it. His ship was the best managed, as well as the fastest sailer, then trading between England and Australia, and many of those who afterwards became leaders in every walk of life in the colonies, journeyed out in Captain Towns' vessel. In 1833 he married a sister of William Wentworth, and, nine years after, he settled in Sydney and established the large mercantile business of Robert Towns and Company. He employed a large number of vessels in the Island trade, collecting bêche-de-mer, cocoanut oil, sandalwood, and other products. The late Sir Alexander Stuart was at one time a partner in the business. In 1851 the Bank of New South Wales was greatly assisted by Captain Towns, he being then a large capitalist. He not only increased its capital, but also aided to reorganise it on a much larger basis, and place it in a position to cope with the altered conditions of the colony after the discovery of gold. He was a Director of the Bank up to the time of his death. Although he was possessed of a large fortune at this time, he went largely into pastoral pursuits, and held numbers of stations in various parts of Queensland, especially in the northern portion of that colony. Townsville, in that colony, was named after him. He formed a large cotton plantation of 2,000 acres, where he employed between two and three hundred South Sea Islanders, and spent £20,000 on the venture. He, in conjunction with Sir John Robertson and Sir Charles Cowper, held immense tracts of pastoral country, called the "Plains of Promise," on the Norman and Albert Rivers, near the Gulf of Carpentaria. On the passing of the Constitution, in 1856, Mr. Towns was appointed a life member of the Legislative Council. Long after he retired from business he took a deep interest in the shipping and commercial affairs of the colony. To the "Patriotic" and Lancashire cotton funds he was a very liberal contributor. He died at Cranbrook, Rose Bay, Sydney, on 4th April, 1873.

THOMAS SUTCLIFFE MORT.

Prominent among the men who have made New South Wales what it is, was the late Thomas Sutcliffe Mort. No name stood higher in the commercial life of the colony than his. No man of his time worked harder to enlarge the industries of the country than he; no man had a wider grasp of the great possibilities of the country, and certainly no man spent so much time and capital in developing its resources.

Thomas Sutcliffe Mort was born on December 23rd, 1816, in Bolton, Lancashire, England. After receiving a commercial education, he entered the counting house of a firm of warehousemen in Manchester. He arrived in Sydney in 1838, having accepted an appointment in the house of Aspinwall, Brown, & Co. He remained with this firm and their successors, Gosling, Brown, & Co., for some five years —till the year of 1843—when the house was involved in the financial crash which then occurred. This disaster was mainly due to over speculation, more especially in land and all kinds of stock, the banks having advanced money for these purposes with a lavish hand. The Bank of Australia was the first to close its doors, and as it was the first monetary institution in the country, it pulled down nearly all the leading business houses who did business with it. Mr. Justice Burton brought in a new Insolvency Bill to meet the times. This measure was known afterwards as "Burton's Purge," and was intended to relieve the great distress amongst the commercial houses of the city. During the first year of its operation, some seven hundred persons took advantage of the Act. A large public meeting was

held during this year to take into consideration the depressed
state of the monetary affairs of the country. Mr. Wentworth took an active part in the matter, and it was resolved
that the Bank of Australia should be allowed to realise its
securities by holding a public lottery for that purpose.
When the firm of Messrs. Gosling and Brown failed, he
made up his mind to start business on his own account,
which he did, opening as an auctioneer. His connection
with the firm of Gosling, Brown, & Co., had brought him
into contact with a large number of the pastoralists of the
country, this, together with his winning and straightforward
manner, brought him many patrons, and his business
consequently increased rapidly with profit to Mr. Mort,
and great and many advantages to the squatters of the
country. Mr. Mort was one of the promoters of the first
railway in N. S. Wales: the Sydney and Parramatta line.
He also held shares in the Australian Steam Navigation
Company. The gold discovery of 1851, which revolution-
ised the whole of the affairs of the country, found Mr. Mort
ready to take advantage of these altered conditions to
improve his own interest as well as those of the country.
It was he who formed the first company for working gold-
reefs—the "Great Nugget Vein Mining Company." Very
primitive ideas of mining existed at that time, so that people
who invested their money in quartz mining expected an
immediate return upon the capital so invested. In consequence of these mistaken notions, discontent prevailed
amongst the shareholders. Mr. Mort called them together,
and, after explaining matters, offered to take up the shares
of any one who felt dissatisfied. The explanation was so
satisfactory that not one of the shareholders took advantage
of his generous offer. A few years after the discovery of
gold, Mr. Mort, in conjunction with Mr. Hawdon, purchased
14,000 acres of land in the Moruya district, about 200

miles from Sydney, on the South Coast. In 1860 he bought out his partner, having up to that time expended on the property £100,000. The extensive dairying business of Bodalla, the largest in the colonies, is well known throughout Australia, and the products are said to equal the best English. The estate at the present time consists of 38,000 acres. The returns from the place are very large, as might be expected from so well managed a business. In 1857, Mr. Mort requiring rest after years of constant toil, paid a visit to England, where he remained two years, returning to the colony in 1859. On his return, he entered into the cultivation of silk, cotton, and sugar. He sank about £20,000 in the sugar industry. Soon afterwards he found himself involved in the celebrated lawsuit, Wentworth versus Lloyd, Mr. Wentworth moving that the sale should be declared void on the ground that the auctioneer, Mr. Mort, had an interest in the transaction. On appeal it was held by the Master of the Rolls in England, that Mr. Wentworth was aware of Mr. Mort's interest at the time of the sale, the verdict clearing Mr. Mort's character in the matter. Mr. Mort also took a leading part in the copper and coal industries of the colony. It need only be mentioned here that he was the founder of Mort's Dock and Engineering Company, the largest of the kind in the southern hemisphere.

The last undertaking of magnitude to which Mr. Mort bent his energies, was the exportation of Australian beef and mutton to England. In 1843 Mr. Mort made an attempt to export meat cured in the ordinary way, but in this he was not successful. He now made an effort to land meat fresh on the home market. In this undertaking he was assisted by Mr. E. D. Nicolle, who was possessed of high scientific ability. Mr. Mort's knowledge of the prospects of pastoral industry enabled him to forecast a magnificent future for a trade of this sort. Mr. Nicolle's experiments were constant, and he received from Mr. Mort a generous confidence which placed all this gentleman's resources at his disposal. The first point was to invent a cheap means of producing artificial cold, and this difficulty was, after many trials, overcome by the experimentalists in discovering the possibility of the repeated use of the same ammonia. In this respect Messrs. Mort and Nicolle went ahead of European science. According to the first authorities in the old world, "meat frozen was meat spoiled." But partial freezing, it was found, would never do, the meat becoming so rapidly bad when exposed. Mr. Nicolle at last demonstrated that in Australia, at any rate, meat could be thoroughly frozen—that its quality was not thus injured—and that it kept longer after thawing than did other meat after being killed. Feeling convinced that the results of Mr. Nicolle's experiments in this respect had made the project practicable, Mr. Mort entered upon it with enthusiasm. A large establishment rose upon the margin of Darling Harbour, and it was connected with the railway. Costly machinery, in duplicate, was erected, and the "freezing chamber" was covered with five miles of iron piping, through which the liquid ammonia was kept in circulation. A series of most interesting experiments showed that the freezing power could be successfully applied to game, fish, and various sorts of fruits, as well as to meat, and it was a novel sensation to find one's self suddenly transferred from the sultry atmosphere of an Australian summer's day to a region of ice and snow, abounding with oxen and sheep, poultry, wild game and fish, butter and milk, all as hard as rock, their natural qualities kept in complete suspension until the time would come to thaw, cook, and consume them. The belief that the process injured their quality was shown over and over again to be unfounded. Mr. Mort then erected slaughter-houses in the Lithgow Valley, amongst the Blue Mountains, on the Great Western Line of Railway, 96 miles from Sydney. This site was chosen to save cattle their journey over the mountains, which much injured their quality. The buildings and yards were on the most complete plan conceivable. When both establishments were finished, Mr. Mort invited, on September 2nd, 1875, a large number of colonists to make an excursion to Lithgow Valley, beginning with an inspection of the freezing works at Darling Harbour. The party proceeded by special train from the freezing works to the Valley, and there sat down to a luncheon composed of varieties of fish, game, and meat, all of which had been frozen for considerable periods before being cooked. The whole repast was a thorough success, and congratulations were showered upon the chairman and Mr. Nicolle from all sides. The Premier, Sir John Robertson, made a speech full of laudation of the undertaking. Sir John Hay proposed "Success to the Enterprise" in terms similarly enthusiastic. In reply to these congratulatory speeches, Mr. Mort said:—"There shall be no more waste! Yes, gentlemen, I now feel that the time has arrived, or, at all events, is not far distant, when the various portions of the earth will give forth their products for the use of each and all; that the over-abundance of one country shall make up for the deficiency of another; the super-abundance of the year of plenty serving for the scant harvests of its successor; for cold arrests all change. Science has drawn aside the veil, and the plan stands revealed. Faraday's magic wand gave the keynote, and invention has done the rest. Climate, seasons, plenty, scarcity, distance, will shake hands, and out of the commingling will come enough for all, "for the earth is the Lord's and the fulness thereof;" and it is certainly within the compass of man to ensure that all His people shall be partakers of that fulness." The next stage was the fitting up of a vessel—the "Northam"—to take home a shipment of Australian beef and mutton for the London market. Together with the sum of £80,000 which Mr. Mort had expended in the costly enterprise, the squatters of the colony who were interested in the result of his experiment subscribed £20,000 to carry the project out. Owing, however, to the action of the chemical matter employed, the machinery broke down, and the undertaking had to be abandoned for the time, after the many years of toil and the princely fortune sunk in it by Mr. Mort The failure affected Mr. Mort very much, and he did not long survive it. A few months after the failure of the "Northam" he caught a cold while attending a funeral at Bodalla, where he was then staying. He died on May 9th, 1878. His death was mourned throughout Australia by all classes of the community. Some time after his death, a statue was erected to his memory in Macquarie Place, in recognition of the services rendered by him to his adopted country.

Mr. Thomas Sutcliffe Mort. Dr. John D. Lang.
Capt. Robert Johnston.
Mr. George Suttor. Dr. Richard L. Jenkins.

CHAPTER VI.

GEORGE SUTTOR —EARLY SYDNEY—DESPOTIC DAYS—SUTTOR'S VAIN APPEAL FOR JUSTICE—SIR FRANCIS FORBES—A HEAVY INDICTMENT—THE LIBERTY OF THE PRESS ENDANGERED — A JUST TRIBUTE — SIR JOHN ROBERTSON— FREE SELECTION BEFORE SURVEY—SIR JOHN HAY—AN OPPONENT TO SIR JOHN ROBERTSON'S LAND THEORY.

GEORGE SUTTOR.

NO book dealing with the lives of the pioneers of New South Wales would be complete without some reference to one of the sturdiest representative colonists who ever set foot on Australian soil— George Suttor.

George Suttor was born on the 11th June, 1776, at Chelsea, where his father, a young Scotchman, carried on the business of a gardener and farmer, renting land from Lord Cadogan. The grandfather of George Suttor was a member of the Edinburgh University, from which fact it may be inferred he held a good social position if not an affluent one, while his grandmother was said to be a sister of the Countess of Linlithgow. His father was a witness of the battle of Preston Pans. All his family followed the Stuarts, and, consequently, became much reduced in circumstances. Suttor, senior, had studied botany under Mr. Lee, of Hammersmith, who acclimatised the fuschia. In 1796, having read "Cook's Voyages," and become acquainted with several ships' officers who had visited Sydney, and, besides, being engaged to marry, he was determined to try what a future in the far off colony would bring forth. He obtained an introduction to Sir Joseph Banks, who did all he could to further his interest. On the occasion of one of his visits, in 1798, Sir Joseph showed him the camellia, just introduced by Lord Macartney from China, with the remark that "he had been very ill when the plants arrived, and, when somewhat recovered, he went to see them, and the sight made him quite well." As they were walking through the garden, the Tower guns were heard announcing Nelson's victory at the Nile. Sir Joseph introduced the intending emigrant to some members of the Ministry, who approved of him as a collector of plants to be sent from England to the colony, and to take charge of them on the voyage. This was an honorary position, but, on his arrival, he was to have a free grant of 200 acres, a house built for him, and five or six assigned servants of the better class. The plants consisted chiefly of grapes, apples, pears, and hop vines. Two years and one month elapsed after the collection was made before the colony was reached, some of the plants were lost, but some of the best sorts of grape vines were brought to Sydney. In September, 1879, he sailed for Sydney with his wife and shipment of plants in the old ship "Porpoise." Governor King and George Caley, the botanist, were fellow-passengers. When the Bay of Biscay was reached, a storm came on which damaged the "Porpoise" so much that she had to put back. The vessel proved to be unfit for further use, so Suttor had to remain till March 17th, 1800, before another start could be made for Australia. This he did in a vessel recently taken from the Spaniards and refitted and called the "Porpoise." They

arrived at the Cape of Good Hope in the end of May, remained there till the 15th September, and reached Sydney in November, 1800. Sydney at that time looked more like a camp than a town—the streets having dead trees and stumps in them. The New South Wales Corps occupied a large space, living in huts. All the houses were thatched, the walls being made of wattle and plaster, whitewashed inside and out. After landing, he sought advice of Governor King, who told him "he could not be troubled with his affairs, and that he had better go to Parramatta." He went to Parramatta, where he met his old friend Caley, and the Rev. S. Marsden. On their advice and with their assistance he settled at Baulkham Hills, and took his grant of land there. This grant remains in the hands of his family up to the present time. In 1801 Colonel Paterson, of the New South Wales Corps, gave him three young orange trees. They were the first orange trees planted at Baulkham Hills. This district is now celebrated for the production of the fruit. Mr. Suttor, like all the early settlers, had to suffer many hardships, and often wished himself back in his native land. He, however, persevered in cultivating his orchard and farm. He found it very difficult to educate his family, but he and his wife imparted all the instruction they could. In a written memoir of his the following passage occurs:—
"I had by this time (1805) become reconciled to the colony and to the part of life I had chosen with my beloved partner, in whose sweet society, and of our dear children, and of a few choice friends, I felt happy, though I yet retained a longing after my native land. I now saw, with my increasing young family, the necessity of perseverance and industry to succeed and become the founder of a family in Australia. The early days of the colony presented many difficulties. Want of roads and bridges, and better protection from the vicious portion of the convicts, who, at

times, inflicted terrible evils on the unprotected settlers, particularly the free settlers, for whom they generally expressed hatred. The convicts believed the colony to have been founded for them alone." On the 26th January, 1808, being in Sydney, Mr. Suttor followed the troops through the streets to Government House, as they marched to seize Governor Bligh. He has left a bold account of that affair, he says :—

"This year (1808) was marked by a memorable epoch in the history of the colony. The officers of the New South Wales Corps, who had, many of them, been nearly twenty years in the colony, and who were magistrates and extensive dealers in rum and other articles, and who monopolised all influence and power, which they exercised with tyrannic insolence, and deposed the Governor and assumed the Government. They did this, headed by Colonel Johnston, who was the dupe and catspaw of a triumvirate. The whole affair was conducted by the military in a most lawless manner. As a consequence, anarchy and idleness spread over the land, the cultivation of which was neglected, and, this state of things continuing for two years, many families were involved in ruin. This event was productive ultimately of much benefit to the colony, as it became rid of the New South Wales Corps, who had been, for twenty years, masters and monopolists, and generally set a very immoral example."

It was about this time that his real troubles began. He was asked to sign an address to Colonel Johnston, calling upon him to seize the Government and the Governor. This he refused to do, as he considered the document a most treasonable one. This act of loyalty to the King's representative made him very obnoxious to those who had deposed the Governor. Soon after, two of his assigned servants were prevailed upon to bring accusations against him before

Ensign Bell, of the 102nd regiment, recently appointed magistrate by the rebel Government. The charge was to the effect that he (Suttor) had said that "those who had usurped the Government were a set of scoundrels, and they should all be hanged, and their property given to the poor." A summons was issued by the Judge Advocate appointed by Johnston, and Suttor appeared at Sydney to answer the charge. There was no proof that these servants had ever heard him use such words, whatever he may have thought; so he was discharged, but his two servants were taken from him, to the injury of his farm. After the mutiny he was asked to sign addresses recognising the necessity of what had been done. This he emphatically refused to do. He was threatened with further persecution. Colonel Foveaux arrived in the colony on the 28th July, and, on the 31st, issued a proclamation declaring his assumption of supreme authority, although he knew that Governor Bligh was within the territory, and was forcibly withheld from the authority which he alone held from the King. On the 20th November, Foveaux issued an order requiring all free settlers or others occupying or cultivating land in the colony, to attend and be mustered before such persons, and at such places, as he should appoint. Suttor took no notice of this order, which he looked upon as illegal, and stayed at home attending to his business. On Sunday, the 25th of November, a convict visited his house, and, in a most insolent manner, demanded to see him, saying, "he came by order of Colonel Foveaux to know why Mr. Suttor had not attended the muster." Suttor considered a message of that kind, and by such a person, as a personal affront. He told the convict "he would hold no communication with a person of his kind," and ordered him off his premises. On the 8th December, Foveaux sent an order to all persons at Suttor's house, citing them to appear on Saturday morning at

Government House, Parramatta. Suttor had previously received a summons from Captain Kemp, the new Judge Advocate, requiring him to appear in Sydney to answer the charge of non-attendance at the muster. He feared the ruin of his family, and, in the disturbed state of the country, hesitated to leave his family and property. He wrote to the Colonel, appealing to his humanity in the following terms:—

"I am informed that you have given orders for the men in my employment to attend at Government House at six o'clock to-morrow morning. But I beg you will suffer me to tell you that one of them was indented to me by His Excellency Governor King, and the other was indented to me by His Excellency Governor Bligh. If you mean to deprive me of their servitude, I shall consider it an invasion of my rights by taking an advantage of the exigencies of the moment so as to terminate in my ruin. The treatment I have met with since the command was taken from Governor Bligh, gives me reason to believe that conscience has something to do in the business. If, by the present instance, my family should come to destruction, the charge must lay at your door, and I shall be under the painful necessity of representing my case to Sir Joseph Banks, under whose auspices I came to this country, and in whom I have every hope my injured family will find a protector." This letter was delivered by one of Mr. Suttor's servants to Colonel Foveaux, who seized the servants and arrested Suttor, who was committed to gaol by some of the magistrates appointed by Foveaux, to take his trial for the contents of his "threatening letter." Being allowed bail, he appeared before the court on the 15th December to the charge preferred against him—that of writing a "contumelious" letter. He declined to plead either "guilty" or "not guilty," as he considered the court was illegally constituted. When pressed to plead he addressed the court as follows:—"Gentlemen I bow to you with respect, but the same motives which induced me to decline mustering induce me to deny the authority of this court; I stand here a British subject and a freeborn Englishman, and I claim the protection of my King and country. To His Excellency Governor Bligh my allegiance is due, and to him alone as the lawful and rightful Governor of this territory, appointed as such by our Most Gracious Sovereign. As to my person it is in your power, to that power, therefore, I must submit. My unprotected wife and children I leave to Almighty God till such time as the peace of this country shall be restored." He was again urged to plead, but refused. The court was then cleared; he was again taken in; no evidence being taken. He was sentenced by the Judge Advocate, who had taken his seat for the first time on this occasion, and the military officers, of whom the court was wholly composed, to be imprisoned in the gaol at Sydney for six calendar months, and to pay a fine of one shilling. He was confined in the old gaol in George-street, Sydney, in a cell appropriated for convicts under sentence of death, without any sustenance being allowed him, and, only for the humanity of his friends, he might have lain on the stones and died from want. He was detained a close prisoner from the 15th December, 1808, until 5th June, 1809, on which day he was set at liberty. On reaching home he found everything in the greatest confusion, and his family in great distress. On 17th February, 1810, Mr. Suttor was directed by letter from the Secretary of the Colony, John Thomas Campbell, to hold himself in readiness to proceed to England to give evidence in the charges preferred against Colonel Johnston and Mr. McArthur by Governor Bligh. On the 13th April he embarked on board the "Industan," and arrived at Spithead on the 23rd October. Suttor considered from Bligh's conduct on the voyage home that "he was very pleasant and agreeable, very attentive to the women and soldiers in the ship, and a very humane man." The trial over, Johnston was cashiered, and Suttor returned to Sydney. On arrival he says:— "No words can express the anxiety of my mind when we entered the harbour, to learn my beloved wife and children were alive and well. But soon I heard from Mr. R. Campbell, who came on board as deputy harbour-master, that, three days before, he had seen and spoken to her in good health. In 1814 he was offered the appointment of Superintendent of the Lunatic Asylum at Castle Hill, an office hitherto held by the Rev. S. Marsden. He did not find the position a happy one; on the contrary it was vexatious and troublesome. In 1820 he retired from the position and went back to his farm. About this time the colony was visited by a scourge of caterpillars, which ate up the pasture, causing a number of live-stock to perish for want of food. Suttor was desirous of crossing the Blue Mountains, but Governor Macquarie refused him the desired permission, although other persons were allowed to do so. However, he received permission from Governor Brisbane, and started with a few hundred breeding ewes and a few cattle; this was in 1822. And soon prosperity smiled upon his labours. In a few years, under his son's management, the hundreds of sheep became thousands, and the tens of his cattle became hundreds. He built a house in Sydney at a cost of £2,000, where Allan Cunningham, the botanist, lived with him, and where Leichhardt, the explorer, was a frequent visitor. On the completion of the education of one of his sons at Cambridge, in 1839, he went with his wife and daughter to England, in a ship laden with much of his own wool. He visited Ireland and Scotland, and the Continent, and, while at Edinburgh, revised the article in Chambers' "Information for the People," which related to Australia. While in

France he investigated viticulture, recording his observations in a book published by Smith, Elder, & Co., under the title "The Culture of the Grape Vine in Australia and New Zealand." While in London he had the honor, on the motion of that eminent botanist, Robert Brown, of being elected a Fellow of the Linnæan Society. While in France his wife died, and she lies buried in the cemetery of Rouen. He returned to the colony, and, after living a short time at Parramatta and Sydney, he took up his residence at Bathurst, where he died in 1859, at the age of eighty-three, leaving behind him a record and a name which commands the respect and admiration of every Australian on the continent. He was, indeed, a worthy type of a sterling Australian pioneer.

Sir Francis Forbes,
First Chief Justice of New South Wales.

Looking back to the days of those whose names are intimately connected with the growth of the Australian colonies, few will be found to stand out more prominently, and certainly no more honorably, than that of Sir Francis Forbes, the first Chief Justice of New South Wales. The leading events in the career of the late Sir Francis Forbes stand out in bold relief. On his arrival in the colony in 1824, a new order of things was introduced by the promulgation of the new Charter of Justice, by which the old convict system was done away with. The British institution of Trial by Jury took the place of martial law, and, what may be considered a matter of still greater importance, the liberty of the Press was secured. Chief Justice Forbes held office for only twelve years, but, during that time, much social progress was made, and legislative freedom, as well as freedom of the Press, became accomplished facts. It should be here remembered that Sir Francis Forbes was a

Liberal at a time when Liberalism did not exist in England as it does to-day. He stood up against officialdom to battle for the rights of the people, and paved the way for the Constitution which W. C. Wentworth and his colleagues brought soon after to so successful an issue. Francis Forbes was born in the Bermudas in 1784. He was sent to England at an early age to be educated. After going through the usual course, he entered the chambers of Mr. Sugden, afterwards the famous Lord St. Leonards, as a student-at-law, in 1803. Nine years later he was called to the Bar at the age of twenty-six, and the following year, 1813, was appointed Attorney and Advocate-General at Bermuda. He remained there for three years, and was then appointed Chief Justice of Newfoundland. He remained in this position until he was appointed Chief Justice of New South Wales on 1st June, 1823. He arrived in Sydney with his family on 5th March, 1824.

Up to 1800 the colony, as has been stated, was governed by martial law. For the first six years of settlement a large number of persons suffered the extreme penalty of the law, yet only sixteen of those executed were charged with murder. The first victim under this martial law was a youth of seventeen, who was executed for petty theft two months after the arrival of the first fleet. The lash was much in evidence, and, for about forty years, every magistrate had the power to order a flogging for the most trivial offence. One woman, suspected of stealing a flat-iron, hanged herself through sheer terror of the law. In 1839 a man was hanged for receiving stolen property, and, a few years before, six men were hanged together for being mixed up in an uprising against the brutal treatment of their master, whose name was struck off the Commission of the Peace for his atrocities. Owing to the horrible cruelties inflicted on the convicts by some of the masters, large numbers of them took to the bush. This went on to such an extent that, at the Criminal Sessions in October, 1822, thirty-four persons were placed in the dock and sentenced to death for bushranging. In 1800, Judge-Advocate Richard Atkins arrived in the colony. This gentleman had not received any legal training. His appointment was procured for him through influence. Amongst Governor Bligh's papers, after his deposition, a letter addressed to the Secretary of State was found, recommending his dismissal. Here is a passage from the letter— "He has been accustomed to inebriety; he has been the ridicule of the community; sentence of death has been pronounced in moments of intoxication; his determination is weak, his opinion floating and infirm; his knowledge of the law is insignificant, and subject to private inclination, and confidential causes of the Crown, where due secrecy is required, he is not to be trusted with." His conduct during the trial of John Macarthur no doubt had a good deal to do with the deposition of Governor Bligh. He was called to England to give evidence on the court martial held on Major Johnston, in connection with the deposition of Bligh, and another Judge-Advocate was appointed, in the person of Elias Bent, who arrived with Governor Macquarie, in 1809. During his term of office a new Charter of Justice was issued, by which three regular courts were established. The first court consisted of the Judge-Advocate and two magistrates, taking cognisance of "pleas of land or subject matter of action that did not exceed £50." The Supreme Court consisted of a judge appointed by a commission under the King's Royal Manual, and two magistrates appointed by the Governor; and the Lieutenant-Governor's Court, which sat in Tasmania. Judge Baron Field arrived in Sydney in 1817. The foundation of the Supreme Court, King-street, Sydney, was laid on 4th June, 1819, and, in 1822, the first attorney, Mr. George Allen, father of the late Sir Wigram Allen, was admitted to practice. Three months after the arrival of Chief Justice Forbes, Mr. Saxe-Bannister, the Attorney-General, landed, and brought with him a new Charter of Justice, which was promulgated at Government House, the Court House, and the Market-place by the Chief Justice. In 1824 the first Sheriff, Mr. John Mackaness, was appointed. Mr. F. S. Mills was elected first Registrar of the Supreme Court. The first officials were: Master-in-Chancery, Mr. J. Carter; Solicitor-General, Mr. John Stephen. Mr. Judge-Advocate Wylde was appointed temporary Judge during that year. The new Supreme Court of criminal jurisdiction was opened by Chief Justice Forbes on 10th June, 1824. He had, of course, to organise all the courts. It was through and by him that "trial by jury" was first introduced at the Court of Quarter Sessions, held at Liverpool, 14th October, 1824. The first Supreme Court jury was sworn in the case of King versus Cooper, 12th February, 1825, on which occasion the emancipists first made their appearance as a distinct class, demanding their right to be enrolled on the jury lists. To test the question an order was served on the Sheriff, requiring him to show cause why certain names submitted to him should not be included in these lists. The Solicitor-General appeared for the Sheriff, Mr. Wentworth and Dr. Wardell representing the emancipists. The Chief Justice decided that the application on affidavit was irregular, and that when a simple remedy—open in the present case—was available, the "high prerogative writ of *mandamus* could not be applied for." The application was disallowed, and the privileges asked for were not granted till 1833. Meanwhile, in 1827, a great meeting had been held in Sydney by the Patriotic Association to consider the question. On that occasion Mr. Wentworth spoke strongly in favour of the principle, and moved the adoption of a petition in favour of it. Sheriff Mackaness presided at the meeting, and was subsequently removed from his office for not exercising his right and stopping "language offensive to church and State." The petition was forwarded to Sir James Macintosh for presentation, but he was unsuccessful. Another unsuccessful attempt was made next year, on the accession of William IV. Three years later the Full Court decided that under the statute of 6th George IV., all free persons were entitled to the privileges of freedom; this, of course, settled the question. Chief Justice Forbes, who had recommended Sir James Macintosh's petition on the ground that "New South Wales was fully as ripe for such a change as any other dependency of the British Crown," presided on the bench on that occasion, Judges Burton and Dowling assisting. It may not be considered out of place to here touch briefly on the battle waged for the liberty of the Press in this colony. Sir Thomas Brisbane, through an official letter addressed by Secretary Goulburn to the editor of the Sydney *Gazette*, 15th October, 1824, recognised the liberty of the Press. This liberty was threatened in 1826 by Governor Darling. Sir Ralph Darling was then two years in the colony. Two soldiers named Sudds and Thompson had committed an offence in order that they might be convicted, and, on their discharge, have an opportunity of improving their condition in life. After their conviction and sentence, Sir Ralph Darling issued an order by which the two men were taken out of the hands of the civil power, and returned to the ranks. They were stripped of their uniform on parade, in presence of all the soldiers; clothed in the convict garb, and iron collars, with spikes and chains made especially heavy, were rivetted on their necks and legs. They were then drummed out of the regiment, and then marched back to gaol to the tune of the "Rogue's March." Sudds died a few days afterwards from exposure in the sun and the heavy chains, but chiefly from the torture of mind he was subjected to before his comrades, Thompson became insane. This action of the official was condemned by both Press and people. Wentworth wrote a pamphlet on the subject, called "The Impeachment," in which he said he would follow the Governor to the foot of the gallows with the accusation. The editor of the *Monitor* (Mr. E. S. Hall), was sentenced to twelve months' imprisonment for libelling Governor Darling. The editor of the *Australian* was sentenced to six months' imprisonment and fined £100 for a similar offence. It was at this time that Governor Darling attempted to re-establish the censorship of the Press, and Sir Francis Forbes distinguished himself by so strongly protesting against it. The result was that the Governor had to abandon the proposal. This was the last attack made upon the liberty of the Press. In 1827 a measure was proposed by Governor Darling in the Council imposing a heavy duty on all newspapers published in the colony. Under the Constitution Act, all measures passed had to receive the certificate of the Chief Justice that they were in accord with English law. This measure was submitted to him in blank, and was so certified. The Council subsequently filled in the blank with figures representing the proposed duty. It was proposed by one member that one shilling per copy should be charged, but a stamp duty of fourpence was adopted. The Chief Justice at once refused his certificate to this imposition, which, he urged, would effectually crush out of existence every newspaper in the colony. This conduct on the part of the Chief Justice entailed the bitter enmity of the Governor, Sir Ralph Darling, who made grave charges against him. These, however, were easily repelled. The address presented to Chief Justice Forbes on his departure from the colony, remarked, among other things:—"To you, Sir, the first

Chief Justice that was ever appointed to preside in our courts, was delegated on your arrival the arduous duty of organising those courts, so as to render them the means of dispensing justice to the inhabitants of this colony, in conformity, as far as then lay in your power, with the constitutional rights of our fellow subjects in the mother country. This was the object submitted to your care, when, although Chief Justice of the colony, you had no brother judge to aid you in your arduous undertaking, and so well did you perform this duty, that you at once raised the judgment seat in the estimation of the colonists to that state of respect from which it has never, on any occasion since, been suffered to descend—an object of admiration for the ability with which its difficult and arduous duties have been so efficiently performed, and of veneration for, and implicit confidence in, the undeviating purity of its decisions. As a legislator and member of the colonial Government, your character is entitled no less to our unqualified regard, more particularly your uncompromising maintenance of the constitutional rights of the colonists, as far as those rights have been hitherto extended to this colony. Nothing but the highest moral firmness and integrity, combined with that genius and learning, for which you are so eminently distinguished, could have overcome the opposition and the difficulties which you have had to encounter." During Chief Justice Forbes' residence in the colony, he applied himself so closely to his duties, that his health gave way under the strain. He left for England in 1836. While in England he received the honor of knighthood (6th April, 1837). At the expiration of his leave he found his health not sufficiently restored, so he resigned his appointment in July, 1837. In the same year he returned to Sydney, where he resided until his death, which took place on 9th November, 1841. He married, in 1813, Amelia Sophia, daughter of David Grant, M.D., of Jamaica.

The Hon. Sir John Robertson, K.C.M.G.

There is no name in Australian history more honored and venerated by all classes of persons than that of Sir John Robertson. During his lifetime he rallied round him the best spirits of his day, and assuredly if ever a man departed from this earth leaving no enemies behind, that man was John Robertson, "the father of free selection," as he was popularly designated.

Sir John Robertson was born at Bow, Essex, on 15th October, 1816. His father was a Scotchman, his mother English. When he was four years old his father emigrated to Australia. He received his education at Dr. Lang's college, in Jamieson-street, and at Mr. Cape's school, the boy being one of the first to enter Scot's College. Finishing his education, he proceeded to his parents' residence on the Hunter, where they were engaged in pastoral pursuits. He spent a portion of his time near Boggabri, leading the usual life of a squatting youth in those days. He did not take too kindly to this kind of life. Thus, while still a mere youth, we find him working his passage to England on board the ship "Sovereign." He remained at sea for about two years, when he returned to the colony, and started in pastoral pursuits. He married at the age of twenty-one. While attending to the duties which his mode of life required of him, his active brain dwelt a good deal upon political matters as affecting the young colony, and he was looked upon by the inhabitants of the north-western portion of the colony as their leader. He pleaded the cause of the squatters before the Governor, Sir George Gipps, who was at the time curtailing the rights of Crown tenants. Young Robertson's pleading, and clear and forcible statement of the case, proved successful. Still a few years later he was found urging the cause of the free selectors against his own class, which shows the rectitude of his mind when he saw the interests of the people lay one way, and the interest of the class to which he belonged on the other side. He never hesitated, but took the side which he considered beneficial to the general public. After the passing of the "Constitution Act," in 1856, Mr. Robertson was one of the first to be requisitioned to stand for a constituency, and his was the first address issued to the constituencies. He lived to see most of the subjects laid down in that address become the law of the land. Amongst the measures alluded to we may mention the Public Lands, Electoral Reform, National Education, and Abolition of State Aid to Religion. He was elected for the Bligh, Brisbane, and Phillip constituencies to the first Parliament under Responsible Government. Daniel Henry Deniehy, Thomas Holt, W. Macleay, W. B. Dalley, and James Martin were elected at the same time for other constituencies. Some two years after he became Minister for Lands in Mr. Cowper's administration. When Sir John Robertson first brought in his motion for free-selection before survey, he only found nine members supporting him. When Sir Charles Cowper formed his second Ministry, in 1857, Sir John Robertson joined him as Minister for Lands and Works, which office he held from January 13, 1858, to September 30, 1859. The chief measure which that Ministry passed was the Electoral Bill; soon after, they were defeated on their Education Bill. The Forster Ministry, which succeeded them, lasted only a few months. Taking office again in March, 1860, Mr. Robertson brought in his famous Land Bill, which was, however, defeated by a small majority on a motion brought forward by Sir John Hay. Mr. Robertson at once appealed to the people, and came back with a large majority, all the members of the Cabinet being re-elected. The Bill was re-introduced, and was carried easily in the Legislative Assembly. The measure, however, met with the most determined opposition in the Legislative Council. Mr. Robertson resigned his seat in the Lower Chamber, and had himself appointed to the Council, where, notwithstanding the Conservative opposition, he secured the passing of the bill into law.

Sir John Robertson was five times Premier: March 9, 1860; January 12, 1870; February 9, 1875, and August 17, 1877. He was Minister for Lands and Works in the Cabinet of Sir Charles Cowper, January 13, 1858; Secretary for Lands in the fourth Cowper Ministry, February 3, 1865, and in the fifth Cowper Ministry, August 17, 1870; he was Colonial Secretary in the Martin Ministry, December 16, 1870; he also represented the Parkes Ministry in the Upper House, 1878; he became Minister for Public Instruction in June, 1880. He again became Premier and Colonial Secretary on December 22, 1885. This Ministry was only a sort of scratch Ministry, and retired from office 25th February, holding office for two months. In 1877 Sir John Robertson was honored by a knighthood, in recognition of his eminent services to the colony, he receiving the title of K.C.M.G. at the same time as Sir Henry Parkes. A writer in the *Australian Portrait Gallery*, some years before Sir John Robertson's death, thus sketched his career:—" Sir John Robertson's career has proceeded *pari passu* with the development of our constitutional history. The dates of its chief events are epochs in his public life, and the one lends light and shade to the other. That public life has been full of colour and character, presenting very few half tones, and no neutral tints whatever. All things about the man, even his mistakes, are clear and well defined. It is difficult to gauge with strict accuracy the vast influence for good of such tough fibre, interwoven so completely as it has been through and through the variegated woof of our colonial political life. The national character of a young country like this is widely tinged and deeply impregnated with that of its political rulers. Their individuality insensibly impresses the public spirit which commits itself to their care. The strong virility of Sir John Robertson has established him from the first in the front rank, and his individual personality has never since failed to impress itself on the opinions and political faith of his followers, as well as on the entire political life of the country. On the whole, it must be admitted that his general influence, apart from his acts, has been for good. He has ever been a staunch friend, always in the face of expediency or prudence, though sometimes in the teeth of justice. As a political leader he has never committed himself to those mock oracular deliverances, meaningless and vapid in themselves, by which some politicians defraud the popular faith and throw dust in the eyes of the people. He has never stirred up class differences to bolster up a weak position, nor revived those rabid sectarian cries and old-world bitternesses, so much out of place in Australia, to strengthen failing political power. His liberality has been consistent throughout, and his disregard of class differences is only equal to his contempt for those who profited by them. Though never despising party tactics, his career has been singularly free from petty subterfuges and whining cant, ever taking his reverses and defeats manfully. As a speaker he has always been eloquent, prompt, and effective. Throughout his life and work, Sir John Robertson has amply justified the popular choice of a leader in the very beginning of Responsible Government. In reviewing both from their commencement, the observer cannot but recognise the great and varied use both have been to our political history, at a time when it was of the first importance, that the general character of its impressions should be good. In sounding the heart of the country he will find, far down in its depths, a deep strain of tenderness for the noble veteran whose face and form are so familiar to every unit in the community. When most of the callow statesmen and immature politicians of to-day, who essay to gain a perilous notoriety by criticism of his work, have found their proper and native level, the feeling of the country will be glad to glance back at the history of the past, illustrated as it was by the virile life and manful efforts of this fearless and intrepid leader of the people."

After his retirement from public life, Parliament voted him £10,000 in recognition of his public services. When the Federation movement was foremost in men's minds, Sir John Robertson always took up a most determined stand in opposition, and, on the very day of his death, a letter, written by him the previous day, was published in the *Herald* in opposition to the Commonwealth Bill. He was present at a picnic at Vaucluse the day before his death, at which he made a speech against Federation. His death took place at his home, "Clovely," Watson's Bay, on 8th May, 1891. His funeral, which was a public one, was attended by all classes and all creeds. The Governor (Lord Jersey), His Eminence Cardinal Moran, the Admiral, and all the high dignitaries, both civil and military, attended. Speaking at a meeting held at the Cathedral on the Sunday evening of the funeral, Cardinal Moran made the following reference to the late statesman:—"Within the last few hours he had the privilege of assisting at the great and well-deserved tribute paid by the citizens of Sydney to the veteran statesman who had been summoned by death, and relieved from all the troubles and trials of the field of politics, and all the cares and anxieties of our daily life. The veteran who had passed away, had not among his compeers during his long and eventful public career, one more remarkable for his wholeheartedness in the building up and preservation of those rights which he believed to be so essential to the greatness of Australia. None had more faithfully served the colony than he, none had been more jealous of the guardianship, and none more courageous in the defence of the liberties he had helped to win for the people of this fair land. It was the duty of all true citizens and all true colonists to cherish and guard the great liberties which were Australia's boast, and the honor which had been paid that day to the remains of their veteran statesman and champion, was but a fitting manifestation of their grateful appreciation of Sir John Robertson's services in defence of their rights and liberties. During his long public life, the distinguished statesman recognised and respected both the political and religious rights of all classes in the community, and it was a cheering thing, now that he had passed away, to be able to say of him, as one of their representative Australian statesmen, that he had never used his high position and great opportunities save for the public good; that he had never lent his aid to the creation of discord in the community, or to the stirring up of the embers of religious strife. Recognising, as a statesman having the country's welfare at heart, that peace and concord were essential to Australia's prosperity, he did his best, and for many years, to foster and extend the growth of a broad and generous spirit in the land."

SIR JOHN HAY, K.C.M.G.

The name of John Hay is thoroughly representative of the pastoralist class. Upon his arrival in the colony he commenced his squatting career, and, during the whole of that life, he always stood up for the claims of his class, both in and out of Parliament. John Hay was born in Scotland, at Little Ythsie, Aberdeenshire, and was educated at King's College, Aberdeen. He proved a successful student, carrying off the highest honors every year. In 1834 he took his degree at the University, and then went to Edinburgh to study law. He spent two or three years in Edinburgh, when he heard such good accounts of the colony that he gave up his studies and took passage for Australia. He arrived in Sydney in 1838, and during that year he went into the country and settled at Weleragang, above Albury, on the Upper Murray. Mr. Hay remained there about eighteen years, working hard for success all the time. Although living so far from the seat of Government, Mr. Hay studied all the political questions which agitated the colony. Consequently it was no surprise to find him offering himself for a seat in Parliament at the first election under Responsible Government in 1856. Before this he uncompromisingly opposed the Border Duties over the Murray. He was looked upon as one of the most prominent men in this Parliament, as was shown by his being chosen to move the vote of censure on the Cowper Ministry, 17th September, 1856, the vote being carried. Mr. Cowper having failed to induce Governor Denison to grant a dissolution, Mr. Hay was sent for to form a new administration. But he declined the responsibility. Mr. Watson Parker was then sent for. This gentleman was at one time Private Secretary to Sir George Gipps. Mr. Parker was successful in forming a Ministry, Mr. Hay taking the position of Minister for Lands and Works. Mr. Stuart Donaldson, who had formed the first Ministry under Responsible Government, took the Treasurership. Mr. Manning and Mr. Darvall assumed the posts of Attorney-General and Solicitor-General respectively, Mr. Deas-Thomson being Vice-President of the Executive Council. This Ministry remained in office for about eleven months, when they brought in a new Electoral Bill. They were defeated by Mr. Cowper, who moved that the Bill be read that day six months, which motion was carried by twenty-six to twenty-three. The Government tendered their resignation. Mr. Cowper again took office. In 1858, under the new Electoral Act, the Murrumbidgee electorate was divided, Mr. Hay sitting as member for the Murray until 1864. In this year he was elected for Central Cumberland, which constituency he represented till 1867, when he was appointed to the Legislative Council.

During the agitation for free-selection before survey, Mr. Hay took a determined stand on behalf of the squatters, and raised the greatest opposition to the principle. His resolution against the clause was carried by thirty-three votes to twenty-eight. The Ministry appealed to the constituencies, and came back with a large majority. But such was Mr. Hay's personal popularity, that, notwithstanding his pronounced opposition to the free-selection before survey clause, he was again returned by his constituents. On October 14, 1862, Mr. Hay was elected Speaker of the Legislative Assembly, in succession to Sir Terence Aubrey Murray. He held the position till October 21st, 1865. He remained in the Assembly until his appointment to the Legislative Council on June 26th, 1867, and, on the death of Sir Terence Aubrey Murray, Mr. Hay was appointed to the position of President of the Council, which position he held up to the time of his death, which took place at Rose Bay, on January 20th, 1892.

CHAPTER VII.

EARLY MEN OF GENIUS AND POWER—THE LIST CONTINUED—DR. LANG—A BLOW TO CONVICTISM—DR. LANG AS A REFORMER—THE FIGHT FOR FREEDOM—DR. RICHARD L. JENKINS—THE EDUCATION OF THE MASSES—WILLIAM COX—THE TRACK OVER THE BLUE MOUNTAINS—HON. HENRY DANGAR—MYALL CREEK—HON. JAMES WHITE—HON. DAVID JONES—ALEXANDER BERRY—WILLIAM H. HOVELL—HON. HENRY MORT.

THE REV. JOHN DUNMORE LANG, D.D.

IN the early days of settlement in New South Wales, clergymen of different denominations took a very active part in shaping the affairs of the colony. But none of them were more active than Dr. Lang. This was so not only in the political movements of his time, but in the work of settling a desirable class of settlers on the lands of Australia. Similarly was he energetic in prosecuting all movements taken to obtain free institutions. From the day he first set foot on Australian soil, his life may be said to have been directed towards advancing the various interests of his adopted country. There is no doubt that there were blemishes in his method of attaining the ends which he fought for. But who can be said to be entirely free of fault? One thing must be said of John Dunmore Lang: his faults were faults of the head, and not of the heart. To use his own words, "Although my course may have been somewhat unusual and erratic, the candid reader will come to the conclusion that it has been uniformly the result of a sincere desire to promote the best interests of the Australian colonies."

John Dunmore Lang was born at Greenock, in Scotland, August 25th, 1799. His parents were Scotch, and true adherents of the Kirk, and had suffered in earlier years for the Solemn League and Covenant. His parent moved to Largs, in Ayrshire, when the subject of this memoir was seven years old. He attended the parish school until he was old enough to go to the Glasgow University. Like a large number of the better educated of his countrymen, he chose the church as his calling. In 1821, his brother, George Lang, came to Australia, and the accounts which he sent home of this country directed the attention of the divinity student to Australia, as likely to give ample scope to his missionary zeal. About a year after, having been ordained to the Ministry by the Presbytery of Irvine, and taking his degree as Master of Arts, he sailed for Australia, arriving in Sydney in May, 1823. Sir Thomas Brisbane was then Governor of the colony. He came from the same place as the Langs, in the west of Scotland.

In the same year, 1824, the Scots' Church, in Jamieson-street, was built and opened. Dr. Lang officiated in this place up to the time of his death. About five years after his arrival in the colony, he was desirous of establishing a college for the education of young men for the Presbyterian Church, as well as for other educational purposes. He endeavoured to obtain convict labour for the purpose, but Governor Darling refused to assist the project in any way. In 1830, Dr. Lang went to England, and, whilst there, obtained from Lord Goderich, who was then Secretary of State for the Colonies, an order on the colonial Government for £3,500, on condition that a similar amount was previously spent by the promoters on the undertaking. £1,500 of this were allowed by Lord Goderich to be applied to the payment of passages of a party of Scotch mechanics, to be selected by Dr. Lang, the party to consist of fifty or sixty. Those mechanics were to be employed in the erection of the buildings, and the cost of their passages was to be deducted from their wages. About sixty Scotch families—blacksmiths, carpenters, stonemasons, plasterers—arrived in the colony by the "Stirling Castle" in October, 1831. Dr. Lang had another object in view in bringing out this class of immigrants, which he expressed at the time. He says:— "Previous to this period, there were only two classes in the colony—the free emigrant gentlemen settlers, with their large grant of land of from one to two thousand acres and upwards, their flocks and herds, and their numerous convict servants. These were, in their own estimation at least, the aristocracy of the colony. The other class consisted exclusively of the emancipated convict labourers and mechanics, who were congregated chiefly in the towns. In such circumstances it appeared to me that the formation of a middle class in the colony was indispensably necessary to its moral welfare and social advancement."

This project met with great opposition, and Dr. Lang took another trip to England in 1833. He returned to Sydney in 1835, and started the *Colonist* newspaper, "for the furtherance of the moral and intellectual development of the colony." He conducted this paper with his usual vigour, and it was not long ere he was called upon to defend more than one libel action. One of the actions was taken against him by the emancipists, a class of persons whom he steadily opposed, from the first, with all the talent and influence which he could possibly command. In this case the writer defended himself in an address of remarkable strength and point, which resulted in the withdrawal of the prosecution. Subsequently the *Colonist* commented upon some of the vices of the day, coupling with them the names of some well-known members of the community. For this he was fined £100, which was promptly subscribed and paid by the public. In 1851 Dr. Lang was sentenced to four months imprisonment, and a fine of £100, for criminally libelling Mr. Thomas Icely. In this case his fine and legal expenses were paid by a shilling subscription.

In 1836 Dr. Lang made another voyage to England, bringing back with him about two hundred and fifty vine-dressers for New South Wales, under engagement to his brother, Mr. Andrew Lang. However, on the way out, they altered their determination and settled at Rio de Janeiro. A number of missionaries from Berlin came out with the Doctor, and established an aboriginal mission at Nundah, near Brisbane, in 1838. During this visit he arranged for the bringing out to the colony about four thousand Scotch artizans and herdsmen. Dr. Lang was elected in 1843 as member for Port Phillip in the first Legislative Council.

On the motion of Dr. Lang, a select committee was appointed in 1844 to consider the subject of franchise and representation; Dr. Lang was appointed chairman. The committee recommended that the franchise be extended to farmers and squatters; the recommendations were not, however, carried into effect. He was the first to move for the adoption of a twopenny postage rate for the colony, which was vetoed by Sir George Gipps. It became law during the reign of his successor. It was he, too, who moved that Port Phillip should be erected into a separate and independent colony. At that time six members represented what is now the colony of Victoria, and, from among all the members representing New South Wales, only one solitary vote was cast in favour of the motion for separation, and that vote was given by Mr. Robert Lowe. Dr. Lang recommended that the members for Port Phillip should send to Her Majesty the Queen a petition on the subject through the Governor. He drew up the petition, which was forwarded in due course, and, about nine months after, a reply came from Lord Stanley, then Secretary of State for the colonies, favourable to the petition. It was not, however, till July 1st, 1851, that Port Phillip was proclaimed a separate colony under the name of Victoria. In 1846 Dr. Lang took another trip to England, for the purpose, he acknowledged, of counteracting the effects of the inflow into the colony of large numbers of Irish immigrants. He considered this could only be checked by bringing out larger numbers of protestant immigrants. The only thing he accomplished in this direction was that he selected a number of Scotch immigrants, with a view to settling them in the northern portion of the colony, on a cotton plantation which he proposed starting. This project fell through owing to the fact that land grants, which he expected to be given to the immigrants, were refused. Most of the immigrants were landed and settled in the Moreton Bay country, and they assisted largely in making that colony what it is to-day. Many of them rose to eminence in the young colony, and became wealthy as time went on.

Shortly after his return to the colony in 1850, he was elected to represent the city of Sydney. He was accused of having made money out of his immigration scheme, by the Parliament and the Press. He issued an address to his constituents, offering to resign his seat if they approved of the course taken by his accusers. His supporters held a public meeting, at which they expressed their entire satisfaction with their representative. This induced him to hold his seat. At the next elections, 1851, he was serving four months' incarceration in Parramatta gaol for the Icely libel. He was nevertheless elected at the head of the poll, Messrs. Wentworth and Lamb being his colleagues, Messrs. Longmore and Charles Cowper being defeated. After his release he made a speech in the following terms:—" He congratulated his fellow citizens on the position which the city had taken up as the heart of the whole Australian group. The heart of the colony was in right action, and the blood it would send into the limbs and branches of the other colonies would infuse life into the whole political system. Personally he thanked them for the certificate of character which they had given him, and which, he doubted not, would serve a future purpose, not only in the colony, but in England, if it should be his fate to go once more home. They were all aware of his efforts to arouse public feeling at home, in order to obtain justice for the colonists of the empire generally; but in making those efforts he had aroused the wrath of the Colonial Office against himself. Some comments had appeared in the London *Daily News*, stating his election last year had been accidental, and that the constituency took no part in the extreme views he held, particularly as to the right of a colony to entire freedom and independence. He had risked his present election, however, on a strong expression of that opinion. It was from no feeling of disloyalty that he professed these opinions. God forbid that he should feel disrespect for the authorities of the old Fatherland! But while he yielded to no man in respect, in veneration, for the constituted authorities of the mother country, he would never hesitate to express his conviction of the right of any colony of the Crown as soon as it could stand on its own legs, to entire freedom and independence. He held that a common language, a common literature, a common law, and a common religion, constituted an infinitely stronger and more binding tie than those which kept them now under the domination of Downing-street, and whenever the day came that they should have a flag of their own floating over the splendid series of colonies founded in Australia, he felt confident that Great Britain would rejoice with them, and would say, 'Many daughters have done virtuously, but thou, Australia, hast excelled them all.'" In the following February he resigned his seat in the Council, and paid another visit to England. Dr. Lang died 8th August, 1878, the immediate cause being a rupture of a vessel in the brain.

Liberty may be taken here to give a few extracts from a speech delivered by Sir Henry Parkes at a meeting held at St. Leonard's, on the first anniversary of Dr. Lang's death, for the purpose of promoting the erection of a statue to his memory. The well-known statesman said " he came to Australia with an expansive intellect, a brave spirit, a capacity for work and mastering the details of life, and with a quality which has been accounted the greatest of all human qualities—the power of gentleness. It has been said that the quality of all others that wins a man's way in the world —that conquers difficulties, that makes friends, that plants a reputation—is not brilliant attainments in science, not great learning, not the endowment of an eloquent tongue, but tenderness of disposition. . . . He attended to public matters, promoted public movements, all of which had a tendency to dispel the midnight darkness of those days, and teach the people to fit themselves for the good time which was in store for them, and which, full of all the liberties of true-born Britons, was sure to come, which was fervently believed in, and which, in the fulness of time, came with all its plentitude of power and privilege. A man who presented this noble figure in those early days, and struggled ever with a brave heart, and a loving disposition towards his fellow men, his one object being to place his fellow-colonists safely and deeply in the land, to educate them and fit them for the making of a great nation—a man who did all this is worthy of some testimony to his undoubted greatness, and the fruits which have flowed from his exertions, it is, I am afraid, and I must say it, hardly a compliment to the well-to-do citizens of this part of the metropolis that they stay at home, even on a night like this, on such an occasion as the present. A man moving in that circle of thoughtfulness and cultivated men who form, as it were, a kind of zone between the privileged and aristocratic classes and the mercantile and working classes of England —that zone, if I may use the word, of intellectual force which is so attractive to us all in the mother country—a man conspicuous in that band of intellectual progress has said that great men grow, like grapes, in bunches. It is a homely expression, but one with a wonderful power of truth. In the history of the world we see periods of barrenness— the period of little minds. The history of England gives you many such sterile and uneventful periods ; and occasionally a group of men arise, and they nearly always do arise in groups, fitted in the most supreme manner for the work of forming society and directing its' movements, and constructing the machinery of government. Such a group of men, in an eminent degree, appeared in England in the time of the Stuarts—Pym, Hampden, and their great associates. Such a group of men, by something like a miracle, appeared in the throes of the American revolution—Washington, Franklin, Adams, Jefferson. Probably never on the face of the earth was there a company of great minds more fit for laying the foundation of a great nation. Though the population of the American colonies in that day did not excel in numbers the population in Australasia to-day, still in that population appeared a group of men who have no superiors in the work of government in all the range of human history. In a less remarkable manner there appeared in this country, in its early days, a group of men who certainly were eminently fitted to struggle with the dark times. Of those the very father of the Australian Press was Edward Smith Hall. If there ever was a journalist with a true conception of his great functions, it was this early conductor of a Sydney newspaper. There was William Bland, a man who had all the faculties for conceiving the true position and the true duties of a free citizen. Then there was William Charles Wentworth, who had a colossal power which has seldom been equalled. And then there was John Dunmore Lang, who perhaps excelled them all in the combination of the qualities which form real human greatness—that is, his bravery, ready to face anything if he thought he was right, his grasp of intellect, his untiring capacity for work, and, above all, that tenderness of spirit, that power of gentleness, without which it has been said, and, I believe, truly said, that no man can ever be truly great."

RICHARD LEWIS JENKINS, M.R.C.S. ENG., L.S.A. LONDON.

One feels privileged in placing on record even what must be an imperfect sketch of such a man as the late Dr. Jenkins. He was a man of gentle birth and high culture, broad views, advanced ideas, and of a humane and philanthropical mind. He paid much attention to the subject of popular education for the masses. He favoured compulsory and free education. Some of his views were regarded as quite eccentric. Yet they have since been embodied in the "Public Instruction Act." But while advocating compulsory and free education, he did not forget to point out that the religious training of the children should be attended to as well as the training of the intellect.

Hon. David Jones. Hon. James White.
Hon. John Fairfax.
Hon. Henry Mort. Capt. O'Reilly.

DR. R. L. JENKINS.

Richard Lewis Jenkins was the fourth son of Richard Jenkins, of Newport, Monmouthshire, and Elizabeth, his wife, eldest daughter of the late William Vaughan, of Caerphilly, Glamorganshire. He was descended from the Jenkins family of Panty Nawell, members of which, in the sixteenth century, and frequently since, held the office of High Sheriff of Glamorganshire. After receiving his diplomas he practiced for some time at home, but, his health becoming impaired, he was obliged to leave England and seek a warmer clime. He came to this colony in 1841 as medical officer on board the ship "James Moran." The passengers of that vessel presented him with an address and testimonial expressing their gratitude for the kindness and services rendered by their medical officer to every one on board. He practiced his profession for some time on the Hunter River, and afterwards turned his attention to pastoral pursuits. He gradually accumulated stock, and soon became the owner of several stations on the Peel and Namoi Rivers. Being possessed of great energy and tact, he forced that success which always comes to him who exercises those qualities. In 1857 he removed to Sydney, where he took a very active part in the political life of the colony, and was soon elected to represent a large constituency. At this time Responsible Government was just commencing in the colony, and Dr. Jenkins' fitness for public life being acknowledged, he was at once elected to a seat in Parliament. His chief desire was to elevate the masses, and he worked hard to bring this about. He delivered a lecture in the hall of the Mechanics' School of Arts on the subject on 21st November, 1859.

Sir Charles Nicholson occupied the chair on the occasion, and among those present were Professors Woolley and Smith, of the Sydney University, the Hon. Saul Samuel, Messrs. Plunkett, Parkes, and Macarthur. In the course of his lecture Dr. Jenkins remarked :—" A few years ago a friend of mine who had not paid much attention himself to public education, hearing me advocate my views in perhaps rather an earnest manner, observed that he thought I was rather mad on the subject. Taking leave to differ from my friend, I, on the contrary, am more disposed to believe that I have a mission in the matter—a mission inconceivably grand— of no less magnitude than to assist you fellow-colonists, in placing within the reach of every child an intellectual, a moral, and a religious education. If this be madness, then my desire is that not only my friend, but that all present and all absent should become equally touched, and that there should be no sanity in this community until the cause of the madness is removed, or, in other words, until we have universal education."

This quotation indicates the state of public opinion at that time. Liberal and advanced as were the views of Dr. Jenkins, few persons at that time were prepared to go so far in the matter of education. Most of those of the old school believed more in the lash and the hangman than in the ameliorative policy as laid down by Dr. Jenkins. The old leaven of the Imperial régime had not died out. It takes a long time to forget the teachings of the school. Further on in the same lecture Dr. Jenkins said:—" Experience has but too often proved that the best way to make a confirmed villain of a young thief is to sentence him to a common gaol. Many a young rogue would be restored to society through the agency of a reformatory school who would otherwise have had his evil habits confirmed if allowed to mix with older prisoners in gaol. It must be apparent that both reformatory and industrial schools are well adapted to dry up the very sources of crime."

These words contain a principle which is now acknowledged, and voiced through the statute book of the colony, and no doubt as occasion arises will be even more fully recognised and acted upon. Reformatory schools have been established and have done a vast amount of good; still there is plenty of room for far greater developments in this direction.

After three years work in Parliament he retired from political life, partly through having purchased the Nepean Towers Estate, near Penrith, and partly owing to failing health. At Nepean Towers he carried out to perfection the breeding of shorthorn cattle, for which, at the shows held in the principal towns in the colonies, he received the highest prizes. In 1873 he read before the Agricultural Society a valuable paper on the "Considerations which should guide the graziers and breeders in New South Wales," Sir Hercules Robinson, the Governor of the colony and President of the Society, being in the chair. This paper caused a good deal of discussion, and contained a large amount of valuable information. Dr. Jenkins was a leading churchman, and a regular attendant and speaker at the annual meetings of the Synod. He died at Brisbane on the 13th August, 1883. He left a wife and eight children, three sons and five daughters. The second son is Dr. Edward Johnstone Jenkins, born 24th October, 1854, and educated at Macquarie Fields, and King's school, Parramatta. At King's school he took the Broughton and Campbell scholarships. He went from there to Trinity College, Oxford, taking degrees as Bachelor and Master of Arts, with honors in natural science and Doctor of Medicine. He was House and Ophthalmic Surgeon at St. Bartholomew's, London, and qualified M.R.C.S. in 1881, and M.R.C.P. and L.S.A. in 1883. He arrived in Sydney in February, 1884, where he has practiced his profession. His elder brother married a niece of the present Earl of Powis, and of the Dean of Hereford. Dr. Jenkins was married in Sydney on 1st January, 1852, to Mary Rae, eldest daughter of the late Major Edward Johnstone, of H.M. 50th Regiment. The tidings of his death caused a feeling of profound sorrow in Sydney, where he was universally honored and respected. But the good work he did has left enduring traces. His influence was an elevating one.

WILLIAM COX.

The name of William Cox takes us back to the early days of the colony; to the beginning of this century. The history of the Cox family, if written at length, would, in many respects, be the history of the colony. William Cox came to the colony in the first year of the present century. He occupied both a military and official position, a position he held with credit to himself and benefit to the land of his adoption. As a magistrate of the territory he fulfilled his duties most efficiently, always remembering that his lot was cast, as well as the lot of his family, with the colony and its future. As a contractor in the time of Governor Macquarie, Mr. Cox also did good work. Later on he started in pastoral pursuits with such energy and success as to place him in the front rank of the wool growers of the colony. He took special interest in the breeding of fine-woolled sheep at Mudgee, and spared neither time nor expense to improve the staple of the wool until he placed the name of his station (Clarendon) at the head of the list.

Mr. Cox was born in 1764, at Devizes Wilts, being the second son of Robert Cox, of Wimbourne, Dorset. He joined the army as a commissioned officer in 1795, and came to New South Wales in 1801 as paymaster of the New South Wales Corps. Mr. Cox succeeded Mr. John MacArthur at the time the corps was ordered to India for its part in the Bligh episode in 1810. Mr. Cox and other officers resigned their commissions and remained in the colony. He first settled at Brush Farm, on the Parramatta River, and afterwards at Clarendon, on the Hawkesbury. He gave all his time to agricultural pursuits for some years, and made large profits. At Brush Farm he had the notorious General Holt as manager. Holt had been transported for his share in the Irish rebellion of 1798. Holt published his recollections, which throw a light on the manner in which things were conducted in those early days of the colony. The detachment of the corps to which Mr. Cox belonged had charge of some of the deported Irish "patriots" who had been concerned in the uprising—Holt being one of the leaders. In his position of manager, Holt proved himself thoroughly efficient. In 1814, when Wentworth, Blaxland, and Lawson discovered the track across the Blue Mountains to Bathurst Plains, Mr. Cox was chosen by Governor Macquarie to construct the road. He had command of unlimited labour, and his aptitude in selecting and his ability to direct men, enabled him to form an excellent road in a very short space of time over this very rough and dangerous pass. The road, one hundred and thirty miles in length, crossed the Blue Mountains from Sydney, bridged Cox's River, which was thereby connecting Bathurst Plains with the coast. Governor and Lady Macquarie, the year after its formation, drove in a carriage over this road, which was highly spoken of by Surveyor Oxley in his published reports. For this service Mr. Cox received a grant of land on the Bathurst Plains, which he called Hereford. He next went into pastoral pursuits, and purchased some of the first shipments of merinos from the Cape, the progeny of which now form the celebrated Mudgee flocks. He gave considerable time and attention to the staple of wool and breeding of colonial sheep, with the best results. Later on Mr. Cox took up land in the Mulgoa Valley, his three sons, George, Henry, and Edward, following in his footsteps, his eldest son settled at Hobartville, Richmond. His second son "sat down" in Tasmania, where he acquired a large estate called Clarendon. He also formed stations on the Macquarie River, naming them Burrendong, and on the Coolah Creek. In 1833 he removed from Clarendon to Fairfield, near Windsor, where he resided up to the time of his death, which occurred in 1837. He was buried in the family vault of St. Matthew's Church.

A recently published memoir says of Mr. Cox :—" There is nothing in his career either questionable or unmanly, and his name does not occur in connection with any of the old records of misused influence or abused power that tell the reader of our history of to-day how little fit many of the early official military officers were to conduct the delicate experiment which the home authorities heedlessly committed to their care. Mr. Cox fought his way in the open, and what he won was the fair reward for his personal energy and sound practical sense. His influence over men in his employ as a contractor and agriculturist, was largely the outcome of his manliness towards them. Treating them as men, he earned from them the respect and regard which such treatment always produces, with the effect that they never shirked work, and the detachments under his command were always noticeable for their results in the shape of honest labour. As a consequence his contracts were numerous, and he was deservedly held in high estimation by the different Governors who held office during his time. Mr. Cox was a magistrate of the territory, and was looked upon as the local representative of the Government in the district in which he lived."

Henry Dangar.

Mr. Dangar was descended from a French protestant family, which settled in Jersey at the time of the revocation of the Edict of Nantes. The family came over to Cornwall early in the eighteenth century. His father owned a farm at Neots, in that county. Here Mr. Dangar was born in 1798. Being of an adventurous turn of mind, he and his brothers came to Australia. He was then about twenty-three years of age, and was blessed with a robust constitution. He obtained a situation as assistant Government surveyor, and was occupied for about six years in a survey of the Hunter River district. In those days land was easily obtained from the Government, the one condition being that a portion of the grant should be cultivated. In this way, in 1826, he obtained seven hundred acres, which now forms portion of the Neotsfield Estate, one of the finest in the district. It is related how Mr. Dangar was chased over this very land by wild blackfellows. During the time Mr. Dangar was employed as a surveyor he laid out the town of Newcastle. In 1828 Mr. Dangar returned to England for the purpose of publishing his map of the Hunter district, and a directory or immigrants' guide in connection with it. Both of these works are now obsolete, but the accuracy of their topographical observations were never questioned. He returned to the colony in 1830, and was for two years under Sir Edward Parry, the Arctic explorer, who was then general manager of the Australian Agricultural Company at Carrington, their headquarters. It was at this time Mr. Dangar took up, for that Company, Warrah, Liverpool Plains. In 1832 Mr. Dangar ascended the Hunter in a boat, and settled at Neotsfield, devoting himself from that time to pastoral pursuits. At this time he fitted out an expedition under the charge of William Gostwyck Cann, about as fine a specimen of the Australian bushman as ever trod the soil. After encountering many obstacles, and suffering many privations, they came upon the country now known as Armidale, close to the city of that name, now the capital of New England. Mr. Dangar's sons still retain large and valuable tracts of magnificent land in that part of the colony. About the year 1836, pushing their way in a north-westerly direction, they took up the splendid tract of country known as Myall Creek—the scene of a terrible massacre in the early times. The true motive for this historical occurrence may never be known. Mr. Dangar unavailingly exerted himself in behalf of the perpetrators of the crime.

In 1845 he was elected as the representative of Northumberland in the first partly elective and partly nominated Legislative Council. Previous to this, in conjunction with Messrs. Wentworth, Macarthur, and others, he espoused the unpopular side by supporting Earl Grey in his policy of continuing transportation to the colony. As is well known the agitation led to the total cessation of transportation. He was re-elected in 1848, but, beyond opposing the land policy of Sir George Gipps, he abstained from party strife. Mr. Dangar was one of the first in this colony who practically tested the tinning of meat as a paying industry. He established a factory at Newcastle for the purpose, and, although the mode of preserving was a success, the cost of labour and the uncertain market led eventually to the closing of the works.

After spending some twenty-five years improving his property and his stock, he visited England in 1853, where he remained three years, but, his health failing, he returned to Sydney. After five years of continuous infirmity, he died on 2nd March, 1861. "Mr. Dangar (says a late writer), was a favourable specimen of one of the numerous sturdy young sons of England who seemed specially formed for the creation of a Greater Britain in Australia. Favoured by none of the special gifts of intellect or fortune, but possessing the particular qualities essential to the attainment of success—strong common sense and resolute energy—he availed himself of the opportunities of the times, and, in gaining a moderate share of that success, he had the gratification of contributing to the development of a great colony, within the limits of which his name was well known.

The Hon. James White, M.L.C.

The Hon. James White's reputation stands, both as owner and racer, absolutely above reproach. His successes on the course, as well as at the stud, were simply phenomenal. As a pastoralist and large station owner he was equally well-known. Indeed, in every walk of life in which he moved, he was honored and respected by all classes of the community. James White was born at Stroud, near Port Stephens, New South Wales, on 19th July, 1828, being the eldest son of Mr. James White, of that place, and afterwards of Edenglassie, near Muswellbrook, Hunter River. James White was educated at the King's School, Parramatta, during the head-mastership of the late Rev. Robert Forrest. He studied at the King's School for four years, and for another four years with the Rev. Mr. McGregor, at West Maitland. At this time his father died, and he left his studies somewhat earlier than he would have done but for his father's demise. His father owned the estates of Edenglassie, Timor (which is a property on the Isis, a tributary of the Hunter), and Baroona, on the Barwon River, about forty miles below the junction of the Namoi, and above the junction of the Castlereagh. Mr. White had to commence the management of these estates at the early age of sixteen years, residing at Edenglassie. A few years later he took up the Narran Lake, a fine stretch of country some twenty or thirty miles from the Barwon Station. In those days the aboriginals were numerous, and, in many parts of the country, hostile to the settlers. They gave no trouble to Mr. White though, a fact which bears testimony to the statement that they were always well treated. Some time after, he purchased Belltrees, a large freehold estate on the Upper Hunter. This he bought from Mr. W. C. Wentworth. He also purchased the Waverley Estate, the two forming perhaps the finest estate in the settled districts of the colony. He stocked all these properties with cattle, horses, and sheep. Belltrees wool fetched the highest price in the English market. Later on Mr. White purchased Martindale, below the junction of the Hunter and Goulburn Rivers. Afterwards he bought Merton and Dalowinton, opposite Martindale, and, while on a visit to England, he secured Segenhoe, one of the largest freehold estates in the colony. All these properties were extensively improved. The fat cattle from Martindale always took the highest prizes at the different shows on the Hunter. Bando Station, on Cox's Creek, Liverpool Plains, and Ferridgerie (near Coonamble), on the Castlereagh, were also added to his properties.

In 1866 Mr. White was returned to Parliament for the Upper Hunter, which he represented for three years, when he resigned prior to leaving for England and the continent. He was absent for some years, visiting the principal cities of Europe and America. He purchased Cranbrook, Rose Bay, on his return from this trip.

In 1876 Mr. White bought the fine racehorse Chester from Mr. E. K. Cox, of Mulgoa. Chester was by Yattendon, a son of the famous Sir Hercules. His new owner won with him the Melbourne Cup and Derby, known as "the great double," and several other races. Mr. White kept his breeding stud at Kirkham, and his racing stables at Randwick. He never had fewer than ten to fifteen horses in training at one time, and with one or other of his horses he won every important race in the colonies. In 1888, at the Autumn Meeting, he won nine principal races in Victoria, the prizes in all amounting to about £8,000. Hales, the well-known jockey, rode on these occasions. Mr. White was nominated to the Upper House in 1874, a seat in which he held up to the time of his death, which took place at Cranbrook, on July 12, 1890.

The Hon. David Jones, M.L.C.

The name of David Jones is a household word all over Australia. It required no small amount of energy and enterprise to lay the foundation and continue the superstructure of one of the very first business houses in a country. David Jones was born in Caermarthen, South Wales, in the year 1792. At that time the English language was not much used in Wales. Young David was brought up quite ignorant of English, and when he left Wales he could only speak in Cymric. While still young he went to London and obtained employment, and soon mastered the language. By steady application and much industry he made himself useful to his employers, Messrs. Nicholls, wholesale drapers. After some years spent in London, finding his prospects not up to his desires, he looked elsewhere for advancement. Thus it was that, in 1834, he determined to leave England, and sailed with the other members of his family for Hobart Town, Tasmania. He there opened a drapery establishment under the name of "Appleton and Jones." He did not long remain there. In the following year he reached Sydney. He opened a retail drapery establishment on the site now occupied by Farmer & Co., and for some years did a large and increasing business. The partnership with Appleton was dissolved in 1838. Mr. Jones removed to premises at the corner of George and Barrack-streets, where the business is still carried on. Mr. Appleton remained in the old shop in Pitt-street, Mr. Jones carrying on under the style of David Jones & Co. He continued in the management of the business up to 1857, when he retired into private life. But he soon after went back into business. His successors, from various causes, were unable to carry on. At the age of seventy years he started to rebuild the old business, and, in a few years, succeeded in doing so, and was in a position to retire into private life with an assured income for the remainder of his days. Mr. Jones was always ready to acknowledge and reward merit in others. During his business career he took into partnership nine of his employees. He was at one time an alderman of the city, and for years a member of the Legislative Council.

Mr. David Jones died on 29th March, 1873, at Lyons-terrace, Sydney, at the advanced age of eighty years. The leading Sydney print made the following observations on his demise:—"As the head of a numerous family and large establishment, he exercised a valuable influence, always on the side of religion, order, and progress. Though for some years a member of the Legislative Council, he did not take a conspicuous part in politics, but during many years he maintained a high commercial reputation, chequered indeed by the vicissitudes which no one could escape. An event so long expected, and at so late a date, must confine the sense of bereavement to immediate connections and friends. But the loss of a citizen who has always done his part in advancing the welfare of the city, and assisted in every beneficent undertaking, must always produce a sense of regret. Mr. Jones held the office of deacon in the Congregational Church, in Pitt-street, for five and thirty years. The religious denomination to which, by conviction, he belonged, shared largely in the donations and subscriptions; but he was generous to other churches, and contributed considerably to our public charitable institutions."

ALEXANDER BERRY.

The strong personality, the physical strength, the indomitable will and energy, together with the high scholastic training, fitted Alexander Berry in every way to achieve the success which he attained. The impress of the man's powerful personality is visible to-day in that part of the country over which he held sway for so many years. For productiveness, wealth, and contentedness, it may be truly said that the Shoalhaven district will bear the most favourable comparison with any district in Australia.

Alexander Berry was born in Fifeshire, Scotland, in the year 1781. He received his earlier education in the county town, the late Sir David Wilkie and Lord Campbell being his school mates. Later on he studied at St. Andrew's, and at Edinburgh. At the latter university he studied with a view to take his degree in medicine. On leaving the University of Edinburgh he entered the East India Company's service, and was a passenger from England to India in the same ship as Colonel Despard, who, at a later date, was in command of the 17th Regiment in Sydney. Mr. Berry having left the East India Company's service, settled in New South Wales during the administration of Governor Macquarie, and commenced mercantile pursuits. He made several voyages to New Zealand and other parts of the South Pacific, which turned out profitable to him. For this description of work he was well qualified, being possessed of high courage as well as great intelligence. It was in 1808 that he first visited Port Jackson as master of the "City of Edinburgh." In 1809 he was in command of this vessel at the Bay of Islands, New Zealand, to obtain a cargo of spars for the Cape of Good Hope. While obtaining his cargo of spars he distinguished himself by rescuing the survivors of the "Boyd." In December, 1809, the Maoris at the Bay of Islands came to Captain Berry and told him that a British ship had been taken by the natives at Whangaroa, a harbour some fifty miles south of where he then was. After he finished taking in his cargo, he determined to go round to Whangaroa, with a view to saving any of the missing crew. He started with three armed boats, leaving only a small number of his men to look after his vessel. Very bad weather overtook the party, and they were obliged to return to the ship. However, he made a second attempt, which brought him to the harbour of Whangaroa, where he found the "Boyd" in shoal water, with her cables cut, and burned to the water's edge. In her hold were the remains of her cargo—coals, salted sealskins, and planks. Her guns, iron standards, etc., were lying on top, having fallen in as the vessel burned.

Captain Berry was very popular among the Maoris, and to this popularity he undoubtedly owed his life on this occasion. He opened direct communication with the native chiefs and their people. He soon learned the fate of the captain and most of the crew, the mate being the last man killed about a fortnight after the vessel had been seized, the Maoris holding a high cannibal feast during the time. Only four Europeans escaped—one woman, two female children, and a ship's boy named Davies. It was only by the determined stand Captain Berry took in dealing with the chief, Tipahi, and other chiefs, that he succeeded in getting possession of the four survivors, and taking them off in the boats to his own ship and away from New Zealand. The mother of one of these two girls had been a passenger from New South Wales to England, and was brutally murdered by the Maoris. The child was the daughter of Mr. Commissary Broughton, of Appin. The woman who was saved died at Lima. The rescued lad Davis was given work by Mr. Brown, the owner of the "Boyd," but was drowned at sea some years later. It would appear that the master of the "Boyd" was not blameless in the matter, as he had unnecessarily provoked the natives. Captain Berry wrote from Lima to Mr. Brown, 20th December, 1810, reporting the loss of the "Boyd" and the rescue of the survivors. He afterwards, at the request of Mr. Archibald

Constable, published a further and more extended account of the affair. From this it appeared that the chiefs, Tupi and Tarra, took Captain Berry with them to where the wreck was lying, and caused the survivors to be handed over, seeing them safely placed on board the "City of Edinburgh." Those who had been concerned in the outrage, frankly, and not without pride, confessed to their participation in the massacre. The natives alleged that the ship was attacked because the master, Captain Thompson, had subjected a chief to some degrading punishment for a theft committed by one of his people. Having succeeded in rescuing the survivors of the "Boyd," and completing his cargo, Captain Berry finally sailed from New Zealand on the 6th January, 1810. Captain Berry returned to Sydney and settled in the colony. In those early days he was also a cultivator of the land in a large way, and received a large grant of land in the Shoalhaven district, which he discovered and explored about the year 1820. His clear and active mind was alive to the fact that it would greatly improve the district if the Shoalhaven River could be opened out to the sea, instead of terminating in a sand bar over which shallow water washed. The difficulties in the way of carrying out such an enterprise in the early days of the colony were looked upon, by most people, as practically insurmountable. But the determined and educated Scotchman set to work and started the cutting of a channel from the lower end of the Shoalhaven River, near Coolangatta, to the Crookhaven River. Having obtained a large number of assigned servants, the work was proceeded with until the waters of the Shoalhaven flowed into the Crookhaven, thus making the Shoalhaven a navigable river.

In a paper read before the Philosophical Society of Australia, in the year 1822, Mr. Berry gives a description of his first trip to the Shoalhaven River. He went there with Lieutenant Johnson. They got across the sandy isthmus of the mouth of the river into the deep waters of the river, and pulled twenty miles up the stream until stopped by a rapid. This paper was published in 1825 by Baron Field, in his geographical memoirs of Australia. Mr. Berry was a man of extensive knowledge, thoroughly well read in most subjects, and was possessed of a wonderful memory. He was literally brimful of anecdotes of the early days of the colony. Some years before his death he was assailed in an objectionable manner by a colonial newspaper. The Berry tenants, by way of marking their sense of the absolute injustice of such an attack, entertained Mr. Berry and his two brothers, David and John Berry, at a great dinner at Numba, nearly every person in the district being present.

Mr. Berry was one of a numerous family. He was married to Miss Elizabeth Wolstoncroft, sister to Mr. Edward Wolstoncroft, who was at one time in partnership with Mr. Berry, and who died in Sydney on the 7th December, 1832. Mrs. Berry died on 11th April, 1845, aged 63. She left no children. She is buried with her brother at the St. Leonard's cemetery.

Mr. Berry was a member of the Legislative Council at the time when there were only three non-official members, and, after the modification of that body, he retained a seat. In May, 1856, he was re-appointed a member of the Upper House, and remained there till May, 1861, when he resigned in consequence of failing health. He resided for some time before his death at the "Crow's Nest," St. Leonards. He died on 17th September, 1873, at the ripe age of 92. He is buried beside his wife at the cemetery, St. Leonard's.

HON. ALEX. BERRY.   MR. J. LANSDALE.
MR. W. H. WISEMAN.
MR. N. V. MORRISSET.   CAPT. W. H. HOVELL.

William Hilton Hovell.

Scarcely sufficient prominence has been given by writers of our early historical events, to the work performed by Hume and Hovell, in the first days of the colony's history. It is well to bear in mind that in those times there were no camels with elaborate appointments to carry comparatively large supplies long and swift journeys. On the contrary the equipments were both rude and limited.

W. H. Hovell was born at Yarmouth, April 26th, 1786. He became a master mariner, and arrived in Sydney, accompanied by his wife and two children, in the year 1813. He followed the sea for about six years, trading to New Zealand and along the coast until 1819, when he retired from the sea and settled on a farm at Narellan. From his home he made several short exploratory trips. In 1824 he joined Mr. Hamilton Hume on the great journey overland to Western Port, or Port Phillip. The party consisted of Mr. Hamilton Hume, Mr. W. H. Hovell, and six convicts; three horses, and two carts drawn by four bullocks. The party started from Appin on October 2nd, 1824, and arrived at Hume's station, Lake George, on the 13th of that month, starting on the 17th towards Yass. Space will not permit a lengthy notice of the trip. Here is a description of how they crossed the Murrumbidgee:— They determined to make the attempt, without further delay and whatever the risk, of crossing the river—an operation no sooner determined on than effected. The body of a cart being substituted for a punt or boat, and the end of the tow-rope having been conveyed across the river, in the course of four or five hours the whole of the supplies, including the cart, were landed, without loss or injury, on the left bank of the Murrumbidgee. The horses and bullocks were then conducted separately across the stream, though not without considerable risk, by means of the tow-rope. "The details of the crossing are given thus:—"The green timber not being sufficiently buoyant, and not being the season of the year when the bark could be peeled off the trees, a raft or boat could not be made. One was, however, improvised out of one of the carts, which was stripped of its axle, wheels, and shafts, and covered with a tarpaulin. The next step was to convey the stout end of a stout rope to the opposite bank, for the purpose of plying their boat backwards and forwards across the stream, to effect which object, Mr. Hume, with one of the men, undertook the dangerous enterprise of swimming across the river, taking with them a small line of about six feet long, which they carried between their teeth, and to the middle of which was attached a line of a similar description, but of sufficient length to reach across the stream. This was not done without great difficulty and some danger, both from the rapidity of the torrent and the great pressure of water on a length of line so considerable, the weight of the latter not only retarding the progress of the swimmers, but at times dragging them almost under the water, so that they were swept down the river a considerable distance ere they could reach the opposite bank. One of the ends of their intended tow-rope was now conveyed across the river by means of the line, and, everything being in readiness, and the boat, not carrying less than six or seven cwt., made its first trip. The bullocks and horses were then conducted across separately, some of the bullocks being in a state of almost complete submersion during the operation, and, one of them becoming turned upon its back, remained in that position a considerable part of the passage. These difficulties were attributable partly to the cattle not being accustomed to swimming, and partly to the dangerous rapidity of the stream, which, with the roughness of the weather, and the coldness of the water, contributed to render this undertaking, to the swimmers at least, not less unpleasant than it was evidently hazardous." Following the Murrumbidgee down some distance they steered a south-westerly course, passing over very good country. On 8th November they came in sight of snow-capped mountains, this being the first time that snow had been seen by white men in Australia. After eight days further travelling they came upon a large river, which they called the Hume, after Mr. Hamilton Hume's father, but which is now known as the Murray, the king of Australian rivers. This river was crossed in somewhat the same fashion as the Murrumbidgee, minus the dray. On the 24th they crossed the Ovens River, on 3rd December they came upon another river, which they named the Hovell, which is now known as the Goulburn. On the 16th December they arrived at the sea shore, close to where the town of Geelong is now built. After two days rest the party started back and arrived at Lake George, on the 18th January.

This trip led to the settlement of Victoria, and it is pleasing to note that the party was led by a young native-born Australian. The only regrettable feature was that unpleasantness should have arisen between Hume and Hovell as to which was the leader of the party. The results of the expedition were ample to cover both with sufficient honor to gratify most men. In 1826 Mr. Hovell accompanied Captain Wright, of the Buffs, to form a settlement at Western Port. They sailed in H.M.S. "Fly," October 9th, 1826. In 1829 Mr. Hovell went to reside at Goulburn. He died in Sydney in 1876.

The Hon. Henry Mort, M.L.C.

One of the men instrumental in a large degree in developing the vast resources of Australia is Henry Mort. He was born at Willow Field, near Bolton, Lancashire, England on 31st December, 1818. He was educated at Manchester, his youth was spent there, in fact he lived there up to the age of twenty-three. In 1838 his brother, Thomas Sutcliffe Mort, who had been engaged in that city, came to New South Wales. Henry followed three years later, in 1840. Soon after his arrival he went up country. In 1842 he went to Moreton Bay, where he engaged in pastoral pursuits, that country being at the time part of New South Wales. He remained there for fourteen years, and saw the successes and reverses, the good seasons and the bad ones, the floods and the droughts, the high prices and the low prices of wool which ruled during those early days of Moreton Bay. He was one of the pioneers of Queensland, in fact, and was acquainted with the country long before its great prospects could be gauged, or its untold wealth dreamt of by the most sanguine well-wishers. In 1855 he returned to Sydney. A year later he joined the great wool-broking firm of Mort and Company, which was founded by his brother in 1843. At this time the market for the sale of the squatters' wool was most precarious. The starting of the Messrs. Mort in this business gave them a reliable and assured outlet for their produce, having regular public sales in Sydney instead of sending the wool to England through middlemen, they could sell for cash on the spot, thereby saving the heavy charges made by the middlemen, as well as heavy banking interest on advances.

Thus commenced the great wool-broking business of Mort and Co., so well known throughout Australia, and, for that matter, all over the mercantile world. Within the last few years Goldsbrough and Co., of Melbourne, amalgamated with Mort and Company, the firm being now known as Goldsbrough, Mort, and Co., the largest wool-broking business in the southern hemisphere. Attention to business concerns has not withdrawn Henry Mort from other duties of citizenship. In the second Parliament of the country he occupied a seat as member for West Moreton. On the separation of the colony of Queensland in 1859, he threw in his lot with the mother colony, where his chief interests lay, and was elected member for West Macquarie. In 1861 he stood for Paddington, but was defeated by Mr. John Sutherland, who was elected for many years a member for that electorate without opposition. In 1879 Mr. Henry Mort was appointed a life member of the Legislative Council of New South Wales, a position which he still holds. He married, in 1846, Maria, the third daughter of Commissary-General Laidley, by whom he had issue three sons and three daughters. In 1878 he married a second wife, the widow of Dr. Rowland Traill.

And now, having looked into the past, and by memories of men of genius and power who helped to make the Present, viewed the gradual uplifting of the mother colony, let us peep into the antecedents of her youngest offspring—QUEENSLAND.

CHAPTER VIII.

The Youngest Colony — Early Days of Queensland — The Western Men — The First Squatters — The Leslies — The Condamine, McIntyre and Weir Rivers — The Incursions of the Blacks — A Western Notable — Paddy Macinnon — William Miles — The Dearth of Labour — Rough Times — An Early Election — A Risky Undertaking — Beck and Brown.

Early Days of Queensland.

COOK in 1770, and Flinders about 1802, were the earliest of our own countrymen to touch the shores of Queensland, and, in 1822, convicts were sent up from Sydney, Moreton Bay being made a sort of a "chapel of ease" for Port Jackson in that line of merchandise. Brisbane succeeded Humpybong as the "settlement," and a fence was put across the neck of land where our metropolis now is, with slip rails at Petrie's Bight and the North Quay, and when the bullock teams meandered in at one and out at the other, they made a track which afterwards became Queen-street. Allan Cunningham found his way later on over the Main Range from the west, and then the Leslies and others *circa* 1840 over from the Darling Downs.

The area of pastoral occupation was extended yet more into the blackfellows' territory, but not without bloodshed. Many a terrible *melée* took place, with a whiz of brutal spears and the ominous hum of the boomerang and nullah mingling with the sharp report of the double-barrelled gun and rifled carbine, with now and then a rush and a vicious dash in the open, and anon a crafty ambush behind some huge rock or tree, and bore witness to the bloodshed, and many a life in God's image on both sides was quenched ere the dusky warriors, all red and white ribbed alternately in their battle paint, yielded up their hunting grounds to the whites. Many a pretty bush station, where ladies in muslin and silks now safely dwell, and walk or ride as they please, has its humble mound neatly fenced where sleeps the stockman or shepherd untimely slain by spear, boomerang, or tomahawk, between '43 and '55.

Yes! Time was when the blacks of Queensland used their spears and boomerangs on the whites. Now that is all changed. You see warlike King Jacky, of Caboolture, in the streets of the city with a brass plate hung by a chain round his neck, setting forth his name and birth. He carries a bundle of clothes-props, while his wife bears an assortment of some of the loveliest and most stately ferns from distant scrubs, which you can buy at 3d. and 6d. a-piece.

It is difficult to say who were the first white men who roamed northwards over the border that now separates Queensland from New South Wales. Most probably it was some nameless runaway and unrecorded convicts ; but Major (Sir Thomas) Mitchell and Allan Cunningham were the first recognised white men over the line, followed, some years later, by Mr. Patrick Leslie, in March, 1840.

I believe the late John Campbell, of Redbank, Ipswich, was the first man to take up pastoral country and form a cattle camp in what is now known as Queensland territory, on the north side of the Dumaresq or Severn River. That was in January, 1840. He was quickly followed by Patrick Leslie, in March of the same year, who struck out still further north on Allan Cunningham's track, guided by a chart of his route. Toolburra was his first location, a neat little station not far from Warwick. The Upper Condamine and its boggy affluents watered this splendid country, where experienced station hands asked £100 to £150 a-year and their food as the lowest price at which, in 1840, they would work for the "boss," and face the plentiful wild blacks as well. New South Wales, of course, at this period, included Victoria and Queensland, up to the South Australian border, and the enterprising "pushing out" spirit was just as active westerly as northerly, for at this time Mr. Samuel Macgregor, afterwards of Brisbane, was helping to take up Eumarella, near the South Australian border, in Western Victoria, for Hughes and Hosking, of Sydney, a station which, in after years, was owned by Ben. Boyd, of Twofold Bay. But, to return to the northern pioneers. Joe King and Sibley followed George and Patrick Leslie on the march, and "sat down" on another of the Condamine affluents, and called it King's Creek, now the Clifton run. Arthur Hodgson and his partner, Elliot, took up Eton Vale. Never before nor since was a choicer district for pasture lotted out amongst plucky even if not always lucky explorers. Joe King was a brother-in-law of the late Hon. James Taylor, M.L.C., of Cecil Plains, both having married sisters of Martin Boulton, another early Downs man. Cecil Plains, I believe, were named after Cecil Hodgson, a brother of Sir Arthur, of that ilk. John Campbell pushed out and took up that magnificent run "Westbrook," while Henry Hughes and Fred Isaac " collared " " Gowrie " from the Crown, two as faultless and flower-carpeted *ranches* for sheep and cattle as wide Australia holds, and the summer and the winter made up the year 1841 when all these events happened. R. Scougall, of Liverpool Plains, near the Upper Hunter country, sent Henry Dennis up north exploring, and the huge Jimbour run was the prize that fell to his lot. Dennis took up Jondaryan (smaller but richer than Jimbour), for himself.

Irvingdale, which adjoined it, was named after Mr. Irving, for whom the Warra run (afterwards Thorn's), was taken up by Dennis, who also secured Myall Creek (Dalby), for Charles Coxen, a nephew of Gould, the great ornithologist of Australia. Yandilla and Tummaville, two huge principalities like average English counties in size, were taken up by the Gores in those early days, and they were richly grassed like all the rest of the Downs. There was, however, another direction from which the Darling Downs were being approached, viz., from the east. Sir Thomas MacDougall Brisbane, of Makerstown (N.B.), an old lieutenant of Sir Arthur Wellesley in the Peninsular war, had come to succeed Lachlan Macquarie as Governor of New South Wales in 1822, and gave his name to the deepest navigable river in Australia, on the banks of which a penal settlement, to relieve Sydney and Port Macquarie, was founded. Traces of him and his are to be found on that river. He had a young officer named Ovens in his suite, whose youthful wife died soon after her arrival in Australia, and "Ovens'" Head (as that point on the Brisbane River where the picturesque Boggo cemetery lies used to be called in the olden days), was, no doubt, named after Lieutenant Ovens. The lion-hearted Patrick Leslie, a Bayard amongst explorers, was accompanied only by one man, a "prisoner of the Crown," named Peter Murphy, in his dauntless strike out into the wilderness of the then unknown Downs. "Darkey Flat" (near Warwick), where they get gold now, is the only place where the blacks came near Pat. Leslie, and a shot frightened them away. Peter Murphy, at Leslie's intercession, got his freedom from Sir George Gipps, and died a sergeant of police at Bowen, Port Denison, a few years later.

The Leslies, Patrick, Walter, and George, came from county Aberdeen, where their father was a "laird" or landholder, and their first effort in Australian life was dairy farming near Parramatta. Their father sent out his groom, George Macadam (who afterwards kept the Sovereign Hotel, in Queen-street, Brisbane), to help and work for them, as well as other of his Scottish servants, as being more reliable than the convict labour then available. Mrs. P. Leslie, who, as well as Mrs. Geo. Leslie, was a Macarthur—a name mixed up as inseparably with the first wool growth of Australia as is the name of Leslie with the exploration of Darling Downs. His wife was the first white woman who set foot on the said Downs. The Leslies never had any trouble with the blacks, for they kept them at a distance, and never allowed them to hover about the station and the men's huts, which is how most quarrels originate that end in the use of spear, boomerang, and carbine bullet. Patrick Leslie sold Goomburra to Robert Tooth, of the Kent Brewery, Sydney, in 1856, and went home to Scotland, but afterwards came out again and bought an estate at Waikato, in New Zealand, where he was in 1877, and, after selling that, he settled and died in Sydney, a "white man" to the end of his days—modest, brave, chivalrous, fearless of danger, and ready to face any odds at all times.

Yes, Patrick Leslie was as white a man as ever walked the earth. He was a Scotsman, too; at any rate he was a native of Aberdeen, and I doubt whether Scotsmen will quarrel with this qualification. He came out in the interests of his uncle Davidson, a banker, of London, to manage a station property near Cassillis, on the Hunter. This uncle Davidson, I might mention, was father of Gilbert and Walter Davidson, who once owned Canning Downs. "Darkey Flat," near Warwick, owes its name to Patrick Leslie, who so named it because it was the only place the niggers would approach in those days, and then a shot in the air would frighten them away.

But let us go more into detail and discover the pioneers

out of whose efforts has sprung the great staple industry of the colony.

In 1850 the settlers on the Condamine, M'Intyre, and Weir Rivers were, as I have already mentioned, Patrick Leslie (Canning Downs), Fred. Bracker (manager for the Rosenthal Company, at Rosenthal Station, near Warwick township), John Crowther, general manager for the Company at St. Ruth, Lochinvar, and other runs in New South Wales. Bracker shortly afterwards selected on his own account at Warroo, on the M'Intyre Brook, when John Deuchar became manager of Rosenthal and St. Ruth. The Downs men were—John Gammil, of Clifton and Talgai; Captain Mallard, at Felton; Hughes and Isaacs, of Gowrie and Westbrook; Andrews, of Jondaryan; Russell and Taylor, Cecil Plains (James Taylor residing on the station); Gore and Co., Yandilla, with Willis as manager; Captain Vignolles, Western Creek; Thomas De Lacy Moffatt, at Stonehenge; Michael Daisey, McIntyre Brook. Canal Creek Station was then owned by Ben. Boyd, and was without stock. Beck and Brown's sheep were on Hamilton. Morris, Young, and Goodfellow were the owners of Callandoon. T. De Lacy Moffatt at this time stocked Wyaga with sheep, Chas E. S. Bowler being in charge. Canal Creek Township, or, as we know it, Leyburn, was just forming, and Graham's inn was hardly completed. In January, 1850, Paddy Murrin's blacksmith's shop and Martin Boulton's had just been opened, and in March of the following year Harry Kirby had completed and opened the second public house in the mushroom township.

From Myall Creek (now Dalby) down the Condamine, the country was occupied something in this way:—Finlay Ross on Greenbank, J. P. Wilkie on Daandine, Sir Joshua Peter Bell on Jimbour, R. R. Mackenzie on Warra Warra (or Cobble Cobble), Matthew Goggs on Chinchilla, J. G.

Ewar on Wombo, and Leonard Edward Lester on Tieryboo. Lester brought about 10,000 sheep from Bundarra, New South Wales, to stock this run, which stock reached the station at the end of 1850 or early in 1851. The former owner, Perrier, of Tieryboo, had sheep there, but had to remove them and abandon the run on account of the blacks. Edwards also had sheep on the Dogwood at the same time as Perrier was at Tieryboo, but he also had to remove the sheep and quit the run, afterwards named Bindian by Charles Coxen, who took it up and formed the station, stocking it with sheep in June, 1851. About the same time Beck and Brown's sheep settled on a part of Bindian run (about six miles down the Dogwood Creek, below the spot where Bindian head station was then forming). Beck and Brown's sheep, with Brown in charge, remained on Bindian run about a year or so, being the furthest out sheep. A couple of Wallan shepherds were killed by the blacks just after the native police settled at their barracks at Wandaganba, on Channing Creek, about the end of 1851. The former police barracks were at Callandoon. The police, with John Ferritt, went southerly with the view to capturing the murderers, but failed. Later on, however, the police went out again and brought back a black known as Simpson, who, according to some accounts at least, had had nothing to do with the business. But the police in those days were by no means particular. It was only a *blackfellow* after all! Brown, who had named the blackfellow, urged that Simpson was innocent, and declared that he had never left his camp for days before the murders were committed, having during that time been minding lambs. But Brown's pleading was useless. That night, Beck (Brown's partner), arrived at the camp, and was told of what had happened, and that the police had gone on with the unfortunate blackfellow in charge. Beck at once decided to follow up the tracks of the police, which he did by the aid of a black. Beck pulled up the police in the scrub, making for Wallan, with Simpson in irons. Beck explained the circumstances connected with Simpson, who was liberated, and accompanied his rescuer back to Brown's camp. Simpson was never able to clearly express himself in plain English, but he several times gave a practical demonstration of the fact that he had not forgotten those who had saved his life.

Dulacca country was taken up by John Crowder, of Weranga, but it was not occupied till about 1854. All the country for hundreds of miles west from Beck and Brown's sheep camp on Dogwood Creek had been taken up some years, but not a single acre at this date was occupied with the exception of Noorandoo, taken up by the Halls, of Dartbrook, and stocked with cattle. Weribone was also taken up and occupied by cattle of Dartbrook. Talavera was secured by Joseph Flemming, and stocked with cattle. Yamboogle was then close to Talavera, and not very far from the present town of Surat. It was occupied by the Crown Lands Commissioner, whose name for the moment escapes me. Noorandoo, Weribone, Talavera, and Yamboogle were all formed about 1849, the occupiers coming in by the Maitland route from the New South Wales side by what is now known as St. George, but which at that time had never been approached from Moreton Bay.

About 1849 James Alexander Blythe (Blythe and Chauvel, the latter a son of Major Chauvel, of Sydney and Clarence), took out sheep to settle on the fine country west, and "sat down" for a time on what is now known as Bungewarra or Mount Abundance, and for a time at what is now known as Blythedale. But the blacks proved too many for them. Blythe was speared in the thigh, and, as he said, only saved himself by having a good horse. After this they cleared out, selling their sheep. Blythe, however, took up Undulla after this—a well watered place, but very poor country. Blythe knew from previous experience what the want of water was, and, if anything, was a too great believer in watered country. He often erred in this respect, but, in 1851, had settled down at Undulla, or Palmy Creek, which he stocked with cattle. One of the stories told of Blythe and Chauvel shows the sort of stuff both pioneers were made of. They had been reduced to the last piece of dried damper, which, on being cut, stuck to the two table requisites. One of them then closed his eyes, and was asked by the other which he would have — knife or fork — and thus it was decided who should have the best or largest piece, if there was anything to choose between them. There are good men now, but I question whether mankind hasn't degenerated considerably since the Blythe and Chauvel days. The old lot were stickers in every sense of the term, and, ah! so unlike the "pioneers" of the present day, who have had the country opened up for them, and in reality have only to walk in and make themselves at ease. Many of the old hands deserved better treatment at the hands of the more recent generation. Poor old Blythe died in Sydney some ten years ago, the only friend to watch over him in his last moments being Ewar, at one time of Wombo.

McPherson formerly took up Bungeworgorai, and had cattle on it, about the time that Blythe and Chauvel were out (1849), but he, too, abandoned all, and made Paddy Macinnon a present of the cattle remaining. Paddy was bullock driver or stockman for McPherson; a second blackfellow in nature, something like Duramboi. He lived with the blacks for years, but managed to keep a few cattle and quiet milkers with plenty of fat beef for all hands. Every year or oftener, when he wanted a spree, he brought down a few of his herd and disposed of them at Dalby or Drayton. He seldom, however, got farther than Dalby.

He travelled down with the blacks, and with a cart loaded with gins and piccaninnies of all sorts. He would return perhaps with a bag of flour, and drapery for his family of blacks, and with cotton and silk handkerchiefs, twill shirts, mole and tweed trousers for himself as a turn out for his next trip, but spending most of the proceeds of the sale and not infrequently leaving a good score at the pub to pay next time. I believe Paddy Macinnon died at Forster's inn, in the Condamine township, about 1860, and with him died also M'Pherson's legacy. Rens Bingham and Macdonald took up Collingull Lagoons (now Myall Grove Station), and had just formed the head station in 1851—somewhere near where the Condamine township now is—which township was formed about 1857 or 1858.

Early in 1852, Henry William Coxen arrived at his uncle's station, "Bindian." W. P. Gordon was then managing for Charles Coxen, at Bindian, and stocked Wallambilla with sheep during this year. Charles Coxen took up the run. Gordon sold out well in 1861 or 1862. Henry Coxen also took up Alderton, and stocked it with sheep. Some years afterwards he likewise stocked Bendemere, selling out to Macfarlane Bros. in 1866, at, I think, £1 a head for the sheep—and bad sheep too—at any rate Macfarlane Bros. "went bung" about two years afterwards. This year Rens Bingham and Macdonald drew sheep from their Collingull station for the Workin run, while Beck and Brown took up 1,100 square miles of country on the Moonie fall of water on the creeks. This country was previously unknown, and Beck and Brown only came to a knowledge of it through the blacks. Acting under their guidance they set out, and, after viewing a portion of it, took steps to secure it. It turned out that the greater portion of it was beautiful open undulating blue grass country, with myall and salt-bush running through it, and with plenty of good water, though Beck and Brown did not consider it of a permanent nature. This country remained long hidden owing to the frontage being scrubby and sandy, consequently that at the back on the small creeks escaped the eagle eye of the exploration parties which went out from time to time. Beck and Brown did not stock until 1856, but paid the rent from the time they found it.

In this year (1852) things began to look up, and many surprises were occasioned by what were considered the high prices station properties realised. For instance J. D. M'Lean purchased Westbrook with about 12,000 sheep at something like 12s. 6d. per head, with the run given in. James Taylor, about the same time, purchased a large portion of the swamp (now Toowoomba), it was said, for £10,000. John Deuchar secured Canal Creek station at 10s. a head for the sheep. Gillespie, of Sydney, afterwards bought this run from Deuchar. Logan sold Dunmore, on Weir River, during this year or early in 1853, to James Taylor, of Cecil Plains, and Watson Bros. purchased Halliford and Wa-Wa with sheep at good prices. John Crowder, at Weranga, on the head of Moonie River station (which was formed in 1848 or 1849), stocked with sheep in '52, and put John Miller in charge. John Crowder was formerly general manager for Lochinvar, Rosenthal, and St. Ruth company. Alfred Crowder, brother to John Crowder, died at Commissioner Roleston's, at Cambooya, in 1850, and was buried close to the road. A tombstone and iron railings marked the spot, but it was sadly neglected and became a wreck. It was Alfred Crowder who formed Weranga, where he resided until his illness. John Crowder sold out Weranga in 1856 to James Hook and Campbell. Some years afterwards Weranga was purchased by Mort and Laidley from Hook. Dulacca was another station taken up by John Crowder, but it was not formed or stocked by

Mr. T. B. Stephens.   Hon. R. G. W. Herbert.
Sir Maurice O'Connell.
Mr. Samuel Brown.   Mr. John Beck.

him, John Miller — mentioned as an early manager of Weranga — having purchased 4,000 sheep and formed it in 1855. Miller held the station on his own account until 1857, when he took William Miles in as a partner in Dulacca, Miles bringing his 7,000 sheep from Kinnoul, on the Dawson, which he had previously rented from Miller and Turnbull, together with the sheep. Both Miller and Turnbull took a trip home during the two years of Miles' lease. Miles about 1860 bought John Miller's share of Dulacca. Dulacca was a small run, its capabilities being about 15,000 sheep, and, being about fully stocked, it enabled the owner to make an annual sale of sheep equal to the increase. Just at this time a demand for stocking the western country arose Sheep were then fetching from 20s. for maidens, and averaging 15s. for breeding ewes. This gave William Miles his start. Magechie Brothers had taken up Retreat, on the Weir River, about 1848, and in this year (1852) stocked it with breeding mares. These may be said to have been the ancestors of the wild brombies which afterwards swarmed the whole country from the M'Intyre to the Condamine, and even to the north of the latter stream. Tarawinnabar, which had been formed by Smith contemporaneously with Retreat, was stocked just about the same year, and the same may be said of Easton and Robertson's Billa Billa, both runs being devoted to sheep. Paddy Clyres put cattle on Tallwood, and Atkins, Jarrott, and Gardner, in January of 1852, arrived from Goulburn, and rented Mulleelee run on the Moonie River, as well as the sheep that were on it.

In 1853 Beck and Brown moved their sheep from the head of Undullah Creek from a block of country named Tara, which was within eighteen miles of Weranga, and took them down the Moonie to Gideon Lang's country. This country was then owned by Atkins, Jarrott, and

Gardner, and had never been occupied until Beck and Brown's sheep were put on it. The sheep remained on Tartha until 1856. Working country then was no easy task, for without shepherds it was impossible to keep sheep or anything else on it—the blacks were so bad. And shepherds were not so plentiful. The two shiploads of German immigrants who arrived in the "Aurora" and the "Merbz" in 1855 were a perfect godsend. They had the greatest difficulty in getting here. These immigrants were the result of a special effort put forward by the squatters and paid for by them too. Kirchner, one of the firm of Kirchner & Co., merchants, of Sydney, went to Germany and engaged them under an agreement for two years, the squatters paying on arrival here £16 for each man. The immigrants had, according to the agreement, to pay off the £16 during the two years, but only a few of the squatters deducted the amount. I remember Beck and Brown engaged thirteen of these people, and did not deduct anything from their earnings. The majority of the men turned out to be excellent servants. Many of them remained in the service of the squatters for years after their term had expired, and, in some cases, they took up land themselves. They certainly filled a gap which sadly wanted bridging at the time. From this out, things went better so far as the labour was concerned, for the two ship loads acted as a sort of advertisement, and others were only too glad to immigrate on their own accord. At any rate there was never the same dearth, for bye and bye English immigrants were also attracted to the colony. Generally speaking these latter were a good class, too, being drawn principally from the farming districts of England, Scotland, and Ireland. Like the Germans, many of these remained in the service of the squatters for as long as fifteen years, and developed into some of the best selectors that have ever taken up their residence in any country. When, however, the system of immigration was so changed as to cover practically only artisans, things changed for the worse so far as the squatters were concerned, and, if I mistake not, neither the colony nor the immigrants themselves profited much. Many a lot of these artisans were got up to the stations at a deal of expense to the Crown lessees, who voted them a nuisance, and who, in many cases, were only too glad to get rid of them. In 1857, Beck and Brown, who, like many others, had become thoroughly sick of what was termed the "riff raff of London," got seven hands up from Ipswich by the drays which were taking up loading. This season was a most extraordinary one : rain, rain, little else but rain; it prevailed from that August to the following August. And a nice time these men had. They were six months on the road. The carrier (Marks) got £2 10s. per man, the squatters providing them with rations for the period as well as paying their wages, which had been going on for seven weeks before they started. When they set out it was thought that five weeks would see them at their journey's end, and, on this basis, Walter Gray, who was then the squatter's man—forwarding and receiving their wool—acted. Of course when these rations were done the men attacked the loading, a very considerable "hole" in which was made before they got to the station. But the greatest loss was perhaps caused by the waste. What all this meant may be better understood when it is stated that the rate to Beck and Brown's station from Ipswich was 18s. per 100 lbs. Add to this the interest on cost of rations and the fact that wool had to be kept on hand for as long as nine or twelve months before there was any prospect of a return, and the reader will observe how very different squatting was in those days as compared with what it is now—and there is enough trouble even now, goodness knows.

After Walter Gray's death in 1862, G. H. Wilson became the squatter's man, and a worthy successor to Gray he proved.

In 1854 or 1855 John S. Scott took over Magechie's Retreat station, on the Weir River, and stocked it with sheep. The year following, Beck and Brown moved their sheep from Tartha (about 18,000) to form the 1,100 square miles of country taken up by them in 1852. Brown in the same year took down about 1,800 old ewes to Flemming's boiling-down works, near Ipswich, but the unusually wet season was against them, and they lost fat in travelling and in swimming the creeks. The returns of tallow was on this account very poor, and made the squatters wonder why they bothered with the sheep at all. Owing to this continued wet weather, nearly the whole of the stations ran out of rations, even those on the Downs, which, by comparison, were close to Ipswich. Some of the drays were fourteen months on the roads, and, in order that those on the stations might not die of starvation altogether, small quantities of flour were carried periodically from the benighted drays to the stations on pack horses. Even then on some of the runs the squatters did not touch flour for three weeks at a time. There was practically nothing but mutton. From morning to night the iron pot was on the fire, the greasy chops in it being stirred around with a long stick. This really was the only food they had; there was not even a pinch of tea to be had at most of the places. When at length the drays did turn up there was great jollification. Damper and scones never tasted sweeter.

In 1858 J. B. Atkins formed Kooroon station, on the Moonie River, stocking it with a mixture of sheep and cattle. About two years later Captain M'Carthy joined Atkins, but in 1863 both fell, owing to the bank putting on the screw on other parties, through whose failure the two collapsed. After this Atkins got the management of Womblebank (in the Maranoa) into his hand, while his partner dropped into the more congenial position of a Government servant in Brisbane.

Gideon Lang had been the first to take up the country, over which Atkins had the management, but never occupied it, and eventually threw it up. Atkins then came into possession of it, paying rent for it from 1856, and forming it in 1858. Beck and Brown had in 1859 established their country, Canmaroo, Coomrith, Ingleston, and Cooroora as a going concern, and quickly stocked up, getting good increases of lambs. These were rough times for the two pioneers, for with sheep here, there, and everywhere, they were constantly on the travel. Indeed Brown has often related that in three years he was not at the head station of any one of the runs a week on a stretch.

As showing how elections were conducted in these times it may be stated that in 1859 Beck, Brown, and two or three men whom they took over, went to record their vote at the Condamine township. D. M'Lean, of Westbrook, and William Handcock, of Drayton, were the candidates. It was thought that Beck and Brown's five votes would just about run M'Lean in, but they were out of their reckoning, for Handcock crept in and took his seat in the old Sydney Parliament.

Murilla station was formed about 1859, and stocked with sheep by Joshua Peter Bell, of Jimbour, and about the same time Barton and Beck Bros. "sat down" at Wandungal, on the Dogwood. These Becks were not related to the partner of Brown, but Barton was a brother of the medico of that ilk in the early days of Brisbane, and the same man who in partnership with Lamb owned squattages on the Burnett and the Dawson.

Roma was in process of formation in this year, Spencer settling on Bugyuagorie, and an inn, kept by one Ware, was opened at Surat. Lloyd Bros., of Tasmania, too, were forming a station near Noorindoo, while Yankee Brown was doing something in the same line close by. The latter, however, did not long remain, for he went over to Maitland, and, as a speculation, bought dogs and goats for shipment to California!

Donald Ross, of Noondaroo, manager for and a relative of the Halls, became the owner of Yankee Brown's station, Cambarngo. In the same year the country on Donga Creek, owned by Jacob and Low, was being formed and partially stocked with cattle, though some time afterward these were withdrawn and sheep substituted, and the run re-named "Glenearn." The same may be said of the country down the Balonne from Surat, and also down the Moonie River, while at St. George it had been decided that they had become sufficiently civilised to warrant the erection of a wayside house.

In 1860, Dr. Nelson bought Tartha from Beck and Brown, and remained there a couple of years, and, in 1866, Brown bought the run back from F. A. Forbes and John Pettigrew, of Ipswich. This was a good deal for Brown, for the run was without stock, and, as a severe drought was being experienced, and there was plenty of grass on Tartha, he was able to weather the trouble tolerably well. When this drought came to an end he sold again to William Dockrill, who for years had worked with Brown as a horse driver and as a shearer.

In 1862 Beck and Brown dissolved partnership, the former taking Canmaroo, and Brown Coomrith, the 40,000 sheep being equally divided. The floods of two years later, however, played sad havoc with both, as indeed they did with other pastoral lessees. In one fell swoop Brown lost 1,700, the flock being swept away down the Condamine.

It was about this time that William Miles came politically

into prominence, being returned for the Maranoa by either two or three votes. The squatters travelled far and wide to record their votes. Brown travelled to Surat, some seventy miles from his station, and took with him three men to vote for Miles, whom Brown had up to this time known very intimately. He afterwards expressed himself as sorry for having taken so much trouble, for he averred that although his votes had practically put Miles in, that gentleman always avoided him and never so much as noticed him. But such are politics.

1866 saw another drought, and, profiting by past experience, Brown got rid of 29,000 sheep at an average of 9s. 6d., the buyers being Youll and Francis, of Melbourne. From this to 1872 sheep went down to any price, and, in the meantime, Brown re-stocked at something like half-a-crown a head.

This may be said to bring me down to the railway days, which rapidly opened the country westwards for hundreds of miles. How many of these old pioneers are left, and how many of those who are living still hold the stations on which they spent the best part of their lives, and the whole of their hard-earned money? And let me ask how many have actually fallen into the hands of those who were servants for the then holders. I am afraid, however, that the individual squatter is nowadays a relic of the past, for, with few exceptions, the stations are held either by banks, or by combinations of so-called squatters who, in the early days at all events, had not even been heard of. I have been fortunate in securing a few particulars of Beck and Brown, who formed, in the early days, one of the best known squatter firms of the back country.

John Beck arrived in Sydney in 1843 or 1844, and immediately took the management of one of Benjamin Boyd's stations—"Capartel," Bathurst district, New South

Wales. In 1847-48 Beck purchased, on his own account, some two or three thousand sheep, principally ewes, and started the sheep for Moreton Bay in charge of Mr. Thomas Nicholson, ultimately reaching Canal Creek, where they settled down until early in 1851 on a block of country named "Hamilton," within three miles of what is now the township of Leyburn. On 4th April, 1849, Samuel Brown arrived in Melbourne. Brown was then a youth approaching the age of twenty-one years. He immediately went up to his brother's station, "Mopianimum," Wardy Yallock, Geelong district. Samuel Brown remained at Mopianimum, learning "colonial experience" till December, 1849, — about nine months — when he proceeded to Sydney to join Beck, his brother-in-law. Both went on to Moreton Bay, and landed at Kangaroo Point on 1st January, 1850. From Ipswich they went on to Canal Creek on horseback. Brown became full partner by purchasing and paying Beck in cash for half share of the sheep, etc. The firm of Beck and Brown thus commenced in January, 1850. The partnership continued till March, 1862. In March, 1851, Mr. Nicholson got the management of Stonehenge station from Thomas De Lacy Moffatt, who was then residing there.

In May, 1851, Brown started from Canal Creek with sheep, travelling down the Condamine (Beck with his family remaining at Canal Creek for a time, but afterwards removed and resided at Kangaroo Point, Brisbane). Brown pulled up at Dogwood Creek, on Charles Coxen's "Bindian" run. Brown was then the farthest out with sheep. However, shortly after, Walker, with the native police, came from Callandoon and settled their barracks on Channing Creek. Brown had hardly got the yards up for the sheep on the Dogwood when he was surprised by the arrival of a special messenger from Beck at Canal Creek requesting him to return with the sheep at once, in consequence of the gold discoveries in the south having caused much alarm among the settlers on the Downs. John Gammil, of Talgai, Clifton, etc., was talking of boiling down all sheep except the very best quality for wool, as the scarcity of labour of all kinds, and especially shepherds, with consequent extravagant demand for wages would, it was then generally thought, compel the squatters to succumb altogether. However, in the face of these prognostications, Brown refused to return with the sheep. Brown had one man at least --"John Davies"--a trustworthy, good shepherd whom he could depend upon By forming two flocks into one, and with the assistance of the blacks as shepherds, he considered he would be all right, especially as the native police had settled within twenty miles of him. And so it turned out. He got two blacks shepherding, with all the assistance he required for lambing. The blacks did their work well. Brown said of them--"I always found the blacks reliable if reliance were placed in them, and were treated fairly and kindly, though firmly, and as human beings. In the course of a year or so the gold fever abated a little, though shepherds and shearers were actually masters for three or four years after. The Chinese who were afterwards introduced assisted somewhat in forcing white labour down to a workable level.

In 1852 Beck and Brown took up about 1,100 square miles of country on the creeks falling into the Moonie River, but being then isolated, with no neighbours nearer than 100 miles, with a scarcity and high rates of labour, they could not occupy the country for some years after they had taken it up and paid rent for it. In the meantime Brown wandered about from place to place with the sheep —a year or so here, a year or so there—but gradually working towards the country they had taken up. He settled for about two years on the country secured by Gideon Lang, but then unoccupied, and in a natural state, on the Moonie River, about fifty miles from Weranga (then John Crowther's). There was no road down beyond a track from Weranga to the farthest out sheep station of Crowther's. All beyond to Lang's country Brown named "Tartha," a black's name, one which still clings to it.

In 1856 Beck and Brown first formed the 1,100 square miles. They placed two flocks on it, then another two flocks, and so on as the yards were ready to receive them, until the whole of the sheep were removed from Lang's country, "Tartha"—in all, approaching 18,000. They thus formed Canmaroo head station (commenced May, 1856). The 1,100 square miles taken up and formed by Beck and Brown are now in four stations, known as Canmaroo, Coomrith, North Ingleston, and Cooroora.

In March, 1862, Beck and Brown dissolved partnership, Beck taking Canmaroo, and Brown Coomrith, dividing the sheep equally—about 40,000—or about 20,000 sheep each. Beck died at Coomrith in 1866. Brown sold part of Coomrith, with 27,000 odd sheep, in 1873, to William Graham (Hon. William Graham and Daniel Williams, railway contractor). The other part of Coomrith was reserved by him with part also of Cooroora, which he held up to the end of '86 — the wind-up of the two years' drought. During this time there was practically no rain — in fact from July, 1884, to May, 1886. Brown lost quite two-thirds of his sheep, and the greater part of his cash, in endeavouring to keep alive those he saved. Brown had been equally unfortunate in other droughts. In 1875 he lost 11,000 sheep, what with drought and the results of three days' continuous rain immediately after being shorn when the drought broke up. Other droughts followed, but Brown has often remarked that the one of 1885 was the worst he ever experienced. In the sixties, stock was a very uncertain quantity. From 1860 to 1867, sheep were restricted from crossing into Queensland from New South Wales. At this time there was a demand from the northern parts of the colony, which was then being stocked; and what with the short supply and the heavy demand, values jumped up tremendously. Maiden ewes fetched £1 a head, average breeding ewes about 15s., and other classes in proportion. Unfortunately many of the southern men were unable to foresee events sufficiently well to sell. Most of them stocked up their country instead of selling. With remarkable suddenness sheep then fell to half-a-crown, and few sales at that, and, in addition, from '67 to '72, wool had fallen so terribly that it was scarcely worth while cutting it off the sheep's back. Prices ruling in Sydney ran from $5\frac{1}{4}$d. to 11d. per lb.

After 1872 the price of wool improved much, and continued to fetch a fair price, but the droughts became more general after then, and the quality of country got worse and worse every year, consequent upon the heavy stocking and the eating out of the roots of all the good blue grass and natural herbage. It is questionable whether the wethers bred on the same country now average 40 lbs., much less 70 lbs., which was regarded there twenty years ago as a fair average.

Both Beck and Brown were born in the parish of Borgue, Kirkcudbrightshire, Scotland. Beck was the youngest son of the late William Beck, of Balmangan. Brown is the youngest son of the late Alexander Brown, of Ingleston and Casleton, Borgue, and, strange to say, both were educated at the same academy in the latter town. As has been stated, Beck died at Coomrith in April of 1866, at the age of about 57 years. Brown, though over 60 years of age, is still hale and hearty—as he describes himself: "I am still a bushranger."

CHAPTER IX.

NORTH QUEENSLAND LEGENDS AND MYTHS—A DARING "DUFFER" —THE GULF COUNTRY—A RUN-HUNTING EXPEDITION— BREAKING IN A "BROMBIE"—A TERROR TO DROVERS—AN ABANDONED TRACK—BACK TO THE EARLY FORTIES—A CURIOUS MISTAKE—MAJOR GORMAN—PATRICK LESLIE—D. C. McCONNEL—THE FIRST SQUATTER ON THE BRISBANE— A BURNETT PIONEER—"BLOOD FOR BLOOD."

NORTH QUEENSLAND is not without its legends and myths, chiefly criminal. There are still a few men living who are the heroes of some stories which would compare with the fabled exploits of many a Highland cateran or border mosstrooper—Rob Roy or William of Deloraine. I have a few particulars of one of them which are worth giving. One of his most daring feats was the taking of over 1,000 cattle from a station on the Thompson, and travelling them overland to Adelaide by way of Cooper's Creek and the Barcoo. Fortune favoured the enterprising cattle lifter more than he deserved, for he had to fear something more than the peril of the law. There was the more terrible danger of dying of thirst. There were really no means of learning that when one waterhole was left in the morning, the next and the next again would not be found to be dry. One wonders what could have been this man's thoughts as he and his companions went on day after day with their lives in their hands. Of course, if the worst had come to the worst, and the drought-fiend had descended on them in all his terrors, they would have left the cattle to their fate, and tried to save their own lives by hard riding. But could they have saved themselves? The question is not easy to answer. A single shower might make all the difference for them between prolonged life and a miserable death. At that time the pioneer squatter had not pushed out very far into the dry interior. The cattle were regularly auctioned in Adelaide, and, probably, the enterprising drover would have escaped scot free if he had been content to take only herd cattle, and left behind a very remarkable white stud bull, which was bought and sent to the Darling Downs, where he was promptly recognised. The result was the arrest of the enterprising drover aforesaid, who had spent his share of the proceeds of the cattle in riotous living in Sydney. He was tried in the Roma Circuit Court, and acquitted on the clearest evidence (of his guilt). Thereupon Roma was, on the report of the presiding judge, sentenced to lose its Circuit Court. This story has furnished the groundwork for an episode in a well known Australian romance; but the novelist has made the drover get into gaol, and come generally to grief, which did not happen, and, as a rule, seldom does in real life, where the greatest rascals commonly "flourish like a green bay tree," so long as their rascality is tempered with a proper amount of discretion.

The above overlanding exploit was not, however, the first of its kind. A person, now dead, was instructed by an Adelaide squatting firm to take delivery of 2,000 Darling Downs cattle, and drive them over to Adelaide. Men were engaged, horses and supplies bought, and a start was made. All would probably have gone well if Mr. X, as we will call the leader of the party, had chosen to follow the then usual route down the Darling and Murray. For very excellent reasons of his own, however, he preferred to keep away from the rivers in the interior, where he knew there had been good rains, the cattle would have feed and water, and be less liable to interference than on the frontage. It was, at the time, a bold thing to do, and the men who had been engaged for the trip, finding that the cattle were not being headed for the Barwon frontage, got panic-stricken, and one night after they had passed the last outpost of civilisation on the Maranoa, fairly bolted in a body. Mr. X was in a predicament. Out in the wilderness with 2,000 cattle, and only one blackboy to help him with them! There were certainly plenty of supplies on the dray, and a superabundance of horseflesh. There were several good dogs, too, and their help was not to be despised under the circumstances. X determined to go on. He knew there were no serious obstacles in his way, no rivers to cross, or station cattle "to box" with his own. The blackboy, who had been with him on exploring trips, was not afraid, and the glory of succeeding in such an attempt was by no means to be despised. So on they went. Of course the travelling was slow. The cattle could not be hurried. They had to be allowed to feed leisurely along all day, spreading a mile or two wide when the grass or herbage was abundant. That ensured their camping at night. When the feed was bad they were driven fast, and compensated with a good rest when there was feed to justify it. The result of this careful management was that very few of the cattle were lost, and they had actually improved in condition when they arrived near Adelaide. So much for careful, steady droving.

Live stock fetched good prices in the early seventies, when the country south of the Gulf of Carpentaria began to be taken up in earnest. It was nearly all taken up in the first instance as "unwatered," in consequence of the absurd then-existing law which required all "watered" country to be stocked before being applied for. Of course this law, like many others, was simply productive of perjury. A wise legislature, in deference to popular clamour, decided that the "cormorant squatter" should not be allowed to take up new country and keep it unstocked for sale as a speculation unless it absolutely would not carry stock. The legislature did not apparently know that a man looking for new country did not usually take his flocks and herds and family about with him—that he often had neither flocks nor herds to speak of of his own; but went out with two or three horses into the wilderness to hunt for a run that he could sell to somebody else who had flocks and herds to stock it. The consequence was that, as the run was not a saleable property till the rent was paid and the license to occupy issued, the discoverer had to declare that it was unwatered even if a river ran through the middle of it. Nobody, not even the officials of the Lands Office, regarded these little fibs seriously.

A gentleman who, in company with a friend named Wilson, was once on a run-hunting expedition to the far north-west, related to me the following:—"We had three pack-horses, but the travelling had been bad, and feed and water scarce. We found nothing like good available country; and the horses were visibly giving out. At last we made up our minds to leave all but the two best on a few acres of good grass which surrounded a small waterhole fed by a spring. Next morning we started as lightly loaded as possible. All day we rode, but there was no sign of water, though the country improved a little. That night we gave the horses a pannikin of water each from our bags, and camped on the desolate lonely downs. The next day was much the same, and as the sun declined in the west I said to Wilson, 'we might as well look out for a place to camp.' 'Yes,' he said; 'it's no use knocking up the horses.' Just then the ground gave way under his horse's forefeet, and out rushed a little brown bandicoot. Wilson drew the revolver he carried, and shot it. He dismounted, and picked it up. It was very fat. I was just going to dismount when the horses raised their heads, pricked their ears, sniffed the air, and mine began to walk briskly on. Wilson mounted and followed, carrying his bandicoot. We crossed the next low ridge, and then the horses, tired and weak though they were, broke into a shambling trot, and began to pull. Over the next ridge, and then we saw before us a long line of huge gums, with the glitter of water between their ghostly white trunks. It was a long lagoon, and we could hear the ducks (they must have been in millions) feeding. We camped, lit a fire, and roasted our bandicoot. Our horses, having satisfied their thirst, revelled in the rich Mitchell grass around."

"When we had rested ourselves and our horses, and marked out the boundaries of our run, we set out on our return. We found a way through better country; but still there were one or two stages on which, with stock, it would be necessary to depend on clay pans. The country was duly taken up as "unwatered," and offered for sale by our agents as "unstocked, but well watered by numerous permanent creeks and lagoons." We soon found a purchaser, a Mr.— say Stokes—from Adelaide. Mr. Stokes wanted to go at once to his new run, taking with him 1,500 mixed cattle he had bought. He had engaged a newly-arrived immigrant, a hard-headed, resolute-looking Yorkshire farming man, and I picked up a blackboy who had already been with me on two droving trips."

"We got on allright till we were well out of the settled country. I had warned Mr. Stokes of the two or three possibly dry stages we should have to pass, but he was inclined to make little of them. We got over one of them well enough, and came to a good permanent spring. There were two stages beyond that where the only water was in

HON. LOUIS HOPE.   JUDGE LUTWYCHE.
MR. J. TURNER.   MR. GORDON SANDEMAN.
MR R. LITTLE.   SIR JOSHUA P. BELL.

clay pans, and there had apparently been little or no rain since Wilson and I had been there some months before. I went forward, and found both the pans dry. It would be nearly a fifty-mile stage to the next permanent water—too much for the cattle—and I went back and reported. I advised that the cattle should be camped for a few weeks, as they were on good and plentiful feed. Next morning Mr. Stokes, taking one of the best horses, started out to look for water, declaring he would take the cattle on at all hazards. That night he did not return. The next morning I rode out with the blackboy to follow Mr. Stokes' track. It led us to a patch of stony desert, the whole covered with flat waterworn pebbles of red sandstone. Tracking was impossible there. We returned to camp."

"Mr. Stokes was never again seen alive or dead. He got out into the stony desert, and must have pushed on till his horse fell exhausted, and perished with his rider. In such country there can be no hope of escape for man or beast. I and the blackboy did not spare ourselves in the effort to find traces of the lost man. We went out day after day, but failed to find, in the stony waste, any sign of a track. At last, after waiting a fortnight, a heavy thunderstorm came, and the next day we pushed on. The two clay pans were full of a thick yellow fluid, which sufficed for the cattle, and on the third day we got to the fifty-mile spring. Thence to our destination the stages were short and easy.

"We proceeded to settle the cattle on the run. I found the Yorkshireman a treasure. He was taciturn, and, perhaps, a little surly in manner, but readily learned the work of a stockman, and became a good and bold horseman. He willingly agreed to remain in charge of the new station when I returned to Brisbane, as I must needs do, as soon as I had put things in order, to communicate with Mr. Stokes' representatives. It was clearly a case of natural inborn fitness for life in a new country. The blackboy was, for all the purposes of station work, far less useful than the new arrival. Not only was he less industrious and less inured to labour, but he really knew less of the ways of cattle, and, in everything except tracking, the new chum, in a month, was his master."

In '73, when some of the cattle stations on the Belyando were being stocked with sheep, a mob of 10,000 ewes was started from the Dawson for one of these runs. They were to travel through the abandoned Tierywoomba and Wandoo country, across Funnel and Denison Creeks, and round the head of the Isaacs. When camped near Nebo, the party, consisting of "the boss," five shepherds, and a Chinese cook, heard of the gold discovery on the Palmer. The shepherds at once told the overseer they would go no further unless their wages were raised to 30s. a week. He simply told them he would do nothing of the sort. They promptly rolled up their blankets, got their cheques, and went off to the township. (They were originally engaged for £1 a week, and the increase of 10s. was a serious matter). It might have been worse, however, if, for instance, they had chosen to strike when further on, where men could not be got at any price. The Chinese cook remained, and made a few strong remarks on the folly of men who were actually travelling in the direction they wanted to go, and being paid for it, throwing away their chance. He then said he could get five of his countrymen to take the place of the strikers, and, being told to get them, soon brought the required relief. They were evidently men accustomed to the work, which some of the strikers were not, and all had good dogs. They agreed to go through for 25s. a week—not an unreasonable demand under the circumstances.

A little earlier some of those same Belyando cattle, which were to be replaced by sheep, were being moved to new country on the Mitchell River. The horses sent with them were collected without much regard to anything but condition and cheapness, and they were, in some cases, notorious for vice. One in particular, a fine, powerful grey, which had come from no one knew where, soon distinguished himself by throwing in succession all the best riders of the party, till no one would attempt to back him. When the party came to the Burdekin crossing, they determined to try an experiment. The terrible grey was run into an old stockyard near the river, roped, and thrown. A strong pack-saddle was put on his back, and two strong canvas pack-saddle bags, filled with sand, were securely attached to it. A greenhide rope was then passed round everything, and the grey was let go. He got up and made one or two vigorous attempts to buck, but they were useless. It had hitherto been as impossible to keep an ordinary pack as a rider on the brute's back; but this pack, which could not have been less than four hundredweight, was too much. A smart application of the stockwhip sent the grey forward among the other horses. There was a mile of deep sand before the water was reached, then two miles more sand to the firm ground on the other bank. That night the grey came quietly to be relieved of his pack. Anyone could ride him or do anything with him after that; but his spirit was utterly broken. He turned out an unmitigated slug. It was impossible to get a gallop out of him, and he was good for very little except carrying a pack. That is always the result of breaking a really bad buckjumper, or any other vicious horse. The vice may be apparently cured for the time being by firmness, or kindness, and judicious management, but if the horse changes hands, and comes under the control of someone who is not firm and judicious, it will break out again.

In the old times, when Hodgkinson reigned at Burketown, the Gulf country was a terror to drovers. The Norman especially, flowing through what had been most unjustly named the Plains of Promise, acquired a most unenviable notoriety for its sudden and capricious floods which, in an hour or two, would convert the wide level plains on either bank into an impassable sea of mud and water. The eastern, or right bank, was timbered, but the tall straight stems of the vast gum trees were inaccessible to anybody but a blackfellow with a tomahawk, and the best mounted horseman would try in vain to keep ahead of the advancing flood, while sheep or cattle would be at once swallowed up. The western, or left bank, was entirely destitute of trees, and the daring bushman who ventured into those solitudes had to boil his tea with a wisp of grass, while there was not a tree for miles to afford him a refuge in flood time. After the crisis of 1866, pastoral settlement on the Gulf receded instead of advanced. Money was of course scarce, the coasting steamers in those days did not go beyond Bowen, and very rarely got so far, while the rates for carriage either from Rockhampton or that port were prohibitive. Flour could not be bought on the Gulf—when it could be bought at all—for less than 1s. per lb. Under such conditions the harassed squatter could not hope to make ends meet, and he succumbed, or, in other words, sold his stock for what it would fetch, and returned to civilisation, or as near it as he could earn a living for himself. True, a few hardy old bushmen held on with grim determination, living on beef and pigweed, and hoping for better times.

When things were at the worst, a southern capitalist, who had managed for a trifle, to buy a half-stocked cattle run on the Flinders, thought it worth his while to send up a small mob of well-bred shorthorns to improve the stock which, even on the seller's showing, was, to say the least, indifferent, consisting chiefly of the very roughest culls from the old down-country herds. The mob were mustered at

Tooloomba, near Broadsound, and placed in charge of an overseer with two half-castes, one as bullock-driver, the other as stockman. There were 250 breeders, including fifty good herd bulls, and there were added twenty working bullocks, a good dray heavily laden with stores, twenty horses, and a spring cart. The deep and boulder-strewn crossing of Salt-water Creek came near wrecking the dray, and lamed many of the cattle; but gentle driving and good management put them nearly right when the climb over the Connor's Range had to be faced. There was no time to lose, as the range must be crossed in a day, and Collaroy run in another. The cattle were in a woful plight by the time they got on to the unoccupied country beyond; but there was then no need to hurry. The grass was good and sweet, and there was plenty of water, and a week's spell put things right. The mob slowly fed their way northward, passed in view of the remarkable table-topped, perpendicular-sided hill of Fort Cooper, named after Sir (then Mr.) Daniel Cooper, of Sydney. Then on, without any adventure worth recording, to Richmond Downs.

It was the old track from Bowen to the Thomson, chosen in preference to that from Rockhampton by the Peak Downs on account of the shortness of the land carriage. Two stages from Richmond Downs began the dreaded dry stage—forty miles of stony desert, without grass or water. At the eastern end of this desert track was a fine, well grassed plain, watered by springs which gushed from a great isolated mass of rock. Beyond was the stony desert, as sharply divided from the grassy plain as is a well kept gravel path from the lawn beside it in an English pleasure ground. Here the cattle were allowed a three days' spell, for there could be no rest in the desert. Then, just before sunset on the third day, the bullocks were yoked, the unwilling cattle rounded up, and headed for the pebble-strewn desert. On they went, and the rising sun found them still moving. The horses were changed, each being refreshed with a pannikin of water squirted into his nostrils from the mouth of his rider. The team was changed too. Then on through the scorching heat of the day. The cattle begun to hang their heads, and their tongues lolled out, but forward they must go. Again the men changed horses. The cool night air seemed to refresh the animals, but only cruel flogging made some of them keep up—that and the dogs, which had been allowed to drink. But before dawn a change came. Horses and cattle raised their heads, and the pace mended. The loose horses started at a gallop, the cattle followed, and even the bullocks got up a lumbering trot. What was it?

It was the scent of water, still some miles away, but plainly perceptible to the senses of the thirsty tired beasts. No flogging or cruel biting at their heels was now needed to keep the stragglers up with the mob. Even the footsore and lame forgot their pain, and made the pace hotter and hotter as the welcome scent became more distinct. Then the surface of the desert began to gently rise, and soon the flat pebbles disappeared, and the hoofs of the animals no longer clattered over them, but trod with a dull dead sound the grassy soil. In front were dimly seen a long line of gum trees, and the rising sun showed the cattle and horses rushing pell mell to quench their burning thirst in a gently flowing creek. It was no easy task to restrain the team from rushing after their companions with the yokes and chains still on them. However, by the strenuous exertions of all three men, they were at last released, and took their share of the refreshing element. Then, thirst allayed, hunger was to be satisfied; and the whole of the animals began greedily to crop the rich succulent herbage. The men made their camp, and, after a refreshing meal of dried beef, damper, and tea, prepared to enjoy the rest they so much needed. Two nights and a day without sleep, and with constant demands on their care and vigilance, had tried their powers of endurance to the utmost. Sleep was a necessity, and it may well be believed that the sun was declining in the west before any of the three showed signs of returning animation.

The overseer, sensible of the responsibility of his position, was the first to rise and look round him. The cattle, their hunger allayed, had evidently gone into camp in the heat of the day, and were just stringing out in long files to begin feeding again for the evening. The horses were nibbling daintily at the short grass round the camp. The overseer caught and saddled one of them, and rode round. He satisfied himself that all was right, rode back to camp, made up the fire, and got a bucket of water. Then the camp woke in earnest. The tent was pitched, and cooking went on merrily, for there was to be another three days' halt, to rest and refresh the cattle after their passage of that terrible dry stage. The route has long been abandoned. Then teams were paid for at the rate of £7 per ton for each hundred miles. A saving of one hundred miles in carriage was a consideration not to be despised. The case was entirely altered when enterprising carriers with good horse-teams would do the round trip from Rockhampton and back in a fortnight for less than a third of the money each way. Then the railway was extended by degrees to the Dawson, the Comet, and finally to Emerald, and beyond into what used, in the memory of men still young, to be called the Never Never. The teams became things of the past, and Bowen, which once believed itself destined to a great future as a seaport, became a very small factor in the progress of the colony.

There is little more to record of the journey. There were no serious difficulties to surmount after the dry stage was passed. The overseer was an intelligent and careful man, and his charge being, for those days, a valuable one, he handled it tenderly. A few days more or less were of little consequence in comparison with the imperative necessity of bringing the cattle on to the station in good condition and with undiminished numbers. The country he had to pass over was then unfenced. The few stations were worked in the old-fashioned way, and were very lightly stocked. Therefore there was little trouble with the occupiers, and it was possible to make short stages, and let the cattle spread and feed freely as they went along.

When their destination was at last reached, the overseer found that the deplorable account he had received of the property he was to work had been by no means exaggerated, but very much the reverse. Those who remember what many of the Riverina cattle stations were like in the forties, will have no difficulty in forming a faint conception of what he saw. The home station consisted of two small and ill-built bark huts, and a stockyard of logs. A cockatoo fence enclosed a small horse paddock, and the river ran swiftly by, bordered by high, steep banks. Such of the cattle as could be seen were of the worst kind possible for profit, and miserably bred. When the stores had been put under cover an attempt was made to muster; but it was soon apparent that the cattle were too wild to be properly worked. Many of them, indeed, were excessively fat, but if disturbed they would charge with such fury and determination that it was clear they had run wild.

The run was fortunately not very heavily timbered, and there was no scrub. It was therefore not difficult to accustom the cattle to the presence of horsemen. The men always carried rifles, and when an old bull with horns like scythes refused, as often happened, to respond to the persuasive eloquence of the stockwhip and go into camp with his harem, he usually found his career cut short by a bullet. The old bulls were shot, and the young ones so dealt with as to be harmless. Then those which had been brought from the south, were gradually distributed to the different mobs, and a small stud herd was formed in a paddock which, with much labour, the three men managed to fence for it. In this way was established one of the best of the North Queensland herds, not exclusively of pure shorthorn cattle, but of inferior stock gradually improved by a judicious infusion of shorthorn blood. It is a typical example of what can be done by a well arranged admixture of breeds when carried out under competent guidance, with a very small expenditure of money. The Australian merino owes its existence to much the same combination of skill, good fortune, and judgment. Nothing could be more unpromising than the progenitors of some of the best Australian flocks.

But to go back to the early forties. In 1840 Major Gorman was commandant of the military at the penal establishment at Brisbane, where Captain Clunie of the 17th Regiment had been in charge with 102 rank and file eight years before. And it was reported to the Major by the blacks that "plenty white fellow sit down." And so up went the troops over the mountains explored years before by Major Mitchell and Allan Cunningham, and on Goomburra Creek they captured Walter Leslie and two of his men, and the mistake was not rectified till at Canning Downs head station some credentials were forthcoming which set the blunder right, and over some real "fighting rum" the Major's health was pledged again and again. This serves to remind me of what happened in Moreton Bay some twenty years later. Constable Boe, stationed at Sandgate, had been instructed to keep a sharp look out for some runaway sailors who had stolen a ship's boat out in the Bay and deserted, and could not be traced. Constable Boe therefore kept a bright watch, and it seemed as if his zeal was to be rewarded. It happened unfortunately, however, that Boe was at times given to the habit of "looking upon the wine when it was red," and on those occasions his views on all subjects were apt to be too positive and decided, and not so answerable to argument as should be. It often happens so when people are "bemused with beer," being confused, they also become irritable and obstinate, for, as one of our poets has happily expressed it,

" 'Tis enough to put a climax on the patience of a saint
When no clearer seems the things that are, than are the things that aint."

A man does get angry when he can't manage to distinguish substance from shadow. Constable Boe saw a boat approaching the shore, and in it was Captain Claudius Buchanan Whish, a well-set, handsome, aquiline man, who looked not one bit like a runaway sailor, but what he really was, namely, an ex-officer of Hussars. Still all this availed nothing when John Boe, of the " foorce," had made up his mind on a certain course impelled by inner potations, so he arrested Captain Whish and took him (disciplined, and of course, unresisting), to Brisbane, where, in place of promotion, the only result was that Boe was told that the police authorities would not need his valuable but too zealous services any longer.

What brought Mr. Patrick Leslie out to Australia at all was the fact that his uncle, Mr. Davidson, an English banker—and the father of Gilbert and Walter Davidson, subsequently of Canning Downs—sent him out to manage an estate at Cassilis, in the Upper Hunter district, in New South Wales. Thence he cast longing eyes northward towards the *terra incognita* that lay beyond the Dumaresq. David Cannon McConnel was the first pastoral settler on the head waters of the

Brisbane. That was in 1841. Born in Manchester, of Scotch extraction, in 1818, he was educated for a chemist and calico printer; but, attracted by the glowing reports of Australian prosperity before the collapse of 1843, he sailed for Sydney, and arrived there in June, 1840. He explored south to the Moruya River, and north to New England, and decided to commence squatting life to the north. He had heard of the Leslie's progress to Darling Downs, and of the facilities which the Brisbane River presented for shipping produce. So he determined to strike out in that direction, and to locate himself and his stock in some equable climate near the sea coast, where the rainfall could be depended on. He had brought plenty of money into Australia with him, so, purchasing sheep and cattle on the Williams and Gloucester Rivers, in New South Wales, he pushed on to the Severn, at which point he diverged from the track taken by the Leslies, Denis, and other pioneers, and passed to near the present sites of Tenterfield and Stanthorpe, and followed up the creek on which Stanthorpe is now built, hoping to find a suitable run on the heads of the Clarence River or the Logan. But the country was very broken, and not tempting; so the tableland was followed till the Upper Condamine was reached. Thence he travelled northward and eastward over the Great Dividing Range, and, settling on Cressbrook Creek, a tributary of the Upper Brisbane River, he became the first man to settle with stock on a run to the east of the Main Range in Queensland. He marked his trees on Cressbrook on 15th July, 1841, as the country appeared to offer all the advantages he had sought for, and he never had occasion to subsequently alter his opinion on the merits of the run. He now went south again and brought up some splendid pedigree shorthorn bulls from the Australian Agricultural Company's place at Port Stephens, to which stock he added some more of the same class shipped from England to Brisbane, and the herd enriched from time to time with new blood, is still in full excellence at Cressbrook. Weathering the monetary crisis of 1843, Mr. McConnel, in 1847, returned to England and married Miss McLeod, of Edinburgh, since well known in connection with hospitals and charitable institutions in Brisbane. This was in 1848, and for a year Mr. McConnell studied farming in one of the leading farming counties in England, and sailed for Brisbane in 1849 in the "Chaseley," a ship that brought so many well known colonists, such as Dr. Hobbs, to Queensland. He then bought the point of land in Brisbane on the river now known as Bulimba, built a fine two-story brick house there, and farmed the point with lucerne, Italian rye grass, sweet potatoes, maize, and cotton, and made them all pay. Mr. D. McConnel helped from 1849 to 1853 to form the Presbyterian Church in Brisbane, first erected on the south side July 15, 1850. The clearing of the Bulimba scrub injuring his wife's health, he sold the property, which was afterwards occupied by Sir R. R. Mackenzie and Donald Coutts. He was always of opinion that a shorter, cheaper, and better railway line from Ipswich to Toowoomba could have been made by crossing the Little Liverpool Range some miles to the east of the present site and where the range is lower and narrower; thence over Lockyer's Creek, near Tarampa, and up easily graded spurs to near Crow's Nest, and so over the Main Range direct to Gowrie, which would have commanded Toowoomba just as well, and avoided, in his opinion, the sharp turn now in use.

I have been thus lengthy in writing of David McConnel, because he combined the triple character of a pioneer squatter, farmer, and philanthropist. He united the agriculturist and pastoralist, and showed how they could be combined.

He was one of the earliest advocates of inoculation for pleuro-pneumonia, and was very kind to young and inexperienced colonists, many of whom he assisted with advice and maintenance, and who now remember him gratefully, and, as one of them remarked (now in a high position in Central Queensland), "the example of David McConnel's life as a christian gentleman always fully before the public amongst whom he moved, proved clearly how a man may "fear God, and keep His commandments," and yet be an active practical worker in new fields of enterprise. He became the first director of the first bank that started business in Queensland — a branch of the Bank of New South Wales, in Brisbane; Captain R. J. Coley (Lloyd's agent), being his colleague. Mr. William Richardson, a brother-in-law of Dr. Hobbs, was the first manager; and Mr. A. L Knowles, of Kangaroo Point, the first accountant. A bank note, No. 1, dated May 1st, 1852, may be seen (framed and glazed), in the inspector's room in the Brisbane office, being the first bank note ever issued in Queensland.

A pioneer of the Burnett district was Mr. William Harvey Holt, one of the many men from the great public schools of England who have made their mark in early Australia. Born at Eton in 1833, and educated at its college, he found himself, in 1851, at the age of eighteen, getting his "colonial experience" at Yendah, near Gayndah, with Mr. Robert Wilkin, with whom, in 1859, he entered into partnership, and formed Kolonga station for cattle, about thirty miles up from the mouth of the Kolan River, near the Talkiberan Creek, a famous and mysterious rocky wild spot where gold and copper lie plentifully concealed in reefs and ledges that are not workable by the ordinary unskilled miner. He removed, in 1872, to "Glen Prairie," in Broad Sound, which he worked most successfully with cattle, and whence in a fine and specially fitted steamer, called the "Yeoman," sailing alternately from Gladstone or Port Clinton, he shipped cattle abundantly to New Zealand and other places. Another pioneer of what was then the "north countree" was Mr. William Young, who, on the 29th May, 1855, took up country with sheep near Mount Larcombe, in the Port Curtis district, just before the Archers, in August, 1856, began on the Fitzroy River, at Gracemere, Mr. Young's nearest neighbors being the Archers on that side, and Mr. Blackman, some seventy miles away, in the other direction; and as Mr. Young and his people gave no provocation to the blacks, he forms a good example of how the early pioneers had to suffer the "manner and customs" of the aborigines.

One day a man in Mr. Young's employ was accidentally drowned while bathing in a waterhole on the run, and the master had to go on to the nearest township (a far ride, indeed), to report the matter. Taking advantage of the absence of the boss, the blacks fell upon the run, killed five shepherds, raided the sheep, rifled the store and house, and when Mr. Young returned he had only a couple of woolpacks for bed and blanket that night, but that, of course, was the least part of his trouble. The nearest police and magistrates were at Captain O'Connell's place, at Gladstone, and the course of orthodox law all over New South Wales was, in such a case, for the sufferer to ride to the settlement and procure a warrant for the offenders, and take a constable with him to execute the same, having, of course, to be careful to identify the real offenders (whom he had never seen, and whom the dead victims could, of course, never testify against). This farcical style of business was fully explained to me in 1853, when I was overlanding, and by old Donald Macrae, a settler on the Lower Lachlan River, near Balranald, in which he referred to the absurdity and "disconvenience" of riding 250 miles to Bathurst or elsewhere for a warrant and a constable for a black who had stolen sheep or killed a shepherd, and Macrae hinted that the business was often settled in a much more summary style. The statute, supine as to black men's sins, was, however, keenly alive when a white man (even by deputy) crossed the border line between law and its breach. One early settler "up north" had his run raided and eight of his men killed without provocation, and his sheep in their charge were driven off for slaughter and feasting.

He was, of course, very angry, and, with two friendly half civilized natives from another part of the colony whom he employed as stockmen (the whole three having loaded carbines, and the "boss" a revolver as well), set out to track the ringleader of the massacre, one "Billy," who had "cleared out" and was just then comfortably camped with some "tame" blacks at a police depôt fifty miles away till the matter should "blow over," the depôt being due to the residence of the Crown Lands Commissioner for the district. And here was "Billy" sure enough; and when he was asked for, the gins replied "here Billy," and he, seeing the game to be "up," at once made for the water nearest at hand, which happened to be an arm of the sea. But as soon as he plunged and was about to dive, the two black stockmen who had followed him up emptied their carbines into him, and killed him on the spot.

Their idea was "blood for blood," after seeing the corpses of the shepherds, whom they knew so well. But the "outrage" of a white squatter thus allowing "lynch law" by his servants under the very nose and almost under the very verandah of a Crown Lands Commissioner, was a matter not to be overlooked, and a warrant was issued for the said pastoralist, and he duly appeared before a bench consisting of the Police Magistrate and two squatters named T. L.

M. Prior and R. R. Mackenzie, the latter of whom, at all events, had known what it was in New England to be robbed of shepherds and sheep by the blacks in the by-gone days. The Police Magistrate, who had once been a schoolmaster, and never owned any sheep, was all for refusing bail, but he was overruled by the majority, and it was granted with a remand to the place where the shooting occurred. The news of the trouble soon spread, and our grazier found himself "shadowed" at every little bush place on his way up to the *locus in quo* wherever there was an inn, a lockup, a blacksmith's shop, and a few people; but the magic words "out on bail till the 30th at————" made the police fall back at once on each occasion, and when finally before the bench at the place of remand he was "discharged for lack of evidence." And so ended the matter of that tragedy.

Mr. Robert Cribb.   Mr. T. L. Murray-Prior.
Col. Gray.
Mr. James Warner.   Mr. John Petrie.

CHAPTER X.

EARLY QUEENSLANDERS—THE SURVIVING FEW—ONCE MORE THE
ROLL CALL—SOME OF THE OLD HANDS—JOHN PETRIE—
GEORGE THORNE—ROBERT LITTLE—FREDERIC BIGGE—T. L.
MURRAY-PRIOR—SIR JOSHUA P. BELL—EDWIN NORRIS—
JAMES WARNER—ROBERT DOUGLAS—SIMEON LORD—CAPTAIN
TAYLOR WINSHIP—JAMES S. MITCHELL.

OLD residents of south Queensland, those with good memories for the past, live in a world of their own, with sympathies and associations peculiar and unique, into which modern Queensland cannot enter any more than New South Wales or Victoria could.

Ours was a strange early history. We were a happy limited community set down in a strange, new, and wonderful part of the world, and our sorrows took their colour from the dear old but then new locality, so unlike any other place that any one of us had come from, but in which we found we had to live and work out our destinies, and where we soon grew only too content to dwell. Some soon passed from us—passed away in the early days; scriptural names like Moses Adsett and others, suggestive of quiet Sabbath afternoons at chapel or school in the wattle-scented bush; others, again, like "honest delving" Thorpe Riding (our early agriculturist), who passed away near their three score years and ten, and all of whom will leave their pioneer names behind them in the persons of their descendants, even as did the Rouses in the sister colony after they landed in the good ship "Nile," in 1801. Foremost in all the list stands John Petrie, identified alike with the old past and the developed present of our new country, and conspicuous by his good work all through.

John Petrie.

When I first knew him he was "young Petrie," for old Andrew, his father, the foreman of works under Colonel Barney, was the family head — sightless, but clever, old Andrew. Other sons there were, not to name the ancestral cockatoo, rival of "Grip the raven," and who lived for 45 years with the Petries and was only excelled by the 70-year-old "sulphur crest" who domiciled with the Sydney Wentworths, patriarchs there like the Petries were here, a bird who lived till his bald chest made him fain in the wintry July to singe his featherless bosom by the hearth fire logs. Many are the memories of those who, long ago, came to us consumptive—some in time, and some too late; Anglican clergymen who came, married, and died, all within three or four years of their arrival. Others, like the Rev. Mr. Mowbray, who came intending to die, but altered his mind and lived for thirty years in the kindly, healthy air of Brisbane, as it was in the forties and fifties, before local sanitary science (?) was invented. Young John Petrie was then only 25 years old—no gray hairs, and an honest "sonsie" Scotch face, redolent of the "bluid" of the auld land, where generations, full of hard work and self-respect, had prepared a race fit to battle with all the labours and problems of a new country, be it Queensland, India, or what not. But he who formed the one strongest link that bound us to the fast fleeting bygone days has gone with the rest—an inevitable, but none the less painful, rending of ties which have been long growing, and are now severed for ever, save for memory's sad offices.

Yes, leading and prominent survivors of early Queensland are now few and far between. They were good men who lived forty years ago, and who settled this land. I wonder do those who have come after them and pushed on the place the pioneers really made, ever think of those who did the hard work? I wonder, indeed!

The old hands of 1822 are all gone. Tom Brookes and "Red" Smith at 86 years old were the last survivors of them, and only the men of the late thirties, the forties, and the early fifties are left, and the youngest of them is at least 60 years old. Conspicuous at the head of the list stands Thomas Petrie, dating back to 1837. The early Burnett and Brisbane River settlers are only represented now by Gordon Sandeman (an absentee), and C. R. Haly (unless the Logan can be said to claim him). The Logan men who are left are considerably more numerous—P. Pinnock, A. W. Compigné, Collins, of Mundoolan, and Pollett Cardew, of Mount Flinders. The clergy one only, in the person of Canon Glennie. Turning to the Darling Downs, we find H. W. Coxen, J. F. M'Dougall, and John Ferrett; while Sir Arthur Hodgson, H. S. Russell, and Arnold Wienholt (of the same place) are absentees in England. W. Tillman, a survivor of the German Mission at Nundah introduces us to another department. Messrs. P. O'Sullivan, R. Gill, Christopher Gorry, H. M. Reeve, and Wm. Vowles, date far back into the early history of the colony. J. S. Turner and Wm. Brookes recall the early Union Bank in Brisbane, and R. A. Kingsford, Sir Chas. Lilley, E. B. Southerden, W. Southerden, John Hardgrave, James Collins, George Appel, Reuben Oliver, A. Raff, John Little, Joseph Baynes, John Leckie, C. J. Trundle, are some of the metropolitan representatives, to whom must be added Pilot Bousfield. Sir Arthur

Palmer, E. Morey, John Scott, and P. Sellheim, now of this colony, are all colonists of ancient dates, but whether ever in Queensland before 1855 is unknown to the writer; when the present century has waned there will, doubtless, be an annual reunion of the survivors of the early life battle of old "Moreton Bay," and perhaps, all things considered, and King David's dictum about "three score years and ten," it would be hardly advisable to postpone the "gathering" of the fossils till the year 1900, or "Auld Lang Syne" will have faded quite away into the "Land of the Leal."

Let us call the roll. Let us lift the veil which hides from the present the past, and those who made the present—the good old have-beens. What of Little, "Bobby" Cribb, George Harris, Frederick Bigge, T. L. Murray Prior, James Warner, George Thorn, Robert Douglas, Taylor Winship, and all the others? Gone! eh gone. Like Tom Moore,

> When I remember all
>   The friends so linked together
> I've seen around me fall
>   Like leaves in wintry weather;
> I feel like one who treads alone
>   Some banquet hall deserted,
> Whose lights are fled, whose garlands dead,
>   And all but he departed.

GEORGE THORN.

George Thorn left us some years ago. He was the oldest free resident. Older even than Andrew Petrie as a Moreton Bay settler; and unless it was Tom Brooks, who came here in 1822, George was the oldest white inhabitant. Pleasant, genial old George! the exploring associate of rollicking Arthur Hodgson in many a midnight camp about the time when the Prince of Wales was a baby, and when the disciples of Bright and Cobden had begun to multiply in the land. 'Twas then, and even earlier still, that he first crossed that serrated limestone backbone, dotted with grasstrees, which overlooked the basin of fair Ipswich, nigh unto the site where Challinor's paddock now commands a full sight of the hoary battlements of the Main Range, the portal of Darling Downs; and there, under the name we have mentioned, sprung up a town that could a tale unfold, if its old ironbark plates, sills, and slabs would but speak. A tale of nights of wit, when Gore Jones, Frank Lucas, and many more, bandied flashes of fun, that recalled the *Noctes* of old *Blackwood's Magazine:* for there was bone and vitality in the limestone waters of our town, and men ate and drank of the best. George Holt made bread of the flour of Hart, and the volcanic pastures of Mount Flinders sent in the purest butter. Faircloth saw that the Club cellars were replete with *Veuve Clequot*, and Yaldwyn was responsible for the four-year-old turkeys; and what even if Lightfoot and Van Tromp *would* now finish considerably in the ruck of Richmond and Goldsbrough? We'll warrant you their hearts were none the less right, and even if double distanced they would rush in with open mouths and extended tails; and as the racehorses were gallant, so the women who came to see them compete were aye fair to view, and many a Queensland love-match was cemented in old Ipswich, where the hard water would never make good tea. We never seem to have such sunsets and sunrises now-a-days as used to be witnessed from that old Limestone Ridge, between 1855 and 1860. Perhaps it is that we are getting older and cannot see them so well; and the early cup of coffee, too, on the old racecourse about 5 a.m., at the end of May, tastes quite differently in 1876 from what it used to in 1859, in the year of Mincemeat and Lizard's match; for things and people grow quickly and fade quickly in 27° south latitude, and the babies of yesterday are the brides of to-day, and the bridegroom of *that* hour has perchance his will proved by a proctor in *this* one.

How well do I remember one sunset. It certainly was a glorious one, and of the real Australian type, too. First of all the sky generally was cloudless, with blue above and golden-yellow in the west to about 5° above the horizon and from thence to the zenith was a dense cloud of brown, umber, red, and gold, the background being an iron grey tinted with chocolate everywhere, and the light red that lit it up had its brown and its gold also inseparably blended with it, a delicious brown, too, that was wedded to the red and wedded the grey impartially and improved them both. And the dark cloud looked like curtain after curtain, brilliant edged and hung each behind and a little below the other in endless terraces, and the vanished sun had tipped each hanging edge with this red gold light on the brown. And there were places and patches where a whiter cloud, flecked with the all-pervading red, looked like a blood-stained half-washed cloth. And away to the east, where the nearly full moon had risen, were more but isolated patches of the iron grey, brown tinted, and with the warm blood-red glow in the centre of each one of them. Then red-brown wavelets of colour broke across the western grey-brown sky field, like parallel ripples on a sea beach; and these four items, brown, red, gold, and grey, made up a sunset effect unsurpassable, even if approachable for beauty, but, alas! so short-lived. One had to drink it in and engrave it sharply on the memory, for, anon, the bright brilliant and beautiful reds and golds and browns had all departed with their father, the sun, and the iron-grey reigned, solitary and unattractive, by itself once more.

Robert Little.

Robert Little was something more than a local solicitor; he was a man of tact and benevolence, a consistent Churchman, and served the office of warden at St. John's before "separation." He was not unknown in athletics forty years ago, and many were the pair-oared contests on our river before it could be finally decided whether "Bob" Little *cum* "Harry" Buttanshaw were or were not superior to "Tom" Jones, of Burambah, and another oarsman whose name I forget. Another sculler and friend of Mr. Little's was Mr. Bigge, of Mount Brisbane, and local wits rang the changes on Mr. " Big" and Mr. Little. Indeed, the little impromptu Saturday afternoon regattas from some private house or other on the river bank were a feature in the social life of early Brisbane days, when "everybody knew everybody," and there was no ceremony. Pair-oared contests were in vogue, and the contestants drew in a hat for boats and partners, and the ladies' delight was supreme when a tall young man of 11st. was in some "tub," mated with and outweighed by a short, fat, elderly one of 15 ditto, and the boat with a heavy "list" all the way round the course, for the sex are mischievous, and fun was the one element sought for at these little meetings. It need hardly be said that everyone manfully accepted his position, and pulled to the bitter end, be the task what it might, for there were no Sybarites among the early "Moreton Bay" men. A proof of Little's tact and quick wit was furnished in the early '50 days, when squatters and immigrants took opposite political views. A noisy crowd of "Liberals" vociferated near a house where a lady lay sick. Out came Little with another lady on his arm, and being a known "squatters' man," they followed him up with their noise, which was all he wanted—namely, to draw the disturbance away from the place where the patient was lying. When the first court was established here in 1857, with Mr. Milford as Judge and Mr. Pring as Crown Prosecutor, Little was appointed Crown Solicitor, and the extra work necessitating a partner, Mr. William Rawlins joined him. The Brisbane climate did not suit Mrs. Raw

lins, who was a daughter of Captain Murchison, of South
Australia, and Mr. Rawlins left for New Zealand. After
this, in 1860, Mr. E. I. C. Browne joined the business.

FREDERIC BIGGE.

Frederic Bigge died in England. He was one of our
Moreton Bay pioneer squatters of the early days. A good
oarsman, his muscle was as often proved as that of his friend,
the late Mr. Robert Little. "Bigge's Camp" (renamed "Grand-
chester" by the classic Sir George Bowen) derived its title from
the deceased gentleman, and Mr. Henry Mort (afterwards of
Franklyn Vale) was at one time manager for the Messrs.
Bigge (Frederic and Francis). The Mount Brisbane station,
managed by Mr. William Bowman, a son of Dr. Bowman,
of the Hawkesbury, New South Wales, was another property of the same firm's, and famous for the Westminster
and Touchstone strains of racing blood in the horses bred
there. Many a Queensland turf winner came from the
pretty station near Wivenhoe. "Bigge's Folly," a conspicuous building in the "early fifties" at Cleveland—the
great seaport and Brisbane extinguisher that was to have
been, and where wool in abundance really was shipped during
the days of the Crimean War—is another memento of the
name that forms one more of the very few now left of the
early band of pioneers who cleared the way for us in Moreton Bay.

T. L. MURRAY-PRIOR

T. L. Murray-Prior was a Moreton Bay man of the early
Leslie and Gammie days, and one whose name is inseparably
mixed with all its pleasantest memories. His father, Colonel
Prior, was a genial Irishman, and the inevitable returning-
officer and chairman of hospital and similar election meetings
in the infant days of Brisbane; for tact and good temper

were essential in those days of open voting, and it was often
"a hard row to hoe," even then, ere the peaceful ballot
system came in. The son inherited the father's suavity, and
would smile under the most trying circumstances in the bush,
the Senate, or the drawing-room. I well remember one evening after a pleasant dance at James Warner's, on Kangaroo
Point, Prior and I from pure jollity indulged in a fistic open-
handed spar in the presence of two or three ladies, who had
not yet put on their cloaks, and who were highly amused at
the harmless fun. Nearly forty years later I met him strolling on the North Quay. He told me he had been walking
to the old Milton Cemetery, and I remarked casually that
Robert Little's first wife was buried there, and Prior said,
"Yes; and by the way, do you know there is news by cable
that Robert Little himself is dead in Ceylon?" I was the
first one to tell him of the awful wreck of the "Quetta,"
where so many of his friends were lost, and I shall not
readily forget his change of countenance at the sad news.
The last time I saw Mr. Prior was at his rooms in Parliament House, when he spoke of H. Stuart Russell, who
wrote the "Genesis of Queensland," and whom Prior saw
shortly before at Adelaide, en route to London, and so altered
from *the* Russell of the "fifties" that he did not recognise
him until he began, as Prior said, to "talk Queensland."
Mr. Prior was certainly the most courtly and polished of
the early pioneers here, and spoken disloyalty about the
Queen was one of the few matters that had power to make
him openly angry.

Joshua Peter Bell.

And Sir Joshua Peter Bell. His death was an awfully
sudden one. How well I remember the shock which was
occasioned the community when the news of the death of
the one man whom everybody admired and respected was

circulated. His demise occurred on the 20th December, 1881. He had a day or two before returned from a trip to the South, and, if anything, was apparently in a better state of health than usual. On the day of the sad event he was engaged in finishing whatever business he had to do in Brisbane, in order that he might spend Christmas with his family at his home—Jimbour. Thus engaged, he called at the Bank of Australasia, and, while there, spoke to Mr. Dixon, the manager, of a passing sensation of illness. It seemed to be nothing serious, however, and both gentlemen got into a cab to drive up Queen-street. They had hardly gone a hundred yards when Sir Joshua's head drooped forward, and he became partly unconscious. The cab was of course stopped, and everything possible done, but it was of no avail, and he expired shortly afterwards.

Sir Joshua was born in Kildare, Ireland, on the 19th of January, 1827, and had therefore nearly completed his 55th year at the time of his death. Although not actually a native of this continent, he was virtually an Australian, having been brought to Sydney as a child four years old and educated in that city. He came to Queensland in 1847, and, in conjunction with other members of his family, became part owner of what was then the magnificent station Jimbour, which has remained his home ever since. When Queensland was separated from New South Wales, Mr. Bell's prominent position as a leading squatter naturally induced him to enter public life, and he was first elected to the Assembly as one of the members for West Moreton in 1863. He soon made his mark in Parliament, and in December, 1864, was offered and accepted the position of Treasurer in the Herbert Ministry. He kept the position when that Ministry merged into the Macalister Government, the last-named gentleman taking the departments of Lands and Works, Mr. Mackenzie that of Colonial Secretary, and

Mr. Lilley becoming Attorney-General. In further reorganisations of the Government, Mr. Bell took charge of the Lands Office in August, 1866, and became Acting-Minister for Works in May, 1867. At the general election of June, 1867, Mr. Bell was again returned for West Moreton in conjunction with Messrs. P. O'Sullivan and G. Thorn. Next year, 1868, Mr. Bell was elected for Northern Downs, and continued to sit for that constituency for some years. In March, 1871, he again accepted the position of Treasurer in the Ministry formed by Mr. Palmer, and held it till that gentleman resigned in January, 1874. At the general election of the preceding year, 1873, under the new Act which had re-distributed and increased the number of electorates, Mr. Bell was returned for Dalby (the seat now held by Mr. Joshua T. Bell—a worthy son of a worthy father), which seat he held till the general election of 1878, when he was again returned by Northern Downs. On the 3rd April, 1879, he resigned his seat in the Assembly to accept the position of President of the Legislative Council, which he held till his death. About three weeks prior to his death he received the honour of knighthood from Her Majesty.

Mr. Bell's career as a public man was characterised by the strictest integrity and honourable dealing. Though not a brilliant orator, his words were well chosen, and he always commanded the respect and attention of Parliament. As Treasurer he displayed a good deal of practical ability, and as a politician he was liked and respected, even by those divided from him by the broadest lines of party demarcation. As a citizen he was a thoroughly popular man. The sentiment entertained for him was not merely respect and esteem, but positive personal liking among thousands who hardly even knew him by sight. This was due in great part to the unfailing courtesy which he always displayed in his intercourse with high and low. It was a courtesy which was natural, the index to a kindly disposition. He had the rare gift of being able to maintain his own views, and take his own part in politics and business, without making enemies of his opponents. Always freely tolerating those who differed from him, he earned from them the same consideration. It is a significant fact that, although a squatter whose run was in part given up to selection, and although associated in politics with what was known as the squatting party, he was always on the best of terms with the selectors. So great was his personal popularity and influence that the electorates in his own district furnished seats which might almost be said to have been at his disposal. And bushmen from one end of Queensland to another spoke of Jimbour as the place where the old-fashioned Australian hospitality was to be found in its perfection. Enterprising in business, ready to take part in all schemes for the industrial advancement of the colony, Sir Joshua was equally active in the encouragement of its sports and pastimes. He was a great patron of the turf, and, as owner of racing stock, had made a reputation throughout Australia for honourable dealing.

Sir Joshua Peter Bell was a singularly fortunate man. Blessed with an even temper, possessed of everything which was calculated to lend zest to existence, in the full strength and vigour of manhood, surrounded by friends and companions not one of whom ever grudged him for a moment the honour and the distinction which had come to him, what mortal man could have been deemed more fortunate? If at times there were difficulties to be overcome, they were met with an even mind, which maintained its supremacy and asserted its superiority with confident ability. Sir Joshua Peter Bell was not an ambitious man in the sense of putting forward any great efforts to attain the rewards of office or of political position. Equably and unostentatiously he went on his way, without apparently attempting to win anything, and yet he won many things which are regarded as well worth having—wealth, honour, distinction, and, more than all these, the unaffected regard and esteem of his countrymen. He was a typical representative of the first generation of his Australian countrymen. He was a public-spirited man, patriotic in the best sense, a man who would make no ostentatious professions, but one who would dare a good deal, one who would have done much and sacrificed much if he had been called upon to do so in the path of duty.

> 'Twas ever so ; and those we least would spare
> Are taken from us in what seems their prime
> But is not ; in a life like his has been
> Years fifty-five stand good for three-score ten.
> For there was work to do in those old days
> When youthful Joshua—he of Jimbour—stirred
> And laid foundation of those princely farms
> Which dazzle moderns with their wealth of fleece.
> A genial Celt ; he spared not himself ;
> Rode hard, by night or day 'twas all the same,
> For he had cattle good, and ne'er could creep
> Nor planned to lengthen out a slippered age.
>
> Peace to him, gentles : we who knew him young.
> And watched him as he journeyed to mid-age,
> Swear knighthood added nothing to *his* shield.
> He's passed : a pioneer of Darling Downs,
> Gone to join Deuchar, Kent, and good men true :
> And maids and children of that region fair,
> In days to come, shall speak of Joshua Bell.
> We, holding faith in the unhurried past,
> Will trust the unhurrying future and its God
> To do what seems Him best in His good time,
> Whose centuries are but moments to the wise.

Edwin Norris.

Edwin Norris, solicitor, died at Townsville. He was, nevertheless, an old *Brisbane* identity, and was once in the office of Mr. Robert Little. He was an enthusiastic yachtsman and astronomer, and purchased the telescope and observatory fittings of the late Captain O'Reilly. He was one of the few now left of those who took part in the historical cricket match between Brisbane and Ipswich, played at Chuwar, the "North Shore" of Ipswich, during the June race week of 1859, when Dr. Cannan, Shepherd Smith, Edwin Norris, Colin Munro (now of the Burdekin River), C. F. Bell, Walter Birley (of Kangaroo Point), and others made up the Brisbane team, and the Ipswich eleven were recruited from a host of batting and bowling talent then newly imported by the Banks of Australasia and New South Wales in the shape of tellers and accountants from those two "hives" of cricket—Maitland and Launceston; Coulson, Manighan, Logan, Harry Glassford, T. O. Bryant, &c. Mr. Sladen, M.L.A., of Melbourne, was a spectator, and the scores were: Ipswich, 99 and 43; Brisbane, 65 and 14, Shepherd Smith getting crippled by a blow on the ankle early in the game. The return match came off in October, in Brisbane, near the North Quay. It was a hollow win for the metropolis with 322 runs on the first innings—Bolger, top score with 118, including an 8, hit into the river from the back of Aubigny.

JAMES WARNER.

James Warner was one of the three surveyors—Dixon (chief), Warner, and Staplyton, the latter being, with a man named Tuck, cruelly butchered near Mount Lindsay—who, about the year 1839, were sent by Governor Gipps to Moreton Bay, first to make a coastal survey, and afterwards to survey the place prior to free settlement. He also assisted in the survey of Ipswich and other towns now included in Queensland, and played an important part in the attempted settlement of "Northern Australia" about 1847, when, owing to the dearth of labour, it was sought to revive convicts and ticket-of-leave immigration. This scheme, however, as most colonists know, was rudely shattered by the striking of the "Lord Auckland" on a rock just prior to landing—in fact while an impressive ceremony of landing was being arranged. Up to 1884 the deceased gentleman filled the position of a surveyor in the Lands Department, and on the retirement of Mr. Douglas was, on on the recommendation of the then Speaker, appointed Sergeant-at-Arms. This position he filled up to his death. A better man never left us; full of genial fun and jokes. He could read aloud the Bible to youthful hearers with a pathos and heartfelt intonation which some archbishop might envy. He learned to sail a boat in early life on dark stormy nights in the English Channel, and could handle one with anybody in Moreton Bay. During the fifty years he was connected with the Survey Office he got through an incredible amount of field and office work in connection with his profession. He married the widow of Captain Lindo, of the merchant service, and his hospitable home on Kangaroo Point will be long remembered by those who were young in 1850-60, when a dance at Warner's was the best in Brisbane. He left several daughters, one married to Mr. W. V. Brown, M.L.A., of Townsville; another to Mr. F. Lord, of Eskdale, and a third to Mr. A. Briggs, of Darling Downs. His genial good humour was with him to the last. He comically complained to the writer that he was getting old and cross, for he found that if after spending three weeks at a map, some one upset the ink over it, he was apt to lose his temper, as he would not have done thirty years ago.

ROBERT DOUGLAS.

Robert Douglas was in Brisbane over fifty years ago. He began life in his new home as a farmer near Ipswich, and afterwards established the first complete soap-boiling plant in Moreton Bay. A huge boiler, rolled over before being put in position at his works on Kangaroo Point in 1854, by its noise caused terrified people in North Brisbane to imagine that a Russian and English frigate were fighting in the Bay, and to contemplate sending the women and children to the back of Mount Coot-tha for safety in case of the worst. Mr. Douglas had a happy knack of making all friends and no enemies through life, and his breezy waterside place on Kangaroo Point was (in any year that began with 185—) the scene of those pleasant Saturday afternoon reunions, when "every one knew everybody" in Brisbane, and when impromptu pulling races and quoits for the gentlemen, assisted by "square gin," with tea and music for the ladies, and a round game or dance in the evening, used to finish the week's work pleasantly, and "round off" the Saturday afternoons all the year round in a satisfactory manner. *Eheu fugaces*, &c. Mr. Douglas was Sergeant-at-Arms in the Legislative Assembly of Queensland from 1874 till 1884, when he resigned.

SIMEON LORD.

Simeon Lord, of Brisbane, was not merely an old resident of Brisbane, but also of Tasmania in bygone days. He was the father of the late Robert Lord, one time member for Gympie, and he owned the fine pastoral property known as Eskdale, on the Upper Brisbane River. The name of Lord is borne by a large number of disconnected families in Australia; there was Mr. Edward Lord, of Drayton, in this colony, a pioneer of 1841, and father of Mrs. George Raff; they are numerous also in Sydney, where a Mr. Lord was city treasurer at one time; while in Tasmania there were three or four distinct families of the name: Edward Lord, of Lawrenny; Lord, of Orielton; and Simeon Lord, of

Hon. A. Macalister.   Hon. John Douglas.
    Sir Charles Lilley.
Hon. James Taylor.   Sir A. Hodgson.

Avoca; another Simeon Lord, who owned property at Botany, near Sydney, died, more than fifty years back, in that city. The Simeon Lord, of Brisbane, was a man of business energy and sterling integrity, in whom the healthy climate of Tasmania laid (as it has done with many others) the foundation of a long, useful, and busy life.

Taylor Winship.

Captain Taylor Winship, of Cleveland, was one of the oldest residents in Brisbane. He arrived here before 1848, and one of his first tasks was the building, for Messrs. James Reid and Thomas Boyland, of the river steamer "Hawk," the successor to James Canning Pearce's "Experiment," and which, unlike the latter boat, was a financial success. In the building of the "Hawk," Mr. James Barr, shipwright, assisted. Boyland commanded her, and her "bones" now lie in a river of North Queensland after some twelve or fifteen years of successful trade on the Brisbane and Bremer Rivers. Mr. Reid afterwards had Camboon station, on the Dawson River. Mr. Barr rebuilt Harris's wharf in 1855, when it slid one morning into the river through one of those vexatious landslips for which the North Quay has always been so notorious. Captain Winship and his family had a beautiful orangery and garden on the river bank in 1853 and 1854, near the south end of Victoria Bridge. He was one of the marine experts who, with Captain Richard James Coley (Lloyd's agent and surveyor), officially visited the wreck of the "Phœbe Dunbar," immigrant ship, Captain Tucker, in the South Passage in May, 1856. He was one of the few remaining types of the old school of Australian master mariners, and was a sailor and agriculturist in one. Captain Winship also built the "Swallow" and the "Bremer."

JAMES SUTHERLAND MITCHELL.

James Sutherland Mitchell died in Sydney a year or two ago. He was a very old Australian colonist, and connected to some extent with Queensland also. He was originally, in the "forties," in the Commissariat Department at Hobart, and married a daughter of Commissary James Laidley, who died at Sydney in 1835. Mr. Mitchell was consequently a brother-in-law of Messrs. T. S. Mort and Henry Mort. He subsequently became manager of a fire insurance company in Sydney, and in the year 1856 the managership of the Kent Brewery was offered to the author, and on his declining it in favour of the then brighter prospects of the projected new colony, Mr. Mitchell was offered and accepted the position, and died extremely wealthy. He was a director of the Joint Stock Bank and Peak Downs Copper Mine in 1872, and visited Queensland in 1863 with Mr. Abraham Fitzgibbon, the projector of the first local railway from Ipswich to Toowoomba. After the death of his first wife Mr. Mitchell married a sister of the late Sir George Wigram Allen, Speaker of the New South Wales Assembly. He was a gifted and scientific man, and author of some very valuable experiments on the strength and tenacity of Australian timber; while, as a wood carver, his amateur efforts in the way of gigantic picture frames, reproducing birds, fruits, and flowers with marvellous fidelity, would almost vie with the masterly productions of artists like Grinling Gibbons. He was a genial and large-hearted man, and left a stainless record behind him as one more of the now fast sundering links left us with the Australia of the "quiet forties."

CHAPTER XI.

The Roll Call—Old Time Queenslanders—Additions to the List—Richard F. Phelan—Walter Scott—H. P. Fox—Richard S. Warry—George Harris—W. J. Munce—Thomas Lade—Robert Cribb—Henry Jordan—T. B. Stephens—A New Generation.

Richard Fitzgerald Phelan.

RICHARD FITZGERALD PHELAN could claim to be one of the pioneer colonists of Brisbane; and, by "pioneers," I mean those who were here not only before separation, but before the Crimean War. Mr. Phelan was one of the early storekeepers of Brisbane, and built his wooden warehouse and carried on business where the valuable "Australian" corner now is. He subsequently sold the building and land to the late Henry Buckley for £900 (a fair price in those days), and Charles Trundle, sen., carried on the business till Thomas Hayes bought the corner from Mr. Buckley. Mr. Phelan afterwards held office for many years in the local branch of the Bank of New South Wales, and must have been well advanced in years at the time of his death, his brother, in the sheriff's office at Sydney, having passed away fully eighteen years ago. Mr. Phelan married a lady from Philadelphia, and was a prominent and zealous member of the Anglican Church in Brisbane, and highly esteemed for his genuine and sterling integrity. The men who linked ancient with modern Brisbane are rapidly passing from us, and none were more respected, or more worthy of it, than the late R. F. Phelan.

Walter Scott.

The death of Walter Scott, of Taromeo station, removed the last survivor of the old resident pioneer squatters of the Upper Brisbane River and South Burnett districts, all so well known in "Brisbane town," in the "forties" and the "fifties." All have now passed away. Balfour and Forbes, of Colinton, and Donald Mackenzie, of the same; Barker, of Nanango; David M'Connel and Alpin Cameron, of Cressbrook; Ivory, of Eskdale; Mortimer, of Manumbar; Clapperton, of Tarong; Mactaggart, of Kilkivan; Lawless, of Boobyjan; T. Jones, of Barambah; and D. M. Jones, of Boonara, are, one and all, mere memories now; as is also Tooth, of Widgee, where Gympie now is. It will be noted how most of the above were from the land of the tartan and "pibroch," the very cradle of pioneers and explorers —time-honoured old Scotland! Mr. Scott lived for forty years at Taromeo, longer than is usual on most Queensland stations by their occupants; though in New South Wales, the older colony, the Suttors held Wyagden for sixty-five years, and the Rouses, of Guntawang (whose grandparents landed in Sydney in 1801), could possibly show a still longer holding. Turning from the past to the future, it is probable that in another fifty years' time Widgee, Glastonbury, Nanango, Kilkivan, Boobyjan, Manumbar, and other places in the "golden belt" of the South Burnett district, will employ more hands in mining operations than in pastoral and agricultural work combined, when time, capital, and labour shall have brought their mineral capabilities more into notice than at present.

H. P. Fox.

H. P. Fox, of New Farm-road, was also a very old colonist, one of the arrivals in the forties. He belonged to an old Kentish family, and was a brother-in-law of Mr. Wm. Bailey (another of the Kentish waterside boat-building fraternity), who used to "fix up" yachts and skiffs for Thomas Jones, of Barambah and New Farm (brother-in-law of Sir R. R. Mackenzie), in 1856 and thereabouts, in the early boat-racing days of Brisbane, and when the better classes of Brisbane who lived by the river side used to come to town as often in a boat as in a buggy, for the river was always a well-kept road, which the other one was not. Mr. Fox was father of Mr. Fox the lithographer to the Survey Department, and of Mr. Fox the partner of Mr. Unmack, the solicitor. He belonged to a class, happily numerous in Queensland—the noncomformist teetotaller one. He had daughters, as well as sons, of whom were Mrs. Carvosso, Mrs. G. J. Walker, and Mrs. Buck, of Sandgate, and his descendants must be pretty numerous. Like all Kentish people he was an enthusiastic admirer of cricket, and could be seen every Saturday in the Queen's Park on the same seat, year after year, till near his death, when his failing eyesight rendered him unable to distinguish his favourite bats, and he had to part with that long enjoyed pleasure.

Richard S. Warry.

Richard S. Warry began business in Queen-street, Brisbane, about the year 1853. He afterwards built that fine brick store next to the Royal Hotel, and subsequently the Q.N. Bank's first office. When first erected, in 1862, it was the most substantial edifice in Queen-street. The deceased gentleman long survived his brothers. Thomas, who died in 1864, was a chemist, on the site of Mr. Beesley's present establishment, and Charles Warry was a chemist in

Ipswich, and died at the early age of 38. Soon afterwards, their father, when hale and hearty at the age of 78, lost his life by a slip between a steamer and wharf down the river, and the consequent shock to the system. The sisters, Mrs. Hugh Bell and Mrs. G. L. Pratten, are now the only local survivors of the family, which came from Dorset, in the old country.

GEORGE HARRIS.

George Harris spent his early youth in Victoria and New South Wales, and, like most Australian young men of spirit, worked at the diggings in the former place, his "mates" (if I remember rightly) being Captain Sholl and the late Donald Coutts, of Jondaryan and Bulimba. Mr. Harris, with his brother John, his sister and mother, arrived in Brisbane about 1847, and carried on business first at South Brisbane, and afterwards at Short-street, on a site purchased from James Gibbon. George Harris was a gentleman of great vital business energy and hospitality. The writer has known him in 1855 and 1857 to clear out and pile up the merchandise in his capacious store at the Short-street wharf, cover it up with red and blue blankets and white calico in a decorative style, and give a grand dance and supper on the premises to the leading people of Brisbane, the proceedings lasting till 4 a.m., when he, having shaken hands with the last guest, would set to work, replace the merchandise, and be at full swing of business again at 9 a.m., without one minute of sleep, and without having lost a moment of the working business hours in the twenty-four. But "sanitary" science (from a municipal standpoint) was then unknown in Brisbane, and every one was strong and healthy.

W. J. MUNCE.

W. J. Munce was an "old identity" alike of Sydney and of Brisbane. Bott, one of the shipping and mercantile pioneers of Sydney, left his property at death to his old friend Munce, who arrived in Brisbane in October, 1859, to open business for Christopher Newton and Co., of Sydney. He was an ardent and practical supporter of the Volunteer movement, which sprung into existence in Brisbane and all over the British Empire in 1860. He purchased from me the land on Wickham-terrace, where he built the house successively occupied by Dr. Fullerton, Sir James Garrick, Mr. Alexander Stewart, and Dr. Rendle. Messrs. Christopher Newton and Co.'s store in Eagle-street, where that of Messrs. D. L. Brown and Co.'s now stands, was the only building in Brisbane which, in 1868, was considered large enough and safe enough to give a ball to the Duke of Edinburgh in, when H.R.H. proposed the health of "The Ladies."

Thomas Lade.

Thomas Lade, of Upper Kedron Brook, was a veteran colonist, and died in his 89th year, after forty-two years of residence here. A farmer in Kent, he was a farmer here also, and in the early days his Isabella grapes, poultry, honeycomb, and butter were famous. Had there been a "social column" in those days we should have read of the pleasant riding parties organised amongst the "upper ten" to "Lade's" which used to be the fashion in Brisbane in the afternoon of a summer's day in the "fifties and sixties," the pleasure-seekers coming back laden with grapes or other spoil, which gave an object to the "outing." Mr. Lade delighted to climb in summer time to the level summit of Mount Bartley, a big hill which extended from Upper Kedron to The Gap, and he used to say that it was at midsummer "a blanket and a suit of clothes cooler than Brisbane was." His "young friend," Mott, another ancient, missed him like many more of us did, and he was the last of the aged trio who held out so long, the others being W. Duckett White and Robert Cribb. Mr. Lade was the father of Mr. J. J. Lade, and uncle of the late Mr. N. Lade.

ROBERT CRIBB.

The death of Robert Cribb would, in the mind of an ordinary modern Queenslander, only give rise to a passing feeling of wonder that any one could live to be 88 in such an enervating climate. But, to the old residents of the "fifties," the well known and time-honoured name recalls the days when Brisbane was sylvan, primitive, and sweet-aired, up to its very heart in Queen-street. The "Pascoe Fawkner" of Queensland remembered the battle of Waterloo, and was alive when Nelson breathed his last in the cockpit of the "Victory," the last surviving "youths" of Trafalgar (such as Sartorius and Tynmore) being now for some time dead and aged high up in the "nineties." How well I remember "Bob" Cribb on the paddle box of the old "Yarra" (September, 1859) eating his basin of bread and milk in the open, as he voyaged to take his seat for Moreton Bay in the Sydney Parliament. He was "aye sound" on the subject of coolies and convicts in South Queensland, for North Queensland and its wants did not then exist. He held that £1 an acre was the lowest sensible price for land, to keep the Jay Goulds at bay. And the *Courier* spoke of him as "that indefatigable old 'die-hard,' honest Bob Cribb" during the hot political separation days. His simplicity and kindness in rendering assistance to others, to his own detriment at times, were only paralleled by what another old resident once did. Walking with a friend, he was accosted by a borrower, who asked for £12 and tendered a £20 diamond ring as security. The £12 was handed over, and the ring as well. When the borrower had gone the friend said, "Why did you part with the ring? you have now no security." "Oh! (said the lender, with exquisite simplicity) if I had taken his ring I should have stopped him from getting more money when he wanted it."

HENRY JORDAN.

Henry Jordan, who represented South Brisbane so long and so well, and than whom no man was better or more favourably known in Queensland politics, was the son of a Wesleyan minister, and, although born at Lincoln, was descended from an old Devonshire family, who possessed a considerable estate in Dartmoor, which, though long since passed into Chancery, still bears the family name. In early life he had unusual advantages in the tuition of his father, a man of broad views and scholarly attainments, who combined with the studies of languages and science, that of political economy. He was for some time at Kingswood College, Bristol, and afterwards studied medicine with Dr. Body, of London. His health failing, he went to America, and after seeing and enjoying the wonders of the New World, returned to work, choosing dentistry as his profession. He studied at the London Institution, and also under Mr. Crampton and Sir Edwin Saunders, and practised successfully in the good old town of Derby for ten years. Being a man of deep religious feeling, he felt at length compelled to offer himself for the Church, and thought of taking orders under the Bishop of Nottingham, but the Wesleyan Missionary Society urged his coming to Australia. Uncertain of his health, he came out at his own expense (not wishing to burden the Society) and entered upon mission work in a country district at Mount Barker, South Australia, where the unusual fatigue and exposure were too great for him, and he was compelled to abandon the work for which he had given up his practice, his country, and his home.

He then went to Sydney, and resumed his old profession,

entering into partnership with Mr. David Fletcher, the well-known dentist of that city. In 1856 he came to Brisbane. He at once entered heartily into all the interests of the young colony, ever ready to sacrifice his own for his country's good. He was a member of the first Parliament. For several successive Parliaments he represented important constituencies, and, as Agent-General for Immigration, Registrar-General, and Minister for Lands, did faithful service, and his enthusiasm, self-sacrifice, and great success in the cause of immigration are historical records. In religion he was a member and lay preacher of the Wesleyan Church, though greatly deploring her secession from the mother Church, and her many unhappy divisions. He called himself "an old Church Methodist." At the request of Bishop Hale, for more than two years he acted as chaplain to the Brisbane Gaol. In private life Mr. Jordan was reserved and somewhat exclusive, and possessed the old-fashioned courtesy and high code of honour, too rare, unhappily, in these modern days. It may be claimed for him that he was, to use the words of his early friend, Sir Charles Nicholson, the first President of the Queensland Legislative Council, "A scholar, a gentleman, and a Christian." He married a daughter of the Rev. Nathaniel Turner, whose name, as one of the earliest missionaries to New Zealand and the South Seas, is well known and revered.

Mr. Jordan was also a member of the first Board of Education in Queensland, and represented the city of Brisbane in the first session of the first Parliament. He was Commissioner and Agent-General for Immigration from January, 1861, to December, 1866; and subsequent to his return from England engaged in sugar planting in the Logan district. Mr. Jordan sat in the Legislative Assembly as representative of East Moreton from 1868 to 1871; and four years later was appointed Registrar-General, an office which he held till 1883. In that year he was elected junior member for South Brisbane, his colleague being the late Mr. Simon Fraser. On the death of the Hon. W. Miles (Minister for Works), the Hon. C. B. Dutton, then Minister for Lands, was transferred to the Department of Mines and Works, and Mr. Jordan was intrusted with the care of the Lands Department. At the general election of 1888 Mr. Jordan was elected senior member for South Brisbane, which position he held up to the time of his death. In 1889 he was offered a seat in the Upper House, but declined it.

Henry Jordan was a good man. There is a spot in one of the lobbies of the House, where he paused for a moment or two every day when on his way to the Legislative Chamber, to ask Divine aid and blessing. The one action in all his Parliamentary career on which he looked back with satisfaction, was his motion for opening the House with prayer, thus laying the foundation stone of the new colony on Christian principles. One other mistake he would not have wished uncorrected, and that was his statement that his want of success in sugar-planting was "the result of white labour." The white labour was highly successful. He employed thirty or forty men at good wages; these men were chiefly farmers or sons of farmers around, who came to him season after season, and a feeling of mutual goodwill and esteem was then formed, which has lasted as long as his life, and to some of these men, or their children, he owed his frequent return to Parliament. He has stated that he made more money in one year's sugar-growing than in any other one year of his life. Insufficient capital, high rate of interest, and three successive years of frost, induced him to discontinue the work. He gave up good practice and prospects to go home in the cause of emigration, for an inadequate allowance, which he had to supplement with his own private means. He was afterwards reimbursed by the

Government, but not until after great loss and anxiety. When the Australian Land and Mortgage Company offered him the position of their first manager, with a salary of £1500 per annum and other emoluments, he refused, and kept his faith with his adopted country. He has had presented to him many means of enriching himself, but these, with his sensitive code of honour, he deemed questionable, and he steadfastly declined them all. He kept his hands pure to the end. He was content to live and die a comparatively poor man, but he left to his children a rich legacy—the record of a noble, patient, self-denying life.

T. B. STEPHENS.

T. B. Stephens! Yes! we remember him, a long time ago; as far back as 1852. It was our lot, then, to stand behind the counter of the old Bank of New South Wales in Sydney, a "crib" long since pulled down, and the site covered with busy offices. We used to stand behind the counter and take the money, and "T. B." (then of the firm of Maude and Stephens, and in the wool line) used to come to pay plenty of it in. He looked young enough then, but he always affected the same quiet suit of homespun-looking colonial tweed. We were destined to meet again and live in the same house, and, a couple of years later, Brisbane was the scene of our operations, at the time when the Siege of Sebastopol was in its infancy, which we used to discuss as mortals now do the Shipka Pass. He was seldom without his faithful pipe, even then forming perhaps the only weakness alike in his character and constitution. His pungent Lancastrian dialect was unmistakeable, and he sought out his countrymen clannishly; and Grimes the elder — one of those wiry men, who never show age till the final moment comes — was an early quest in Stephens' rambles in those bygone days. We had no politics, no caste, no officials here during the Crimean War, and it was both amusing and amazing to hear Robert Ramsay Mackenzie, *circa* 1856, a high Australian Tory of the day, knowing chiefly such *ultra* men as Stuart Donaldson, the first Premier of New South Wales—it was "immense," we repeat, to hear R. R. M. say, of the homespun, plain spoken, tweed clad T. B. S., and after a short and sharp confab on the wharf—Where was it, by the way? Raff's? Ah! we forget now : n'importe—that he had never met with a more respectable man in his life, nor one who had so mightily convinced and surprised him as did the earnest, broad-tongued, Chartist sort of individual he had encountered so casually. R. R. M. never entered the Sydney Parliament. He drew the line "somewheres" you know, but in his Queensland politics we fancy there was, perhaps, just a soupçon of the Stephens proselyting leaven. Well! the world kept on moving round, and we got "separation," and T. B. was grievously "licked" by John Watts, at Toowoomba first election, but the Lancaster man, like more of his race, was not to be denied. He came again and was, for fifteen or twenty years, more before the public and less with the writer than of yore. We ourselves don't like to pester Colonial Treasurers and Ministers for Lands. Goodness knows! they have enough of it with others; and we like to leave them alone, no matter how well we may have previously known them, as we would not willingly be even suspected of requiring Government office or patronage. Not that "T. B." would have been a bad friend, if one had been so situate; for he never forgot an old chum. We first met and lived at M'Cabe's old hotel in South Brisbane in 1854, and he remained faithful to his first love till the last, bought land and built and made his workshops on that side of the river. He was not the stuff of which poets or painters are made, but neither England nor Australia would be what they are without the aid and presence of such men, and in abundance, too. Happy is the man who knows his own faults and his own perfections, for we all have some of both, though variedly dealt out. Happy the man who cultivates the possible in his character, and lets the impossible "rip," and who does not blindly mistake his faults for his perfections, as too many of us are apt to do. And now for the subject of our discourse, we will

> "No longer seek his merits to disclose,
> Nor draw his frailties from that dread abode
> Where both alike in trembling hope repose—
> The bosom of his Father and his God."

From the archives of the not very distant past, I could take down the records of many more pioneers. But necessity knows no law: especially that necessity which takes the shape of a printer's fiat, which demands that you shall say what you have to say in so many pages and no more.

The old folks go, and the young generation of youths and maidens spring up in Brisbane and elsewhere in Queensland, but the steamy torrid Decembers never change nor fail with the damp breeze; and the saturating heat and the strong tremendous resultant life that shoots forth in every scion of the tree and vegetable kingdom. And the ferry boats carry over the gay and smartly dressed folk to church in 1894 even as they did in 1854, only it is not the same river, nor the same boat; and it is the grand-children of the grand-parents who figure on the scene to-day. Two generations have passed, and cemeteries have been filled and biographies have been written since the fifties you know. Yes! old Job Pratten, Tom Perrin, Geo. Thorn (shall I mention the list?) were with us, and the twang of the "Zummerzetsheer" and the "Hampsheer" man echoed time and again in the tropic scrub mid the orchids and staghorns of Queensland, where erst "Biro" and Yarran and Weurum-neurum were the only sounds. But now both tongues are silent, and English as she is spoke in mother Queensland by the new generation reigns in their stead.

How delightful were the early mornings? How pure the mountain air on the neutral ground between the Darling Downs above, and Tent Hill and Helidon below the range? What strong life it put into one even to breathe it? How the girls of '43 who were grandmothers in '93 used to "set their caps" at the comely youths of the manly "cross-country" breed, but generally married the other fellow after all. For though money was scarce and fortunes few, and business matters seemed petty by comparison with present expansion, yet life was never since the creation more thoroughly enjoyed than it was by "boys and girls" alike in the scanty settled districts country of early Australian days. For indeed it was life! life! life! that thrilled and pulsated through every fibre of the body, and every idea and aim of the mind as well.

CHAPTER XII.

The Capital of Queensland—Brisbane—Its Features and Characteristics—The First Survey—Sir George Gipps—Old Day Ocean Travelling—Amusing Incidents—Mc Scotty's Triumph—Road Making Extraordinary—Philip D. Vigers—Jovial Evenings—Early Sugar Days—South Brisbane—Sea Sick Travellers—The Queensland Club—Its Founders—The Financial Crisis of '66—How it all Happened.

BRISBANE cannot be said to head the list of Australian cities in point of beauty, but still it is equally far from being at the tail of the race. It lacks two great essentials in scenery, viz., church spires and snow-topped mountains. There is plenty of water, an element without which no scenery is perfect; and divested of which the finest landscape is but as a beautiful woman with her eyes put out. Brisbane is little, if any, inferior to Hobart and Sydney, as we will presently prove, and far surpasses Melbourne and Adelaide from the artists' point of view. Hobart—with its clean, sharp-cut, whitey-brown stone streets, rising in terraces from the harbour, its open blue bay and its lofty but lesser hill sites, which would be reckoned giants anywhere near Brisbane, but which nestle dwarfed at the foot of Mount Wellington 4,196 feet high, snow-topped, with a broad saddle summit; and a noble overhung basaltic cliff, 700 feet sheer, near the summit, and which looks

Mr. Christopher Rolleston.   Sir A. H. Palmer.
Mr. G. E. Dalrymple.   Mr. Matthew Goggs.
Mr. W. Bowman.   Sir R. R. Mackenzie.

more like seventy feet poised up there in the air—sits supreme in ostentatious beauty amongst her Australian sisters. This splendid background of mountain, only some three or four miles from the city, is to Hobart what Vesuvius is to Naples, and the Table Mountain to Cape Town, except that old "Wellington" is a cool thousand feet or so over the heads of the pair of these lesser lights. Sydney, again, with its harbour, like a delicious sandy beached Highland loch, embosomed in bold, shrub-clad hills; and its church spires and dense city glimmering in the haze of the setting sun as seen from the heights over Vaucluse at eventide, and backed up by the distant sandstone gorges and trackless defiles of the Blue Mountains, is almost a perfect picture, and the "almost" could be rewritten "quite" were there a snow-clad peak handy to the spot, for everything else about it is complete. But Melbourne, with all its fine public buildings and broad streets, its handsome suburbs and grand shops, lies too flat by the banks of the Yarra ditch; and with never a mountain to swear by save distant solitary Macedon, a mere dwarf of some 2,400 feet or so, and the still lower ranges of the Plenty and Dandenong. Melbourne, therefore, must look for her laurels in some other line than the picturesque. Adelaide, too, with all its well-built streets and busy marts, can raise no admiration for its dried up little brooklet of a Torrens River. And Geelong, despite its "Station Peak," its blue mud bay, and its rising terrace site, fails somehow to catch and fill the eye as such a place ought to do. Brisbane is more comparable with Launceston than with any other Australian town. There is the same fine broad tidal river, tapping the up-country and stretching away in time to the blue water. But the Bremer hardly can rank with the lovely South Esk, neither is there any roaring cataract of 100 feet at Brisbane; nor would the highest bank on the Brisbane River, viz., Mount Ommanney,

Q

barely 200 feet high, near Woogaroo, make any show by the side of the bold hills, 900 feet high, which border the Tamar below Launceston, near where is, or was, the seat of Captain Niley. Neither, again, does the Brisbane ever spread out into such a noble lake as Swan Bay, on the Tamar. But Brisbane can crow, too; for her river is navigable higher up, while Launceston is at the very head of hers, and the scenery of Brisbane proper surpasses that of Launceston almost as much as the climate of the latter is preferable to the other; in proof of which, let us ascend Wickham-terrace by way of a commencement, and make a few notes. We find that Brisbane city proper lies chiefly on a bend of the river, which makes a cape pointing to the south-east. And the city is well provided with "lungs," for on the north-west are the Wickham-terrace reserves; on the south-east are the Queen's Park and Botanic Gardens; and on the north-east and south-west lies the river, fully a thousand feet wide. These four breathing spots, which encircle a straggling built city of less than a hundred acres in area, should give it air enough in all conscience. And, looking from Wickham-terrace, to the south-west are just visible the Darling Downs, those famous pastoral reservoirs of nutritious herbage, which have filled so many purses; made fat so many bank accounts; caused so many lawsuits; engendered so much political "bile," and rancour; broken so many hearts and firms in early pioneer days; but which are still, for all that, the brightest gem for their size in the mammoth crown of our Queensland. And before proceeding any further we will briefly dwell on the one particular advantage which Brisbane possesses over any other city in Australia. She is environed by scattered irregular hills, which vary from 150 feet to 2,000 feet in height, and all within a radius of fifteen miles of the General Post Office; then, secondly, she has a very wide and very winding river; and, thirdly, the sea in all its glory is only ten miles away. Now, to any one who knows what scenery is, these three elements of beauty will tell a tale of ever-changing and diversified arrangements of forest, water, farm, ocean, buildings, mountain, gardens, as the point of view is shifted from hill to hill. You can see the beauty of Sydney and Hobart by standing close in front of them; but the beauties of Brisbane (and they are far beyond what any stranger, or casual visitor, would suppose), must be seen from the surrounding points of view; when so viewed, they are unequalled by any city or town inland or seaboard in the colonies.

The surveyor who laid out Brisbane had been to Batavia, and wanted to make each allotment half-an-acre in this warm climate, so as to allow of fresh air and a garden round each building, but Sir George Gipps, the Governor of New South Wales, who, poor man! was but mortal and could not have been expected to foresee that in ten years more the destiny of Australia would be revolutionized by a gold discovery, protested against this "waste of Her Majesty's land," and ordered the lots to be five to the acre, put up in Brisbane at £100 per acre upset, and £8 per acre in Ipswich. It will be useful for local residents to remember that all the female named streets in Brisbane have lots of 66 feet frontage by 150 feet deep, while in the male-named streets the frontage is 74 feet by 132 feet deep. Allotments now worth £50,000 each in Queen-street were then bought at £20 over and over again; £2 deposit paid and forfeited repeatedly, as not worth the money. Notably those where the Joint Stock Bank now is.

Modern residents of Brisbane cannot realise the intense calm and quiet which reigned in our simple village forty years ago. So let me try to bring it home to them now. There are several hundreds of constables to keep the peace in Brisbane in 1892, but, in 1853 and 1854, there were *six* only : one at Kangaroo Point, two at South Brisbane, the chief (Sam. Sneyd), and two in North Brisbane, one of whom was the lock-up keeper, Mr. A. S. Wright. Sneyd was inspector of slaughter-houses, and went to see one of P. Mayne's, where "Kingsholme" is now, and he blew his whistle there, and the lockup-keeper in Queen-street heard and replied to it. Fortitude Valley was mostly bush, and had no constable, while Ipswich, Gayndah, Warwick, Maryborough, Drayton, and Dalby were allowed one or two constables each by the Sydney headquarters people : proud metropolitan Brisbane revelling in a whole six of them. No doubt the time has been when a loud whistle, aided by the wind, could have been heard in London from St. Paul's to the Elephant and Castle, or in Sydney from Dawe's Point to the Haymarket. But those days have long since passed.

There was always a great difference in the style of the departure by steamer from Sydney and Brisbane in the olden days. The Sydney boats left at night, and friends who came to see you off, lined the staircase and the cabin for the sake of the light, and took their farewells standing, and in haste, for the steamer had to call in at Newcastle and fill up with coal. Many of the northern passengers followed her on later; so late that an extra three hours could be spent at the theatre, the Brisbane boat being picked up by 11 o'clock by the Newcastle one, and then they would get aboard the Brisbane packet long before she got away. This coaling at Newcastle took place regularly in the 1855-65 era, before the Ipswich coal had begun to assert itself properly. But, to return. How different was the departure by steam from Brisbane to Sydney. All daylight work, and there was often a few hours anchorage at the bar, waiting for the tide. None of your transition in a single short hour from perfect repose to wretched sea-sickness as when coming out of Sydney, but a jolly sit-down dinner for all hands in mild water, lulled by the rattle of the rudder-chains; the sweets and viands and fruit lit up in the spink saloon by brilliant lamps. All the well-dressed ladies were in full view, and for the men New Zealand hit on with Clermont and the Condamine, while Bathurst fraternised with Adelaide, and so on. All Australia, as it were, welded into one under the introductory auspices of the genial skipper, who knew everybody, of course. Never on shore at any time, or anywhere where such rare social meetings, such bringing together of the representative people as were consummated in the old Moreton Bay coasting days in the saloons of the "Yarra," "City of Brisbane," "Telegraph," and other of the "primeval" boats—passed away like the good captains who sailed them, and the busy passengers who travelled in them.

A comic event happened after Separation. A parliamentary commission, consisting of some half-dozen, or more, of members, was appointed to travel, per rail, up country, and report on a question that affected the interior of the colony. I mention no names except two, and those will be borrowed ones. There were McScotty, the astute, and Rathmoyle, the jovial amongst the number. On the way up in the train, and in a carriage in which the former party was not, his character for drinking at other people's expense, and never "shouting" himself, was freely discussed. Good old Rathmoyle, against whom no such indictment could lie, took the absent one's part, and contended that he might not, perhaps, be as bad as he seemed, and his triumph was complete when, at the roadside inn at "Bigge's Camp," a whole case of champagne was ordered in by McScotty, to be drunk on the way up. Great was the triumph of Rathmoyle over the detractors. "There now, boys," said he, "what did I tell ye? Ye'll believe, *now*, that McScotty's not a bad fellow." The commission were silenced, and all went well up the country, where they duly performed their task, and returned to Brisbane. It was noticed that McScotty, before they got back to "Bigge's Camp," had hurried on in advance of the rest, pleading urgent business in Brisbane. The landlord at that place called Rathmoyle privately on one side, and asked him in a low voice those cabalistic words: "How about that there case of champagne, sir?" "What case?" said R. "Why, the one you gents had on the way up. Mr. McScotty said as how it was to be booked to you and no one else, Sir." There was no photographer by to perpetuate the expression on poor Rathmoyle's visage at that supreme moment, and it is a great pity, too. It would have made a picture indeed.

A Mr. Philip Doyne Vigers was, in 1855, an official of the New South Wales Government in Brisbane. He had been an army lieutenant, a fact which, in early Australian days, seemed to be held sufficient qualification for a man to fill any office outside of the church. He was appointed Superintendent of Roads for Moreton Bay, and set to work to clear the road between Brisbane and Ipswich. But, in place of stumping and clearing the trees off in the old orthodox fashion, he put men on with crosscut saws to shave the trees down at the level of the earth, and the ungrateful bushmen, who used the road, used to complain that in wet weather these wooden "tables" were more slippery than a wood pavement to a galloping horse, besides tripping him up as the earth washed away from the edge of the stump. The experiment was *not* a success, as the trees soon grew up again, and a bit of straight road near Ipswich, got up in this fashion, was known, long afterwards, as "Virger's Avenue." He was, of course, known by the witty young ladies of the period as "Poor, dear Virger," and nothing else; but there was nothing remarkable in that, seeing that Peter Dalgarno Anderson, from up north, was also known as "Poor, dear Anderson." "P. D." was an undesirable initial to bear in those days. I first met Vigers at Jerry Laidley's, at Franklyn Vale, where Jerry used to whistle the "Dewdrop" waltz, which he had newly learned, and evidently much admired. C. F. D. Parkinson made the fourth at whist with us in the evenings. The blacks were still dangerous outside Brisbane then. Sylvester Diggles and a clerk of Harris's, named Kerfoot, were in 1855 each with a double-barrelled gun across Breakfast Creek beyond where Bowen Bridge now is, and up near the present Eildon Hill, when fifty blacks came up to them, not armed with spears, but who took up stones in such a threatening manner that the guns, which had been brought out to shoot birds for stuffing, were levelled at the mob, who took the hint and did not "operate." One could get dollar birds and other rare specimens in plenty then all around Brisbane. Wild ducks and those named could be got at Kingsholme and Bowen Hills. But "*nous avons changé tout cela*" now. Even as have some Brisbane greybeards of the present day who used, as squatters, in the February of 1855, to sit up till 5 a.m. discussing politics and talking "bullock," but who keep much earlier hours now. I mention no names. At this time G. C. M'Donald and John Crowder had not started on the grand tour to Europe, but they did go not long afterwards.

Godfrey Gammon was a thick-headed city drayman, Hawkeye Boss was an astute and refined city gentleman. Hawkeye had a "farm" on the Logan, which he had bought in error for the next lot, and, sad to say, it contained fifty acres all stones and swamp, not worth a shilling an acre. Hawkeye badly wanted to "plant" this "farm," not *with* sugar, you know, but *on* to some one. But he could not hit on a plan. Godfrey Gammon owned a really nice little five-acre bit on the south side, worth £50, but no more. Godfrey wanted to knock out £150 for it, so he smoked a pipe, and he did hit on a plan. Result: Enter Gammon to Hawkeye, and *loq.*: "Please, sir, ain't you got a nice farm on the Logan to sell?" To him Boss, fixing his eyeglass: "Very much so, my man." G. G., in reply: "Please, sir, I want to buy it, but I ain't got no money, but I'll give you £150 if you'll take my paddock in South Brisbane in payment." Rapid mental debate goes on behind Boss's eyeglass, and resolution silently carried *nem. con.* that £50 worth of paddock will do well for 50s. worth of Logan swamp. Bargain clenched, there and then; Gammon speaks again, "You see, sir, I ain't no scollard, so the best plan will be for you and me, both on us, to sign the deeds, and a three months' bill each, and leave the deeds in the bank till such time as the bill is paid." Hawkeye has no fault to find with this idea either, and the job is duly perpetrated. Strange to relate, it fell out that Godfrey Gammon, the thick-headed drayman, discounted Boss's bill, and left the colony a week after. Boss met his own bill, of course, and had to take up the levanting Gammon's P.N. as well, and so somehow he finds himself minus £150 in cash, plus a £50 lot in South Brisbane, and with his Logan farm still on hand. He poked his stick savagely into the front garden bed, and muttered something about a "plant," but whether a horticultural one or otherwise we leave the reader to determine.

The Queensland sugar industry is hardly as old as that of New South Wales. The first experimental plantings were on the Brisbane River, and in East Moreton. The first considerable plantation was that of the Hon. Louis Hope, at Cleveland, and he was succeeded by Colonel Mackenzie, at Tingalpa. The latter had extraordinary difficulties to contend with, for his land, though it had a very rich volcanic soil, was so stony that it could never have been ploughed, and could only be worked with the hoe. Still the returns were good so long as the rank-growing bourbon cane, which was first introduced, remained free from disease; but the number of small farmers in East Moreton required the introduction of a system analogous to that of the central mills, which are supposed to be a quite recent invention. Mr. Day, at Oxley, and the Messrs. Grimes put up mills with a capacity far in excess of the requirements of their own small farms, and either bought cane from their neighbours, or crushed it for them "on halves." The latter was long the favourite plan. Mr. Day increased his plant till he had one of the largest mills with vacuum pan, and all the newest devices for manufacture. The first attempt at co-operation was made by the settlers on Doughboy Creek—many of them Germans—who put up a mill to crush the cane grown on their own farms, and entrusted its management to a Mr. Burrell, who, like many of the best and most successful Australian sugar men, was an engineer with a good clear head, and a smattering of chemical knowledge.

The settlers on the Mary River, chiefly through the capital and enterprise of Messrs. Tooth and Cran, early gave this district a leading position, and kept it till the almost greater climatic advantages of the northern districts brought them to the front. Bundaberg and the Lower Burnett, which now contribute so largely to Queensland's total sugar yield, long lagged behind. In 1874 there were hardly a dozen houses in North Bundaberg, and Stewart Brothers had only just finished their sugar-mill, the first on the Burnett. The Rubiana Estate, with all its improvements was, in that year, sold for about £1 an acre. What is it worth now?

I first landed in Brisbane in February of 1854, when the steamers always berthed near the present Parbury's wharf, on the south side. Stanley-street of now was scrub then. There were a few business houses round about. There was McCabe's wooden hotel close to the wharf, and next door Daniel Peterson, storekeeper, held sway. Orr was the butcher, and was located on the site of the present "Graziers." Close by was George Appel, John Ocock, the solicitor, and M'Conolly (*pater* to the late Colonial Architect), who had a wharf. Appel was the official inspector of stock. I remember a flock of about 300 sheep were landed affected with scab. These were ordered to be killed, and burnt, at once, which was done in an open allotment, in front of Orr's place, in sight of all, females and children, who passed by. Volunteers (to save time) were pressed into the service, and even the butcher's clerk, a college man, had to wield a knife, and, oh! how he did perspire under the unwonted exertion, so different from ordinary quill driving. And the wood to burn such a heap of carcases was another heavy drain on the limited resources of "our village," in order to be up to time with it. Then there was Kent, the chemist, Toppin, the baker, and Thomas Grenier's well-kept hostelry. These, with J. and George Harris' store, just about filled the bill.

There was no Woolloongabba; it was "the one mile swamp;" and a dense, sweet, wattle-scented grove extended the whole way round what is now River-terrace. How the place has grown during the last twenty years!

Whoever would have thought that the mere 994 feet 6 inches (be the same a little more or less) of muddy, brackish water, which separates North from South Brisbane, marked the boundary of two townships so closely dissimilar in all respects? Joined though they may be by a bridge, the intervening water seems to forbid any assimilation in character between the two places. Is it a fact that crossing water changes character, either in long or short voyages; or what is it? Be this as it may, we must confess, that when we visit the south side, we feel at once as if transported all the way to Ipswich, or Maitland, or Balranald, or some other bush township 1000 miles away from Queen-street.

The smaller hotels of South Brisbane were, in 1875, all

of the same kind of houses you find scattered thirty miles apart in the bush, and whose hospitable doors you arrive at after a long, dusty, weary day's ride. There was a fine old work-a-day bush twang of the stockwhip and bullock yokes, the branding iron and stock-yard, still left about South Brisbane, and which was totally unknown in finicking North Brisbane, sacred more to wealthy tradesmen, German missionaries, and the "Fortitude" immigrants, the very race of people, in short, whom a "true blue" blacksoil squatter hated (politically, of course) like poison, even as his cattle would their sour sea grass paddocks. The little boys of South Brisbane would (at a surprisingly tender age of infancy) energetically and successfully track and chase for you the active working bullock and the shy sweet milking cow alike from their secret forest lairs to your very doors, and would wield the resonant stockwhip, and sit "to the manner born" the propping stock-horse in a way and a style which no effeminate North Brisbane boy could attain under double the age of the miraculously precocious South side infant Hercules.

And then the gentle ladies too, and the healthy children one met with in the grassy suburban streets, outside their cottage gates, around the outskirts of South Brisbane and Kangaroo Point. They didn't resemble the North Brisbane ladies one bit. There was more of the garden glove, thick veil, sunshade style about them. They were just as prettily, but less fashionably, attired. They were more like the ladies and children one meets with at a comfortable 30,000 sheep station up country. There was a primitive, shy, kindly, healthy look about them, and nothing in the least degree civic or urban in their manner or appearance. Provided always, and be it understood, that none of these remarks be held in any way to apply to Kangaroo Point Proper, which, in the year of which I write (1875) was more like a tiny colony from Darling Point, Sydney, than anything else. We are speaking now rather of the sylvan Shafston, the rural Norman's Creek, the beauteous River-terrace with its unrivalled *coup d'œil* of the great city ; we are writing now more of grassy Coorparoo, and of the aspiring crest of lofty Highgate Hill. And so, dear old South Brisbane, farewell for the present. Our wish was that the days be many and long withal, ere branch banks and shilling ordinaries, free counter-lunches and typhoid fever, railways and cab-stands, and all the other delightful *agrémens* of " civilisation " invade thy quiet precincts and primitive haunts. We would fain have had thee remain as thou wert, innocent of all "progress," for it was indeed not everywhere that one could travel 500 miles from home, by simply crossing a short bridge with a penny toll.

In 1854 the ferries of Brisbane were only two in number, one kept by William Baxter, which plied to the foot of the next street parallel to Melbourne-street, and the other, carried on by Carter, from the Custom House to Kangaroo Point. The latter was the first to treat his passengers to an awning for the sun in the boat. Mr. John Stephen Ferriter, R.N., was the agent for immigration then, and lived in the cottage adjacent to the stone barracks, between George and William-streets, which were afterwards the Queensland Colonial Treasurer's office. He was somewhat addicted to bad puns, but, otherwise, of a kind and genial disposition. I remember one hot Sunday when he arrived at St. John's Church and sat in front of me, he turned round and remarked to me as he wiped his heated face, "Well! if a man gets no other promotion by coming to church in this weather, he, at all events, gets made a Knight of the Bath."

The old commissariat stores of 1822, and Pettigrew's saw mills, were the only places besides Tom Dowse's and a small public house on that part of the river bank in 1854, and the

Botanic Gardens, barring the old bunya and lebeck trees, were in a very premature state till Walter Hill came along in 1855 to put a new face on them. York's hollow, below the present site of Gregory-terrace, was a pleasant glade, full of clear water lagoons.

I remember a sea trip about this time, with A. H. Yaldwyn and Mark Farrell, the contractor for Cape Moreton lighthouse, as fellow passengers. I was down at once, of course, when Cape Moreton was cleared, and the south-easter freshened up, but they were case-hardened, and sat below out of the rain at night and amused themselves with brandy pawnee and by trying whose gold repeater had the most musical bell. I think Farrell's watch had a little the best of it. And here a word or two about that miserable affliction of sea sickness. How that eternal "beam sea" which rolls in on the east coast of Australia is responsible for bilious misery! Why, oh! why does everything you have eaten for the previous six months appear to rise in judgment against you all at once, as you wrestle with your agony in the creaking "state room," where your coats and "belongings" swing mournfully from the hooks? Why do young people, with their strong, vital, biliary organs, suffer so much more than the aged do? Who can tell? It is certain that those who do not suffer at sea are not any longer lived (but rather the contrary) than those who do so suffer. It is a mystery. I remember one sturdy scion of the Yorkshire Lumleys, who, with his ancestors, I suppose, had known neither dyspepsia nor starvation for 800 years, and whose stomach was of cast iron strength. I remember him in a frightful gale, where even the seasoned captain and stewards were all sick. He came up smiling and *alone* at each meal; but every one is not so gifted as this. But, as Shakspeare says, "there is a soul of good in all things evil, would men, observingly, distil it out," and so I used to construct, as I lay on my back, rules of diet to be observed on shore based on what experience I get in the hours of agony at sea. What to take and what to avoid were learnt there. Oranges *before* breakfast were grateful at sea. Memorandum : To continue the habit and freshen the mouth with them on rising through life, when on shore; to avoid vinegar always and salads sometimes, and so forth.

I was heartily amused, once, on board steamer, with John Tait and his racehorses. To see a worthy old member of Parliament, from the Maneroo district, very sea-sick, and saying to his wife, "My dear, I can't think what ails me, for all I had for breakfast was a plate of tinned lobsters and a black pudding." I wonder how he could have proposed to improve upon this? And, then, 'mid the giant waves that roll off Flat Top Island, on the Queensland coast, was a steamer which carried an objectionable fellow, the manager of a "variety troupe." He was noisy and voluble, and bragged that he was never sea-sick in his life, as the mail boat anchored off the island, and, to prove it, he ate an enormous breakfast of raw onions and similar horrors. But old "Flat Top" has a habit of "fetching 'em" when a boat is at anchor there, which the boaster had never bargained for, and I am proud to say that it asserted itself on this occasion, and the onions, etc., went to the fishes in due course—for the first time on record, no doubt, in his case.

I once tried the heroic remedy of two grains of tartar emetic, and one scruple of ipecacuanha the night before going to sea from Melbourne in 1851, and the precious emetic kept me all right and hungry in Bass' Straits, in the month of May. But the same reduced to half, only aggravated the seasickness sailing out of Brisbane in 1857. The best remedy I know is physic before you go to sea. Drink sea water as soon as you feel you are "in for it." Take a dose *after* this *(not* before) of a chloroform and camphor mixture, which any chemist can make up. *Lie down;* eat bananas and sponge cake, which require little chewing or digesting; drink soup, the salt in which keeps the stomach from converting it into vinegar, as it does all drinks. And the orange in the early morning removes the nasty taste in the mouth. My fellow passengers on one trip were Mr. Robert Cribb, then one of our members in the Sydney Parliament, and Judge B. (the "genial") was also on board, and my cabin mate. He it was who used to go circuit out west, and, at one township far out in the "never never" country, where there was no church, chapel, or parson, but only a court house, public houses, stores, etc., the Judge was asked by a deputation to read the Anglican prayers at the court house on the following Sunday, and on no account to omit the prayer for rain, as there had been a twelve months' drought out there. The Judge promised compliance, and duly officiated on the Sunday, but somehow, in place of reading the prayer *for* rain, he turned over the wrong leaf and substituted the "thanksgiving for rain." The subject was mentioned to him after church. His only rejoinder was "Look here, boys; it's never a good plan to open a fresh account before you've squared off the old debt: I'll be bound now ye never thanked Providence for the last batch of rain ye got, and ye owed for it still, and now I've squared that bill for ye and ye can ask for more with a clear conscience!" He left the crowd cogitating.

A gentleman (now no more) once wrote me to ask if I could give him a list of the original or foundation members of the Queensland Club. I was surprised at the request, for I concluded that the early archives and books of the club would have afforded the information required, but when I learnt that they had all been destroyed by an accidental fire, I told him that I knew something of the subject, gathered from old diaries and memoranda. In the month of December, 1859, the great success of the "North Australian" Club in Ipswich made Brisbane people think of starting a club here, and a preliminary meeting of those interested was held at the office of the Hon. D. F. Roberts, and several working sub-committees were appointed. It was resolved to ask the newly-arrived Governor, Sir George Bowen, to become the patron, to name the club after the new colony, and to secure temporary premises at once at Mr. W. A. Brown, the sheriff's house, in Mary-street. The first House Committee were Shepherd Smith, E. S. Elsworth (of the Joint Stock Bank), and N. Bartley. These drafted the rules, bought the furniture, and engaged the first staff of servants, after which R. G. W. Herbert and J. Bramston were added to the committee. Those members who were willing to, and had been invited to join, came in during January and February, 1860, and the first ballot for the election of members was held on the 1st of March, 1860, after which, of course, there were no more "originals." About the year 1876, and during the secretaryship of Mr. Davidson, and before the fire, I remember seeing a list of members, with the foundation ones printed in red in place of black letters. The original members, of whom I am quite certain, were R. Little, R. Douglas, J. Little, W. D. White, D. F. Roberts, A. A. May, J. W. Jackson, E. S. Elsworth, N. Bartley, Shepherd Smith, J. J. Galloway, R. G. W. Herbert, J. Bramston, and, I think, the following might also be included : Dr. Cannan, F. E. Roberts, W. Rawlins, W. Thornton, W. Pickering, and J. F. M'Dougall.

Full often in the long, weary flood throughout the years of bad times does the struggling man wish for death as a release, when he views his haggard wife and foredoomed children—doomed to scant education, social extinction, and early trouble. It is the old-told story repeated every generation in Australia—a spurt of prosperity, a great money

CAPT. JOHN MACKAY.   DR. DORSEY.
MR. F. BIGGE.
MR. T. DE LACY MOFFATT.   HON. R. TOWNS.

scramble, a wide-spread game of "puss in the corner"—at the end of which the wise ones who have picked up and hugged the fleeting money shower, are all on the snug corners, and decline to leave them; while the poor fools left out in the middle of the room are stuck there for ever; and the lessons forgotten by half the community when the next era of money plenty comes round again.

There was a nice financial crisis in Brisbane in 1866. In the month of July, the Bank of Queensland, without a warning of any kind, without a run or panic, put up its shutters one morning. True there had been a firm of bill brokers in London, called Overend, Gurney & Co., who had failed for nine millions just before that, and the Agra and Masterman's Bank, forgetting the old traditions of Masterman, Peters, Mildred & Co., had joined forces, and not succeeded thereby. But no one expected trouble here from it all till it came like a thunderclap, and then everyone of course had foreseen it, only they forgot at the time to mention it, you know. But mistrust soon spread. The Union of Australia was the Government bank then, and there was a weakness about Government cheques, and a run on the bank itself, which was then in Elizabeth-street, near where W. Steele & Co. lately were. It was a comical and suggestive sight to see the fools drawing out their sovereigns at the front door of the bank, and rushing off with them to the other banks, which were quietly all the time carting more and more sovereigns in at the *back* door of the Union. The run could have been withstood for ever. But Queensland was in a bad way. The pace had been fast since 1862, and there was bound to be a pull taken, and it was a real pull and a dead halt, that lasted for six long weary years afterwards. A land boom had sprung up in 1862. Up to that time land had been subdivided and sold in moderation as wanted, but generally sold privately, and in this way a

R

good deal of Fortitude Valley and Spring Hill (so called) had been built on. But in 1862, a ship came from Scotland to Brisbane, called the "Helenslee," with many more. The "Helenslee" passengers brought out £30,000 with them, an average of £100 per passenger, and on the strength of this and similar arrivals, a "land boom" was organised. One enterprising firm of auctioneers found out that "there was money" in the feat of buying suburban land wholesale at £1 an acre, and selling it retail in 32-perch lots at £2 each (half cash, and half at three months), and "estates" on the Enoggera ranges and elsewhere found buyers who paid up but never claimed their land to this day. One astute agent persuaded people that the Ipswich-road was destined to be lined with shops on both sides, and a rush for land took place thither, and he led them just as easily elsewhere when that "fad" was exhausted. The town of Bowen, at Port Denison, originally sold by the Crown in 1861, was "boomed" in the same way about 1863 and 1864. £10 lots for £200 and so on, to the disaster and grief of buyers, who died despairing.

A four million loan had been raised and spent partly on railways, and the country, as usual, seemed all the poorer in place of richer for the expenditure. The panic did not extend in the other colonies nor England as it did in the nineties. It was foretold, in 1867, by myself, that Queensland would, in her vigorous growth, emerge from the 1866 trouble, and think it and its four million loan a flea bite, and I hoped it would be a warning. She did so emerge, and, in one generation, as usual, it and all its lessons had been forgotten, and a new crash—with thirty millions in place of four millions—with loans laughed at in London for all Australia—with things queer and unsettled all over the financial world — came to pass. Queensland, still in its infancy, teeming with natural wealth, will outgrow this crisis also, but it remains to be seen whether the people of 1915 will have overlooked the traditions of the previous generation, and brought on a third cataclysm. The world never does learn wisdom by experience, and the chances are that collapse will then follow inflation as in 1825, 1843, and 1866. Every evil that led here and elsewhere to the affair of 1866 was repeated with aggravation, and on a larger scale, between 1884 and 1889, and the inevitable eruption followed. I recall how in Sydney in 1877 gigantic estate auctions in allotments would last three days, and realize £20,000 a day ; how in Brisbane in 1884 and 1885 a land agent with no auction at all would book land all day long in his day-book privately. A.B., Dr. to C.D., for land at Fortitude Valley, Cleveland, &c., £500, £350 ; booking and selling huge lots like the Civil Service Store books groceries, and with no trouble of putting string round them or sending them out in a cart, in order to earn the commission on them. But it all came to an end, and no wonder. The astute land broker who started the game in 1862, held on bravely at it for twenty-five years, till the numerous land banks arose and snuffed out the private land shark, and then he retired sniffing the coming financial cyclone before anyone else did, and, with topmasts down and twenty anchors out, each of a thousand pounds sterling weight and more, he rode out the cyclone snugly in harbour. He is one type. Now for another and equally (up to a certain point) successful land broker. He, in place of converting all into cash (like the party quoted), used to put all his profits and commissions into land. He showed me his safe one day crammed full up of his title deeds, all clear of lien or mortgage. "Very good," said I ; and have you any money as well." "No," said he. "Then," I replied, "you are in a very unsafe position. Everyone should have a third of his total assets in liquid form, gold or notes. Cash at call. It is *not* 'idle money,' for it helps to *protect* all the rest of his property, and save it from loss and depreciation and forced sale to an extent far beyond the mere loss of interest on the (so-called) 'idle money.'" He could not see it, and when the financial cyclone did come, if he and his condition had been represented by a ship with all sail set (the sails being his parchment deeds), and his sole small anchor out, represented by his slender stock of cash, you will have a full idea of how the tempest wrecked *him*, who put his faith in all land and no money. I have spoken of the land brokers so far, let me now dwell on private land speculators. Class No. 1 buy and hold twenty or thirty properties at a time, make by-sales, and secure large profits. But when the crash comes they are "left" with heavy interest to pay, and to face the "shrinkage" on thirty properties. Result: the absorption of all past profits. A more careful class of operators would never buy a second piece till they had sold the first one, and so only hold one piece at a time, with the result that, when the crisis came, they held on to all past profits, and only had to face the loss on one piece of land; a much better position than the other class held.

In order to illustrate how the 1866 crash affected me personally, I must go back a few years. My grandfather was chief clerk in the Ordnance Department, and had an official residence in the Tower of London. He was born in 1779, and died in 1842, and left me something handsome in his will. I became of age when in Australia, and the money was sent out to me in Queensland. Mr. Robert Little prepared the identification papers, and the money came out through the Bank of New South Wales. Contrary to the advice of all my southern friends, who looked upon Brisbane *then* as we now should at Tongatabu as a field for land investment. I resolved to spend it all in land. I bought it from the Crown at Wickham-terrace, Bowen Hills, village of Lutwyche, Highgate Hill, &c., besides odd lots at Rockhampton, Maryborough, Toowoomba, Bowen, Cleveland, and Tingalpa. Before the crash of 1866, these, which had not cost me £1,500, were valued at £15,000, but after the Bank of Queensland put the shutters up, I could not raise cost price on it. It long since passed into other hands, and then fetched high values.

CHAPTER XIII.

Life by the Sea Shore—Early Sandgate—My First Visit—What the Wild Waves were Saying—An Appreciable Soul—Good Company—Floods in the Brisbane—A Few Records—The Weather and the Seasons—Drought and its Recurrence—Magnificent Queensland.

EVEN in those days we in Brisbane had our marine nooks; and whether there was plenty of money or an absence of it, there was no dearth of enjoyment either at home or at those places were folks used to lie and listen to what the wild waves were saying. Of these Brisbane summer resorts, Sandgate may be considered the oldest.

It is true that as far back as early 1854, Brisbane ladies used to be left at Moreton Island to recruit, being fetched up and down by Sydney steamers in passing. And at Cleveland, too, was a seaside resort, and Captain Towns gave us citizens of Brisbane a picnic thither in the steamer "Breadalbane" in 1856. Certain of the upper families in Brisbane (well off for buggies and horses) and their married friends also, from the Logan, used Cleveland for a summer sojourn, and many a daring side-saddle dash after the cows and the milk for breakfast and tea was made by young married ladies (whose husbands were busy in town), and to see whom dance would give you no idea of their skill in the side-saddle; for they had learned to ride as children far away from Brisbane, and their husbands were then at a desk in town, and were not stockmen, and could not "run in" a cow as their spouses could when the children needed milk. But, for all this, Cleveland was used only by a fashionable and select few. It was twenty-two miles from Brisbane, and Sandgate was only twelve, and the latter soon became the place for all hands to flock to in the summer season. I first went there in September, 1858, in company with Dr. Hobbs and the Rev. George Wight. I remember how Lieut. Williams, of the native police, and I, threw spears over the fork of a high gum tree near the Ein Bunpin Lagoon, in a style which Dr. Hobbs (who had never been in the bush) could not emulate. The population of Sandgate was then, I should estimate, about twenty-five souls. The "hotel" was kept by one Charles F. Davie, a consumptive little man, who came there to try and prolong his days on earth, by the soft sea air. Butchers and bakers and shops there were none, so all the fare was salt beef and damper, unless you liked "to bring a few pounds of steak with you in your valise," which was just what *we* did. Bottled beer, wine, and spirits were procurable. We slept well, and, in the morning, Dr. Hobbs went for a bathe under the very *hibiscus* tree which still gives its grateful shade at the land end of the pier, after which we strolled to "Shorncliffe," where Mr. Wight noticed the coal measures jutting out on the beach. Months after this, again, the blacks from the north end of the Bay (Bribie way) came down and made the place uncomfortable. They bailed Tom Dowse up in a slab hut which, fortunately for him, had no glass windows, but only an opening to which a thick wooden shutter fitted like a hatchway. This was spear-proof, and he escaped, and after this Lieut. Wheeler, of the native police, cleared out the aboriginals, who never again troubled Sandgate, except as men and brothers, on the look out for tobacco and pennies, and the place soon became a fine resort for children who needed to get rid of the troublesome tail end of a whooping cough, measles, or scarlet fever. Cabbagetree Creek was a "teazer" to cross at high water, but, after 1861, it got a bridge, and so *that* little trouble was at an end, and a picnic to Sandgate and back on the same day soon became a recognised institution in Brisbane life, and the little town grew, and stores and hotels were run up, and cottages were built to let for the summer season furnished. But it was still advisable to bring down bread and poultry, &c., from time to time, as supplies were precarious, and visitors came unexpected. "Jordan Cottage" was built about 1860. Loudon's about the same time. McConnel's house (now D. L. Brown's), was put up in 1866.

There is, at Sandgate, no thunderous roar of curling breakers thirty feet high, sounding forever by day and night in front of your verandah, and only fifty feet away from you. Your eye does not range over an open ocean unbroken and undefiled by so much as a sandbank for ten thousand miles clean away to distant Valparaiso. There are no beautiful cone shells and tiger cowries and ear shells and other conchological delights. In fact Sandgate is chiefly remarkable for what is *not* there. There is no pier, no yachts, no bazaars, no German band, no docks, no shipping, no circulating libraries, no donkeys (four legged ones with saddles on, I mean), no Ethiopian serenaders, no fishwives, no bathing machines, no steamers, no society—and no scandal, I was going to add, but I am not so sure about this last item on my first visit.

I had been informed that mine ancient whilom and famous hostelry, the Elephant and Shoestrings, had fallen into decay somewhat, and that if I wanted to be comfortable I must transfer my patronage to the Goat and Compasses (strange how the old Puritan inn sign of "God encompasses us," should have been corrupted into the above). So to the "Goat and Compasses" I went. Alas! the potatoes there were stone cold; but, by way of set off, the claret was very warm; the kidneys were raw and bloody; but the leg of mutton was done to a cinder, and ah me! the Board of 'Elth had *not* visited the premises very recently, I fear.

But, still, for a' that and a' that, Sandgate is not all a dreary waste. Oh dear no! Albeit the male strollers on the beach are annoyed at times by coming suddenly upon bands of female Naiads bathing in the surf, and although the female strollers are now and again similarly offended at coming quite unexpectedly upon a squad of male Tritons disporting themselves in the rollers, these things will and must happen in primitive Sandgate, and possibly in 1975, when Sandgate is very highly civilised, the people will look back with interest to the simple, early, Knickerbocker days of old Queensland. No, indeed! Sandgate is not all a waste. There is God's pure breeze laid on daily in full force, and nothing to pay for it; the quality never varies. There is no adulteration in that, no municipal stinks commingled with it. There is the murmur of the mimic waves on the beach, soothing you to sleep all night, and seeming to say, "Take your rest, and I will keep watch, for I never slumber nor sleep." Many a sickly baby, and people of larger growth, marked for disease and death in Brisbane, have revived under the doses of ozone which they must inhale at Sandgate whether they like it or not; for, with all the force of ten thousand punkahs, the fresh sea air fattens you and is pumped into you to your great and permanent benefit.

In the year 1872, when, for the first time since 1858 and 1861 I stayed there, Sandgate had grown, and in the winter

I had a bad cold, caught at the time of the maddening tin fever of the period, when the amber and black crystals of cassiterite, of 70 per cent. purity, from the 3,000 feet Highlands of Stanthorpe, drove Greville's Rooms and Sydney Exchange brokers into a frenzy of delight (rivalling that of the simultaneous Hill End gold, and Peak Downs copper mania) and hand rubbing, at the prospective fortunes in store for them, and all skilful operators, who could "bull" and "bear," each in their allotted season. So, to cure this cold, I hied me to the hospitable home of jolly Frank Raymond, of the "Sandgate Hotel," and, over a steaming glass of "Burnett's Old Tom," with lemon and sugar, and by a cheerful fire, necessitated by the "shrewd" winds "of the period," I listened then—as I often do now—through the closed doors and windows, to "what the wild waves were saying;" and how they *did* discourse and babble to us, in their own universal language, about the former travels of some friends; about the old woman who used to sell the polished pebbles at Scarborough; of the consumptive curate, with his splendidly handsome and healthy sister and nurse (in one) at Biarritz; of the lovely oysters and the pretty milliners at Dieppe; of the heiress at old Bournemouth, who was so quiet and demure, and proved to be no heiress, after all; of the natty fishwives of Calais; of the "cavalry officer," who was always so lucky at loo, at Brighton; of the plentiful mackerel on the beach at Boulogne, shot from the hold of the fishing smacks.

Truly a prophet has no honor in his own country, and it is not in Brisbane that Sandgate is fully appreciated—it is too near at hand, too easily got at to be considered the luxury it really is. Ebriosus, that least sentimental of all possible souls, is put into a trap in Queen-street by his friends, and they and he "tool it" down in one hour and forty minutes, Ebriosus being fast asleep all the while, and totally unaware whether he is going to South Brisbane or the "Valley," or whether he has been one minute or one hundred minutes *en route*; and then he wakes up and finds he has exchanged the sewer and drain essences which distinguish the Brisbane perfumery for the pure ozone and iodine of that paradise of all places—a sea beach. But does Ebriosus (who is but a type of many spreeish visitants to that breezy bluff)—does he appreciate his good fortune? I trow not. Sandgate is wasted on all such. Better were it that some of the sick poor, the feeble old and the feeble young, who never see the ocean shore, and thousands of whom do live and die in Brisbane without ever seeing it at all, better were it that they who cannot afford to go there should have some of the useless opportunities of Ebriosus and Co.

The man to appreciate Sandgate is the bushman; the man into whose weary soul the iron of the Condamine Plains and the brigalow scrubs of the Dawson country has fully entered; the man who has tasted no vegetable but "fat hen" for seven years, who has lived on salt beef and damper till his veins are full of land scurvy; the man who is weary of fresh water, its rivers and lagoons and its fishes, its reeds and its lilies; the man to whom sheep and cattle are, for want of a change, a weariness and a desolation. Such a one can appreciate that narrow zone of Paradise which lies just where the continent and the ocean meet. Clap a piece of thick green seaweed under his nose, and the memory, ever sensitive to the call of the olfactory nerves, at once conjures up visions of the far-off Mediterranean and Biscayan shore, where the starfish lie on the sands; and eke of those Norman and English watering-places where buff slippers and camp-stools, organ-grinders and fishing smacks, lovely girls and noisy children, fill up the motley but delightful scene. Nothing on earth equals the place where land and sea meet. How dreary is it five hundred miles up country, among the sandy plains, and how equally dreary is it five hundred miles out at sea among the endless tumbling hillocks of indigo blue which fill up the monotonous scene. But any part of the sea within five miles of a bold shore, or *vice versâ*, how exquisite it is! I hardly know which is preferable, to live seven years, say, on Peak Downs, and then take a couple of months at Manly Beach, with its wild violets in the rocky dells, its purple and white sea-flowers in the rock pools of salt water, and its snorting saline south-easters, with the glass seldom rising over 70 degrees, and the horizon enlivened with as many passing steamers and ships as if one were in the English Channel, and oh! the glory, on a dark stormy night, when the curtained blackness has just swallowed up the pitching and rolling steamer northward and outward bound for dear old Brisbane, to see, after a spell of ebon darkness, the moon rise, and send a stream of silver drops dancing along the floor of the sea in a bee line from east to west, and lighting up the scene where all was Erebus a minute before. I am undecided as to whether all this is preferable to the sensation experienced when after a hundred days buffeting with the waves since leaving the Lizard and Ushant lights behind, and after getting "knocked into a cocked hat" amongst the seething mountains of water which rage where the Mozambique Channel and the Agulhas bank currents meet in dire conflict off the Cape of Storms—when, after all this, the crippled barque comes within smelling range of the aromatic hay-fields of Tasmania, and her sea-weary passengers sniff the new sylvan odours of the South-west Cape, and tremble at the black Mewstone, a giant to its English namesake, and which sits on the sea like a lion in basalt as big as Gibraltar, and defies the angry waves which clothe its blackness in white foam ever and anon. Yes, it is truly a toss-up which is the better, to smell the sea after too much of the land, or the land after too much of the sea.

Sandgate is still a place of delight for the soul that can appreciate Nature, and is in no way fallen off (albeit somewhat Cockneytied now) from the good old days when we had to follow the marked tree line to it, carry our own provisions down, and think ourselves lucky if no aboriginal spear or boomerang interrupted the al fresco meal by the sea; which was too often the case before the energetic Sicilian who afterwards officered the native police there, taught the darkies better manners and customs.

But Sandgate is nothing without good company. For my part I like that of my cousins Lucy and Laura down there; Lucy is a half-golden, half-silver blonde of 19; Laura, a tall, fair brunette of 17; Lucy wears gloves No. 6, and weighs 9 stone; Laura wears $6\frac{1}{2}$, and she actually weighs 11 stone, despite her slender wrists and ankles, for she is of that noble, vital type of womanhood which sculptors of the first rank assign to Eve—the brooding and grandly mysterious mother of all the nations. Blondes are my usual weakness; yet am I powerfully affected by the large, dark, deep eyes of my Laura and her clear, firm profile; and all the little men, of course, are mad after her, for she is devoid of conceit and sentiment alike. What a Juno she will be in ten years time, I vow. Where do they live, do you say? Why, on their father's station, a hundred miles, more or less, west or so of Sandgate; at a spot where the western escarpment of the Australian Cordillera melts into swelling downs of rich herbage—a place where (so to speak) lagoons of treeless grass are environed by shores of timberland which jut out in picturesque capes, points, and promontories, into the said dry lagoons of grass, and enclose snug little bays of verdure—a place where the eye and ear are refreshed with the sight and the sound of waters falling over rocks, and where, at day-dawn, the early carol of the magpie rises in melodious chorus to heaven, at the same time as the wholesome white wood smoke from the station chimneys mingles upward and lazily with the pure ether overhead ; for the breeze which sweeps the wattle-scented forest later in the day, as yet is not. Yes, the name of the station is Wyndômel, and it lies just under the shadow of Kunghi, that monarch mountain which marks the junction of the Main Range, and one which crosses it from east to west— a fine, venerable old swell of the cloud-capt breed, in whose heavily-timbered sides you could easily get lost, yet whose beneficent peak catches all the thunder clouds on a sultry day, and sends them down in showers of cooling water and ozone on the parched people of the tableland and the lower country alike, and it then smiles like a benevolent giant, as the setting sun gilds its head, and seems to say, "There, see how I've refreshed you all ; I'm not half so grim as I look !"

Yes, that is where Lucy and Laura live when they are at home, and every lamb and calf that is born there is unconsciously adding a half-sovereign or a couple of pound notes to the heritage of these two charming girls. Upon my word, I have a great mind to write an Australian novel about them ; for I don't mean to marry either of them, they being my cousins, and their father having £15,000 a-year. But, bless my life ! how discursive I am. I have got right clear away from Sandgate altogether, and by the same powers, I had almost lost sight of Brisbane.

There was considerable controversy in 1887 as to whether the flood in Brisbane of that year exceeded those of 1864 and 1870. The weight of evidence showed the 1887 one, I think, to have been more severe than any since 1841. No one flood rises proportionately high at all parts of the river, and hence these disputes. In 1841 the Brisbane River, from its heads above Colinton and Taromeo, was in full flood, as was also its great affluent, the Stanley Creek, while at the same time the Bremer, with its tributaries, Purga and Warrill Creeks, was in high flood also, and the rivers dammed each other back, and thus the whole basin from the Main Range on the west to the Mary Range on the south, was inundated. The water rose 70ft. at Ipswich, and as there were only 4ft. at low tide on the Brisbane River Bar at that time, you may be sure the water was well kept back, and no such flood was again seen until the 1893 trouble. In the floods of 1857, 1863, 1864, and 1870, the water rose 45ft. to 50ft. in Ipswich. As the Brisbane River above the junction was not in flood to any extent, the highest point reached in Brisbane in any of these was 6ft. 8in. above spring tide, and it was marked on the post at the South Brisbane ferry, the post that carried the punt rope. Since 1870, of course the river bar has much changed, and there is a better "get away" for the water. The 1887 flood is said to have risen 50ft. in Ipswich, which is 5ft. above 1864 and 1870. The flood of May, 1857, was the outcome of six weeks' long continued rather than heavy rain. That of 1863 was a February autumn one, 15·14in. of rain fell in sixteen days, electricity negative. August, 1860, gave us 12·39in. of rain, but no flood. February, 1863, gave 9·70in. between the 13th and 17th of the month. In March, 1864, an equinoctial gale brought the flood. The night of the 18th was terrific. A hurricane blew. The river rose 50ft. in twelve hours at Ipswich. A heavy lifeboat was blown over like a hat for 200 yards on the beach at Moreton Island. Steamer collisions in the river were plentiful. Boats rowed in Mary-street opposite Perkins's brewery in 1863 and 1864. But no rain above 7in. in twenty-four hours fell this time. South-east gales brought all these floods. The deluge of March, 1870, consisted of 24·25in. of rain in a little over four days, 8·20in. being the maximum fall in twelve hours. Maryborough got 14in. in twenty-four hours at the same time.

On the 9th March the flood was over Bowen Bridge, and breast high at that place and the Waterloo Hotel; a perfect typhoon blew from the east all the night of the 8th March, 1870, in Brisbane. The swamps had not been much built on then, and there was no "manure depôt," and it was not so bad as 1887, on the whole. I pass over the minor floods of 1873, '75, and '79 as of little consequence, except that they killed the seafish in the river, and made an unpleasant smell. Eighteen inches of rain really fell on 21st January, 1887. It may fairly be inferred that, spite of the 24ft. of water at the Bar, such a concentrated fall of rain must have caused a worse flood than any of those quoted, except 1841; and when such a one as that year's flood comes again, as it assuredly will do some day, people who live on the hills will be better off than the swamp dwellers of our suburbs. The Brisbane River, after all, except for the matchless depth of water on its so-called "bar," looks small by the Fitzroy and Burdekin rivers. The Brisbane drains a country but little larger than Yorkshire. It is a "soon up, soon down" river in flood time. The Fitzroy and Burdekin together drain a country the size of France or Germany, and a flood in them rises slowly and keeps up for weeks. We have no record of the rainfall that led to the 1841 flood, but, as we have seen, a flood may come on in twenty-four hours, or be six weeks in brewing, and in the former case little warning is given. The severity of the floods can be safely reckoned by the severity of the droughts, of which we have had such a terrible example in 1883-86. And talking of floods suggests the weather.

The principle of "compensation," of which Ralph Waldo Emerson writes so ably, obtains universally in nature. This system of material double entry, by which every debit has, so to speak, its credit, can be traced far and wide in the physical world, and even further. Gamblers, for instance,

OFF THE ISLANDS.

A SHELTERED BAY.

with cards and dice will tell you of an ebb and flow in luck, of certain occult laws which govern the succession of what are called chances, and this tendency to action and reaction is observable wherever we turn our attention.

It is of this irresistible propensity in nature to oscillation that I would now speak more particularly, as it affects our weather and our seasons ; and here is apparent the great contrast between the European and the Australian climates. In Europe the tendency to action and reaction finds its outlet in cycles of abnormally hot and of abnormally cold seasons. We hear of brandy frozen in cellars ; of frost biting into the solid earth to the depth of many feet ; and anon we hear of tropical thunderstorms in the latitude of 50 degrees, and of mosquitoes, where such things ought not to be. But in Europe, nevertheless, there is no startling variation in the rainfall, even in the course of a century.

All these things are totally different in Australia. Nature in this country exhibits her tendency to the ebb and flow system by cycles of abnormally wet and abnormally dry years, while the average heat of one year varies but little from that of another, at any time ; and there are no startling contrasts. Thus it follows that the average yearly rainfall of Europe is steady, while the average yearly heat and cold vary much in the course of fifty years ; and at the same time in Australia the average temperature is steady, while the rainfall varies greatly. Such is the marked and great contrast which the two places exhibit as regards weather and climate.

The power of this great law of nature in Australia is exemplified by the fact that the monsoon itself which brings rain in the Indian Ocean, and generally floods Northern Australia in autumn, has sometimes to pass over the latter place very lightly. The first three months of the year 1871 were a notable instance of this. There was little or no wet season that year in the Gulf country. The 1875 season was a very dry one; clouds formed, it is true, but there was lacking that peculiar electric condition, or quality, in the upper air, which alone can turn clouds into rain, and there they hung, tantalising us with false hopes. Sometimes this electric quality or condition was in excess, and then we had in a clear sky and without a moment's warning a little black is formed directly overhead, and apparently out of nothing, and coming down like a bucket of water; all over in five minutes, and the sky clear again. There was plenty of this weather in the first three months of 1872.

The 1875 dry season somewhat resembled that of 1862, and still more so that of 1854. The dry spring of 1862-63 was followed by a sickly wet autumn, and the most unhealthy weather ever known in Brisbane was in February, 1863. Rain water, caught in clean open vessels, putrified the next day, and all in the open air. The hills about Brisbane were covered with new arrivals camped in tents. The rain and heat were incessant, and the mortality great, the sea breeze being almost entirely absent. December, 1854, marked the end of seven months' dry weather. Great was the scarcity of water on the Darling Downs. The stations of Westbrook and Western Creek were in especial straits just then. Well sinking and dams were not yet in vogue, and many an angry squatter wished aloud that some of "Dr. Lang's 'agriculturists' were farming up there just then." The heat was insufferable. It ranged in Warwick and Drayton between 105 degrees and 108 degrees in the shade for a whole fortnight. At Franklyn Vale, below the Downs, it was 112 degrees, while on the Lower Condamine 117, 119, and 122 degrees were the quotations in the shade. But February, 1855, brought refreshing showers, and it was all over. The most unendurable months in Brisbane since regular observations have been taken, were February, 1863, and December,

1869; the average heat of the latter month was the same as that of Calcutta in the hottest summer month. They have punkahs, however, and stone palaces in Calcutta; but in Brisbane we have just half an inch of hardwood only between us and the heat. At present I have spoken only of minor droughts. I come now to the very serious question of the great and terrible ones which about *four times in each century* visit Australia.

Captain Flinders, cruising about the coasts of Australia at the commencement of the present century, found, everywhere, the bush on fire, grass burnt and withered, and every sign of great and long-continued drought. In 1828 and 1829 came the drought of the century, with water at fourpence a gallon in Sydney—the great Murrumbidgee River dried up, and the fish dead in the dry mud of it; and yet this river, in ordinary seasons, overflows like the Nile, and is ten miles across it (as I have found in a canoe). Then in 1849 and 1850 came the terrible drought, which culminated in "Black Thursday," in February, 1851, when burnt leaves were blown across Bass' Straits by the fury of that north wind, which amalgamated into one huge blaze the previously scattered bush fires of "Port Phillip." The rain came, and the drought broke up in May, 1851, when the streets of Melbourne became so many mud-banks in no time.

The question for us now to consider is this: will the great periodic droughts, extending over eighteen months or two years at a time, which has already happened three times in a century, and at apparent intervals of twenty-five years, more or less; will it come again to us, and how soon? I don't think it is on us yet, but I think it is only a year or two away from us—that is to say, if past experience be any guide, and if any dependence can be placed on statistics. It is a serious matter to contemplate; we can store water but we cannot store grass. The sheep and cattle of 1875 will outnumber those of 1825 and 1850 by an amount so vast as to render the prospect all the more terrible. Much can be done in agriculture by irrigation. I once lived at a station on an "ana" branch of the Murrumbidgee River. The country was flat for hundreds of miles round, and it seldom rained there, for there were no mountains to catch the clouds, but we had a garden on the river bank, and had vegetables and fruit all the year round by means of a pump made of four pieces of wood and a long hose of osnaburgh. Twenty minutes of pumping every morning sent the water flowing from the top bed in the garden, which was about three feet above the water level, zigzagging its way back to the river, and saturating all the beds thoroughly as it runs backwards and forwards, but always towards the river, and this was all done by white people, as there were no Chinamen there in 1853.

But this relates only to fruit and vegetables. The question of food for stock is another and a terrible one, but that phase of the subject need not be discussed here. In the year 1864 I read before the Philosophical Society of Queensland a paper on Meteorology, which had the effect of causing the establishment of observing stations throughout the colony. I remarked then that cycles of about ten years of unusually wet and dry seasons, alternately, appeared to be about the rule in Australia. The year 1854 was unusually dry, 1864 was unusually wet, 1874 again was dry, and 1884 wet; while in 1894 we had a mixture—floods in the north and drought in the west,—thus, each decade appears to mark the commencement or end of a more than ordinary wet or dry epoch.

Magnificent Queensland! great storehouse of gifts and riches, how shall I best describe thee? Where even begin, when so many sterling claims to notice offer all at once? Let me first soar, and then, borne on wings calmly over thee, and so look down on thy domain, and, as I behold, I perforce must own that if I were compelled to sum up thy greatness in one word, that one magic word would have to be "Basalt"— the basalt of the columned cliffs. The volcanic work which, under various names and disguises, "chums" with the gold, and is a guarantee for the plentiful presence thereof, and other rich metals *galore*. And the dear old basalt, the mother of the agate, is not confined to the minerals. Oh! dear no. Behold it now decomposed on the swelling western plains, and giving birth to the matchless grasses (world-challengers) which fatten the beeves over a space like unto France and Germany combined. Let us mount higher and take a more comprehensive view. Here lies *the* champion colony spread out below us, and, 'mid ravine and tableland, water course and mountain chain, dark crag and green savannah, let us mark the countless citadels scattered broadcast where Nature has her treasures of gold locked up—Charters Towers and the Cape River, Ravenswood and the Gilbert, Mount Morgan and Clermont, Gympie and Kilkivan, Croydon and the Etheridge—enough! I will not fill the book, as I could with all the rocky gold fortresses that are dotted o'er the land, or speak of the granites of Herberton, saturated with tin oxide; the scrubs of Bundaberg and Mackay; the Johnston, the Burdekin, and more, boiling over and effervescing with bright sugar crystals, or the unregarded and too plentiful coal and copper. See, below us, Buckland's Tableland and Lake Salvator, memories of Sir Thomas Mitchell, the veteran Peninsula man and explorer. Note all the exquisite show scenery in parts where pastoral pursuits "don't pay," and the turfed flats where millions of quadrupeds fatten and make money for their owners. And regarding, too, the race of men which a land like this produces, the hardy, free overlander, the hard, dogged miner, what matters it whether they be bold natives of the Victorian Wimmera, or the Valley of the Hunter, or the broad-loined sons of Staffordshire? Queensland can toughen and weld them all into sons of her own if they only will live the life that she calls them to.

CHAPTER XIV.

The Islands—At Tahiti—Eimeo—Papiete—A Mountain Climb—A Hearty Welcome—Ladrone Island Wonders—Among the Lonely Islets—Racatu—Hachin—Bora Boru—Gems of the South Pacific—The Marquesas—Female Types—The International Patrol—The Mountains of Raiatea—Fear Dispelled—Aripah's Farewell—A Story.

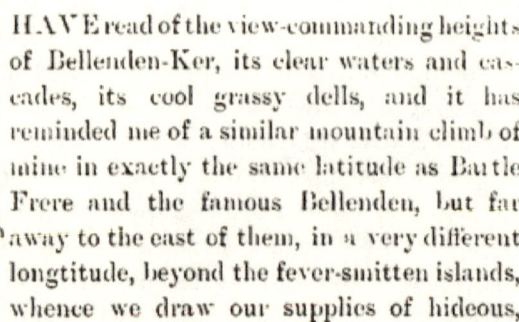

I HAVE read of the view-commanding heights of Bellenden-Ker, its clear waters and cascades, its cool grassy dells, and it has reminded me of a similar mountain climb of mine in exactly the same latitude as Bartle Frere and the famous Bellenden, but far away to the east of them, in a very different longtitude, beyond the fever-smitten islands, whence we draw our supplies of hideous, woolly, not to say sometimes murderous kanakas, beyond even the distant and handsomer Samoan's group of islets; in fact about as far east as you can get, without losing Polynesia altogether. I allude to Tahiti, whose men had the form and beauty of Greek gods, as we see them sculptured in marble, and whose women, with luminous eyes (like amber black fire) and faultless forms, made one regret that the feminine discipline and culture of Europe had never been engrafted on their many innate good qualities.

Off the island of Eimeo, near Tahiti, I had climbed to the topgallant crosstrees of our 'Frisco-bound barque, the "Eudora," to see its conical, spiky peaks the better, and, when I came down, my example was followed by young Wales, the son of the police-magistrate at Morven, Tasmania; and two of the sailors (not liking this intrusion on their domain) followed him up the rigging, with ropeyarns round their necks wherewith to bind, till he paid a forfeit, this too aspiring youth: but he was clear grit;" for, coolly waiting till "Johnny Flatfoot" was within a few inches of him, Wales slid like lightning down the topgallant backstay to the deck, ruining his pants with tar and barking his palms a bit, but triumphant, as a native Australian should be, and leaving his would-be captors lamenting and laughed at by all hands. The boy had "been to sea" before.

Anon came an outrigger canoe alongside from the shore of Eimeo, bringing some young men, who, as they sat on our bulwarks, had the profiles and heads of Antinous and Achilles, and an air of unpretentious and unconscious dignity and manners only met with in the higher class of European youth. They bartered with us their beautiful mother-of-pearl fishhooks for any trifle we could spare, and their noble heads, bound with fillet and a feather, disappeared over the side as we sailed on towards Otaheite and its harbour of Papiete, where we were to water; for, be it known to the reader, eighty of us in the "Eudora," cabin, steerage, and crew alike, had been on a ration of $1\frac{1}{2}$-pint of fresh water *per diem* for three weeks in the month of February, south of the line, mark you, as well as in and near the tropic, and you need only to try this to know what it is like. There was, of course, no tea, no soup, &c., for the cook would have boiled it all away; no "grog," either, for this would have caused thirst, but salt-water soap sufficed us for baths. We had plenty of champagne and bottled beer, yet it was melan-

choly at night for us bachelors to hear the thirsty babes and
children through the saloon bulkheads talk in their sleep
and murmur, "Drint o' water, ma." My plan was to mix
a little limejuice and sherry with the water and drink once
in twenty-four hours. Nobody died ; some suffered and
some did not. I was amongst the latter, for I never even
carried a pannikin in my thousands of miles of solitary bush
rides in Queensland summer; but, if some of us had not
"subscribed" a daily gill apiece of our scanty allowance,
to help the "hot coppers" of the brandy drinkers on board,
some of them might have gone under. We started from
Hobart short of water, intending to fill up at New Zealand,
but deceived, like the captain of St. Paul's ship, by a spanking fair wind, we sailed past it for Tahiti, and were caught,
half-way, with a ceaseless north-easter, and were kept at
sea till we got down to 10in. of water in the last tank, a
tight fit for eighty people, as we entered the harbour of
Papiete, in Otaheite, a semicircular bay in the shore like a
bow, the string of which was a coral reef with one opening
in it, enclosing a harbour smooth as the docks of London,
which I had left not long before, and now found myself in
an atmosphere and temperature like the Palm-house at Kew.

Papiete was not the dull place one would have expected
forty years ago in a remote Pacific Island ; the French had
just taken Tahiti by force from the natives, and there had
been a fight on a large scale, and under a lofty monument,
duly inscribed, reposed forty - one men and officers of
"L'Uranie" frigate who had fallen in the conflict, quite as
disastrous as the German loss in Samoa. The middle-aged
Queen, called by the family and titular name of "Pomare,"
had a husband much younger and handsomer than herself—
she 40, he 30 years old. She dressed in a black satin cassock,
and the girls of Tahiti in the same, only the material was
coloured print, and with a flower in each ear for an earring,

and some sweet-scented native oil on their straight black
hair. Never walking far, never carrying burdens, always
swimming or canoeing, they had diminutive hands and feet
to match; not so some old chiefs, who were pointed out to
me as having remembered Captain Cook's visit in their
early childhood, and their white heads and their legs and
feet swollen to the size and shape of a log of wood with
elephantiasis, certainly gave them as they sat in a row an
air of great antiquity. They appear to be a longer-lived race
than the Sandwich Islanders, as well as far handsomer.

The kings of Hawaii follow each other in quick succession,
as well as the queens. I met one of the latter, Emma Rooke,
a slender creole-looking half-caste girl of 14, in 1850. I
sold to her father, Dr. Rooke, of Honolulu, a frame house,
ex "Eudora," and on calling to collect the doubloons she
officiated for him, as he was out. She was a granddaughter
of John Young, and married the fourth Kamehameha.
She became the plump Queen Emma, who was made so much
of by Queen Victoria in England in 1865-66, and who died,
untimely, like most Hawaiians of rank, in 1885, the death
of their only child having killed her husband with grief
many years before.

But to return to Tahiti. It was, as I said before, anything but dull. The military bands and the men-of-war's
bands together discoursed evening music on the beach such
as neither the Melbourne nor the Sydney, of those days,
could match. The massive foreyard of the frigate "Sybille,"
fifty-two guns, lay on the shore like a fallen gum-tree, a
well-kept tropical-looking hotel on the sea strand dispensed
claret, with a divine, rough bouquet, and we drank it out
of coffee-cups; also tomatoes, cunningly fried with vinegar
and eschalots; bananas, worked up into all sorts of artful
pastry; and execrable, thin, pale, sour, bottled beer from
Paisley, though the *parfait amour* and other liqueurs were

quite up to the mark—for a Polynesian island so far from all civilisation. Queen Pomare's 70ft. carved canoe was sheltered from the sun under a thatched roof, on a bed of bamboo leaves, and here, for the first time in life, I heard the romantic Æolian hum of the tropical mosquito, suggestive of verandah courtship by starlight at 80deg., what time the land breeze would cut off the heads of every roller that moaned on the coral reef which bounds the harbour, and blew the spray out to sea again.

We had to stop several days to get in all the water we required with primitive appliances, so an excursion was planned for three of us—namely, Wales, Turner (a surveyor, who afterwards settled at Oaku), and myself, to ascend the mountain stronghold of the island, the last defence from which the natives had been driven, and only then because they deemed it inaccessible, and therefore impregnable, and not necessary to be guarded; but they had to deal with the active Zouave breed of biped cats, who, five years later, scaled the Malakoff at Sebastopol, a Niagara of irrepressible red breeches; and the Tahiti warriors (who had never heard of such things as ladders) found the enemy, armed to the teeth, suddenly in the midst of their garrison, and all was over. It was to this mountain fastness, nearly 4,000ft. above the sea, that we started to climb. Five times we had to ford a beautiful little pellucid river, 60ft. wide and 5ft. deep, and didn't I get a fine sore throat next day from the wetting, but our doctor (a brother of Eusebius Lloyd, of St. Bartholomew's) soon sent it flying with a gargle of dilute sulphuric acid. Lovely was the scenery and fertile the soil, as we began the ascent. Cones of rock, 1,000ft. high, rich in lichens and veiled with flowery creepers, towered by the side of our route. The wild ginger threw out its gnarled tubers under our feet; grand timber trees, solid and hard as ebony, made up the forest, in company with the breadfruit, guava (which scented the air), mammee apple, papaw, oranges, lemons, bananas, &c. It will be noted that, unlike the forest of Australia, nearly everything that grew here was food of some sort, and, with the easily-caught fish of the country, made up a bill-of-fare that caused anything like hunting or labour to be as out of fashion as hunger or thirst or want were.

We were made heartily welcome by the Gaelic lieutenant, who, with 100 soldiers, kept the "Pah Fattawah," as the fastness was called, and some excellent cognac, with pure cascade water, made Turner and myself recollect our French, and find out all the history of the capture of the place. Full in view of the officers' quarters, was the loveliest waterfall imaginable, not a broken one or in a mountain gully hidden by scrub, and only visible here and there, but a sheer fall of 700ft., over a wide, clean, perpendicular white wall of rock of double that in width: and poised high in air above it hovered, clear out against the sky, a beautiful bird, called, I think, the "frigate" bird. Anyway it has one, and only one, long amber feather in its tail; the feather from which the priceless State cloak of the Kings of Hawaii has been for 200 years a making, at the rate of one bird, one feather, and no more. This wall of rock bounded our view in that direction, and the tumbling water became mere mist and spray ere it reached the foot of the fall. But it was a sight never to be forgotten; and we dwelt on it as long as we could compatible with the necessity of being back to town before "gunfire" and on board our ship again, for matters were strict, and martial law was not quite in abeyance, and the institution known in "nigger" countries as the "calaboose" (synonym for watchhouse) was open for the reception of belated travellers who might be away from their proper domicile at night without a passport.

The magnificent and massive ruins in the Ladrone Islands

open up a new and still stranger phase of the mystery of the mammoth trilithon and other marvels of savage places where engineering is unknown. The huge images and carvings on Easter Island, near the west coast of South America, are not so wonderful, being, most likely, on land that was once continental. The vast ruined temples and carvings of Guatemala and Central America are exactly like those of Hindustan in character, and totally dissimilar to those of Egypt and Asia Minor, at Baalbec, Luxor, Palmyra, and Nineveh. The mystery of these last is somewhat modified by the fact of their having had some sort of a contemporary papyrus literature, some form of stone inscriptions open to interpretation, left behind them. But where is the literature (if any ever existed) of ancient Guatemala? older far, in its buildings, than Moses and Homer and their days. Where is the literary legacy of the Ladrones and those other islands to the north-east of us, where the gigantic cross stone rests high on two upright monsters, and where, apparently, no human hands nor machinery could ever have placed its enormous size and weight. Could it have been done by people who could engineer and reckon but not read nor write? But the mystery of the Ladrones far surpasses all this. Here we have not only the gigantic work in masonry, but not a trace of any similar kind of work is to be found elsewhere on the island, whence it might have been quarried. This brings us face to face (on the theory of land submergment) with the carriage of massive stones over an impossible distance by land or water, in short, we confront a miracle, a paradox, which overstrains the intellect and faculty of comprehension, even as did the awful hypnotism, or will-power, of the Incarnate Deity, eighteen centuries back, in the presence of diseased human organisms, which obeyed their Creator's command, and became sound in a moment; and even these miracles present no stronger shock of the "possible-impossible" to the mere reasoning faculty than do those wonders of the Ladrone Island. The evidence of the mere senses seem still to be as incredible, as when the Infinite will-power hypnotises matter and gives it mind, and then hypnotises mind and gives to it more than one can speak of. For words are all powerless to paint some ideas, and, great as these last may be, they cannot even go near to grasping the unlimited, which has neither size, weight, dimensions, distance, nor any other mere vulgar material attribute. Yet, in the pride of intellect, one does not like to recoil baffled from a solution of this lithic mystery. The stone in the Ladrones ruins is described as being like basalt, like granite, and *unlike* that of any on the other island. Now, a "rule of thumb" engineer would account for the trilithon in the "recruiting" islands to the north-east of us by supposing that the inhabitants (past or present) "up ended" the two upright stones, and then filled in an easy gradient mound of earth to the top of them, and, with rollers, placed the top stone in position afterwards removing the earth again; but this solution of the riddle would not apply in the case of the Ladrone Island ruins, where the pillars and walls were of an unknown and non-local stone. I once went down the Thames on an excursion to Rochester, and explored the ruins of the castle I found a cement, full of flints, said to have been the work of the Romans, and which time had rendered as hard as any granite. May there not once have been a "concrete" or artificial stone, the secret of which is as lost as the art of carving a ruby, or burning colours into glass, but which was known to former inhabitants of these islands, and which concrete could be put up piecemeal with wooden moulds while it was soft, and then hardened gradually till it became what it now is, one solid piece of work apparently? Failing some such theory as this, we are still face to face with a miracle. And a few words on miracles. When a man catches cold, the College of Physicians, being mere mortals, discourse learnedly of capillaries and congestion, and counter irritants, and then mechanical remedies, which only touch the *outside* of the matter, and half cures it, Nature herself doing the rest; while an omniscient and Creative Being *sees* the other and subtle conditions (all unseen of man) both in their natural structure itself and in the ailment and disorder thereof. which conditions underlie and are behind, and which cause the outward signs seen by the mortal College of Physicians, and He, the Maker, can wend also, and, with His hypnotism, calls on those occult conditions, and they respond and obey and return to health as invisibly and irresistibly as they fell out of it, and because *we* cannot see the unseen and unseeable work behind the scenes it is called by us, and very naturally, a "miracle."

It is not generally considered a solitary place, and yet it is really the most far removed and isolated one upon the face of the earth. I allude to the Sandwich Islands, where lofty Hawaii, smaller than Yorkshire, but tall as the Alps, and snug Oahu, with its Honolulu harbour, and a few more clustered islets, lie alone. The sole oasis in a wilderness of ocean, stretching eastward till Mexico, nearly 4,000 miles off, is the first land; looking northward till naught but Kamschatka, 5,000 miles away, breaks the ocean's monotony; westward, the far off shores of China, 6,000 miles distant, alone bar the ship's progress over the water, while, to the south, an expanse of 8,000 miles of sea reaches to the Pole itself. There is no continental spot so lonely as this, no oasis in such a desert of size, solitary as are none of the beautiful islets in the Southern Pacific. These last all nestle, more or less closely and sociably, to each other a species of extended Venice with the beauties of nature as a good substitute for those of art. From exquisite Tahiti,

and moored down to the low coral "atolls" where some
honest stalwart son of the sea from the waterside tarry,
Wapping of cockney Sydney, has taken up his permanent
abode with the cocoa nuts, and proved conclusively that the
male Caucasian race mates well with the rounded soft-eyed
houris of the eastern cyclades, whose kindly salutation is
Yurana takn eti; and, if you doubt it, behold his strapping
sons and winsome irresistible creole daughters, all healthy,
happy, simple-hearted workers. How suggestive are some
of the white man's names for some of the lonely islets in
the South Pacific, to say nothing of the beauty and euphony
of the native appellations. Pylstaart Island, for instance.
Here we have the old Dutch Vanderdecken revealed. He
was amongst the early maritime explorers of the Southern
Pacific, one of the first whites to see the dusky syrens of
the palm groves and coral reefs, and "Starbuck," too!
What need to trace *this* name beyond Nantucket on the
thrifty north-east states of Uncle Sam. English it may
have been originally, or German corrupted with English,
but it proves now that the enterprising whaler, of Maine
and Massachusetts, went and poked his nose out west from
Valparaiso, and the "sparm whale on the coast of Pe-ru"
till he found the magnetic nymphs who knew the oil of the
cocoanut better than that of the whale.

Maddalena and Dominica, in the Marquesas group, are
as lovely amongst the islands of the world as are Milan and
Freiburg amongst its cathedrals; while Hackim and Bora
Boru, in the Society group, give us glimpses of Eden in
their matchless scenic beauty beyond the dreams of the
India drug smoker; and there is health with it all, too.
Yes, and romance and association to Byron's "Island," the
romantic tale of the Bounty. You are far from baleful
Asia and India, far east and away from them and their
diseases, those fearful changes that are rung upon the end-

less types of disordered livers, born of heat, hunger, and malaria. You find these in Java and New Guinea, and all the other tropical groups which hail old Asia for a parent and neighbour, and peculiar to whom as are crocodiles, serpents, and minerals, all quite unknown in our eastern dream as lands of bliss; for measles will sweep as a scourge over Fiji and the New Hebrides, and a disease which those best able to judge class as cholera, is not unknown. In some of the "atoll" islands which cluster near the equator and lie to the north and east of Australia, there is at times a scarcity of water, and a small and unwholesome choice of food. Stunted cocoa nuts, drought smitten, is not the diet to ward off depressing disease, and when the poor islanders are taken to sea in ships, to sail to where they *can* be properly fed, the Destroyer is at work early amongst them. They grasp their bellies where the pain is, and fail to come on deck; putrid blood bursts from the mouth, aggravated with frightful purging. Sometimes even this is surpassed, and you see a "boy" bringing you coffee at breakfast, and you miss him at dinner at 1 p.m. Search for him at 4, and find him already cold, with the froth at his lips, behind a coil of rope. At 4 p.m., overboard they go, half-a-dozen a-day. It would take twelve doctors, not one, to keep the five hundred of them alive to the extent of even 60 per cent. And oh! the suggestive smell that pervades the ship; it would break down the pluck of a buccaneer. Not even the deadly dysenteries of China are "in the same street" with this nigger cholera; for you can't keep men in full stamina without appropriate diet. We grieve over the death of a neighbour, and go over all the details of the illness, but who notes the pain and the death of these poor islanders, each one of whom suffers his full martyrdom alone and uncomforted.

As regards the relative beauties of Racatu, Hachin, Bora Boru, and Eimio, all I can say is that the world does not

WOMEN OF TAHITI.

hold the equal of them elsewhere, but if you ask me to decide which amongst them bears the palm, I can only tell you that you might as well set me the task of awarding the prize to the best essay in the various Epistles of Saul, of Tarsus, each one a glorious gem in itself, but all differing like choice flowers in a bouquet.

The South Pacific Islands round Tahiti are, as a rule, not large enough to exhibit extensive bays, but one exception is at Marchard Island, or Nukubera, discovered by Captain Ingraham, of Boston, Massachusetts, about 1790, and lying to the north of the main Marquesas group, first made known by Mendana, the Spaniard, 200 years before that. There is a real bay in Nukubera, and it makes a grand harbour, too. Like Rio Janeiro, it has conical islands in it, and two of them, higher than St. Peter's at Rome, guard the entrance, and then it spreads out both ways and forms a nearly circular basin for anchorage, from which rises a green amphitheatre, sloping upwards gently at first, but rising anon into steeper acclivities, the green at the water's edge shading into deep blue where the serrated summit outline cuts the sky and hems in the view all round, at a height of nearly four thousand feet. But this is only a part of the picture. Profound and picturesque gorges radiate from the bay and pierce up to the dim summits of the cordon range. Each glen with its own particular tumbling white torrent appearing and disappearing 'mid the green, till it at last soberly enters the little harbour, which has about nine miles of circular frontage. As an amphitheatre, it is about the biggest and most beautiful in the South Pacific, and like a Titanic coliseum in scenery. Creeping and hanging vines and other plants covering, as well as they can, the rocky furrows and stony wrinkles, all on an enormous scale, which time seems to have worn on the aged face of dame nature just here. And the natives are no mild vegetarians; they have

T

not solved the problem of how to live solely on fruits of the earth, as the Hindoos have. A keen lust for that which once had blood in it, be it fish, fowl, or animal, rules their appetite. I do them the justice to think that cannibalism first arose through the vile habit of human sacrifices, originated by the dominant priestly caste, long before the early sandal-wood hunting days of the South Pacific. *A propos* of which our sailors 200 years ago used to sail from the locality of the present London Docks to the Marquesas for sandal wood.

> Isles, with the mystic spell,
>   Tonga! Tabu!
> Lands, where pride rose—and fell,
>   Vanua! Levu!
> Haunts of some vanished race
> Lacking in God-born grace,
> Stone now—their only trace,
>   Vengeance their due.

In speculating as to the origin of these Pacific Islands, several matters strike us: there are no fossil remains, and no animal or aqueous survivors of the pre-Adamite era such as the ceratodus or ornithorhynchus of Australia; there are no dangerous beasts, birds, or reptiles of any kind. Paradise itself was not more free from them nor more abounding in edible fruits by the wayside; the present inhabitants are not of the highest intellectual type, such as the arithmetical and mathematical Arabs and Jews of old, though they retain many of their traditions and customs; but, in gentle courtesy and homely domestic common sense, as applied to political, religious, and social daily life, they are very simple and "human," even if a little common-place, and not aspiring; still less do the present people belong to the past and vanished race who could "up end" stones of 15 x 12 x 8 and place an 18ft. one across the top of them and mortice it in; Polynesia, I think, must be geologically young, far behind Australia, but ethnologically the oldest place in the World and inhabited perhaps before any other spot was, and by a race who could carve and hew stone, but of whose graving tools no trace can now be found; the mystic, potent, awful "Tabu" being the only fragmentary spirit and symbol now remaining of the wisdom and the interdiction of those whom the whirlwind of Time hath swept away for ever from this planet.

Tahiti and Marquesas! A region of scenic wonders indeed! Large gorges; perpendicular ravines—all of giant dimensions; lilac and amber peaks, whose jagged points pierce the sky and are flecked and cut with tinted cloudrings, hardly one round-shouldered hill visible anywhere, but gothic peaks of bright hues against a darker background; mysterious abysses, sunlit cones, superb and awe-aspiring, though made up of basalt and other homely geologic products of extinct volcanic warriors of bygone igneous ages, and now almost clothed in green vegetation beautifully contrasted with a peep of sterile rock here and there; and inhabited by a race of women who are beautiful and don't know it, who are not vain, not "dressy," talk no scandal and envy no one; for they have not known the temptation of the white woman who *is* vain, and no wonder for white men make her so, thusly:— A beautiful girl, not vain, is approached by a common-place man who seeks to attract her attention and interest. Well! there is nothing in *him* to do *that*, so the animal resorts to strategem and begins to tell her that her hands, feet, ears, eyes, hair, figure, bonnet, mantle, dress, gloves, what not, are perfection; loads her with fulsome flattery in order that he may leave on her mind that pleasant impression of himself which his looks, his wit, or his manliness never would or could do; and so it comes to pass that he spoils and mars a fresh bit of Nature's work, in order, forsooth! that *he* may feed in forbidden pastures, and she becomes vain from that day forth, who never was so before *he* intruded on the scene.

The girls at the island, like Tahiti where there is a crowd, and where people see hundreds of others and fresh faces every day, are staid to a certain extent in their demeanour, but this is no criterion for some of the lonely groups and solitary islets where ever new and varying types of exquisite female loveliness are to be met with. One would wonder where the variety came from: for the Tahitian differs from the Marquesan, and both again vary from the Samoan, the Prumoto, and the Chain Island girl; in one group, the eyes and lashes surpass the world, in another the sweet expression of the features, in another the littleness of the ears, hands, and feet, in another the superb development and symmetry of the limbs and body; but, in the solitary places where they rarely see a white man in the pride of his youth, they are not what Mrs. Grundy calls "modest." Why should they be? or rather, how can they be? Did they ever read a book? Is the word "propriety," or its equivalent, met with in their language; did even Mother Eve ever hear it spoken, or read of it in a novel?; and what does Lukeeha, of the lonely "atoll" know more than Eve did. Lukeeha is kind, she would give you all, or any of her poor barbaric ornaments, would feed you, nurse you, worship you, for she never saw a white young man before and knows nothing of him, or his civilization, except that he is a new ideal for her, and she is no more backward or retiring in his presence than would be a London *debutante* in the presence of a diamond necklace, that could be got for the asking and handling.

These islands form the largest "beat" in the world for police supervision. Scattered cruisers from England and France, from Germany and the United States, patrol the groups the whole way from Espiritu Santo to Nukahiva more or less, and do what they can where all the fleets afloat could not do what *is* wanted; and the Pacific paradises are mostly a "law to themselves"; the long pennants cannot fly

everywhere, and even then "international" law is a clumsy
weapon at best, in the strange and lovely unannexed islets,
so pirates and buccaneers of the "handsome Hayes'" type
do much as they please, in the way of fraud, "kidnap,"
violence, and cajolery; long before his day, the fun went on,
and women's beauty and men's labours, and men's property,
the fruit of labour, were preyed upon as freely as in the
lawless and unpatrolled land ocean of Central Africa.

The art of committing sham suicide is not, as is generally
supposed, one of quite modern invention. True, we do hear
nowadays of young men who have failed in some praise-
worthy attempt to select beforehand the winner, say, of the
Caulfield Cup, and who "borrowed" some money from the till
over it, which they could not replace before its absence was
found out, and who disappeared from view, leaving no trace
beyond a suit of clothes on the cliffs or sea-beach, and a
loaded revolver with two chambers recently discharged.
The finder is placed in a blissful state of uncertainty as to
whether the absentee had fired the two bullets into his head
and then swam out and drowned himself, or whether he first
of all tried to drown himself and then came back and used
the revolver, winding up with a lead sinker and an emptied
air belt half-a-mile out at sea, uncharitable and cynical
folks, of course, asserting that no suicide at all had taken
place. But these are mere modern episodes; the art itself
was invented hundreds of years ago at Raiatea, a large and
beautiful island of the Society Group, near Tahiti, in the
dark ages, tracing back to the year 1400 or so, when the
great "Hiro" was reputed to be the founder of the Pacific
race, it was customary for the priests to select, from time
to time, victims for human sacrifice from amongst the poorer
and less influential islanders, who were not acquainted with
the secret signs, and, so to speak, the freemasonry which
the chiefs used in talking to each other. The victim was

never warned; he was only silently selected and missed by his friends. The stealthy blow with a stone axe from behind did the work in a moment, and no one except the priests knew who was to be the next one. The result was that these poor islanders (to use a bootmakers' phrase) got "full" about this.

Now Raiatea is a curious and lovely island, an earthly Paradise in climate, beauty, and scenery. It has the inevitable beach all round it, narrow in places where the mountains come down to the sea, wide and stretching back into fertile plains where the mountains recede from the ocean; the usual glorious coral shallows environ it, of course, and on their edge ever beats the curling and musically booming surf, the upper crystal drops of which are blown out to sea in an opposite direction to the advancing waves by the land breeze, and look like lancers' pennons when they "charge" to windward.

And then these mountains of Raiatea! How shall I describe them? Their sides are verdant, but unscaleable, clothed with dense jungle and rich vegetation, cleft with narrow deep ravines at their outlying edges, down which the cascades pour 1000 feet at a leap from the terraces and tablelands above. High above all this lies the inhabited but inaccessible "downs" of the interior, where a race lives who never visit nor are visited by the dwellers in the plains below. Wild fowl, fish, and fruit are plentiful on this upper country, and before describing it further, I will relate how it came to be inhabited. Smoke and fires had been seen on it with telescopes, and from passing ships, so the existence of human beings was a certainty, and this is how they originally got there. One poor fellow who had lost some of his near and dear relatives by the priests in the old idolatrous days before Mendana, the Spaniard, in 1594, burst into the eastern Pacific. This one poor fellow plotted with the survivors of his family tribe a happy idea. They took their well-known canoes to a distant point of the island, and there so damaged them that they appeared to have been wrecked on the coral, and for themselves they hied them to a spot high up on the mountains, where some overhanging lianas or vines gave access upwards by a route where no foot could find a resting place.

Travelling a great distance along the narrow ledge of a lofty eminence, a sharp corner is turned, leading into a verdant fertile hollow, buttressed all round by sheer and awful abysses. In this dell grew a profusion of the mountain plantain and other fruits, and a herbal bark of great use in the mild fevers and skin eruptions peculiar to the islands. The only outlets to this hollow dell were the ledge already spoken of and some hanging vines which led up a precipice to safe, clear, and widely extending ground above. Thither came the priest dreading fugitives, climbed the vines, drew them up, and were never seen again on the island below. Their canoes were found, and they themselves were supposed to have been drowned at sea, and the priests had to travel further for victims. And this is the first case on record of "sham" suicide, of which modern Australia is but a feeble imitation. The race which sprung up on these tablelands of Eden grew to be the most expert climbers amongst the human race. The eight or ten families who started this new departure throve and multiplied on the wide-spread land of plenty, which they thus found in those glorious undulating mountains of happiness. But the vines being once drawn up, no one could follow them, while they could, if they liked, make secret excursions below. Their language, of course, remained the same as that of the people below, but they held no communication with them, and till the early missionaries brought telescopes with them no unassisted human eye could scan the dim recesses, cloud, peaks, and shoulders of this divine spot, or view the living people who there flitted about and were happy, though as invisible to those below as the inhabitants of the planet Mars are to us on the earth. Only on two occasions up to the date of George the Fourth's death were any of those mountain people captured. On the first occasion, two children and one old man were surprised in the dell alluded to. The children screamed, and, like monkeys, soon climbed beyond reach of capture. No lowlander could follow *them*. The old man in escaping slipped and fell, and fatally injured himself. He survived his capture a week, and told how his forefathers had fled at the season when the one fruit, which was always then eaten with human sacrifices, was known to be nearly ripe, a season always fatal to the poor islander, as the green pea season is to ducks.

Mr. Robert Bourne, of the Congregational Union, went out as missionary to the Tahiti and Society Group about the latter years of King George the Third's life. His children were some of them born at Raiatea. He was, twenty years later, in the drapery business in Pitt-street, Sydney, and, forty years later again, he was secretary to the Board of Public Education in Brisbane. He was the grandfather of the Registrar of Titles for Queensland, Mr. J. Orton Bourne, and of Mr. Robert Orton Bourne, Superintendent of Telegraphs for the same colony; and his son, George Bourne, was Landsborough's colleague in that brave dash across the Australian continent, in 1862. But to return to the Rev. Robert Bourne. He, stationed as a missionary at Raiatea, was, previous to 1822, told of this legend of the captive wild mountaineer, and he burned with a warm desire to get at the rest of this interesting community, and to let them know that the murderous bugbear of centuries was at an end. But all in vain. His most active scouts could never climb the ravine slopes that led to the central fastness to beyond a certain height, where rock walls grew absolutely perpendicular, and the sides of the gullies were much the same. The central upper Paradise was guarded like the gardens of the Hesperides. But after some years, and when his two elder children, a boy (Robert) and a girl (afterwards Mrs. Chisholm) were out walking with him at a new home which he had made in a far corner of the island, his wife also being with them, he was startled to see a crowd of natives, three of whom held a captive by the hair, which flowed wildly about, and long, like a womans'. The poor terrified creature was a man from the upper regions; the foam on his lips, and exhausted partly from struggling and partly from illness; for he had been pounced upon while gathering some of the fever herb which grew only on the lands below the summit centre of the island. He stood trembling and with dilated eyes, as frightened as any wild beast captured by men. His terror was not decreased by the sight of the white gentleman and lady, another startling wonder for him. "Do not kill me! Do not give me to the priests!" he said; and Mr. Bourne was able to reply to him in the same language. "There are no priests here now, and the false gods have left Raiatea for ever, my friend, so have no more fear." The captive could not grasp the meaning of the words, but the kind looks of Mrs. Bourne and the two little white children spoke more reassuringly than any words could. He had no terror of them, but he gazed in such agony at Pomare, who now came up with more natives, that Mr. Bourne, as the only way to soothe him, took him away from them and to his own home for the night. When a few days had elapsed he grew calmer, but the slightest incident would renew his fears and entreaties for mercy. Not a native could come, even to look at him, without his dreading to be murdered. The little white boy and girl helped their father to teach the captive his letters and to spell short words when his fears had subsided, and had it been possible to keep him in sight of them and them only, all would have been well, for Mr. Bourne devoted all his time to the poor wild man. A couple of weeks thus rolled away, and the wild "Orson" seemed to be tame at last. But the fact that Mr. Bourne and his new home were on a remote part of the island, and away from the populated place where whale-ships and white men called in, prevented the poor "myall" from realising by the sight of chapels, etc., that "old things had passed away." On the fifteenth day, Mr. Bourne asked him to come out for a walk with Mrs. Bourne and the two children (this was in 1822). He refused at first, but the two youngsters seizing his hands playfully, dragged him out. All went well till Aripah (this was the man's name) in the stroll along the beach, the only path then in that dense jungle, came in sight at once both of the dear mountains on one side, and of a mob of natives on the other. The crowd drew nearer, and Aripah grew wild in the eyes again. Mr. Bourne waved to them to go back, but curiosity pressed them on. In another moment Aripah broke from Mr. Bourne, who held him by the hand, and fled like a deer to his beloved mountain, pursued by the crowd of shouting natives, who might have spared themselves the trouble, for he was fleeter than they, and was half way up the mountain before they got even to the foot of it, where its abrupt and unknown cliffs forbade all further pursuit by them. Mr. and Mrs. Bourne exchanged saddened glances as the cries of the hunting pack died away in the forest, afraid alike of what might happen, and also that in any case they would never see Aripah again. He had a thirty yards' start, when fear overcame confidence, and he increased it at every stride. Bye and bye a great shout arose, and Mr. Bourne, going out to see the cause, beheld, on the sharp angle of a precipice far above them, Aripah looking down a farewell at him, and even then he had to send for his telescope to be sure it was his lost one. Aripah sat there for thirty minutes looking at him, and then got up and vanished—and for ever as far as the Rev. R. Bourne was concerned, for up to the year 1832, when he finally left Raiatea, neither Aripah nor one of his mates was seen by those below.

The genesis of the South and East Pacific Islands is shrouded in unfathomable impenetrable mystery, alike as to their geologicial inception and their ethnological settlement. Serving for us to recall the lines—

> With what an awful world-revolving power
> Were first th' unwieldly planets launched along
> Th' illimitable void--there to remain
> Amid the lapse of many thousand years.
> *Which oft hath swept the toiling race of men,*
> *And all their boasted monuments away.*

This great ocean, sighted first as regards the earth and by white men — from the mountains on the Isthmus of Darien, which Balboa climbed in 1513, and sighted in 1520 by Magelhan from the other end of the continent that terminates in Cape Horn, contains islands peopled by a race that puzzles the wisest to trace back. And the more their customs, their features, and monuments are studied, the less able are the enquirers to discover what led to present conditions. There was a gentle and handsome female race kept in bondage by a fetish called the "tabu," and not allowed the freedom and privileges due to their sex. There were habits and usages, analagous to those of the ancient Jews, Arabs, and Phœnicians, there was a cast of countenance of the Greek and Caucasian type, and a mythology of the same. Stone monuments, statues, hieroglyphs, and massive terraces, walls, and trilithons, recalling Central America, and the dimmest, darkest ages of the old world.

Yes, the women may well be good-tempered in Tahiti. *They* never have to go, at 11 p.m. on Saturday night, to pull a drunken husband out of the tavern, and with a baby on one arm, and him on the other, as *occasionally* happens in the white man's land, both north and south of the equator. These be matters that shorten the temper and sharpen the tongue of the white girl. They have never happened in Tahiti since time began. Temperance people sometimes foolishly try to reckon up the "drink bill" of the British Empire by the wholesale money that is paid for the liquor. Fudge! *that* does not represent a tithe of the real bill. John Stumps, of Australia, drinks half-a-crown's worth of alcohol, and becomes thereby fearfully and wonderfully drunk for forty-eight hours. He stands at the bar of the public-house and reiterates the wearisome statement that he, and he alone, is the best (sanguinary) shearer, bootmaker, saddler (what does it matter?) in the (gory) colony. He keeps this up till 3 a.m., and, on the third day, is "seedy, and can't work for four days more; losing 10s. a day for six days, or £3 in all in mere money. So that the 1s. 3d. *wholesale* price of the liquor that "knocked him out," and which is all that the temperance statisticians take note of or put in their "drink bill" needs to be multiplied fifty times in order to show even the mere dollars lost for ever. While, as for John Stumps and his broken health, wretched family, ruined soul and prospects, you can't possibly put *them* into practical numerals at all; such things are classified otherwise and elsewhere. Come, now, I will tell you a story *à propos* of all this. There was, at the east end of London, a brilliant gin palace, with cut glasses and candelabra and gas jets, with pork pies on the counter, and ham sandwiches, and stalwart barmen to serve the liquor, and ready to eject noisy customers. A young man (whom I afterwards knew in Australia) was one of these. His father

managed a brewery, and he had a rich uncle, a retired
publican, who wanted him to marry a pretty girl who would
have £5,000 on her wedding day, and to start in hotel
business for himself with her money, and what his uncle
would give him. He was to meet her at the "Licensed
Victuallers' Annual Ball." She was a partner (I can tell
you) worth dancing with—with her splendid black hair
and eyes, her costly golden jewellery, her rich bronze silk
dress, her bronze silk hose, and her neat bronze kid pumps,
and with 5,000 sovereigns and a ready-made business. She
was a bait indeed for any young man to snap at. Well, one
night some time before the ball, was cold and wintry, and
our hero was serving as usual behind the bar, when a girl
child of ten years entered for a jug of beer. The snow was
falling outside "underneath the gaslight glitter," and the
poor little waif had nothing on her head or her feet, and
I am bound to say, very little on her body The snowflakes
as she stood at the counter dripped from her head and melted
between her bosom and the ragged garment which alone
covered it that bleak night. Yet her parents had the money
to send her for beer, poor, half-frozen starveling! The sight
was too much for our barman; he *had* a heart inside him.

He saw the child's hungry eye and shivering form, and he
forced half a pork pie and some ham sandwiches on her and
made her eat them, paying for them himself. He made an
excuse to go home, and swore to himself, that he would
never serve a glass of liquor again, or take wages, or make
profit that arose from, or was in any way connected with
such sights and awful realities, as that poor little snow-
bathed victim. He went to the ball, though, and danced
with Miss Bronze Pumps, inhaled the warm perfume of her
tresses, admired her splendid *physique*, and could have had
her, and competence, too, for the asking, for he was clever,
and could sing and act; but, somehow, between him and her

would come that half-frozen, fragile, snow-dabbled child of half her age, and he could *not* make money or enjoy ease in that way, so he angered his uncle, threw up his situation, and went to sea as steward of an emigrant ship. There was everything to tempt his animal nature and love of comfort in this ballroom heiress and the ready-made business, but he could not somehow "get away from" this child-Lazarus "at his gate," nor enjoy in peace money derived from the misery and wrongs of such pitiful helpless innocents. But there is none of this in Tahiti, you know. For one thing, of course it never snows there.

[EDITOR'S NOTE.]

"Most of the following occasional papers were found among the late Mr. Bartley's manuscripts. They are all more or less important, and are certainly interesting, since nearly the whole of them treat with either Australian men or matters. For that reason, and with a belief that the author intended to give them permanent value, they are included in this his last work."

EDITOR.

SAMOAN TYPES.

MEMORIAL LINES TO HARRY KENDALL.

HERE Idumea's myrtled hills frown dark on Judah's
    land,
Whose summit crags seem castle towers to many a
    pilgrim band,
Where Aroer, by Arnon's stream, 'neath lofty Pisgah's
    springs,
On far-off Harosheth doth gaze, beyond the Gentile
    kings,
Where Midian's dromedaries bore their load to
Ephrah's Vale
With Bozrah's gay-striped garniture, like Afric's lateen sail,
Where Chaldee sages kept the stars on parchment scroll engrossed,
(When Guatemala's hoary fanes crowned Costa Rican coast)
There, singers in the days of old, heard Nature's stirring call,
And David, Deborah, enrapt bade music's cadence fall.

And hath not this our Austral land, a pre-historic claim?
The old world's elder brother it, in everything but name
Ceratodus*—long since a part of Britain's marble stone—
Swims our free waters here to-day strong living flesh and bone.
And other forms, Pre-Adamite, attest it still the same
Since long before on earth man bore a spelt or spoken name.
And should we not *our* singer have to chant in measured rhymes
The weird and wond'rous sights that dawn on wand'rers in these
    climes?

Mazy gulfs of amber glory, winding eastward to the sea,
When the yellow sunrise goldens all the mist that wraps the lea,
On Govett's Leap, the stately Clarence, Miki Falls and Yulgilbar
Hanging Rock and steep Koreelah, mountain, river near and far.
Sandstone bluff, basaltic pillar, granite dyke, deep waterworn
Dolomite and golden quartz reef, wattle bloom and waving corn,
Forest trees that dwarf Cathedral's spire and bid it hide its head †
(Though we own no sculptured cloisters, urning earth's illustrious
    dead).

Kendall sang these, Kendall knew them, gave them each a name
    and form,
And ('like 'Peter') sang them from a true heart deep and warm
Yearned, too, for that mystic Eden, above the amber sunsets hie
When they nightly fade in turquoise from a gold and purple sky.
Sang he once: but, never more upon our ear his note shall fall,
Higher theme, on earth unspoken, *now* upon his soul doth call—
Thankful may we be he left us plenteous music of his soul—
Thankful—for such men as he was ne'er on earth yet found their goal.

---

   * The Burnett Salmon.   † Dandenong trees 471ft. high.
    U

TURTLING ON THE BARRIER REEF.

IN 1873, the manager of the Lake's Creek Meat Works, on the Fitzroy River, a little below Rockhampton, learned that the true green turtle was to be found in considerable numbers on the reefs and islands of the Great Barrier Reef. It occurred to him that it might be worth his while to tin and export turtle as well as beef and mutton. At the time an old fisherman from the Hebrides was in Rockhampton with a little 25-ton ketch which he owned. Donald was on the look out for profitable employment for himself and his craft. He had lately been out of luck, and it is more than likely that it was he who had told the meat works people about the turtle, for he knew more about the coast from the Burnett to Broadsound than perhaps any other living man.

But the ketch wanted new gear, and a number of things, and Donald just then had no money, so he was not sorry when, one fine day, as he was strolling along Quay-street, he was aware, as the old romances have it, of an old acquaintance who had shared in some of his former ventures, approaching from the opposite direction.

"D' ye want a share in a good thing, Mr. Smith?" said Donald.

"What is it, Donald, and how much?" asked the other.

"Turtle from the Barrier, and I want £20 and yourself," said Donald.

"What will it return, and how many are in it?"

"£10 a week, at any rate, and our own two selves, if you'll chance it. It'll be a third for the hooker, and a third apiece for ourselves."

"That'll do; come to the bank and I'll give you your twenty notes."

Donald soon laid in his supplies, and next morning the ketch dropped down the river to Lake's Creek. The manager was on the wharf, and when he understood that Donald was starting for the Barrier, he gave his final instructions: "£1 per cwt., but nothing under 1cwt., but as heavy as you like above that." Then came the weary beat down stream against an easterly wind. The tide served, however, but it was far into the afternoon when they passed Mud Island, and opened the wide expanse of Keppel Bay. It was nearly dark when the light of Cape Capricorn was seen ahead, as the vessel came round on the port tack. Then the land breeze piped up, and they were soon bowling along for Masthead Island and the Bunker Group. It was now necessary to proceed with caution, as the reefs were near, and daylight was necessary to enable them to thread their way through the narrow and intricate channels. Masthead Island was dimly visible, and they lay to, to wait for morning.

The ketch was carefully guided to her anchorage between the Masthead Reef and the island. Donald was at the tiller, and Smith in the bows keeping a sharp look-out for the sharp points and jagged edges of coral which could be plainly seen beneath the surface of the clear water. The island is nothing more than a sandy "cay" (as they are called in the West Indies) an islet of sand overlying the coral, and thinly covered with brushwood. It is surrounded by reefs, with here and there a cap of sand where the coral has grown to the level of the water, forming the nuclei for other islets, which will grow in time till they rival, or even excel, the patriarch of the little group. All are haunted by vast numbers of sea-birds, and there is actually fresh water to be found on Masthead Island, and that was an important consideration on all accounts. Many turtle were swimming about, but they were troublesome and difficult to catch in the water, and, in any case, they must not be harpooned.

The ketch was securely moored head and stern, with lines from each bow and each quarter, to ensure that she should not swing on to any of the jagged points of coral projecting around. The dingy was got over the side; lines, poles, and other appliances were put into her, the main boom topped, and the standing block of a tackle to hoist the turtle on board. Eating and sleeping filled up the rest of the day, for the turtles were to be caught at night, when they came on shore to bury their eggs in the sand.

At nightfall the dingy took on shore "all hands and the cook" to catch turtle. As the two men were lying quietly behind a bush, from which they had a view of nearly a mile of the beach, they noticed two turtles come ashore and push their unwieldy bulk along the sand inland with their flippers. Then another pair landed a little way off, and a third pair further off. There was a vast deal of scuffling while the night's quota of eggs was being buried. Then the two men rushed on the nearest pair of turtles. The larger was seized as he was trying to shuffle off to the water. The long poles were pushed under his body, and while he snapped viciously, turning his snake-like head from side to side, with a sudden heave he was turned over on his broad back, and left to gnash his teeth in impotent rage, while his captors hurried off to attend to the others. Only one more prize was made that night, but it was no easy task to get the monsters into the dingy, and, with the weight of the two men, her gunwale was brought down nearly level with the water. It was a relief when the dingy was fairly brought alongside the ketch, and Donald said it was like hoisting half a bullock on board to lift either turtle, but both were soon safe in the hold.

Next day a respectable supply of the turtles' eggs was disinterred and cooked for breakfast. They made a welcome addition to the larder. Altogether the expedition had turned out better than was expected. The two turtle taken the night before were each of them well over 3cwt. The cautious Donald put down their total weight at 7cwt. at least, and Smith, judging by the strain on his arms when hoisting them in, said that was full 1cwt. too little.

The ketch was, in the afternoon, shifted to a new berth between two of the smaller islets of the group, and that night they got three very fine turtles on one of the islets, and the following night they turned four on the other; but that came near ending all their good fortune, for the smallest of the captives was also the most lively, and while he was on his back he was busy reaching round with his head, in search of something whereon to try his teeth. He eventually succeeded in getting a good grip on Donald's leg, and he held on with such excellent good will that his jaws had to be prized open with a marline-spike, to make him let go his hold. Then there was the surgery—tearing up old shirts for bandages, and nothing would please Donald till a chew of tobacco had been placed on each tooth-mark on his leg. But he would not keep still, and Smith, who really knew a little about such matters, began to get alarmed at the vagaries of his obstreperous patient. However, as it turned out, there was nothing very seriously the matter. Donald had a stiff leg, and occasionally it gave him twinges that made him explode with blasphemy in that picturesque half-Scandinavian dialect used by the fisher-folk of Scotland's western isles.

There was plenty of work to do as the ketch filled up with turtle. It was necessary to give the captives plentiful sluicings with salt water, and provide them with wet pillows —swabs, or gunny bags, or anything that came handy. The weather was not the best imaginable. It grew squally, and the wind piped up from the eastward in a way that threatened unpleasantness; but it was good for business, nevertheless. In the first place, the turtle seemed to get more plentiful in the smooth water among the reefs and islets, and they were not small ones, either. But it was not by any means easy always to get them on board in the wind and rain, and with the spray sometimes flying in sheets over the outer encircling reef, which kept the little channels within the group smooth and still; but the gusts of wind would every now and then catch the masts of the little ketch where she lay moored between the two islets, and make her strain and tug at the chains that held her, till the kedges threatened to come home, and her bottom became perilously near becoming acquainted with the sharp points and knife-like edges of the coral rocks, that were visible under the clear water—almost as clearly visible, except for refraction, as if they had been in air. It is a wonderful thing, this transparency of the tropic seas, which, in many cases, would be almost unnavigable without it.

In less than a fortnight there were twenty-nine large turtles in the hold of the little ketch, and both Donald and Smith began to find it inconveniently crowded. There was little room to pass between the shelly monsters as they lay in close ranks on the dunnage in the boat's bottom. It was high time to get the kedges on board, and to lift the anchor; but it was no easy task for two men to work even so small a vessel through that intricate labyrinth of coral, and before they were clear of the outer reef a squall had caught the corner of the mizzen, which Donald had hoisted in the hope that it would give her head a cant through the opening. In an instant the ketch's stern swung round too far, and some eight or ten feet of her false keel came up and floated alongside. Then she came up again, the squall passed over, and the little vessel was tossing about among the big rollers outside the reef, with Donald's forcible remarks on squalls and coral patches as a running commentary. To make things worse, the loss of part of her false keel made the ketch steer very much worse than before; but the wind was just abaft the beam, and it kicked the little vessel along at a famous rate. She went staggering and plunging through Keppel Bay, and up the river, By sundown she had discharged her uncouth cargo. The twenty-nine turtle totalled 93cwt., and Donald and Smith, after making all snug on board, betook themselves in the dingy to Rockhampton, there to arrange for another trip.

The turtle speculation was an unfortunate one for the Lake's Creek Meat Works. For some inscrutable reason the tinned turtle would not keep. A considerable quantity was exported, but most of the consignments went bad, and had to be destroyed. The trade, while it lasted, was highly profitable to the catchers, though in any case it could only be followed during the three months in which the turtle resort to the lonely islands of the Great Barrier Reef to lay their eggs.

Donald and Smith, being steady fellows, reaped a golden harvest; but everyone was not so prudent. A man, whom we will call Wood, was sailing a cutter owned by a Chinese merchant of Rockhampton. He was a good seaman, but of most intemperate habits. He went turtling in the Bunker Group, and was nearly as successful as Donald & Co. When Wood got his cheque he settled with the owner of the cutter, and then went on the spree, *more suo*. After a two or three days' debauch, he and his mate took the cutter down the river, having with them only one bottle of grog as sea stock. Wood exhibited a highly developed attack of *delirium tremens*, and the cutter was taken alongside a ship lying in Keppel Bay for more grog. A quite insufficient supply was given, and Wood's mate, being afraid to go outside with a man in such a state, and finding that the tide served, ran the cutter through the Narrows, between Curtis Island and the mainland, into Port Curtis, and anchored. It was unfortunate, as all half measures are unfortunate. During the night, Wood became violent, and went about brandishing a tomahawk. His mate hid himself, and, next morning, Wood had disappeared, and so had the cutter's dingy. During the day the people in a passing boat took off the other man. The dingy was found among the mangroves, but, of Wood, no trace was ever found.

THE YELLOW-STONE OF QUEENSLAND.

NCE I owned a copy of "Dampier's Voyages to Australia." It was published nearly 200 years ago, and is now in the Government Library of the Government Botanist. In it old Dampier figures the animals and plants he saw on our north coast—iguanas, bananas, &c.—but he never names gold; nor do Captains Cook or Flinders, in any of their notes on New Holland, hint at it. Sir Thomas Mitchell and Leichhardt, whatever minerals they saw in their explorations, seemed never to have suspected the existence of gold, though the latter traversed the Cape River and the Gilbert River, both the sites of famous golden reefs.

Leichhardt disappeared in 1847, and it was not until the beginning of the next year, when the bullets were flying about in Paris over the Louis Phillipe revolution, that London was startled by the still more momentous news of the gold in California, then newly acquired by the United States from Mexico.

This led, indirectly, to the discovery of the metal in Australia, in 1851, through Hargreaves noticing the resemblance of the formations in Australia with those of California; and—strange to say—it was first found in both countries on the land of a Mr. Suttor. Mr. Toms disputes with Hargreaves the merit of being the first to drop on to the gold in New South Wales, but the latter got the reward.

Neither of them, however, was the first to find it. I was in Melbourne in March, 1851, and, in the window of a jeweller's shop in that city, I saw, suspended by a thread, a lump of pure gold the size of a musket ball, and labelled "from Clunes." Knowing people in Collins-street shrugged their shoulders, and said "from California," and pooh-poohed the Clunes idea, or that of gold in Australia at any price; but Clunes proved golden later on. However, on 10th May, 1851, New Holland attained her majority, and Australia became of age; for, on this day, the Sydney "Government Gazette" officially announced to the world that gold existed in the colony; à propos of which I may here be allowed to express my surprise that such an anniversary is not kept regularly as a supreme holiday, seeing how much more important a bearing the £300,000,000 of gold unearthed in the past has had on the destiny and expansion of Australia, than the few hundred of convicts, landed on the 26th January, 1788, at Port Jackson have had. Yet this latter event is religiously observed. But we shall, I hope, grow wiser in time. I say nothing here of the £1,000,000,000,000 of gold that has yet to be dug out in our continent. My argument is sufficient without that.

The discoveries in New South Wales in 1851 were quite eclipsed by the gold finds in Victoria in 1852, in the November of which year, the gold came rolling into Melbourne at the regular rate of £400,000 a week, enough to demoralise a poverty-stricken city then smaller than Brisbane, and having no export but wool, tallow, and hides up to that period. Let anyone try to imagine what would come over Brisbane, if gold were found at this rate within 100 miles of the General Post Office.

People now began to wonder if "Moreton Bay" (as we were then called) had any gold; but it was voted in Sydney that the Darling Downs (the supposed garden of Australia then) and gold together, would be "too much joy" for any one place, and people there scouted the idea, as the Collins-street men did the Clunes gold of March, 1851. However, at the end of 1853, Mr. Stutchbury, the Government Geologist of New South Wales, was sent up here to explore, and he, in about December of that year, found gold near Port Curtis, at the Calliope, and this was the first authenticated discovery of gold in the territory of Queensland. The Dawson River was at that time the very outside limit of settlement.

Messrs. Charles Moore (of the Sydney Government Gardens) and P. L. C. Shepherd (nurseryman of the same place) were up in Brisbane about the same time on a botanising tour. They stayed at the same hotel with me for a month, and they informed me that, although looking for plants and not for minerals, they had found gold by washing in the same locality that Mr. Stutchbury did.

The next discovery of gold in Queensland was in August, 1856. I was up in Warwick then, and a shepherd on Canning Downs brought in from "Lord John's Swamp" 8 dwts. of gold, which I bought and still have by me, the oldest uncoined specimen now extant of Queensland gold, I suppose. I had as far back as 1854 noticed the quartz formation at Talgai, and anticipated the discovery of gold in the reefs there. About this time further discoveries of gold took place. Brisbane, a village, and weary of waiting for separation, and finding trade dull, sent out expeditions, one of which found gold at Boonoo Boonoo, New South Wales, and another at Emu Creek, on the way to Gympie; but these were small affairs by the side of the Canoona rush, which came off in 1858, and for a time left Brisbane cut off from the world, every northern steamer and schooner from Sydney being diverted to the Fitzroy River trade for the time being. And in this connection I remember writing, from

the Union Club, a letter in 1857 to the Surveyor-General
in Sydney, asking him if he knew that there was a river up
North named the Fitzroy, as wide and deep as the Thames,
where wool was produced, and which had neither a wharf
nor a township. In reply, a surveyor was promised to be
sent up to lay out a township below "the rocks." The
panic in Brisbane in August, 1858, amongst the holders of
Brisbane corner lots, during the Canoona fever, may be
imagined when I state that a full town allotment, corner
of Edward and Mary streets, sold for £300, and the vendor
was only too glad to "pull that out of the fire," as he
thought. However, Canoona died away, Mount Morgan
and the Crocodile as yet "were not."

The Dee River and Westwood were credited with copper
merits only. Gold slept, pretty well, till 1862, about which
period Peak Downs, Gayndah, and the Star River were
heard of. The Gayndah people made an effort and offered
£2,000 reward to anyone who would find a payable goldfield
whose trade would pass their door. The ubiquitous digger
took advantage of every shower of rain with his tin dish;
and it soon became known that in the country that stretched
eastward from Eidsvold and Rawbelle to Reid's Creek and
Mount Perry, alluvial gold existed and could be got out in
wet weather. But nothing worthy of note occurred till, in
October, 1867, Gympie, with its wondrous yield of 350lb.
of gold from 7cwt. of stone, startled Queensland into a
knowledge of the fact that reef and not alluvial gold was
her strong point in that metal. And then the grand mineral
district that extends from Glenbar and Merodian on the
north, eastward to Glastonbury and Gympie, and through
Kilkivan and the Black Snake southerly to the head springs
of the Brisbane River, began to show forth its powers in
gold, cinnabar, and copper production. Similar developments took place up North, where the lamented Richard

Daintree, a geologist and explorer, who carried the camera and lens on a pack-horse wherever he went, brought under notice the golden capabilities of the Cape, Gilbert, and other districts, and gave us those undying realistic pictures of old Queensland life in the bush, and still older eruptions of subterranean forces, that keep his memory green amongst us. Ravenswood and the Cloncurry in 1870, Charters Towers in 1872, now became known and famous, and the latter soon passed the more "patchy" Gympie in the race for auriferous honours.

The ante-Californian prophecies of Sir Roderick Murchison, and especially the later inductions of the Rev. W. B. Clarke, found ample fulfilment in North Queensland as well as further South; and whether it was quartz or gossan, porphyry or limestone, syenite or slate, that formed the matrix, there lurked "El Oro" in all his glory.

I need not follow the subject down to the Mount Morgan era, or tell of the possible glories of the Mackinlay Range and other places that now hide—even as Mount Morgan once did—their gold so well. Suffice it when I say that, great as we think our development in gold and gold-extracting machinery in 1887,* the time is near when we shall consider them as rudimentary as we do the days of Canoona and early Gympie. Our yield will astonish the world and make us famous, when the over-inflated, London-floated Queensland gold mines of 1886-87 have ceased to leave their sting behind them, and have been replaced by mines floated and sold for fair value only, and the grand struggle for supremacy that will take place during the next twenty years between the vast golden mundic beds that lie beneath the surface at Charters Towers and the Etheridge country in North Queensland; in the Crocodile, Cawarral, Rosewood,

---

* It should be borne in mind that the late Mr. Bartley penned the above lines in 1887. EDITOR.

and Morinish districts south of the Fitzroy, in Central Queensland ; and the equally mighty (regarded in nature's grand mineral upheaval) Burnett and Mount Perry districts in Southern Queensland, will—whichever of the three comes finally to the front—be all the while tending to the fame and prosperity of Queensland ; for the three, though seeming rivals, will be always pulling together, and whatever is the outcome of their rivalry, this will go similarly to the credit side of the Queensland ledger.

It is well known that for hundreds and thousands of years there has been a steady export of gold in the shape of alluvial "dust" from the continent of Africa, alike on its west coast, and from those parts that border the Levant and Red Sea, and this has held good from before the days of King Solomon, Ophir, and Tarshish, until now. Statistics are silent as to the quantity of gold, but it must have been very great indeed. Then again, we have it on record that the princes of Hindostan possess uncounted treasures of gold in coin and jewels, the produce of their country, whose alluvial gold resources could alone have furnished them ; for there was neither there nor in Africa any gold quartz crushing machinery fifty years ago. Hence the gold exported from and in use in both places must have been both local in origin and alluvial in character. The same remark may apply to Peru and Mexico, where gold was so abundant and used for domestic utensils 300 years ago, and which must all have been alluvial in the absence of the stampers of our nineteenth century. I cannot speak with certainty of the produce in gold of the Ural Mountains in Russia, but I fancy that reef gold must predominate there. Some massive specimens that I have seen show free gold and malachite, exactly like the early raised stone from the "Alliance" reef at Morinish, near Rockhampton.

We may fairly infer from what I have here stated, that

the confessedly rich alluvial gold deposits of Peru, Mexico, Africa, and India, must have greatly impoverished the reefs in all these places. Indian and African reefs will rarely "pay." No place, with the exception, possibly, of Brazil and the country lying northward between it and the Spanish main, will ever come to rival Queensland in the production per ounce per ton of reef gold. California and New Zealand can never do it, for they are both handicapped in the alloying mixture of silver with their gold, to an extent which affects its value greatly. The colony of Victoria affords us a striking example of the way in which the alluvial gold has "robbed" the reef. The full yield of alluvial, so far, from all Victoria, may be safely put down as between 150 and 200 millions sterling, and to this extent the reefs have suffered, and the result is that something like 9dwts. of gold per ton is the average reef produce of Victoria. Contrast this with Queensland, where, with the exception of the great alluvial deposits on the Palmer River, there was no water-washed gold found in the soil to a large amount anywhere, and so it came to pass that, in the year of which I write (1887), our reefs have yielded all round, as nearly as possible, 40dwts. of gold to the ton—an average result which not only challenged, but (in racing phrase) "distanced" all the world besides.

And there is an advantage in this to our colony that does not appear in the surface of matters. Reef gold has to be (very much) worked for, and one-half at least, of its £3 10s. per ounce value has to be spent and remain in the colony in the shape of wages, machinery, &c. We clearly gain by every ounce of gold won from the reef in our vast territory. There is none of that system of taking £30,000 worth of gold in nuggets and water-worn pieces out of one hole, in one week, that used to obtain in the colony of Victoria, enabling the lucky finders to go home to Europe with their plunder, and leave the colony only the richer by their week's rations and the purchase of their mining tools. Fortunately we in Queensland get considerably more, though indirect benefit, from our gold yield than this.

The Southern limit of payable gold in Queensland may be considered to be at Gympie, where it occurs in a tolerably pure state in quartz that traverses what miners call "slate," but which more resembles diorite (or basalt). There is a little galena and copper, and some calcspar with it, but it is much more "free" than the gold at Kilkivan, which is so mixed up with copper, lead, and other metals as to be difficult to extract, though very plentiful. Eidsvold, in the same district, gives good "straight" quartz and gold. Passing north we come to the Mount Perry, Reid's Creek, and Rawbelle districts, where gold is also plentiful, but much incorporated with the ores of iron, the same as at the Crocodile Creek and Charters Towers. Passing over the minor reefs at Cania and the Boyne, we come to that grand "Central Emporium" of gold in Queensland, that lies grouped to the south of the Fitzroy River. Rosewood and Mount Morgan produce the purest gold in the colony, Clermont and Cloncurry being "well up" in point of fineness also. Ridglands and Blackfellows' Gully show free gold in decomposed sulphuret of lead, and at Morinish it shows free and very pure in iron and copper ores. Mount Britton and Clermont are minor goldfields, but Charters Towers is a proof of the prolific nature of gold mundic in the concealment, entanglement, and useful reservation of gold in wholesale quantities free from all risk of alluvial escape, or of being cheaply raised and borne out of the country without benefiting its native land, as so much of the alluvial gold of Victoria did. Ravenswood, at the Upper Camp, carries some very refractory gold ores, as shareholders have found to their cost, albeit very rich in the

Interior of Chillagoe Cave (Q.)

precious metal. The Cape River reefs have very free, pure, and thread-like filaments of gold in them, and the Etheridge produces beautiful waxy, white needles of cerussite (carbonate of lead) crossing each other in every direction, and with little "pinheads" of pure gold adhering to every intersection, and everyone wonders how it came there.

At some reefs, such as the Aurora, so mixed is the stone that three distinct ores of copper, one of lead, and one of iron may be seen with the native gold on a piece not larger than a boy's fist. The Hodgkinson reefs are much troubled with peacock copper ore. The Croydon is too vast an area, and too little explored for anyone to pronounce as to what form of stone predominates there, beyond saying that there is plenty of iron in it, and much silver with some of the gold. The Palmer reefs, though much "robbed" by the heavy alluvial deposits, are so well in the tropics that there is plenty of gold left in them, for reefs and gems grow rich as you approach the equator. Gold is found to the east of our meridian in New Caledonia and New Zealand, and in the former 64 ounces to the ton has been assayed, but none of it is of high purity; and west of our meridian we have Kimberley and Borneo, as gold-producers of as yet unknown value; but nothing has been found to surpass the Eastern Cordillera of Australia, from Cape York to Gippsland latitude, while for "unrobbed" reefs that will employ labour and produce gold, locked up meantime in trust for future generations, long after the alluvial beds of Victoria have been cleaned out, we shall have to look solely to that vast territory at present known under the general name of Queensland.

THE DISCOVERY OF MACKAY.

REPUDIATION is the destiny which almost invariably awaits the discoverer. The distinction which awaits the man of enterprise in other paths, comes to the explorer posthumously. His labours often unrewarded, his perils unsung, the credit of his success not infrequently accorded to the clamorous pretender, he too late, if ever, receives the tardy recognition of a posterity which reaps the advantage of his discovery, and awards him the empty honour of a name.

That Captain John Mackay proves no exception to what seems a fatality, is found by a perusal of certain parliamentary debates, when a motion was brought forward by Mr. Edward Palmer, member for Carpentaria, calling upon the Government (Sir Samuel Griffith then Premier) to confirm the resolution so unanimously affirmed in 1882, and according Captain Mackay a grant of land for his discoveries. But the motion furnishing an opportune medium for the conveyance of political feeling and resentment, after considerable discussion by an unusually small attendance of members, was negatived by a majority of one—a result when viewed with the former unanimous expression of the House, must be accepted as satisfactory evidence of the justice and equity of his claim, and the willingness of the people of Queensland, through their representatives, to grant such claim.

Sir Samuel Griffith was one of those who most opposed the motion when the question on the last occasion came before the House. He asked "What about the discoverer of Townsville (Mr. Black); I think that a much more valuable discovery than Mackay, and the man who made it is deserving of more than Mackay? What about the discoverer of Port Denison (Mr. Stirling)? He got no reward, and I do not know that the discoverer of Normanton or Burketown ever got anything."

Apart from the historical fact (which one would think such prominent men would be familiar with) that Cleveland Bay was discovered and named by the immortal Cook during his memorable voyage in H.M.S. "Endeavour," Captain King, R.N., in 1818, then engaged surveying the Inner Route, measured a base line on the sandy beach in shore of Magnetic Island, with the view of triangulating the Bay. But observing, like his gifted predecessor, the erratic deflections of the magnetic needle, and being pushed for time, he was reluctantly compelled to abandon the project. Again, early in 1862, Mr. G. Elphinstone Dalrymple made a journey northward to Rockingham Bay with the view of discovering a pass through the coast range to the Valley of Lagoons, where his partners (Messrs. Scott) were then forming a station. On his return to Bowen he found a letter from Captain Robert Towns, of Sydney, asking where, in his opinion, was the most favourable site for the erection of a boiling-down works, that would be available for the cattle stations then forming on the Lower Burdekin. In reply, Mr. Dalrymple recommended the mouth of what is now known as Ross Creek. This was some months before the arrival of Mr. Black. So much for the Griffith version of the discovery of Townsville. Let us see how Port Denison came to be discovered.

On Dalrymple leaving Rockhampton, in 1859, he arranged with Captain Sinclair, of the schooner "Santa Barbara," that four months after his departure he would proceed with stores to the mouth of the Burdekin River, and there await his arrival coming south. Dalrymple, however, being unable to reach the appointed rendezvous, Sinclair, after waiting a reasonable time, returned to Rockhampton, reporting, on his arrival, the discovery of Port Denison. Besides the charter money, I think the Government gave him £100, and offered him the appointment of Harbour-Master, which he declined.

The discovery of the rivers flowing into the Gulf of Carpentaria cannot be claimed for any individual explorer. Leichhardt crossed some of them on his first expedition to Port Essington, others were discovered from seaward two years previously by Captain Stokes, in H.M.S. "Acheron," who, after carefully surveying fully two hundred miles of the southern shores of the Gulf, ascended the Albert River with his boats some distance above where Burketown now stands, naming the flat land on its banks the Plains of Promise.

But, to return to Mackay. When reminded of a promise so frankly made by Sir George Bowen, in the presence of Mr. Gordon Sandeman, Sir Samuel Griffith, as if conscious of the absurdity of his arguments, resorted to the not unusual professional alternative of adding insult to injury, with the persistent rejoinder of "Where is the proof? Where is the proof?" concluding his chapter of subterfuge with the illogical remark that by Captain Mackay's acceptance of a harbour-master's berth, he had forfeited all claim to compensation, apparently forgetting that in Captain Mackay's absence someone equally competent would be required to perform the work.

The then Minister for Lands (Mr. Dutton) taking his cue from his chief, Sir S. W. Griffith, spoke as follows:—
"Although Mackay must ever hold a foremost place among his contemporary pioneers, the men who discovered the Burdekin, the Belyando, the Mitchell, and Warrego, had similar hardships to endure, but we never hear anything about them."

But the Burdekin and Belyando were discovered and named by the long-lost Leichhardt, on his first expedition from Moreton Bay to Port Essington, while in 1845, Sir

THE DISCOVERY OF MACKAY.

Thomas Mitchell, Surveyor-General of New South Wales, fitted out by the Imperial Government with every necessary conducive to success, discovered the Mitchell and Warrego, as well as the Barcoo (Victoria, of Mitchell) with the immense pastoral area now known as Central Queensland. What other discovery has been so fraught to Queensland with commercial and agricultural prosperity as Mackay and district? When Captain Mackay made the discovery he was in search of pastoral country, the finding of which to some extent, it may urged, brought its own reward, but his claim for compensation for having solely at his own expense made known a port and district which in contemporaneous prosperity (no matter how indifferent the former) has to-day no rival in Queensland, rests on such just and equitable grounds that it ill becomes anyone to dispute it.

Captain John Mackay was born in March, 1839, at Inverness, Scotland, and received his education at the Free Church Academy in that town. He first came to Australia in the ship "Australia," (Captain Mowbray Mountain) arriving in Melbourne in 1854, visiting Sydney the following year in the ship "South Carolina," Captain Charles Leisk. While on the Rocky River diggings, in 1859, he was chosen leader of an expedition to northern Queensland, the most notable result of which was the discovery of Mackay and district. Having travelled overland from New England to Rockhampton, a final departure was taken in March, 1860, from Marlborough (the then furthest out station) from where they were absent some five months. During the trip they encountered dire privations from the scarcity of food, and fever and ague, to which one of the party succumbed, and was buried on the head of Denison Creek. They penetrated north as far as 20deg. south latitude on the Burdekin River, but, observing the marked trees of Dalrymple's party (who preceded them by some months) they retraced their steps to the southward, deviating however more to the eastward, then on the outward journey, when the head waters of the Pioneer River were discovered and traced to the sea coast. On the homeward journey they fell in with a party of three white men, comprising Mr. Andrew Scott, of Hornet Bank, Dawson River, a Mr. Ross, and Mr. William Fraser, whose family had been murdered by the blacks at Hornet Bank some years previous. Being destitute of food like themselves, they made common stock of their meagre supplies, and travelled together to Rockhampton.

In 1861 Captain Mackay formed the station of Greenmount, some fourteen miles west of where the town now stands, and, chartering a schooner at Rockhampton, he ascended the river, and afterwards sent by her, to the Crown Lands Office, Brisbane, a map of the locality, correct position of mouth, with soundings and directions for finding it, on which report the Mackay River was shortly afterwards (without any expense to the Government) declared and gazetted a port of entry. In 1863 Commodore Burnett (afterwards lost in H.M.S. "Orpheus," on the Manakau bar, N.Z.) visited Queensland in H.M.S. "Pioneer," and having, in honour of one of his officers, named a stream flowing into Rockingham Bay the Mackay River, he suggested, in order to avoid geographical and other mistakes hereafter, that Captain Mackay's discovery should be named the Pioneer River. But the Queensland Government, not wishing to detract from the merits of discovery, named the town then being surveyed on its banks Mackay.

In 1864 Mackay had the pleasure of travelling from Rockhampton with the Hon. Gordon Sandeman, who, conversant with his labours as a pioneer, induced him, while in Brisbane, to accompany him on a visit to Sir George Bowen, who, with reference to Mackay's claim, expressed himself as follows:—"Were the Government now to recognise your claim, many less deserving applicants would come forward for places of minor importance. But you can rest assured, Mr. Mackay, that if ever the district becomes of any importance, it will be the bounden duty of the Queensland Government to remunerate you."

How Mackay was remembered has been seen. Shortly afterwards he left Queensland and resumed a sea life. For several years he commanded vessels under the agency of the well known Sydney firms of Montefiore, Joseph & Co., and Rabone, Feez & Co., trading to the various groups of the Pacific, and ports of the eastern seas, amongst which he has experienced some hair-breadth escapes and thrilling adventures. He has also commanded vessels under the American and Tahitian (French protectorate) flags.

It was in October, 1882, that a motion by Mr. John Stevenson (member for Clermont) was carried in the Queensland House of Assembly, without division, awarding him a thousand acres of sugar land, as compensation for the discovery of Mackay and district, which, a week later, was passed in committee. But parliament being shortly afterwards prorogued, and a change of ministry unfortunately following, the reward was never made effective. Although under the impression that the grant was complete, Captain Mackay left promising and lucrative professional employment to take possession of it, and, on arrival in Brisbane, was appointed harbour-master at Cooktown.

In 1889 Captain Mackay was promoted as harbour-master to Brisbane, which position he now fills. For five years before coming to Queensland he commanded steam and sailing vessels between the New Zealand ports and Fiji, and when on the point of leaving was offered an appointment by the Union Steamship Company. Captain Mackay holds an extra master's certificate, and exemption for several New Zealand and Australian ports.

OLD MACKAY.

TIMES are changed since the little steamer "Tinonee" did the whole of the A.S.N. Co.'s business north of Keppel Bay, and sufficed for the traffic, too. She could get into the Pioneer River, and lie alongside the wharf at Port Mackay. There was then no bridge across the Pioneer, and all who wanted to cross the stream to the upper plantations had to wade it. Just below the crossing place there was a deep hole, in which a very large crocodile used to lurk. He could be seen sometimes lying on the bottom, with his great jaws expanded, waiting for any nice morsel that the current might carry down to him; but he was reputed to be a peaceable, harmless beast, at any rate he was never known to interfere with man or beast on the crossing.

When Mr. Fitzgerald, the surveyor, first took up the land which is now the Meadowlands Plantation, few people had any idea of the future in store for the district. The dreaded colonial fever was then rife, as it was at first in Illawarra, and in many other districts of New South Wales, which are to-day among the healthiest in Australia. As the land was cleared, and cultivation extended, the fever disappeared, and he would be a bold man who would now assert that there is anything in the climate of Mackay, or its peculiar industry, inimical to the European constitution.

When Meadowlands had been got into full swing, Mr. Fitzgerald, in partnership with Mr. Davidson, took up the Alexandra plantation, and added to the sugar mill a large distillery. Messrs. Amherst and Pocklington, and Hewitt and Romilly, bringing into the business large amounts of English capital, also started plantations on a substantial scale, and Mr. John Spiller established the Pioneer Plantation on the northern bank of the river, above Amherst and Pocklington's. Mr. Spiller was an excellent practical farmer, with a great natural faculty for organisation, and these qualities more than compensated for the want of large pecuniary means. In his time there was no more economically or efficiently managed property in the district than was the Pioneer. He never employed manual labour where he could get a machine to do what he wanted. He never really believed in South Sea Island labour either, though he employed it largely, not from choice, but because he could not get enough of any other. When he left the district, just before he disposed of his plantation, he impressed on the manager whom he left in charge his conviction that Europeans, if they could be got to work steadily, and were efficient, were really cheaper than kanakas. In north Queensland the difficulty has always been to get good, steady, and capable European labour.

In the seventies old Mackay was an isolated place, only accessible by land from the west. Some daring bushmen had occasionally made their way from the southward along the coast; but the journey was full of peril, for the blacks were bad between Broadsound and Saccharopolis, and there were only two small cattle stations along the route, and they were emphatically posts of danger for the stockmen in charge of them. At one of them, Kelvin Grove, two men were murdered in one year. The second of the two was speared in full view of his hut, and in the presence of his wife, who defended the hut for three days against the whole tribe of blacks. The husband had only just gone out to catch his horse, with the intention of riding to Clairvaux, the next station to the southward, to get men to muster. The blacks were evidently waiting for him, and, before he had gone many yards, he had two spears in his body, and was felled by the stroke of a boomerang, which struck him on the temple. Then the savages made a rush for the hut, which was of heavy slabs loopholed for defence, and had an iron roof. The wife slammed the heavy door in their faces, and having plenty of arms and ammunition, began firing from the loopholes. Travellers were not numerous along that lonely track in those days, and the siege might have been prolonged indefinitely, perhaps, till the heroic woman was compelled, by thirst and hunger, to surrender herself, if her husband had not been expected at Clairvaux. A party of half-a-dozen armed horsemen was sent to look for him, and found him dead. They drove away the blacks, and relieved the widow from her terrible position.

On another occasion after the affair just related, a man with two horses was making his way northward. One of the horses was lost near Kelvin Grove, and the stockman in charge kindly offered his help to find the animal. The two men were out all day, but without success, and they camped for the night. The stranger sat by the fire, but the stockman, who was uneasy, went away to take a look round. Before he returned, the traveller, who was no stranger to the bad reputation of the district, became nervous, and stood on his guard. A dim figure appeared through the surrounding darkness. It proved to be the stockman, who said, when he came up to the fire—"We shall have to shift out o' this, mate, or the blacks will be on us. I've been yabberin' with 'em."

No sooner said than done. The horses, which were feeding close to the camp, were caught and saddled, and the hobbles taken off. The men camped again about half-a-mile away, but did not make a fire. In the morning they returned to their former camp. They then saw how wisely they had acted in removing. There were tracks of naked feet all round, and even the wood which they had piled on the fire before they left it was scattered about, as if the blacks had been searching among the embers for the something they hoped to find, but could not. The simple device of camping without fire had baffled even aboriginal cunning. It was impossible to track in the dark.

Deep Creek used to be by far the worst and most dangerous place on the "Coast Track," as it was called. The creek flowed in a narrow channel between high, steep banks, and had a narrow fringe of scrub on each side. A day's rain in the range in which it had its rise would flood it sufficiently to make it impassable, and delay the traveller for a day or two. That would suffice to make him an easy prey to the blacks, who were always on the lookout for such chances of plunder, and generally murder, too, for they were cruel and bloodthirsty, and never spared a white man.

The aborigines all along the coast of Queensland have always been far more dangerous and troublesome than in any other part of Australia. They are far superior, both physically and mentally, to the aborigines of the interior. Their country abounded in all the necessaries of savage life, safe from the sufferings and losses entailed by the prolonged and desolating droughts of Central Australia. They were, and, in the far north, still are, an amphibious race. Fish and game (the latter including not only mammalia and birds, but snakes, lizards, and grubs) abounded, and the pinch of hunger was seldom felt except by the aged and crippled. Most of the tribes were more or less addicted to the practice of cannibalism. This statement has sometimes been denied by people who only know the blackfellow in his partially civilised state; but those who have come into close contact with him in his native wilds will not question it.

The coast blacks never used the woomera, or throwing-stick, for throwing their spear. The boomerang and nulla nulla were their favourite missiles. Their heavily timbered country made them less dependent on such weapons than the dwellers on the open plains of the interior. They were great fish eaters, and caught their fish near the shore in shallow water with an ingenious sort of purse-net, its mouth formed of two wooden semicircles hinged together at the ends. This was dexterously passed under the fish, the half-hoops closed, and the fish tossed on to the bank, or, if that was too far off, into a canoe. Sometimes, when there was a large extent of shoal water, the whole tribe would walk into it, each having one of these nets, and enclose a shoal of fish, catching as many as they could in the nets, and driving the rest on shore. The larger fish were speared, and when this was done from a canoe, the sport was worth watching. An athletic black, standing like a bronze statue in the bow of a fragile bark canoe, paddled by his "meri," whom he directed by a scarcely perceptible motion of his left hand, while the right held the bone-pointed spear poised ready to strike, was a sight to see. Then the spear would descend like lightning, and the struggling fish would be transferred to the canoe.

The canoe itself of the aborigines of the coast was not to be despised. It was not, like that of the interior black, a mere bark dish from the hump of a crooked tree-trunk. It was made from a large sheet of bark, which was first flattened out, smooth side downwards. Then the rough outside was trimmed down, and the trimmings, with a quantity of dried leaves, were spread evenly over the outside surface, and set on fire. When the sheet of bark was softened by the heat, the corners were turned up, each end was doubled on itself, holes were made with a shark's-tooth awl, they were sewn with withes, and the canoe was made. In these little cockle-shells, the blacks were accustomed to make quite long voyages. They would not hesitate to cross over from the mainland to the Percy and Northumberland Islands, and even to the Barrier Reef. At times they would attack the dugong and the porpoise with their spears, and not unfrequently they were successful. One of these monsters would provide a royal feast for the whole tribe, and its capture would be followed by a scene of gluttony such as the civilised imagination can hardly conceive.

So much for the coast aboriginal and his ways. He played no small part in the development of old Mackay, for he helped to supply the labour market when the kanaka was not available in sufficient force. Old John Jack, of Sandy Creek, worked his plantation chiefly with aboriginal labour. This was the last plantation on the Nebo-road, and John was a character. He first appeared at Mackay as a sawyer, and made a good deal of money by providing boards for the buildings put up by the early settlers. In those days timber *was* timber, and commanded a very high price. Pine from Maryborough was scarce and dear, and besides, the white ants made havoc among it, and sound local hard wood at double the price was cheaper in the end. Jack was soon able to equip a sawmill, and lower the price of his timber, without reducing his profits. Then he planted cane, and, as he had the engine and boiler, he added a sugar-mill to the sawmill, and crushed not only his own cane, but that of some neighbours, "on the halves." Jack, however, was by no means a successful manager, and contrived to get into difficulties with the financiers, which ultimately cost him the fruits of years of industry.

Many of the men who helped to make old Mackay have vanished, and some of them have declared that the sugar industry had, in their case at least, belied its brilliant promise. As a matter of fact, too much was expected from it. The glamour of tradition surrounded the West Indian sugar planter of the early nineteenth century, when his profits were swollen by his monopoly of the British market, by the distillery, and the employment of slave labour. The utter collapse of the West India colonies between 1840 and 1850 was not understood. Still, the sugar-cane is a profitable crop, though the loss of waste products through the Australian restrictions on distillation (which, in the West Indies, is practically free) is heavy, and the richest soil will not continue to produce the same crop for ever. This latter fact was brought home to the Mackay planters some years ago by the "cane blight," as they called it, which brought the richest of them to the verge of ruin. Mr. Davidson, of the Alexandra Plantation, did excellent and unrewarded service to his fellow planters and the public in this emergency, not only by the field experiments which he made at his own expense and risk, but by his personal researches in the laboratory. That the practical results were not greater was not his fault. Time and experience, guided by real science, can ultimately solve the great problems of practical agriculture, which affect equally the English and Australian cultivator.

BLACKFELLOW CRIMINALS.

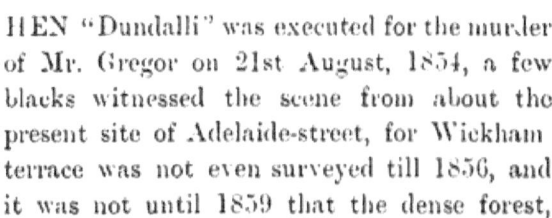HEN "Dundalli" was executed for the murder of Mr. Gregor on 21st August, 1854, a few blacks witnessed the scene from about the present site of Adelaide-street, for Wickham terrace was not even surveyed till 1856, and it was not until 1859 that the dense forest, which covered it, was sufficiently cleared to afford a sight from it of what went on in Queen-street. Still, for all this scanty aboriginal attendance, the spectators were quite too numerous, for they included the little Brisbane children who were then passing on their various morning errands, and it was not a fit sight for them to see. In the same month, five years later, there was a big gathering of the blacks on Wickham-terrace to see the execution, on 4th August, 1859, of "Chamery" and "Dick," two Burnett River lads, sentenced for criminal assault on an old German woman, and whom Sir William Denison refused to reprieve; the authorities—never anxious that the blacks should see a murderer hanged, as "a life for a life" was already a well-known rule with them—caused all the available aboriginals to be sent for to see this execution for rape, in order to teach them that it ranked with murder, a lesson they were slow to learn at that time. "Kipper Billy," two years later, was another notorious black criminal, quite in advance of the two callow Burnett boys already named.

The Upper Brisbane River was the scene of his lawless

exploits; he had an eye for white female beauty, and one handsome lady, the wife of a rich squatter there, carried a small revolver for his benefit, after hearing how he had spoken of her. He was a daring fellow, and, after his capture, he scaled the walls of Brisbane Gaol, and would have got away, but a bullet from the carbine of Warder Armstrong killed him when on the top of the wall, and, strange to say, no hole could be found in his head or any part of his body, and it was supposed that the bullet entered under the eyeball and remained in the skull. His head (like that of Griffin, at Rockhampton, in 1868) was stolen from the grave, greatly to the wrath of Shepherd Smith and Henry Buckley, the churchwardens, or cemetery trustees, of the period, and it were a bold man who "chaffed" either of them on the subject till some time after it happened.

But the blacks were not always the sinners. There is a gruesome legend, hailing from the Macintyre Brook, and setting forth how a bevy of convict stockmen in the early pioneer days, not content with merely murdering a black-fellow, stripped off enough of his skin to make tobacco pouches from, and dried them in the fire smoke; but they had to "dree their weird" for it. It is related that, whenever they camped near the spot at night, they became aware of the figure of a black man sitting in a dejected attitude, with his hands hanging over his knees, at the foot of a tree on which the light of the camp fire shone. The figure was distinctly visible 50ft. away, but faded altogether if you approached within 5ft. of it, and reappeared as you retreated again. It was not at all "canny" (about the latter days of Louis Phillipe) to sleep in the next room, at a primitive hotel of the Southern Downs, to that of some old bushman whose hands had taken human life. You heard words that you would gladly forget—yet words enough to make a man thankful if *he* had never known "drink" or "blood."

THE ROCKS, BURDEKIN RIVER.   LIMESTONE CLIFFS, BURDEKIN RIVER.

BLACKFELLOW CRIMINALS.

The most beautiful strip of country in Australia is that bounded on the north by the road from Warwick to Cunningham's Gap, on the east by the Main Range, and on the south by the border of the colony; a tract which, for beauty, salubrity, and fertility combined, is unsurpassed in the world. Here stood Jubb's hotel (pulled down in 1859), the scene of many an old-time carouse, joke, and yarn. Jubb was formerly a servant of the Leslies, and it was here that brave Pat Leslie went down one night, to fight or silence a whole bar full of noisy bullock-drivers, whose shouts prevented Mrs. Leslie, at the other end of the house, from sleeping. It was at Jubb's, in 1852, that the youthful Lord Ker, and Lord Scott (a son of the Duke of Buccleugh) put up when visiting this mountain scenery after a run through Sydney. Jubb once told me a hideous ghost story of murder, suicide, and a haunted dairy, near Goulburn, in New South Wales, and how the priest laid the ghosts—in his early days; but, as all the parties were white people, and this deals with black folk, it need not be referred to further.

ABOUT BULLOCK DRIVERS.

IT is impossible to be "up" to *all* the tricks of the bullock driver in Australia, as witness the following:—An old hand had often been "bowled out." After sampling the contents of wine and brandy casks, he sometimes filled up the vacuum with water and sometimes not, the result being disastrous in either case. It was to be his last trip on that route, 300 miles from the seaport to the copper mines, and they determined to watch him *that* time. The only liquor on the dray was a quarter-cask of brandy, and Bob was specially forewarned not to touch it, as he would be found out and punished this time without mercy. He was told that the cask had been weighed, and so any abstraction would be noticed, and that, as far as any attempt to fill up his stealings with water, a sample bottle of the brandy had gone up in the mail bag to the copper mines, and that it would be compared with the cask as received from him. They thought they had "stockyarded" Bob this time. But all their precautions, which they were so foolish as to reveal to him, only enabled him to take his own measures accordingly. The brandy was duly conveyed 300 miles to the mines, was weighed, and found allright, and was sampled and found to correspond with that in the bottle which had come up in the mail bags six weeks before, and so Bob got his clear receipt for it and departed. The brandy cask was a 30-gallon one, and, after ten gallons had been used, the tap refused to yield any more. It was supposed to have got choked, as the cask was clearly not empty, nor even nearly empty, as its weight told. But all attempts to make the tap act proved useless. So the bung was appealed to, and then a tale of horror was revealed. Bob had taken his precautions well at the seaside. He had, after he got the "boss's" warning, procured a dozen and more of clean sheep's bladders, and had them on the dray with him. He spiled the cask, and partly filled a bladder with brandy, and through the bung-hole he introduced another bladder with the *same* quantity and weight of water in it, and so on till he had removed twenty gallons of the brandy, the cask on arrival containing ten gallons of spirit and twenty gallons of water in sheep's bladders. But Bob had departed to distant shores before the *eclaircissement* took place.

THE OLD "PARRAMATTA."

DEAR old ship "Parramatta!" Grand old comfortable family sea-waggon! Surely never since the days of the Spanish Armada were more picturesque elaborate quarter-galleries, figure-head, or roomy "chains." I love thee, because thou art built on the model of, and hast even survived, the line of battle-ship of King George's day. They are gone, but thou remainest, and still dost swim and travel the seas, as they do not. All our love for Nelson and his ships of the bygone now centres in thee, old hooker! so much art thou their image and presentment. Away with thy modern sweepers! with no figure-head or galleries to speak of. Away with modern utilitarianism! the spirit of Charles Lamb, of "Elia," ariseth within us and protesteth against the sweeping away of old sea marks.

What to us is their fast sailing and quick passages?
Though other ships may carry us, as fair, perchance, as thou
With all the fine lines of thy "run," the contour of thy "bow,"
They *never* can replace the bark our early fondness nurst,
They may be clippers in their speed, but not, like thee, "The First."
"The First!" how many a memory bright that one sweet word can bring
Of hopes that blossomed, drooped, and died, in life's delightful spring—
Of halcyon times all passed away, and early seeds of bliss,
Which germinate in hearts unseared by such a world as this.

THE AUSTRALIAN SQUATTER.

THE typical Australian squatter is a man quite *sui generis*. You do not meet with his exact double anywhere else in the world. He is generally tall and sinewy. His hair and beard are iron grey, and so is often his suit of clothes. His eyes, too, are frequently grey, and there is an expression on his face the furthest remove possible from vacant idiotcy or trifling. Instead thereof is seen a concentrated, strong, purposeful, earnestness of look, such as is shewn on the faces of a few eminent generals, but never on those who have not seen real service; for the great Australian squatter has to be a general and more than a general. Not only has he to battle with savage nature, and give his muscles and his sleep, his nerves and his life to the task, but also to be his own prime vizier, financier, council of war, and commissary general. To think of everything, and to build up everything, from the start. No adjutants or commissaries lighten *his* labour, or render needless much of his forethought. All falls on *him*, and he responds to the call with a bravery born of old British blood, and of the stimulating surroundings of his new life. He goes from strength to strength, till, at last, others wonder (and he, himself, almost does the same) how one man can face it all and be "ready, aye ready" for aught that turns up, as he is. He has all the tenacity of the Transvaal Boer, with education, *savoir faire*, intelligence, and world knowledge to crown and polish it. See him on his station he is all brave hospitality. See him at the club, in a colonial metropolis, and there is a more than military *aplomb* and precision about him. He has had his discipline, you can affirm at a glance, and there is the same commanding gleaming eye that directed that dangerous wild ride on the mountain side to prevent the escape of the cattle meant for a fine market. That was one of his daughters whom we met yesterday descending the cabin steps of the mail steamer, with a child leading in one hand, and another perched on her shoulder. Her feet are small, but are in loose baggy boots far too large for them, for she is no dresser. Her husband has a station in far northern Queensland, and she remembers as a child the time when father and mother fought the wild blacks for seven hours in their barricaded cottage, 100 miles from help, and beat them off with heavy loss, both firing and loading for themselves. You might have seen a look of resolution on her pretty face such as has often taken the "nonsense" out of untamed horse or bullock, and has luckily never been further called upon; yet it would fare ill with anyone who menaced her little ones even now. But happily those days are passed.

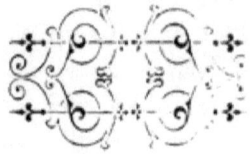

THE SEXES.

YES, the relations between the sexes are strange and wonderful indeed! And who really does know and understand them? A young man meets a pretty girl—he all manhood and fire, she all archness and demure coy coquetry, with womanly love underlying it all. They marry, they kiss, and are familiar both before and after that ceremony. They chaff and joke, and bandy wit with each other all through, and no people (you would imagine) *could* be more intimate than they with one another, and none could more perfectly know and understand their mates' nature and inmost soul. And this, too, from the ages of 20 to that of 70 years. Companions by day, companions by night; every chance, every opportunity, given for inter-knowledge and self revelation on both sides, this, too, for a full half century at a time. The silver wedding, the golden wedding, comes and passes, and yet, I dare to say it, those two true lovers and soul-mates never *really knew* each other at all, nor would they have done it had their joint life been doubled or trebled. For no man ever yet fathomed, or learnt, the depth of a woman's real nature, any more than any woman ever yet did that of a man. A man learns more about another man, or a woman of a woman—each of their own sex—in an hour, than they could read aright of one of the opposite sex in fifty years. No man can track all the feelings of a woman as another woman can, and *vice versâ*.

They are a creation apart from one another are these mysteries—"sexes." The veil of the flesh blinds the eye during life. There is intimacy, there is love, there is happiness, there is oneness, there is all this and more, between the man and the woman, but they never really see the other as the other really is, and never will do it till Charon and the Styx have been passed, and flesh is no more. And, if all this darkness, all these unexplored closets, exist in the case of long married and intimate mates, what must be the ignorance of those who merely flirt with the other sex and never yield their liberty? And, if anyone doubt this line of reasoning of mine, let him or her recall some case in which they have loved a person, whom, from some cause, they could not marry. The loved and loving one dies, and then the survivor at once recalls so many things that he, or she, might have said, might have done, to the lost one, *if* they had only but thought of it and seen it as plainly before death as after it; but it never is and never will be so seen in lifetime, for the veil of the flesh is in the road, and only disappears when life also does, and only then and not till then does it cease to becloud the relations between the spirits of the sexes. Does not a man, does not a woman, perpetually catch himself or herself in the act of saying something to the loved one of the other gender; a something that they did not mean and did not mean to say even, a something that only conceals, in place of revealing, the *real* truth? Who can deny these things? Yet, in spite of this failure to realise each other, how intense is the longing for one another! And what results it leads to! what sexual cruelty! Why! were there no men at all in the world, no woman would ever revel, as some do, in the killing of another woman. Killing her, I mean, with envy and jealousy and mortification over some superior dress or surpassing beauty, or charm of manner; all of which are matters often valued not so much for themselves, as for the pain they can inflict on others of the same sex. There would be no active animal cruelty in men if there were no women, but only cruelty of the passive, neglectful, and heartless type. The only being to whom, and of whom, a woman never talks scandal, and is never envious of or spiteful to, is her baby. Man was not originally created male and female, like the animals and birds were, but created alone and in the image of God, and woman was formed, not of dust, but from the highly organised flesh and bone of man. Hence the purity, the exquisite charm, the archness of the refined delicate real woman, and it hardly leaves her even when she is a little "off colour" in her behaviour. As witness Abraham's beautiful and oft stolen wife, in Genesis 18; how she laughed and how she lied about it, in her poor woman's terror, when the Almighty One announced to her and her husband His controlling power in all creative and sexual matters. How grandly, yet mercifully, He assumes His mantle of omnipotence, as He speaks to the pretty, but doubting, woman, whom (in her mother) He created first in Eden.

ON LOVE.

OE to the man who suppresses love. Either the love that would fain spring in his own heart towards others, or the love that would fain spring in their hearts to himself. He misses an awful chance, kills a possible world of good, and the evil is perhaps most marked when it is the case of a parent with his children, or a husband with his wife. Love is a great power. We cannot murder or rob those whom we really love, and God Himself cannot send to hell one who is all love, for such a one could find hell nowhere. Love would conquer pain, opposition, hatred, and all else in its rapt self absorption. Woe also to the man who is ashamed of being good, afraid to seem good, and who would be mean enough to purchase exemption from ridicule at the price of denying his actual master, and by professing to know nothing of that which is really dear to his good but weak and terrified heart. God give strength to all such, for there comes a time when cause and effect, logic and science, length and weight, definition and argument, money and commerce, learning and knowledge, and all else that pertains to modern thought and material concerns shall be lost, dimmed, swept away, and absorbed in the more real though ineffable essence of something that is indescribable in words, spoken, printed, or written, and which thought can only faintly grasp, but which is near us and around us, and must finally triumph and be all *to* us and all *of* us, when the planets themselves shall have crumbled to decay.

ON MIRACLES.

HOW little is the nature of the deeds, which bear the name "miracles," understood by the world in general! No one tries to imagine *how* they come about. Some sort of magic divination is suspected, and the operator is supposed to be proud and vain of his gifts. How different, surely, must be the reality! When the prophet Elisha heard that the Shunamite's son was dead, how did *he* act? Was there any vainglorious ceremony, posturing, or attitudes? No! any more than there was with St. Paul over the dead body of Eutychus. A divine feeling of intense pity and gentle sorrow; a yearning spirit of love and sympathy that showed itself in soft murmurs of low-voiced, earnest words (as if to a living loved one) and rend itself in a tender touching of the dead loved one. A trance, a rapt ecstacy, of speaking and handling, setting forth a deep longing, to which no rehearsed or remembered words could do justice, the sorrowing one all unconscious of the unseen power that was passing involuntarily from himself into the lifeless form before him. Not trying, for one moment, *to* work a miracle, or to upset the apparently completed act of God, but all the time exerting an occult force (whether in the spirit, or the body, one can no more tell than St. Paul once could) which (he knows not how or why) at last rewards his tender, all-powerful magnetic love and sympathy, with the sight of a revived and responding life, to turn and appreciate the love spent on it, the strong tender will, the strong tender wish, enrapt and ignorant of its own power, unconscious even of what it is doing except that it loves and yearns, is a reflex, albeit a faint one, of the love and the will that first created all things. These described were but men's miracles. Turn we now to the giant miracle performed by the God-man on Lazarus. Four days in the grave bound hand and foot with grave-clothes, he still "comes forth" when bidden. *How* did he come? What awful gait was it that he shewed? What scene of terror and majesty did the people witness? He could not walk nor creep, for he was pinioned. He "came forth bound," and he was *not* "loosed" till he had travelled. But travelled how? Like an awful shadow on the wall, he must have loomed, moved by no muscle or limb, yet still moving. The terrors and the love of that spectacle are beyond all imagination. The one greatest manifestation of semi-material power in Holy Writ.

PROPER NAMES IN AUSTRALIA.

NO doubt there are *some* very ugly-sounding native names, but they are the exceptional few, and the number, even of these, would be diminished if it were not for the grotesque attempts to reduce to English spelling the delicate inflections of the Australian tongue which we then pronounce as spelt in English. People are apt to forget that the Australian names have not been *spelt* by the natives, but only spoken. French is a soft-sounding language; yet I should like to see the French sound of the word "Rheims" exactly reproduced on paper, English fashion. The word "Enoggera" sounds harsh enough, but the native word is "Yewoggera"—the *u*, corrupted to *n*, has been now, to avoid confusion in title deeds, made a recognised error.

Gunniga Mubbur, in New South Wales, Toon doon gonanige and Muttarpilly in Queensland, are also harsh in sound; but what can be softer and prettier than the name of Jullula, one of the most elevated, kingly, and beautiful peaks of the royal Muniong Range of Australian Alps; or Cowra Goara, a peak of the Canobolas, near Orange? Are Mimmurra, Illawarra, Yatilla, Peachilba, Ringarooma, Yulgilbar, and Koreelah, unpleasant to hear? And that string of beautiful lakes which runs out between the Murrumbidgee and Darling, known as Gunarwe, Macormon, Makoombi, Doondoambli, Lymbennaroy, &c —are they badly named? Is the Schreckhorn of the Alps better named or better sounding than Jullula? Has any dialect of Europe got a more poetical name than the Camillaroy of Australia? Even in Victoria, alongside of such horrid names as Cut Pau Pau, we find the redeeming one of Bellerine. It is quite impossible, with English letters, to print the *sound* of Australian words. There is Neurum, or Deurum, or Jeurum, signifying rain, and neither the N, the D, nor the J, but all three combined, conjure an idea of the exact sound as pronounced by the blacks. Bondi, near Sydney; Mildura, on the Lower Murray; Burranjuhi, the north head of Broken Bay, are all examples of euphonious names. The latter is not unlike the Spanish Aranjuez in sound. The Moonbi Pass might have had a far uglier name if an English one, such as Gap Hollow, or what not.

The race of the aboriginals will soon be extinct in Australia; but her beautiful mountains, glens, waterfalls, and other scenes of nature, pure air, and strong life will never, while the world lasts, receive more lovely and appropriate names than those bestowed by these poor uninspired and doomed savages. The softest names that Longfellow writes of, the liquid murmurs of the Polynesian tongue—no language that the world most admires can ever more worthily clothe with titles the scenes of Australia than has been already done by her aborigines. In this, as in the power of tracking, they stand unequalled; in all the rest they are as nothing. Away then with the hundred and one vulgar Sandy Creeks, Oakey Creeks, Stony Rises, Devil's Pinches, Scrub Flats, Brown's Waterholes, and similar abominations of bewilderment and monotony which fill our Australian gazetteers at present, and which will do so in future if some people's taste is to be allowed to prevail against better ones.

CRICKET.

CLUBS may come and clubs may go, but cricket lives for ever. Brisbane cynics may sneer and say that the days are too short from April to October, and the weather too hot from October to April for cricket practice, and that all the rest of the year is available for it. But still the game struggles for an existence, and serves its purpose, namely, to keep the boys out of mischief. There is the "allegretto" style of cricketer, who sings to the air of "Wet Sheet and Flowing Sea"—

> "Oh! for a gently hopping ball"
>   You'll hear some "duffer" cry,
> But give to *me* the "ripper" swift
>   No odds if low or high;
> I'm bound to "give it fits" my boys,
>   For, with my bat, d'ye see
> I cut it slick past "cover point,"
>   And I score another "three."

his time being changed to "penseroso" in the following:—

> They've changed the bowler, now, by jove,
>   And there's mischief in his "hi,"
> And he bares a rounded biceps hard,
>   And he aims one "wicious" shy.
>   . . . . .
> How that ball came I'll never know,
>   Its course I didn't see,
> But it skied my timbers, "leg, mid off,"
>   My fondly cherished three.

Cricket only hibernates in the cold weather. In summer the mighty beaker of genial "shandygaff" rewards the sunburnt and (it must be confessed) somewhat moist hero of half-a-hundred runs and not out; and the "yah! butter fingers," the "run it out," and the "played, sir," and the "oh! good ball," form the outward manifestations of the inward emotions of the pleased, or displeased, spectator, as the ball happens to be fumbled, or swiped, or smothered, or disperses the homogeneity (good word that, but, I fear, of doubtful applicability) of the timbers and bails. Well, boys, let winners remember that losers did their best, and the losers bear in mind that someone *must* be beaten, and let both remember that the "cock-a-doodle-doo" business is out of place in cricket, and that it is "bad form" to ventilate theories as to what *might* have happened *if* Muffins had *not* missed Sloggerson that time in the "slips" in the third ball of the second over, after he had made fifty-six "without a chance." It is unkind alike to Muffins, who, poor fellow! did all he knew, and is, already, sorrowful enough over the mishap; and it is rough on Sloggerson, too, as it takes half the gilt off *his* gingerbread. I must now tell you of two early cricket fights in Moreton Bay—the great match between Brisbane and Ipswich in June, 1859, at the North Shore, the "Chuwar" of Limestone, and the return match, in the same year, on the grassy flat at the back of where the Hon. P. Perkins now resides in Brisbane, and, taken for all in all, the play, the lunch, the speeches, the *tout ensemble*, "Dingley Dell *versus* all Muggleton," even with Alfred Jingle and Sir Thomas Blazo thrown in, was nothing to it. I admire cricket, and always had a reverence for it. It carries all the ceremonious gentlemanly punctilio of the duel, but shorn of its bloodthirsty drawbacks. There is the exactly measured ground, as in the duel; the uniformity of the weapons used on both sides, and the strict

care exercised to ensure fair play, and that no advantage shall be taken on either part. But, to proceed. Ipswich and Brisbane were rival towns from 1843 to 1859, and the former stole a decided march on the latter when the branch Banks of New South Wales and Australasia, at Ipswich, imported some sterling cricketing material in the shape of accountants, tellers, and ledger-keepers (who were also wicket-keepers) from the classic recruiting grounds of Launceston and Maitland—both centres of cricketing skill. So the chance was not lost, and poor Brisbane was challenged to come up and play cricket during the Ipswich race week of June, 1859. Hard work we had to collect a team, and great was the array of talent against us. We took up Dr. K. Cannan, Shepherd Smith, Colin Munro (now of the Burdekin), Edwin Norris (of Townsville), C. F. Bell (manager at D. F. Roberts', solicitor), Walter Birley (of Kangaroo Point), James Bolger (the Kilkenny underhand bowler), a Spring Hill cobbler, who could keep wicket well, and some more whom I forget. We found ourselves faced by the redoubtable Captain George Maughan, of the "Australasia," with his piratical long black beard, red cap and shirt (a W. G. Grace in miniature); by Harry Logan, of the Bank of New South Wales: also F. O. Bryant (6ft. 3in.) of the "Joint Stock:" and Harry Glassford (of Gilchrist, Watt & Co.), all prime bats; and by an awful bowler, Coulson, he was from one of the Maitland banks, and had an extra joint in his shoulder (like a railway semaphore), and could send his arm with the ball backwards and upwards till it stood all but perpendicular. Then, like lightning, his arm would be flat at his side and the ball impelled each time, swift and true, at the middle stump. And let me here remark that the bowler who covers that piece of timber with every ball needs "playing." Then Ipswich had A. D. Broughton (afterwards Sir A. D. B., baronet), and a butcher was there, named Cleary, famous for never sending any kind of ball up. The fray began.

x

W. Sladen, of the Melbourne parliament, was an interested spectator. Shepherd Smith got a knock early, in the ankle, which lamed him, and spoilt his bowling, and Bolger bowled till his shoulder required the chemist, Eldridge, and liniment, when night fell, to fit him to go on next day. Enough! Brisbane was over-matched—99 to 65 first innings; second innings, they 43 and we 44; and they beat us, and proposed our healths, and banqueted us. Then, next day, we had a mixed "scratch" match—Bolger, Bryant, Coulson, Glassford, &c., on one side, Maughan, Arthur Wienholt, Birley, Colin Munro, &c., on the other. The first lot won, and, at the races, all was forgotten. Then came the return match at Brisbane, about October, and Ipswich had not got her crack team, all of whom could not leave; but they brought Charley Fattorini, Jemmie Laidley, Edwin Campbell, and others down; good men all, but "not—not the six hundred"—at least, *not* cricketers. The match was played on the forest flat at the back of the present "Aubigny," North Quay. Bolger was in for three-and-a-half hours, made 118, sent the ball into the river for 8, and Brisbane's first innings closed for 322 runs, and the game was won, in hollow style, by the future metropolis. Club matches have often been played since between the two places, but I believe the foregoing were the only "town against town" games that ever took place. I must plead guilty, personally, to a superstitious distrust of the article called a cricket ball. How innocent but deceitful it looks in the shop windows! And people tell me it is made of cork and leather, and weighs only $5\frac{1}{2}$ ounces. All I know is that when *I* (the amateur) hit it, it seems to be made of cobbler's wax, by the way it sticks to the fielder's fingers; and when I try to catch it, after someone else has hit it, it feels slippery as ice, while hot as fire, and to weigh about as much as a thirty-two pound shot when in motion. And the diabolic tendency which that same impish ball has, to rise up in the air, no matter how I try with the bat to flatten it down to the ground, surpasses all belief.

BLACK LABOUR.

ON what is called the Black Labour "question," much print, time, and tongue have been wasted. There is no more room for debate, sentiment, or politics in it, than there is in a sum of arithmetic with its inevitable and self-evident result. Fahrenheit's thermometer is the only index or guide herein, and it is an instrument quite devoid of theories, imagination, or "fads." Some kind or other of "black" man is bound to "hunt" the white man, in the long run, out of the coast districts of North Queensland altogether. God, climate, and nature silently decree it with a legislation louder than any mere word declamations inside the walls of parliament; the white race can no more thrive and be perpetuated (say) in Cooktown than at Lahore or Demerara; absentee white men may own property possibly, and grow rich on the labour of alien races in North Queensland, but the laws of nature cannot be set aside. Take every coloured person, if you like, out of North Queensland, and keep them out; try and "run" the place with white men only, and see the result. At best, Nature, the wise dame, making the best of a bad job, would, in the course of a couple of centuries (if they did not become extinct altogether), have adapted and turned them all into acclimatised black men, who would (if a phase of 1893 politics still obtained in 2093) have to be expelled once more to make room for the "white" man, for Queensland, you know, sir, is only for the white. What kind of a degraded, fiery-tempered, unnatural, murderous race the white lower orders would gradually become in that climate can be best judged by the annals of America—but with tenfold intensity would it be, for New Orleans, the southernmost and hottest city in the United States, is about 3deg. further from the Equator than is Brisbane, the most southerly and cool of Queensland coast towns. Superficial talkers, when they judge Queensland by the United States, should, first of all, consult their atlas and note the very different parallels of latitude under which the two countries lie ; one place "leaves off" about three degrees before the other "begins." Black labour is not necessary in the States; but it is in Jamaica and Demerara, which are under Queensland parallels ; and let the political side of the (so-called) "question" go as it may, Dame Nature will in the end jump iron-heeled on all and sundry, "Liberal," "Conservative," "Labour party," or what not (with no respect of persons, "views," or creed) who dare to set up their penny trumpet against decrees, ecliptips, and conditions that were and are settled (not for ever, perhaps, but still for thousands of centuries before and after our brief era and strut on the scene and stage). Why, and by whom, and for what purpose, was the coloured man ever created, and to what place do some people propose to banish him ?

THE WORD "SYNDICATE."

OR the life of me, I can't make out why the luckless word "syndicate" should carry with it and excite such feelings of suspicion and distrust. I don't profess to be much of an etymologist, but the word "syndic" used to mean the mayor, or the burgomaster, of a Dutch town, and the syndicate, I presume, were the aldermen thereof. And yet, mayors and aldermen are not, necessarily, swindlers. We borrow other words from the Dutch. There is the word "kop," for instance, imported and much used by low Dutch sailors in the port of London since the year 1680 or so. It means to "steal, thieve, or take possession of," so the Wapping thieves took it up as short and expressive, and in time, an arresting constable came to be called a "Kop-per." The only harm that I can see in the unfortunate word "syndicate" is that it happens to be spelt with almost exactly the same letters as "dynamite," the d y n a i t e being all present in it, and, perhaps, that is why so many syndicates explode, blow up, and get shattered to pieces. There is, evidently, too much of the detonating element in both of these words.

AUSTRALIAN FISH AND FRUIT.

THE fish and fruit of Australia form fertile, and also interesting topics. Touching the former, it may be remarked, by way of introduction, that the sole, turbot, and trout of England are not reproduced in Australia. But the "trumpeter," of Hobart, is *the* champion smoked fish of the world, salmon, haddock, and herring being a bad "second." The "butter fish," of New Zealand, is a luxury like whitebait is in England. The giant crab, of south Queensland, has all the flavour and twice the digestibility of the English lobster, but the great Australian crayfish is far behind it in both respects. I must here mention the "dugong," or sea cow, of south Queensland. People who suffer from lung, or bowel wasting, or defective assimilation and nutrition of any kind, have been greatly relieved by the use of cod liver oil, extracted from a cold-blooded fish in no way analogous to the human species. The dugong (something like a porpoise to look at) is a warm-blooded, mammal, sea animal, and its oil and lard (the residuum of the oil) are the most sovereign remedy on earth for defective assimilation or nutrition, with all the virtues of the cod-extracted article, and a number more of its own. Rich no doubt in iodides and phosphates from the sea and from a warm-blooded and milk-bearing, not a cold fish, source, the white flesh of the "dugong" is a combination, in flavour, of the veal sweetbread, and turtle steak, and with a "melt-in-the-mouth" delicacy that surpasses both of them. There is not one trace of fish flavour about it.

Let me narrate some of its most wonderful cures, which sound almost fabulous. It must be remembered that oil taken into the stomach is not very digestible, or capable of assimilation, and can only be "exhibited" a little at a time. So, it is here that the "lard" comes in. Placed on "spongio-piline," like butter on bread, and applied to the skin of chest and stomach, and kept there, it finds its way through the skin into the blood direct, without fatiguing, or out-raging, the stomach, and does its restorative work quickly and thoroughly. If applied to the skin of a sound person, it remains inert and unabsorbed outside, while the skin of a poor consumptive will suck it in and dry the pad in no time, to his or her lasting benefit. I will cite a few cases of the effects of dugong lard, which it is not sought to "puff," as there is, unluckily, not enough of it to be got, even for local wants. A boy fell into some boiling sugar, and scalded himself from ankle to thigh ; a month in the General, and another in the Childrens' Hospital, only found him unhealed —a skeleton, with his eyes deep in his head, and dying, under all ordinary remedies. The lard was clapped on him all over, as a last resource, and in less than a month it had given him such vitality that the scald, in place of covering thigh and leg, had shrunk to the size of a crown piece, the rest being new skin, and he had regained his ordinary ful-ness of flesh. Another case: An old lady of 73, wife of a high Crown official, was seized with paralysis in her bath ; doctors were called in ; she could not sleep, and opiates maddened her. The lard was applied, sleep came, and she survived five years more. Another cure : A poor milliner, of 23, stitching in a hot workshop, "nourished"—save the mark !—on tea, tepid water, and bread and butter, in Bris-bane, began to lose one lung, could not sleep for the "night sweats," could eat no breakfast, and was in a bad way generally. A pad smeared with lard was applied ; she fell into a sound sleep, woke hungry, ate a breakfast, found her chest had sucked the pad dry of lard, and kept on at it, with the result that she gained seven, nine, and thirteen pounds in weight in the first three months. She then left off the lard, for (as she said) the oil was so perfectly absorbed through the skin into the stomach, that it began to rise in her throat, as newly swallowed castor oil would. She needed no more at the time, but afterwards, when sleepless, she would resort to the lard again, and procure renewed health, appetite, and sleep. The "night sweats" never returned. An overgrown boy of 17, six feet high, seven stone weight, unable to work, was, in one month, by the lard, raised to nine stone, and back to his bench again. A little boy of eighteen months, whose mother had just died of consumption, was fast following her from *marasmus*. His big beautiful eyes were surrounded by purple rings, his long eyelashes shading them. I saw and pitied him in his sister's arms, she and the rest of them looking healthy enough in all conscience. His little flannel was kept soaked in dugong oil day and night, and he was kept clean. At the end of a month I saw him, not dead, but the beauty of his eyes all gone. He had come back from the angels, and was human once more, and, at the end of three months, he was all "beef," like his brothers and sisters. A word now as to another natural remedy found in south Queensland. A medical man of Brisbane suffered terribly from anæmia. He went to the seaside, and bathed daily in a fresh water lagoon with ferruginous sandstone walls. At the end of a fortnight he noticed that the brown leather lining of his hat was turning quite black where it touched his forehead, and he at once surmised that iron from his skin had mingled with the tannin of the leather, and he noticed that his skin had become red, in place of white, and he felt quite well again. He put the matter to the test, and sent a keg of the water to be analysed. Its constituents were discovered, and packages of them were artificially prepared for sale with equally good results when mixed with bath water and so used. There was a master painter in one of the southern towns of Queensland, who had a family of daughters, most of whom, at the age of twelve, sickened with anœmia, grew fretful, peevish, and died. I told him of the remedy. His children could not digest preparations of iron by the mouth and stomach, nor take up enough to be effectual in that way. But the absorbing skin, in the bath, found no such difficulty. As with the lard, as much could be taken into the system through the skin in one day, as in a month by the mouth and stomach, and no digestion required, as it went *direct* to where it was needed. The child thus treated lived.

Having discussed the fish, a word now as to the fruits of Australia and England. The peaches of New South Wales are as good as the French. The apricots of Australia are far inferior to English, and only fit to make jam of. In greengages and plums, sunny France and southern England can show Australia the road for saccharine development and delicious juiciness. These fruits do *not* flourish in Australia, somehow. The cherries of Hobart are quite equal to the Kentish "bigaroons," and the strawberries of New Zealand to the "British Queens" of Myatt. Raspberries are large, woody, and tasteless, but make splendid jam when the absent and lacking sugar is added. Chesnuts and walnuts grow to perfection in the France-like climate of Tasmania. Ribstone pippins are also perfect there as in Devonshire. Grapes and potatoes, of magnificent, world-challenging merit, and that will keep sound and good longer than any others in the wide world, are exported from Adelaide and Hobart respectively. The dry climate of South Australia imparts a "keeping" quality to its products, which those of damp New Zealand are sadly lacking in. With regard to pears, Australia is "all there," and south of the latitude of 35 degrees, the "Bon Chretien," the "Marie Louise," the Bergamot, and the Jargonel, are up to the mark of anything in Europe. The colony of Victoria—while, in ordinary English fruits it vies with its neighbours, Tasmania and New South Wales—is ahead of them both in the excellence, abundance, and variety of its kitchen vegetables, tomatos, asparagus, and the like, and the Cape gooseberry, of southern Queensland, yields, with sugar, a jelly in whose presence the guava preparation cannot compete. Oranges in Australia do *not* defy the world, those of Bahia and even of Tahiti are far before them in all respects.

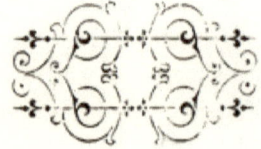

LIFE AND DEATH.

IT is a melancholy truism that all bright things must fade (diamonds, possibly, excepted). One does not like to realise the fact, for instance, that Dickens' charming wilful Dolly Varden, so full of refreshing, wholesome vitality and womanly sweetness combined, was born in the earthquake year of 1755, and would be 137 years old if now alive, and consequently must have slept with her most "Protestant" mother full sixty or seventy years ago, when the Reform Bill and Catholic Emancipation were first agitating the public mind. Nor is it pleasant to go into figures and reckon that, if dear old Pickwick was 60 years of age when (A.D. 1829) he read his famous scientific paper on the "Theory of Tittlebats," then he must have been born 123 years ago, and so must long since have "joined the majority;" unless, indeed, it be (as some folks assert) that his sententious utterances, his rotundity, his spectacles, his childlike simplicity and love of fair play, good fishing, and a good social dinner survived for a time in all their original perfection, in the person of a certain venerable and respected Judge in our modern Queensland. Few of us will live to see the Dickens' Centenary," which is sure to take place in 1912, with all the character creatives of his Shakesperian brain, mingling together in full costume on the stage at one view. We seldom remember a more beautiful or suggestive sight than a similar gathering of Shakespeare's characters, on the old Adelphi stage, and particularly "Hamlet," all bugles and sable, gracefully passing his playful rapier at the philosophic *Touchstone*, to the thrilling music of "Macbeth," at that particular juncture when the witches all resolve *nem. con.* to have "a dance upon the heath." Bright fancies are forever being elbowed off the stage of life by stern realities; and the gorgeous wedding breakfast and blissful honeymoon during which the pretty bride trills out the musical masterpieces of her maidenhood on Pleyel's grand pianoforte are succeeded, at an interval of twelve short months, by the advent of the serious-minded monthly nurse, and by strange noises, unwonted sounds in the house, by sleepless nights, and the piano neglected for evermore in favor of a new musical instrument—the baby's voice. But we venture to say that, if you were to consult the young mother, she would tell you that baby's most incoherent utterances are worth whole volumes of Gung'l, Chopin, and Weber, even when discoursed by the best of Pleyel or Chickering's prize medal productions in walnut and ivory.

BISMARCK'S DESIGNS ON QUEENSLAND.

E once described the terrible plots which are hatching in our peaceful midst, and which even our insignificance and remoteness from the great world's haunts fail to shield us from. We have now, alas! to note a further piece of secret underhand treachery in our very centre, and emanating on this occasion, *mirabile dictu!* from the stronghold of the Bismarck himself! We are, indeed, between two fires. The plot, this time, was hatched in Berlin, where an emissary whom we will here call Herr "Von Slawkenberg" (for want of a better name), received his orders, packed his carpet bag, and made sail for Queensland. Arrived there, did he play the guitar, or make love to the maidens, or call at Government House in kid gloves, or sing the "Watch on the Rhine?" No, he was on a mission, and Herr "Von S." did not come all the way just to fool or rave about Vaterland. We know not whether he took the steamer to Maryborough, or haply even to Bundaberg, but anyway, certes it is that he arrived in due time at Gayndah—which is a town of Queensland, quite unknown to nine-tenths of us, and never heard of at all outside our borders, that is to say never heard of in Australia, but which is well watched and cared for by them of Berlin. Then did Herr "Von S.," for the first time, relax his grim onward Erl King speed, and took to the Izaak Walton business—took to fishing in the broad-banked, sandy-bottomed, deep-pooled waters of the crystal Burnett. Yes,

the gentle angler's craft was now his pastime, for, be it known to you, reader dear, that "Von S." was an able disciple of Cuvier and Humboldt, and came hither to look after that which was neglected by the *savants* of Australia and England alike, but which was valued in Berlin. He fished for, and he found, and he took back with him, the marvellous ceratodus, that piscine wonder with *ribs* and *lungs*, that died out in fossil ages long ago, wearied of the hacknied old world's ways, but which still enjoys existence in ever fresh Australia, and so links the era of the mastodon with that of the sewing machine. Yes; "Von S." fished, and he caught even new and fresh varieties of this wonder-fish, and he found, moreover, a new, or old, but at any rate, living monster, which supplies the link between the tortoise and the serpent. Hear this, ye gods o Elephanta and of Hindostan, and let your so-called mythology be called true science for ever hereafter. And, hear this also, ye sleepy ones of England and Australia, and know that this same "Von S." was a competent expert of the first class, and not a man likely to make mistakes in matters of science. Bismarck chooses no bad tools—that you know, at any rate; and so here we are again check mated, outwitted, outrun, and undermined by strangers in our very midst in matters of science as well as of religion; blind to our own interesting position in the scientific world, and a very laughing-stock to the iron heroes of old Hereynia's Valhalla.

QUEENSLAND REDIVIVUS.

AUSTRALIA in 1893 was under a cloud arising from various sources—over-extravagance and over-prosperity in herself in the past, combined with political jugglery, and the whole crowned by the tactics of the English financial press and Stock Exchange "bears," who "must live," even though Australia's prosperity has to be "boiled down" to furnish the feast. And it must be confessed that the spectacle of bank after bank shutting its doors in the (naturally) richest country in the world was a sorry and unseemly sight. Australia was warned thirty years ago not to borrow money; but she gave no heed, and the day of reckoning came. Still, sarcastic comments of the English financial press did good. They roused a feeling of proud resolve in Australia, and the time will come when not only will all foreign loans be paid off, but nothing more will ever be borrowed. Australia can produce every mineral, every textile fabric, every article of food, drink, and medicine, every necessary and every luxury in the world, in a climate that ranges from that of Edinburgh to that of Demerara. Such a country should be a lender, not a borrower, of money. New Zealand, when her pride was hurt some years ago, led the way in ceasing to borrow; Queensland followed. She exports $9\frac{1}{2}$ millions yearly to $4\frac{1}{4}$ millions of imports on a population of 450,000, and no country in the world can surpass this, and it is bound to tell its tale soon. Normanton, the Gulf port, will be the Singapore of Australia—the great outlet gate of the island continent, starting from a point 300 miles nearer to the heart of the Dominion than Adelaide is, facing a smooth-water sea and showing by thousands of miles the nearest way to Java, China, India, and all the great markets of the East, for meat, gold, and other products, which the country at the back of Singapore does not afford, but which are found, right up to the gates of Normanton, and for thousands of miles back and round from it. A land which exports 5½ millions sterling annually more than it imports, on the labour of only 450,000 people, need not stand long with its hat (so to speak) in its hand. And just look at the imports, too, boots and shoes (to go no further)—how much longer do you suppose will the country, which is far and away the largest cattle holder—per head—in the world, continue to import, and not to export, leather, and boots and shoes? And so with other imports; the time is coming when Queensland will need to import nothing at all, except, perhaps, human beings and literature. So please let us have no more sneers in the English press at a land which has 400 millions of unsold acres, full of grass, water, timber, gold, coal, silver, tin, graphite, pearl-shell, tortoise-shell, asbestos, bismuth, copper, chrome, tellurium, mica, antimony, wool, tallow, sugar, rum, wheat, cotton, indigo, rice, tea, coffee, arrowroot, hemp, wine, fruit, &c., and to which outsiders will one day offer their loans in vain; though I must confess that Australia has erred hitherto in departing from the conservative canons of old Scotch and English banking usage.

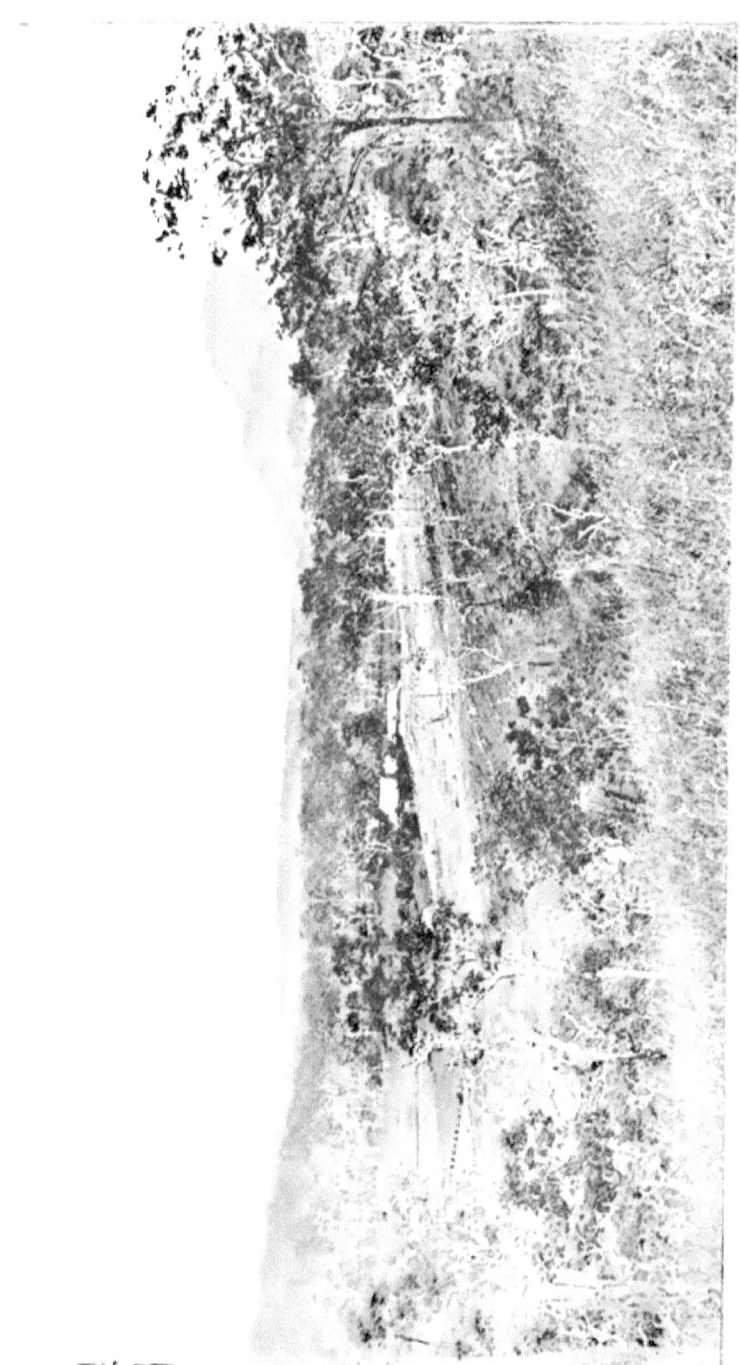

THE AUSTRALIAN CEDAR SCRUB.

TO anyone who knows how endless is the range of the great plant kingdom—which King Solomon is reported to have so well understood, from the beautiful cedar of Lebanon down to the wall hyssop—no botanic gardens in the world serve so much to remind of what *is* there as of what might be but is *not* there, and never can be there. Speaking of the cedars of Lebanon leads us to dwell awhile on the cedars of Australia, and the dense scrubs in which they delight; differing totally from the tangled beautiful forests of Tahiti, away on the east, and those of the Malayan Archipelago on the north, and affording a host of new sub-varieties which the hand of man has never yet gathered, nor the brain of man ever yet classified. And if all these strangers can be met with in the cedar scrub of Australia, where white men and intelligent botanists are at hand, what, then, of the vast and unexplored tropical and extra-tropical lands, where only untutored savages dwell? And who shall even guess at their unknown riches in fruit and flower, timber and foliage, colour and perfume, medicine and art material. And what botanic garden on earth will ever display the whole of them? Less heated than the forests of the Marquesas or Guiana, there is still a very equable temperature and a decidedly tropical aspect in the dim green aisles of the Australian "Cedar Brush." An old volcanic mountain is often the origin of the whole affair, and some ravine on its sides gets full in time of rich mould, replete with trachytic and vegetable elements in decomposition, and thus the little plant colony is started in life, and it soon generously hides the nakedness of its parent. "Soon," that is to say, if regarded as a term in our planet's history, and not measured by the mere span of a man's life, the rainwater in the ravine helps matters along, and the scrub gradually spreads sideways, as well as up and down, being fully proof against bush fires, which cannot penetrate its damp recesses, on which the sun even exerts no power of drought, and but little of heat either. And it is only here and there, too, that the adventurous explorer of these realms of fairyland can find an open space in which to enable him to judge of their enchanted beauties. Their most charming trees, like many fine churches in crowded cities, are too much hemmed in with dwarf companions to be visible in all their glory from any point of view whatever. High up just where the translucent pale emerald light gleams, unearthly, like a stained glass window over some cathedral altar, and scarce breaks through the dense barriers of leafy canopy; seeming to be derived, too, from almost any source except that of the sun itself. High up there is seen the great staghorn fern, gracefully drooping; whilst, lower down, on the irregular sides of the parent tree, its less aspiring dependents, the mosses and orchids, make up those picturesque and eccentric bits of form and colour which nature so much delights thus to hide away for her own glory and to secrete from the vulgar gaze of man. There is none of Australia's drought in these moist retreats, and their pleasant perfume and the subdued light gratify the senses wonderfully. So much for the mere rambler, then! But, alas! for the botanist. How is *he* to explore this place, and to remove all the coveted gems he would like to carry off; unless, indeed, he had the aid of a whole regiment of sappers and miners, of bullocks and elephants? And who shall decide as to the species of this or that lovely tree, whose bark and trunk are so beautiful and gigantic, but whose top foliage is lost overhead in a dark jungle, interlaced with its neighbors in such a manner that you must perforce cut all down, or leave all alone, if you want to successfully gratify your thirst of botanical research. Turning from botany to commerce, I may state that a single tree of the red cedar, *cedrela Australis*, will sometimes yield 30,000 feet of marketable timber.

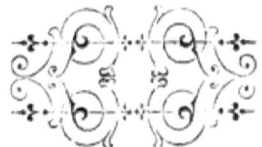

TAMBOURINE MOUNTAIN.

I WAS never near Tambourine Mountain in my life, but I claim the merit of being the first to discover its mission on this earth. Some old residents of one class saw nothing but sugar-growing there, others were all for saw mills, but both missed the real point of its merits—namely, that of being the finest climate on earth, and being the premier sanatorium of Australia. It was this way: I found an old Admiralty chart of Moreton Bay, and figured on it inland was a three-cornered tabletop mountain (unnamed) showing 1,850ft. and 1,790ft. at its angles and buttresses. I saw at a glance what a perfect climate it must possess, but where was it? and what was it called? So I took its Brisbane bearings on the map, and ascended some of our highest hills (Mount Coot-tha, &c.) and did the same from there, and, by a bit of amateur "triangulation," I found the mysterious stranger was no other than Mount Tambourine, of which I had often heard in the early Logan days. People told me of its wonders, how that folks who went up for a day were enchanted, and spent a week instead; how others ate themselves out of "house and home" and exhausted their provisions long before their picnic time was over, all owing to the glorious appetite engendered. I heard of little children residents, fed chiefly on maize porridge, but rosy-faced as Kentish "bairns;" of scrub soil 20ft. deep; of orange trees that you could cut a fishing-rod out of; of cedar trees that would build two houses; of geraniums that would fill a room, and so forth; and it all seemed quite credible, for Tambourine Mountain is just where it should be for a perfect health resort. Were it at Cape York it would be too hot with its moderate elevation; if at Cape Howe it would be too bleak; if ninety miles from the sea, like Toowoomba (at the same height), it would be too variable; if razor-topped it would still have a view, but not be habitable; but as it is, it is perfection. In 28deg. south, ten miles from the sea, flat-topped, only moderate in area, and nearly 2,000ft. high, it is an exceptional wonder, and no other place on earth like it; but in pure air from below and around its precipices it is equable in climate, unlike what a larger tableland would be; and were there even no view at all from it, it would still be worth living and dying on for the climate alone, and I envy the lucky people who, fifty years hence (when it has been "civilised") will enjoy life there.

The late Captain W. B. Brown was himself no poet, but when he was up Tambourine he said, "Well! neither painter nor poet could do justice to this," as he viewed the scene from the north-east angle of the mount. I have, myself, often enjoyed the view from the passes that border Mount Mitchell, Spicer's Peak, and Cunningham's Gap, and looking at the chaotic and beautiful peaks, which mark the sources of the Clarence and Richmond Rivers, there is nothing like it, that I have seen, in Tasmania or Eastern Australia. But, Tambourine must beat it; for you have all the grand mountains to the south and west, and also (what you have not from the Main Range sites) the bay, islands, and sea, and the homes and settlements of civilisation. With a good telescope, or field glass, you can discern, on a fine day, the tawny north buttress of old Tambourine glowing in the sun, and I have no doubt that much of the outlyings of Brisbane can be seen, also, from there. Tambourine Mountain goes down pretty "sheer" on all sides, though, of course, there are leading spurs of access up on the north and east sides, and this is one of the secrets of its grand and unapproached climate, which, it is to be hoped, will never be marred by any injudicious and overdone destruction of timber, or it will become bleak, and arid, and unsheltered, and lose half its charm; clear away the scrub, to some extent, by all means, but spare most of the big timber or you will be sorry. Tambourine is a place where you can enjoy a temperature of 65deg. and your blankets at Christmas time, and, if the old Romans had had it, it would have been converted into a magnificent high-level irrigation reservoir (by gravitation), but I fancy Queensland will do still better with it in the next century.

THE BRISBANE BOTANICAL GARDENS.

WHILE the western up-country stations are sometimes afflicted with an iron drought, our eastern district is generally emerald green, and least of all in our Botanic Gardens is there any sign of the lack of needful moisture. Not only pleasing to the eye, not only grateful in their shade, and soothing for a lounge — while the *susurrus* of the sleepless bamboos imparts an irresistible pleasing drowsiness to the nerves—these gardens have their multifarious and great uses, one of the highest of which is the surrounding of many a poor little bush hut in the suburbs with allamandas, lagerstrœmias, and other plants of tropical beauty, which a duke's hothouse in England can scarcely bring into flower. People cannot all afford a good house, but they can all afford lovely flowers in this climate; and slips from the Botanic Gardens, planted about Brisbane, have grown into trees more beautiful, in some cases, owing to richer soil, even than the original ones they came from.

Although not blessed with a fine outlook like that over the harbour of Port Jackson, yet our gardens in themselves surpass those of Sydney and Melbourne. We can grow all the temperate zone plants as well as they can, while they cannot approach us in the line of the tropical ones. They can no more raise the purple lilac in Sydney than we can here, while their attempts at the bamboo look ludicrous to a Queenslander. One of their greatest successes in Sydney gardens is the Manchineel, a very handsome, but, we believe, poisonous tree, from Madagascar. Two interesting trees in our gardens are suggestive of the Holy Land : one of these is the fine, venerable, hoary old olive tree in the main avenue, the other is the thorn of Judea, near the henna tree. A fine shady evergreen, well-grown, noble-looking, pleasant and profitable tree is this same olive ; and it is a pity there are not whole forests of it in our colony. The then Collector of Customs, Mr. Duncan, twenty years ago, lectured on this topic, and had his advice been taken at the time, the trees would now have been something to look at and to reap the benefit of. A curious contrast is presented by the asparagus of England and the asparagus of Java. The latter is a pretty flowering, sweet-scented creeper, the very thing for children to weave garlands from. The fragrant and beautiful Plumeria acutifolia, the sacred tomb flower of Java, flourishes as bravely as ever, and is rapidly becoming a tree in its proportions. It keeps steadily in flower from November to May, and is clearly quite at home in our climate. The coffee berries are yet green, and the cinnamon trees have not finished shooting out tender leaves yet. Passing near the bamboos, and the drinking fountain, we can travel, in fancy, from the Surrey lanes, where flaxen-haired, rosy-cheeked girls abound, to the volcanic gorges of Honolulu, where the dusky, yet symmetrical, damsels are attired in surplices of blue calico, or satin, according to their rank in life, and the imaginary journey is performed, in a few seconds, by simply rubbing a leaf of tansy and holding it to the nose, which at once suggests Surrey (or any other county you like) ; and then passing

on to the big alocasia, or taro, a gummy blue potato, or
turnip, on which nearly all Polynesia manages to keep its
ribs clothed with fat. That most delicious fruit, the date
plum, does not appear to grow well here, for we never see a
specimen of it for sale in any shop. The gardens show a
fine collection of the Melastoma, with its curious leaf, unlike
any other, and its deep "Humboldt" violet flower. A wild
pretty variety of this, the Melastoma Banksia, grows about
the hill side gullies, in the parish of Toombul, facing the
east. The Spanish Annato, so useful to cheesemakers, who
wish to send a well-colored article to market, is only in
flower as yet; it is a very handsome tree, and its blossom is
fully to match in point of beauty. The Clerodendron
Nutans, from India, is a pretty drooping flower of a hawthorn type and color, to the unbotanical eye, but it is quite
destitute of scent; not so, however, is the Clerodendron
Fragrans, which somewhat reminds us of the hydrangea in
appearance, and possesses all the refreshing fragrance, and
none of the pungency of the choicest smelling salts.

Near the foot of the hill some granadillas of eight pounds
weight each, and as big as a man's hand, are hidden amongst
the leaves of that variety of the passion flower. The henna
tree, as useful to the ladies of the east as belladonna and
kalydor are to our Western belles, diffuses a sweet perfume
so long as you remain ten yards away from it, but a very
close proximity, between its blossoms and the olfactories,
discloses a sickly unpleasant odor. The thorn tree of Judea,
from which, it is reported that, the crown of thorns was
plaited, shows spikes of a moderate length only, and destitute of much stiffness, and we should imagine that either
this is not the same tree, as is alluded to in the New Testa-
ment, or else that it does not take to this climate kindly.

The close of the floral season is at hand, but the still
warm days enable the waterlilies to resist the increasing

chilliness of the nights. The mango and jack fruit are in good, full fruit, considering that they are so far away from home, and though they have much of the flavor, they have neither the overflowing juiciness nor the ponderous weight they attain to in their native *habitat*. The Japanese camphor tree is growing to a dimension that begins to rival some of our gum trees, and the aromatic savor, of its twigs and leaves, strongly remind us of the universal old eucalypt of Australia, with its precious astringent gums, pungent and solvent essential oils, and of the valuable heritage we possess, in a country where it is so plentiful. The decadence of the once splendid Poinciana regia, near the round bed, is being atoned for by the vigorous growth and beauty of the younger trees; one by the Albert-street gate, and the other by the aviary, where it stands just close enough to the Brazilian rosewood to make us regret that they do not exactly blossom at the same time of the year, in order that we might make comparison of the scarlet and the lilac, side by side, and see which of them bears the palm. On the whole, we fancy, the Madagascar red surpasses the Brazilian lilac, for it is set off by a green, so intense, and yet delicate in color, that the somewhat more sombre verdancy of the jacaranda leaf looks dull beside it.

And of the palms, we must say a word for the Cocos flexuosa, of Brazil, which is equal to the Seaforthia Elegans and the Cocos Plumosa for beauty, and which bears a fruit pendant in bunches like elongated ears of bright tawny yellow wheat, fully ripe.

When the sun has again crossed the line to the south, Nature responds to his presence, and the plants of the tropics are unfolding, and gladdening the eye with their unrivalled beauty. October brings out the mimosa-leafed Jacaranda tree of Brazil, a very gem of size and beauty combined. It is not alone that it grows as tall as an oak, nor that its leaf vies with the shamrock for verdure, and with the fern for delicacy of shape, but its clusters of flowers have a color that is neither mauve, lavender, lilac, nor violet, but like them all, and more beautiful than any. They are marked slightly with pure white inside, and I must not forget to describe, if possible, their shape. First of all, they are elaborately "scolloped" round the edges, and they have a curved cornucopia shape, and droop, surpassing in gracefulness of outline any nepenthe campanula, or ixia that I have ever seen. This tree is a conspicuous object half-a-mile away. Its only rival in these gardens, the gorgeous Poinciana Regia, of Madagascar, flowers in December. In greenness and delicacy of its mimosa-like leaf, this latter tree vies with, or surpasses, the Jacaranda ; its foliage shape is dome-like, its spread great, and the dome-curve is observable from beneath as well as from above. The flower is a glorious scarlet, prettily marked with black and white, and, like the Jacaranda, it appears in huge clusters or sprays. Either of these noble trees would be calculated to arrest the notice and attention of people, who had never in their lives before looked with interest at any botanic specimen, and, to those who delight in floral beauty, they afford pleasure beyond all description. This tree also, like the Poinciana, strikes the eye at a great distance with its blaze of colour. The cochineal insect is here at times busy at the cacti. The caper shrub shows its berry here as well as on the Mediterranean. The "wine" palm of Western Africa bears a fruit as nice as the strawberry, and not unlike it in flavour, and the talipot palm shows a sweet-scented spray of flowers. The jutes and sunn hemps of India, are growing here on the same bed with Irish flax, and it is hard to say which looks the best. The "travellers' tree," of Madagascar, not unlike a plantain to unbotanical eyes, affords a fine supply of pure water if tapped at the root of the leaves. Nothing can be more soothing on a warm day than the ceaseless rustle of the breeze shaken bamboo clumps, which makes just noise enough to sing one to sleep on

> "The sweet siesta of a summer day,
> The tropic afternoon of Moreton Bay."

But we must remember that Queensland is no country for laziness, and this hive of bees on the lawn is not very sleepy at all events. The sugar-cane, textile materials, coffee, cotton, tea, &c., which are growing all round, serve to remind us that repose is not the sole, but only an occasional phase of existence, even in warm climates like ours. The "silky oak" is in yellow flower, full of honey and of sweet scent. The honey from this tree has an intoxicating effect on some of the little paroquets, which are easily caught after a long feast on it.

AUSTRALIA FEDERATED.

VERILY, 'tis a grand idea! Not but that Dame Nature made her all in one, at the outset, but she had to be divided in order to be won and conquered. *Divide et impera* is an old adage. In subduing the wilderness we had to save time by instituting several central saps and points of attack, at once; and Adelaide, Melbourne, Sydney, Brisbane, Rockhampton, and Townsville, have each spread out their polypous arms of inland settlement on the more genial southern and eastern shores of the continent, for it would have taken too long to try and radiate the light of civilisation from one depôt alone. Hence the disruption into "colonies," which system will now soon have effected its work, and then Dame Nature's sway must again be resumed—resumed, that is, so far as unity of territory goes. For, be it remembered, that the Darling and Condamine, in their onward flow, neither know nor care, nor pause to ask, which is Queensland and which New South Wales. The great Cordillera throws out, lavishly, its gold reefs and its copper lodes, its veins of tin and its dykes of iron, everywhere alike, and even as the rain of Heaven, it recks not of blue books or boundaries; of orders in Council or differential tariffs. Nature knows nothing of Border Customs or Legislative Halls; of local jealousies or commercial wire-pullings: but, on the contrary, and so far from it, Tamworth cries out to the Barcoo, and the sound is echoed to Gippsland and Warrnambool, even as the forty millions of sheep and cattle answer each other's bleatings and lowings, without a break, over three thousand miles of hill and plain.

The shepherd kings, dwellers in bush palaces, meet and traffic, and exchange productions; and beeves are bartered for ewes, and drovers travel from the Lynd to the Glenelg, swarming to and fro in ceaseless caravans of peripatetic wealth. There is a savor and a spirit of unison in all this, leading us up inevitably to federation, whose inspiring angel must eventually arise from the inland, when it triumphs, as it must do in the end, over the schismatic counsel of the seaboard cities, who know not, as they ought to do, of the homogeneous continent, lying vast at their back. The sun-tanned youthful heir of the Queensland cattle squatter marries the blonde daughter of the New England sheep Crœsus, and her fair-bearded brother is, in turn, the husband of that glowing brunette who will, one day, own half the stock on the Loddon; and shall their respective offspring have need to wonder and enquire what petty country, or little colony, they belong to? They would be called Australians, if travelling in Rome or Vienna; so, why are they to be differently known and designated while under the Southern Cross? The Castlereagh and Talbragar people are allied to the Snowy River folks; it may be by marriage, by business partnership, and by traffic in mild-eyed oxen and woolly lambs. Such ties of blood and money overleap, and will never long brook the restraint of mere departmental administration. The tendrils of trade, of love, and of matrimony, are stretching out and taking hold, and family blood is intermingling in all directions in New Holland, for there is an interchange borderwise of thoroughbred people as well as of blood horses, pedigree bulls, and stud sheep; and, where these ties bind, who shall separate? Viewed in this aspect our venerable continent is rapidly being federated already by the operations of daily human life, by the interchange of material wealth, and by the mutual alliances of well-dowered families. So, let our politicians coquette with the question as they please, still to that complexion must it come at last. They will find that nature and civilisation have combined to forestall, and do their work for them, and all that Australian cabinets will have to do will be, like the heavy father in the play, to affirm gracefully what they can no longer make a show of retarding, and yield their consent to the union of the young colonies who have, so to speak, long since travelled to Gretna Green and back again.

THE CERATODUS.

YEARS ago I bathed daily in the Burnett River, where the fish *ceratodus*, that relic of pre-Adamite life still survives, and survives nowhere else in the world. In England you might see the fossil remains of one imbedded in a marble mantelpiece, part of the marble itself, so long, long ago has it disappeared from life there. It has the gills of a fish, and lungs also, like a sheep, when it is opened. It is reckoned that the *ceratodus*, a plump, full, round scaled, eatable fish, died out in Europe 200,000 years ago. He grows in the Burnett to $2\frac{1}{2}$ft. long, and up to 12lbs. in weight, and the simple villagers there at Gayndah caught and ate him, all unconscious of his status; all ignorant that the Emperor William of Germany had, as I have related, sent a special *savant* to their village to bring specimens to Berlin. I saw one dissected at the Brisbane Museum, and saw the weird, uncanny lungs in the fish's chest. He is said to belong to the Jurassic period, to be contemporary with the awful *Ichthyosaurus*, and still more awful Plesiosaurus and the "wing finger" (beg pardon, the *pterodactyl*), all mere fossils now, of the Mesozoic era. What human pedigree, dating only half way to Adam, can compare with this *ceratodus* family, which was old and *began to die* more than *two thousand centuries* ago, and had the job complete by that early date, so far as the world outside of Australia was concerned? Queensland should surely have this fish on its coat of arms, and no other place on earth could infringe the patent. Talk of ancient heraldry, indeed! after this. The dread and legendary mystery of the bunyip, sacred to Australia only, seems justified and half explained now by the *ceratodus*.

The Glasshouse Mountains—Beerwah.

THE WOMEN FOLK.

COMELY, is she not? in that pretty uniform, and with her smooth skin, good complexion, and rounded, firm limbs! What a partner she would make in a waltz, now, or companion for a moonlit stroll! Gently, gently, enthusiastic male reader, don't be in such a hurry to twine that arm of yours round her waist, she would not appreciate it. No! She has seen too many men of 80, or 90 years, swoon for the *first* time in their long, strong lives. She has inhaled, too often, the odour of wounded human flesh in the military hospitals, after a great battle; she has seen the ending of too many lives, the scared and troubled faces that bore the impress and memory of unrepented and unatoned misdeeds, and so the "grand passion" is not in *her* line. And you *must* believe it, too, if you take one intelligent glance at that alert, kindly, bright, beautiful eye of hers. There are plenty of girls and women in the world with her eyes, but without the matchless expression which hers have so well earned. For *that* can only be acquired and attained to in such a life of devotedness as she has led. Marry you? oh! yes, I daresay she would, and be a good nurse, too, when needful. Marry you? certainly, if she liked you, but you would have to open up preliminary negotiations in some different fashion from passing your arm round her waist at the outset. *Croyez vous mon enfant?*

z

Female beauty is bound to come to the front against all drawbacks. The present style of costume would have been voted "theatrical" by our grandmothers in 1835, and it certainly strives hard to set off every feminine charm and attractiveness to the uttermost, from the high-heeled shoe—with the maker's name in gold letters on the inner arch of the sole—up to the little ears and white neck nape, exposed to full view by the piling up of the hair (black, auburn, or flaxen) high on the back of the head. All this is permissible, though the said grandmothers thought it rude to even expose the *ears* much, and wore no heels, and covered their arms up with long gloves, and so forth. And how they *would* have shuddered at the awful triangular slice of nudity which is cut out at the back of the modern ball dress, and I believe, too, that future generations will join in the reprobation of it. It is no matter how nun-like and modestly and unfashionably you dress a pretty woman and her hair, she *will* attract notice, and the girls of 1835, with their high waists, short skirts, elaborate sandals and lengthy gloves, secured a larger percentage of husbands from the gentlemen in plum-coloured swallowtails and nankeen "tights," than do the "theatrical" damsels of the present era from their swains. Let the poor things have their little triumphs of dress by all means; they have plenty *(per contra)* to put up with. What *would* the men say if the women turned out in armies of 20,000 or 30,000, and proceeded to fight and kill each other with "arms of precision?" How they would howl at this "waste of good material," if on no other ground. But how little they reck of or consult the women's feelings, when they resolve to go to war themselves, and leave the females bereaved on all sides.

DESTINY.

HOW awful is the roar of the lion, heard in the forest at midnight! How impotent, weary of waiting, uncouth, weird, eerie, uncivilized, unconventional! So destitute of, so different, and so far from, the trained and modulated accents of society and diplomacy, of the disciplined repose that "stamps the caste of Vere de Vere." How that roar haunts one! rouses one up! seems to stir the conscience with the voice of retribution! for it appears to blurt out some terrible truth of some unfinished crime, unheard of, undreamt of before; and all the more unwelcome from its startling newness of revelation. The heart feels frozen with a guilty terror at the thunder of that gruesome voice of the night, so harsh, abrupt, so strong, yet so pitiful withal: the cry of the oppressed demon. It is not that the tawny agile brute could crush you with its weight, that its muscles would flatten you at a blow, that its teeth and claws could rend you like a steel rag mill—it is not in all this that the chief horror lies. The inarticulate loud cry of the soulless giant cat is replete with a sadness, a tale of long-felt injustice, of ages and aeons of dire suffering and oppression. A being created by no will and for no wish of its own, sent into a hard world, armed only with muscle, teeth, and claws, and a quenchless hunger, with no gift of brains to mitigate the doom, or reason to see or hew a way out of its life's burden and life curse. No wonder it cries aloud, and that its voice in that one sigh-cry carries to those who have ears to hear withal a whole volume of bitter, pent up remonstrance, against its cruel fate. Terror is all that it conveys to the other animals, but the demi-god, semi-animal, man, can pity the lesser animal whose tones can thus be analyzed as its cries to God and man of its intolerable destiny. Yes, there can be no doubt that the roar of the lion has a subtle sound in it, a mysterious minor key that *accuses* some one. "The lions roaring—do seek their meat from God" (so says King David) and still, as one contemplates the massive red forearm, the spreading claws, the terrible teeth, the fathomless, glowing, yellow eyes, pity still holds her pride of place against fear in the heart of the seer.

And it is not the void and hungry lion alone that raises his awful voice in accusation and remonstrance with "Destiny." The atheist, the scoffer, the "larrikin," he, too, has a grievance. *His* "bitter cry" takes a different sound from the lion, but it has the same basis. He does not roar, but he writes what he thinks. It is useless to tell him that there is a benevolent design in everything; he laughs in your face. What is it to *him* that the active lizard is "designed" to catch the active fly? "What need" (he cries) "of either of them?" He sneers at the well-fed people who see benevolence and purpose in all arrangements of Nature. He admits some of it, of course, but he has eyes only for what is "out of joint," and he wants to know who permitted, or who caused, *that*. Why was he, the larrikin, left to starve, in mind and body and soul, with not an opening or chance in any direction that was not blocked for him or his forefathers, centuries before he was born. He feels deserted and "left," and he summons his resolution and doubts everything, at all events everything that is—or proposes to be—good. Let those who are fed and taught and instructed testify as to how evil ever got loose at all. Why is a young man sent into the world unarmoured against the wiles of women; why does he buy his armour and experience so dear and so late in life? How much more useful it would be at 17 than at 70; and so with the girl, why is she not born wiser about the tricks of the men? Why is that bitter, useless, school, kept by Dame Experience, the only scholastic establishment available for youth of both sexes? Why is not sentimental Horace armed by Nature with the knowledge that pert Celia's pretty pout and toss of the head are her instructive methods of calling him, not of repelling him, and so leave the poor fellow some show in the matter, in place of being impelled and killed by his "love of approbation," to be miserable about her imaginary scorn?

THE BRITISH CAPITALIST.

THE British Capitalist, whom I will, for shortness sake, call "John Bull," is a strange fellow to deal with, and it is quite a miracle if any one can get him to invest in Australian mining. He thinks himself very knowing, but the fact is, that he generally "pitches on" when he ought to hold back, and holds back when he ought to "pitch on," as I will illustrate presently. If you talk to him about Australian mines (and Queensland is Victoria, or Western Australia "just over the way" to him), John Bull waves his hand loftily, and tells you of how utterly he failed in the one or two solitary ventures he made, but you will not hear a word from him about what he made elsewhere.

In 1849, I saw a fine instance of John Bull's perspicuity (?) I was among the early voyagers to California, when gold was discovered. I saw ships from all parts, except England, pouring in and reaping a golden harvest in their cargoes. France, with her sardines, claret, cognacs, velvets, &c. Spain with her sherry and raisins. America, of course, foremost in the dance (no *ad valorem* on her goods); and even Australia well represented by active little hardwood brigs and schooners from Sydney, Melbourne, Hobart Town, &c., with jams and onions, that realised, with apples and potatoes, from 2s. 6d. to 10s. a lb.; even Australia shared in the spoil. But lofty John Bull "knew better, you know; he'd been taken in before, and wasn't to be done like that," and so forth. Well, if John Bull had only been consistent, one might have respected him, even if disagreeing with his views; but, alas! by-and-by, John Bull, as soon as the glut and reaction took place in San Francisco, began to rub his eyes and open them, and think there was something in it after all, and so he shipped heavily, and lost all, and some more; in his usual nice way he swore, a deep oath, never to go into this sort of thing again, and made the matter an excuse, and a "precedent," for holding back on the next opportunity for making money; but, of course, only till the unfavorable time arrived, when he repeats the process. John Bull was nearly as behind-hand when gold was found in his territory of Australia, and he was the last person in the world to believe in it. He always forgets, that those, who venture early win in commercial matters. He will consign recklessly to old-established and overstocked markets, but he shudders at the idea of shipping to a new and untried one. Red tape is as rife in the counting-house as at the Admiralty; and it is a great pity, both for John Bull and the young markets of the world for his capital, that he is at once the richest and nearly the least enterprising person on the face of the earth. He does not know, and nothing possibly would drive it into his head, that he has a dead certainty of making money at Gympie and Ravenswood, if he mined extensively and judiciously. The poor fellow has, doubtless, been victimised in Victoria, which cannot show a coal or a copper mine, and whose average gold yield is below ours; and who has capital enough, of her own, for any really good thing within her own borders, and only offers the refuse to John Bull; but all this is no reason why the old gentleman should mistrust young Queensland, who has not the money to follow up either gold, copper, or any other mines, which would make the fortunes of the people, in no time, if situated in countries with capital at command. Of what use is a solid mountain of 50 per cent. copper ore, without plenty of money to begin operations with?

But the root of the evil lies deeper; it is not in the alleged poverty of our gold-spangled reefs, or of our thick copper lodes, both of which challenge the world, that the drawback is to be sought for. Corruption and jobbery unhappily obtain as freely in mining matters as they do in Government departments, and John Bull is infinitely more deficient in skilful and trustworthy professionals in the mining science, whom he can send forth with confidence to study his interests abroad, than Queensland is deficient in rich metals, which, I again repeat, she can challenge the world for. It has happened that John Bull has started a mining company in Australia (I will not point out the exact colony) entirely on his own capital, and the company never paid expenses whilst *he* was proprietor; but, as soon as he sold out, it began to pay handsomely to the new and colonial owners.

Some wiseacre would here interject: "Oh, but my dear fellow, you know you can't expect John Bull to venture in 16,000 miles away, while your local lucky reefers on the spot are afraid to speculate a mile away from where they are for fear of being robbed!" The reply to this is obvious. The lucky reefer turns up his nose at a dividend which would send John Bull wild with joy—viz., 20 per cent. per annum on capital invested. The lucky reefer likes to buy a claim for a bottle of grog to day, and to sell it a week after for £500. That's his style. As for trusting your employés, that is a matter which any clever business man can encompass, and the "smugging" of an odd specimen or two would never affect the dividends much if economy in working were the rule.

America is not frightened to risk capital in mining. Witness the silver mine which has yielded millions in silver, and to get at which, more favorably, they had to drive a tunnel many miles long into the heart of a mountain, at 3,500 feet from its summit, in order to cut the lode.

Queensland is wide enough, and her laws ought to make provision to accommodate, at the same time, the small reefing parties and the mammoth companies, without clashing, or interfering with each other. The latter will require, in return for large investment of capital, the freehold, or long lease, of mining areas some miles square, or I fear we shall not attract them hither, or make it worth their while.

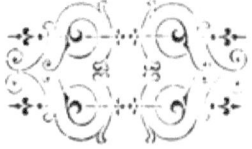

BUSH PUBLIC HOUSES.

IN Queensland, the murders, properly so-called, occasioned by the grog, improperly so-called, dispensed at the "bush hells" where kegs of new rum containing a ground tier of figs of rank new colonial tobacco, afford the best and speediest means of maddening the brain and sickening the stomach, with all the deep deadly anguish of outraged nature, thus compelled to swallow and digest that which it is a narcotic poison even to inhale—these murders, coupled with a perusal of returns as to the crowded state of our lunatic asylums, suggest enquiries as to how long this triple murder of body, mind, and soul, is to escape the legislator's lash. A bank robber, with crape mask and pistols, is a gentleman, an angel almost, by the side of the vendor of tobacco essence, and yet the former comes in for his full share of police attention, proving thereby that "money" is worth more than "life" in the eye of the law—in practice, at any rate, if not in theory. Woogaroo Asylum contains 800 inmates, and it is not the only place of confinement for lunatics in the colony. More than this, Queensland is a wide and thinly-populated place, where a mad person, unless specially obnoxious or dangerous, would not necessarily or readily be immured within four walls for safety all round; so that the number of people, more or less lunatic, who are at large in Queensland, cannot even be approximately estimated; while in densely-populated England, the nuisance of having anyone, ever so little mad, at liberty to trouble and annoy the busy working millions around, causes all such to be kept locked up and out of harm's way. Following up this train of reflection, it would naturally occur to anyone that the lunatic asylums of Great Britain should—or ought to—contain a much larger percentage of the population than those of Queensland, or Australia, do. Yet we scarcely think that it can be proved that from 118,000 to 180,000 people are immured in mad-houses, or asylums for the insane, in England, and yet that proof would have to be adduced before we could truthfully assert that our percentage of lunacy in Australia—or Queensland, at least—was no more than that in England. We have to face the fact that nearly 2·5 people of every thousand here are mad enough to be locked up and kept at the public expense, to say nothing of those who ought to be and are not so confined, which would make the percentage look still more ugly by comparison. Place these terrible figures side by side with the returns of lunatics confined throughout the United Kingdom, and we shall all be startled, if anything in Heaven or earth can startle a legislature, a matter which may at times be doubted.

It is needless to enlarge upon the share, or the monopoly, rather, which the tobacco-steeped "grog" of these bush publics enjoys in the creation of those shattered minds, dethroned souls, and wild staring eyes of horror we so often meet with, where reason, health, and industrial productive use ought to sit supreme and reign in their stead.

BYGONE QUEENSLAND PRESSMEN.

WILLIAM WILKS, who, in 1853, edited the *Courier*, was a racy writer, and smart of speech as well, with a holy horror of "High Church" parsons, one of whom refused to read the burial service over Wilks's little girl (dead of scarlet fever) on the ground that he attended the Wesleyan Chapel. The following is a sketch by Wilks in the *Courier*. In the early days of the Crimean war, a sound was heard at noon in Brisbane as of heavy gun firing down in the Bay (there was no traffic to drown noises then). It was reported that an English and Russian frigate were "fighting it out" somewhere near the Pile Lighthouse of to-day, and expeditions to the back of One-tree Hill were at once planned by the more timorous villagers, but it was only a big boiler being rolled over at Kangaroo Point after all, and Wilks put the whole matter into rhyme in the *Courier*, thus:—

> "To arms! to arms!" became the cry,
> But peaceful cronies said "Not I,
> To legs! to legs! let each one vie
> With each, to scale the mountains high."
> And land shark speculators fly,
>   And corner lots forego.

> Till, ever true to his warlike name,
> Terror-dispelling, the "Douglas" came.
> At Kangaroo Point, where soap is made,
> A monstrous boiler, used in the trade,
> Was rolled along by men that I paid,
> And, as it rolled, "Bong Bong" it gaed,
> Which I deem has sufficed to alarm the blade
> Who has frightened each man, boy, wife, and maid,
> And so my innocent say is said,
>   And you're done extremely brown.

Sylvester Doig edited the *Free Press*, and so did Robert Meston. There was then no paper either in Ipswich or Darling Downs, and I question if there was another journal nearer than the *Maitland Mercury*. In 1855 Ipswich started a newspaper under the Bays Bros., and comic sketches appeared at the time from the pen of Lieutenant Nicoll. A midnight "spree" of the 1858 period at an Ipswich hotel was set forth in verse—

> Three Benedicts, of furious mein, were foremost in the fray,
> Two Bachelors, of aspect mild, by them were led astray.

and the ballad went on to say that—

>   Not to be beat, they brewed their punch
>   In Jack ———'s new hat
>   Made spatchcock of the parrot green,
>   And then clean shaved the cat.

It was a week before the race ball, and as they passed her door it is reported that they heard a young lady from the Darling Downs talking in her sleep at 2 a.m.

>   For as they passed the maiden's door
>   She murmured in her sleep,
>   "Mind ! nothing under twenty yards,
>   And make the flounces deep,"

which goes to prove, unless it all be a base fabrication, that the damsels of 1858 were very like those of—a later era.

Separation soon followed, and newspapers multiplied. John Kent, erst of the commissariat department, was at one time (he landed here about 1840) in a position analogous to that of Government Resident in Brisbane, but in the late "fifties" he edited the Ipswich paper, and was a pungent writer (in the Thady O'Kane style). When Sir George Bowen first landed, Solicitor (now Judge) Chubb, of Ipswich, published an ode of welcome to him, which drew from Kent a comment on the needless cruelty of administering an emetic to a recently seasick man, and when the first Upper House was gazetted in 1860, Kent prefaced a terrific leader and followed up a list of them with the line—

> And the boldest held his breath for a time

(from Campbell's "Battle of the Baltic").

T. P. Pugh was a trenchant political writer when he edited the *Courier*, and a vain attempt was made by the Tory party to prosecute and crush him at the time. Searle then appeared upon the scene, and, writing under the name of "William Nutts," soon gave the public a proof of his comic powers. He was specially happy in his poetic delineations of the feud between Judge Lutwyche and Colonial Secretary Herbert, in one of which the latter chaffs the Judge on being "sacked" for meddling with politics, which evoked from "Alfred James Peter" the couplet—

> The subtle wiles of your revengeful crew
> Misguided youth ! deprived me of my "screw."

I remember, one evening, at the club in Ipswich, during circuit time, and when we were alone after dinner, I "made bold" to ask his Honour how he liked Searle's latest "skit." He (the Judge) laughed heartily, and said that he enjoyed it amazingly, especially the line—

> Ye gods ! my wrath assuage,

which he proceeded to recite with heroic intonation. It was supposed to be spoken in reply to some of Herbert's cruel chaff. Judge Lutwyche always was manly enough to take a joke in good part. Searle afterwards came out with a duet parody on "Polly Hopkins."

HERBERT.
Well my ancient, portly buffer,
  How do you do—oo, how do you do—oo?
LUTWYCHE.
All serene and up to snuff—ah?
  So are not you—oo, so are not you.
HERBERT.
If you don't mind your p's and q's, sir,
  We'll dock your screw—oo, we'll dock your screw—oo.
LUTWYCHE.
To vote it now you daren't refuse, sir,
  Of thousands two—oo, of thousands two.

Herbert and Lutwyche were enthusiastic prize poultry breeders, and met on common friendly ground in the halls where black Spaniards and gray Dorkings competed; and the poem winds up with a reconciliation scene, of which the chorus (still to the same tune) is sung by Herbert and Lutwyche in a duet—

  Let's go fee—eed!
  And poultry bree—eed!

Searle *was* irresistible beyond a doubt. Then blossomed out Walter Cooper with his comic sketches of the early Queensland members, many of whom he photographed and lampooned in print under borrowed names. He was versatile, and could give a good imitation of Captain Feez in "Come where my love lies dreaming," picked up at Rockhampton in 1863. When he went to Sydney he made enemies by his very epigrammatic summing up of the people who "saved their souls in Pitt-street and their bodies in King-street," alluding to the chapel in one place and the Bankruptcy Court in the other one. George Hall ("Bohemian") was a man whom it was a treat to hear read aloud in some of Artemus Ward's sketches; he always dryly put the right accent in the right place, never laughed himself, but made you and every one else do it very much. (I often have wondered who "Zadriel" was whom George Hall used to publish letters from). Bohm was a newspaper man whom one always met at the committee and betting meetings before the races. He and a certain lawyer's clerk were admirers of the fair daughter of an Ipswich hotelkeeper. Bohm married her; the other one killed himself. D. F. T. Jones was on the *Courier* in 1864, and wrote many a racy article, notably one of a trip to Gympie in 1867. L. J. Byrne, in 1863, was the Brisbane correspondent of some Victorian papers.

Wm. O'Carroll, who left us in the cold winter of 1885, was long ago a conspicuous and worthy figure in Queensland journalism, a genial editor, full of the brotherhood of the craft, kindly and helpful to juniors, bold as a lion, comic as *Punch*; his crisp and incisive "specialities" could scarce be distinguished from the "best brands" of Traill and Brunton Stephens. This review is not meant to come down to later dates. There were in the old times other and more ephemeral pressmen, who cannot all be here noted. In 1855, the Rev. W. Smith (Baptist) wrote leaders for the *Courier*, and headed one of them "Blue Sky," in reference to a recovery which Moreton Bay was then suffering from a monetary collapse. We had our little booms and reactions even then, but it was on a small scale, and only when the "New South" put on the "screw" for a trifle of £20,000 or so that the village of Brisbane owed it. The article headed "Blue Sky" was responded to in the opposition

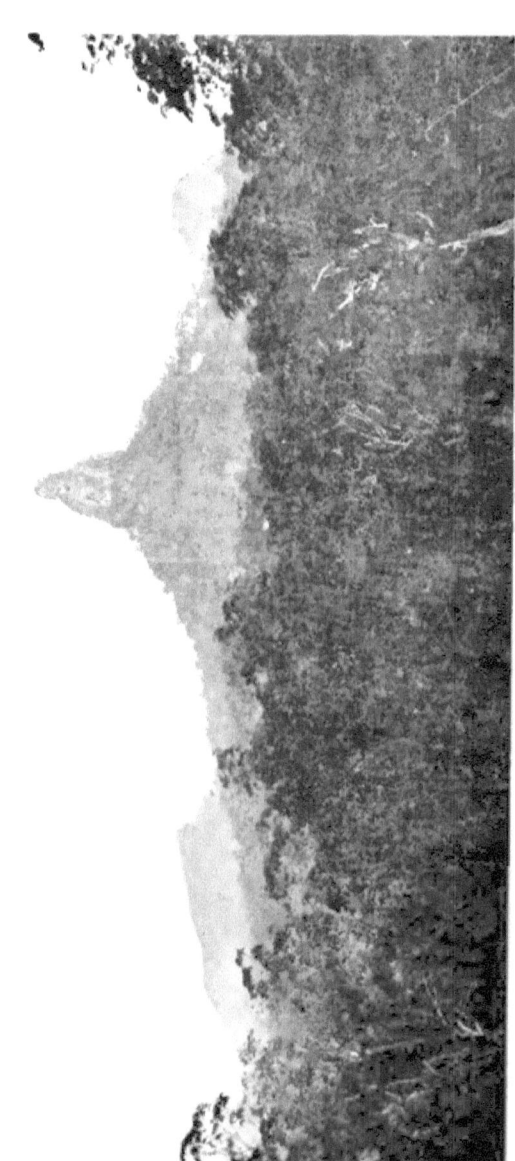

THE GLASSHOUSE MOUNTAINS—NGUNGUN—CROOK NECK—TIBEROOWOCCUM.

paper by one headed "Sky Blue." A very little sufficed in those days to get the "screw" put on. In this case the owner of a waterside property in South Brisbane advertised it for sale, with a footnote that a portion of the purchase money (naming a balance equal to three times the market value of the whole) could remain "on mortgage." This roused the ire and jealousy of a Sydney bank director who owned land near it, and a travelling inspector came down to call in the money due by "those inflated Moreton Bay fellows," and to restore them to a sense of the financial realities of life, and wake them from their silly dreams; and Geoffrey Eagar was the ambassador who came to "fix matters up." The "Blue Sky" was the return of the tide after his departure.

Verily, there is nothing new under the sun! only our creditors were all in Sydney in 1855, in place of being scattered over the world as at present. Thomas Woodward Hill was, perhaps, the last survivor of the old "comps." who wore the black calico apron at the same time that John Fairfax and Samuel Bennett did, in the days when piece work was introduced, and a draughts board was kept under the "frames" to relieve the tedium of the frequent intervals of work in the long ago, when Sir George Gipps was the Imperial Proconsul of Australia.

ON A CORAL ISLE.*

START not! Yawn not! This is *not* going to be any hackneyed, twice-told tale of shipwreck, although there *were* eighty of us on board the "Eudora," barque, bound from Hobart Town, December 18th, 1849, for the new golden land of California, then just annexed from the Mexicans by Uncle Sam. I had but landed from London some two months before, and the gorgeous panorama of Hobart Town, glowing, *a la* Naples, in the sun, backed up by snowy Mount Wellington and the stupendous "organ pipes," and looking like some rich-toned drop-scene at Drury Lane or the Lyceum, had first greeted my eyesight in glorious mid-October, and almost made me cease to regret the Regent-street and Covent Garden, the Lea River and Epping Forest, and the "Ocean" (84 guns), lying, a thing of beauty and of might, as guard-ship two-decker at the limpid anchorage of Sheerness, all of which matters and more, I had left behind me for ever. I had little time, however, for sentiment in those days, and being offered the supercargo's berth on board the "Eudora," laden with "notions" in the shape of timber, shop fronts,

---

* This paper is an old friend in a new dress. The event was treated by Mr. Bartley in his book "Opals and Agates," but, by comparison, the pen picture there depicted is but indifferently drawn. "On a Coral Isle" is certainly one of Mr. Bartley's choicest bits of descriptive writing.—EDITOR.

cottages, jams, potatoes, and onions from thrifty Hobart Town to a market where onions—glorious news!—were a dollar, and "spuds" a "quarter" per lb., I took the office at once when offered, and went in search of fresh scenes and adventures. Cabin, steerage, and crew made up eighty of us, and we sailed, and we sailed, and we sailed, till we made the Snares, the only bit of New Zealand that has hitherto greeted my eyes, and forming the extreme south of the group. We had left Hobart Town short of our full supply of water, intending to call in at the Maori Land and fill up our tanks, for water is good and plentiful at that shop; but there was blowing such a spanking south-wester and fair wind, as we passed, that we resolved not to lose it, but to run on to Tahiti, and there to get the needful *aqua pura*.

But not long after this there arose a tempestuous wind, and, like the Euroclydon, from the north, with just a taste of easting about it, and that too ere we were far from the latitude of Cape "Maria Van Diemen," and so we found we were "in for it." For three weeks in the month of January, 1850, and under a vertical sun, just within the limit of the Southern Tropic, we were on short allowance of water, coming down at last to a pint and a-half per day, served out on the poop daily at 9 a.m. to all hands, fore and aft. I am not a thirsty soul myself, and it troubled me very little; but our doctor, a brother of Eusebius Lloyd, sometime of "Bartholomew's," London, was a man who liked his "pawnee" and he suffered greatly; and some of us, who were able to bear it, used to subscribe a few gills apiece daily to help the "weaker brethren." It was rather melancholy, though, to hear the little babies at night, through the cabin bulkhead, say in their sleep, "Drint of yorter, ma." There came a shower one midnight, and we hung pickle bottles on the mizen belaying-pins and caught some water for the poor doctor's "hot coppers." At last, when but ten inches of fluid remained in the last tank, we sailed into Otaheite's fairy bay. It was a bit of a jump for me, from Regent-street to the land of bread fruit, Captain Cook, and *maitai wahinis*, or beautiful girls, not to say gloriously handsome men too. all in a few months. It was just like stepping into Loddige's nursery at Hackney, or the Palm House at Kew, as far as the temperature and damp, warm feeling went; there was a faint odour of guavas and oranges hanging about everywhere, a pleasant murmur from the coral reefs, and a still fainter hum from the mosquitos; there was the full tropical beauty of India, multiplied by at least three, and with all the *per contra* tiger and cobra business totally eliminated. Otaheite was pronounced a thorough success by all hands, fore and aft. The music of the French men-of-war and military bands was good; the cookery at the hotel was masterly, and they had a way of putting tomatoes, onions, and vinegar together in a frying-pan, in a style that no benighted Britisher *chef* can ever hope to approach. No ! the Frenchman's mission is to cook, and John Bull's department is to eat, ask no questions, and be thankful. But Otaheite has its scenery as well as the handsome men and small-eared women of A.D. 1850. Those last possibly are not there now; but the cascades and the forests of the interior remain for ever. So a party of us set out to explore, and to find the place where the spry little French soldiers had carried ladders unsuspected to the back of the Otaheitean's last central eyrie and fastness in the island, erst impregnable to all Polynesian warfare, invulnerable also to artillery and siege, but not so to ladders, skilfully used by cat-like Zouaves.

We were four in party : Wales, the son of the police magistrate of Morven, Tasmania ; Turner, a surveyor; Tillet, a cotton-broker from Liverpool, and myself. We crossed and recrossed, as we ran it up to its source, a

beautiful pellucid river, eighty feet wide and a yard deep;
we admired the prolific forest, full of wild ginger, sweet
oranges, limes, mammee apples, and noble timber trees of
unknown botanical *genera*; and we came at last to the Pah
Fattawah, the key of the island, 3,600 feet above the sea,
garrisoned by a lieutenant and a hundred men, and full in
view of one of the finest cataracts in the world, made by
the aforesaid river as it leapt, clean and clear, 700 feet over
a straight wide wall of rock, on its way down from the
central peak of the island, which we had no time to explore,
and high over which hovered a solitary tropic bird with its
single long feather tail. The French officer "shouted"
cognac, and told us how they took the island, not without
heavy loss, as the monument of the dead sailors and marines
of "L'Uraine" testifies. That was, I think, the name of
the frigate which bore the brunt of the fray. We got back
to Papieete, admired Hort's store, and the state canoe of
Queen Pomare, 70 feet long, and also her good-looking
young husband. We saw the land breeze cut off and blow
seaward the head of each roller, as old ocean ceased not,
day and night, to assault the guardian reef of enchanted
Tahiti. We bought a cheap hogshead of divine claret, such
as in Sydney not even four sovereigns a dozen would secure;
a claret you could drink out of tea cups and never know
the difference, for it wanted no coddling in this, that, or
the other shaped glass. We hobnobbed with some ancient
elephantiasis-afflicted chiefs, who said they remembered
Captain Cook in their youth. Goodness knows! they looked
old enough and grey enough to have done so, and it was
then only seventy-two years since he had fallen mortally
under the shadow of Mauna Loa, in Owhyhee, further
north. We sailed away from Tahiti; we met the "Herald"
frigate, Captain Kellett, fresh from a fruitless search up
Behring's Straits after Sir John Franklin. We met Ben

Boyd in his yacht, the "Wanderer," with a long brass eighteen amidships, and with a sumptuous cabin and piano, curtains and sofas, and bookshelves, fore and aft of the whole schooner. Ben Boyd of the Royal Bank and Twofold Bay was the man I mean—*the* Ben Boyd of 1843—and we were about the last white people who saw him alive, for he was massacred at the Solomon Islands before he could see Australia again. I climbed the topgallant-yard of the "Eudora" to admire the conical peaks of beautiful Eimeo, sister island to Tahiti, and full of the same sugar-loaf rocks—1,000 feet high, and covered with moss and wild creeping flowers from base to summit—which adorn the road to the Pah Fattawah. Noble-looking young men came off to us in canoes and traded us some wonderful pearl fish-hooks, and we had sailed onward and northward from Otaheite for eight degrees, when at night the "shipmen deemed that we drew nigh to some island," for, strange sight, a very legion of birds, of large size as well as small, loaded every yard and spar on our barque; and where did they come from? was the question asked on all sides. We got out the chart, and found that "Caroline Island, discovered by the English in 1795," was just ahead of us. So solitary, so out of the usual track of all ships, was the isle, that the birds came off to see the unwonted intruders. They all went back before morning, however, and by daylight the island loomed green and right ahead of us, and as we were short of fresh meat, though with plenty of oranges and cocoa-nuts on board, volunteers were asked for to go in the boat and shoot pigs and goats, if any, on this wonderful, lonely, Robinson Crusoe island, that had sent forth its birds to greet us so strangely. Eight of us embarked in the dingy, a square-sterned, sixteen-foot affair, the eight including three of the crew, one of whom was "Rotumah" Tom, and five passengers, viz.:—Mr. Irwin (who had his family on board), Wales, Guthrie, Turner, and myself. We, and our guns, made the boat swim very deep, and well for us was it that the sea was smooth, but we made for the island *con amore*, and a big roller at the edge of the reef caught us fairly on the stern, and sent us flying up the beach. We jumped out, and soon walked the boat up to the water's edge and landed. The shallow water was all coral, and beautiful shells at the bottom; but, on shore, there were no trees except mangroves; no soil, no water, all coral; no animals, but birds *galore* to make up for it all; lovely pure white cranes with crimson ruffs round their throats, birds like small albatrosses, thousands of birds, all so tame and numerous that you could run in among them and they would scarcely rise; and, if they did rise, you could catch one in each hand as easily as with the gnats, on a summer eve, by the brookside, in our buttercup and daisy lanes of Walthamstow and Essex. Their eggs covered the ground like hailstones after a storm, and it was clear that nothing there living had ever seen man's face before.

Well, after a few hours or so of gathering spoils and curiosities, we resolved to go aboard again, and we faced the rollers on a fallen tide, which we found to be a different game from running in before them, especially as ours was not a whaleboat. The island was one of those solitary rings of coral, with a shallow sea lagoon in the centre, and a shallow fringe of water to the edge of the circular reef, which was here red and hard as granite, and went down to the ocean's bed plump all round, perpendicular a thousand fathoms; and when, at low water, the sea receded from the edge of the rock, a fearful gulf yawned between, as the returning thirty-foot breaker came roaring back to cover the dripping, bright, red scarp once more. Imagine, then, our flat-bottomed, deep-laden, square dingy facing *this* "little lot!" At the first essay we broached to, filled, and had

to go back and bale. Some of us now took off clothes and
boots, expecting a swim for life at next attempt. All our
guns, pistols, and powder were thoroughly wet, and I even
lost my hat. At the next essay we nearly got through, but
one of the oars broke, and again the surf beat us back.
Those who had taken off clothes regretted it, for their gar-
ments were all washed away. ·I could not swim a yard and
so did *not* strip, but I sat in the nose of the boat at our
third mad effort to break through a coral surf at low-water
in a deep-laden dingy, a task which was only fitted for a
flying, light, and well-manned whaleboat, properly steered
with the powerful lever of a thirty-foot oar, and that, too,
only at high water; but greenhorns, you know, will face
any danger. Well, at our third attempt we got clear, for a
moment, of the reef, and as we climbed the side of the lofty
roller that was just going to curl over, I looked with horror
at the red coral edge high above us behind, and the green
curler high above us in front. I realised our fearful position,
and the risk of being crushed between the wall of water
and the wall of rock. The tide was falling all this time,
and nature seemed angry at our third dogged rush. Sus-
pense did not last long, however; the wave rose, barely
covered the red bastion, lifted us without our striking the
rock, and turned us over endways, shooting us out, like a
sack of coals, on the top of each other in the water. I fell
on Wales, who was swimming prettily on his back, and kept
me up finely. Mr. Irwin, who had lost almost all his
clothes, here caught his foot in a crevice of the coral, and
was nearly overtaken by the next sea, but extricated himself just in time. The boat righted as she came down, and
bumped a hole in herself on a coral boulder, so there was,
happily, no more chance of our renewing our mad tempta-
tions of Providence. We grasped the dingy's gunwale, let
each sea lift us and float us gradually ashore, and were soon

back at the beach again, where we spread ourselves out, thirty feet apart, so that the people on board the "Eudora," which was now standing close in, might, if they chose, see that we were all safe. My light-rowing experiences on the placid Lea—sacred to crack "rodsters," beguiling fat bream, chub, and barbel under the pollared willows of dear old Broxbourne—had barely prepared me (then still in my "teens") for this heavy boat work amongst coral reefs; but I picked the art up soon, and I saved—by towing a longboat to the scene of disaster—all the sails, stores, and band of a thousand-ton New York and Havre liner, burnt in the Bay of San Francisco not long after. But all this is by the way. At present we are on Caroline Island, and it does not appear by any means clear how we are to get off from it again.

I had read of

> The sweet siesta of a summer's day,
> The tropic afternoon of Tooboonai :

but did not quite realise it here : still it was evident that we must pass the night on shore, at any rate ; our position was unpleasant ; we were very thirsty, having swallowed more than *quant. suff.* of salt water, and yet there was nothing to drink. We longed for the claret-cup of Blackwall and Greenwich, and even the humble ginger-pop of Hobart Town would have been "accepted at sight." But there was nothing for it but to suck raw eggs, which are *not* a thirst-quencher. Rotumah Tom rubbed sticks and lit a fire, and we dug up and roasted a few turtle's eggs, but they sadly wanted washing down. I slept in the boat, and so escaped the polite attentions of the land-crabs, and had only the mosquitos to deal with. Some of us who had lost boots and "breeks" alike, found out that large carnivorous crabs, on the seabeach of a tropical island, experimenting at night on unwonted human flesh, were worse than any fleas ever invented. So passed the darkness away, and in the morning Guthrie and I had an early bathe at day dawn, regardless of a few minor seven-foot sharks who swam near us in the shallow water, flecked with shells of Tyrian purple, pink and all hues, lying at the bottom of its clear pale green. By the way, how I *do* love sea shells! beautiful fresh ones; they never grow old, but are the same to-day on the shores of Sandgate, Manly, or Queenscliff, as they were on the Mediterranean beach in the gilded days of Antony and Cleopatra. I well remember a little gem picture, by Gerard Douw; only three shells on a strip of sand, with a bit of seaweed among them; and yet, what an idyll they seemed to sing about cool briny breezes, of green surges ever roaring out their diapason lullaby, with its soothing sense of drowsy comfort for the nerve-worn pen-toiler, or sick bushman, bidding him cast his care to the winds, and go in for dinner at the Pier Hotel, and try the rock cod and boiled schnapper with oyster sauce, washed down by the Verdeilho and Reisling of Australia, or the Rudesheimer of the Rhine; after which, he might stroll forth once more, seat him on some weedy rock, what time the tide came in; and, as he watched the crabs all "skedaddle" and the *octopus* change its matchless colours, and while he gazed to the bottom of the clear shallow wavelets around him, he might well raise his hat, and ask himself, what great good he had ever done, or evil left undone, that *he* should be so blest in his surroundings, at this most pleasant of all spots, that one where sea and land meet, and "mutually improve" each other. But I am digressing, and must hie me to the island again. Well! after Guthrie and I had bathed, Rotumah and I went to look for water. He dug a hole in a particular part of the sand, and it filled presently with a milky-looking sort of fluid, fresh enough to quench thirst, but still "for a' that" not the kind of drink which an old Indian staff-surgeon, who understood troops and dysentery, would prescribe in anything like quantity. We drank some shellsful of it, and then returned to tell our companions of the discovery, when lo! we found Captain Gourlay, of the "Eudora," had come ashore in the whaleboat with two hands; and he wanted to know why we stopped spreeing on shore all night. We wanted to know why he had brought us nothing to eat, and whilst we were palavering and telling him of our mishaps, we all became suddenly conscious of a group of people, bearing a white flag, approaching us, and just visible on a point of the island where it trended north-east. Here was a discovery; the island inhabited, possibly by enemies, and not an ounce of dry powder in the crowd! But, as I said, *that* was no reason why we should let them know it, so I tied a red kerchief round my head, stuck two horse pistols in my belt, gave my old Sierra Leone rifle to Wales, who had the previous day been "potting" birds at long ranges therewith, and we strode up, eleven in number, to meet "the enemy."

On nearing the group we found it to consist of only three persons, the principal one of whom was a most striking and Robinson-Crusoe-looking personage, burnt a dark coffee colour by the sun; his clothes in tatters, and kept on by pieces of string tied here and there; and with a long beard, and boots in the very last stage of dilapidation. We asked him who he was, and how he got there. He explained that he was an American sailor, named Lewis, and was left on the island by the Tahitian firm of Lewsett and Colley, to make cocoa nut oil for them; they sent a schooner, once a year, for the produce, allowed him 400 dollars per annum for wages, and all his rations and clothes, needles, canvas, &c.; the two men with him, he said, were natives of the Chain Islands, a neighbouring group; and he had, at the other side of the island, a cocoanut plantation on fairly rich soil.

He and his two men had each a girl-wife, from the same group, the youngest and prettiest being, of course, assigned to the old Yankee. He accounted for his weather-worn attire by telling us that the schooner would be due in a month to take away the oil, and bring him his fresh supply of wages, rations, and clothes; he was now "out of everything except tobacco and tea; no biscuit, flour, needles, sugar, canvas, vinegar, &c., on hand. He said the island was a ring of coral (sometimes called an "atoll") with a shallow sea lagoon, just wadeable, in its centre, and that there was, as is usual on all these islands, a smooth water break in the reef where a boat could come in and out, but this was opposite his place and near the cocoanut plantation, and away on the opposite side of the (circular) island to where we now were; it was half a mile "thick" all round, from inner to outer beach. His advice to us was, that the Captain should go back aboard the "Eudora" and take her round to his place, that two sailors should walk the broken and stove boat round by the shallow water on the beach, to the channel, and take advantage of the smooth water passage to tow her out; and that the rest of us should wade with him across the lagoon, on a bee line to his homestead.

We agreed thereto, and set out to wade, in the course of which proceeding we made some discoveries; the bottom was clearly visible, at a depth of from two to four feet, and consisted of the loveliest coral, such as we Brisbanites buy to put under glass cases; brain coral, stags' horns, lettuce coral, &c.; it had a fine cutting edge on some of it, and those of us who were bootless had to watch their footsteps. I had Wellington boots, my only shortcoming being in the hat line, but I was little, if any, better off than the barefooted ones, for the labour of lifting some ten pounds of water, at every step, "totted up" considerably in a five mile wade, and seemed to wrench my legs off. Immense clams laid picturesque at the bottom of the water with their mouths open; a good old sort, about 400 lbs. weight apiece, and equally ready to take off the leg, or the head, of any unwary intruder, between the serrated edges of those bivalve *Tridacnas*.

There are heaps of these fellows on the Queensland Barrier Reef. I have one, myself, of three hundred weight, the "oyster" from which weighed just forty-five pounds, but these are as nothing to the old gentleman (from the "keys" of the West Indies) whose upright shells once guarded, like Gog and Magog, each side of the doorway at an oyster shop in Maiden Lane, Covent Garden. *He* weighed six hundred pounds in his life time, and is, in his turn, surpassed by the king of all the Tridacnas, who holds his court on an island in Torres' Straits, and is estimated at fully half-a-ton, and whom no one has yet ventured to disturb.

But, all this time, we were following Lewis and the two Chain Island "boys" towards the now fast nearing, and particularly welcome, cocoa grove, and just as I thought I could not lift another leg, so terrible was the strain of the few pounds of water, raised at every step, of this weary five miles in the water, and with a sun overhead that made poor Mr. Irwin cry out with the pain of his blistered legs and thighs, just then we emerged from the lagoon and clasped the stems of the cocoa palms; up went Rotumah Tom, and the two Chain Islanders, and down came the green nuts, and "drinks-round" was the one idea.

We "Eudoras" *were* thirsty, none of us, except Tom and myself, having drunk aught but half-a-gallon of sea water each, for nearly thirty-six hours. I don't know how many "cocoas" the others emptied, but I know that seven of them, each with a good tumbler full of milk inside, barely satisfied me, for that long wade had been the most killing job of all for us; and now we strolled over to Lewis' homestead, a comfortable thatched abode, with a square hole of clear fresh water hollowed in the solid coral rock near it, the pool well garnished with wholesome green moss, at the side and top, and looking home-like and normal as a reservoir or tank.

We were next introduced to the three voluptuous looking Chain Island girls, whose eyes and lashes were a "caution." I have never seen black fire, and yet, if fire *could* be black, it would shine through such eyes as these; and, if this should fail to convey the idea of them, then let the reader imagine a clear amber, deepening in darker shade, by succesive degrees, till it threatens to merge at last, in pure black, and arrested just *before* the beautiful brown lustre disappears, and he will have the eyes of these girls before him. The men's optics were scarcely less brilliant, but smaller, and without the female wealth of eyelash.

In other respects these children of the South Pacific were less handsome in feature, and form, than the perfect Greek gods, and fairy-footed goddesses, who were still to be found in Eimeo and Tahiti, in 1850; but, if you come to eyes, why, then I never saw *dark* eyes, at any rate, like those the Chain Island girls had.

How great a pity it is that these nymphs, who are beautiful, and look clever enough to be the mothers of a race of Tennysons and Byrons, should, by their generally libidinous nature, be the easy prey of any low European sailor. But, we were, now that thirst was satisfied, most confoundedly hungry, a matter which caused the untimely death of a small pig, whom I should most willingly have helped to eat, but for the fact of his being cooked on that vile, smoky, Maori, subterranean fashion of hot stones and leaves. Much more palatable, in every way, were some jew and parrot fish, which one of the boys, taking his outrigger canoe to the smooth water channel, hooked and brought in, and for which there was no lack of lard to fry them, in this isle of pumpkins, cocoa palms, and pigs. And now, just as we had finished, there "arrove" the Captain, who had brought the whale-boat through the break in the reef, and eke a consignment of corned beef, bread, rum, &c.

I did not stay to witness the scene, though I heard, subsequently, that old Lewis, overcome by the unwonted rum, "made a night" of it, but Mr. Irwin and I, now that there was a respectable smooth water passage, to be availed of, and a decent whale-boat to go in, responded to the skipper's invitation for volunteers to return to the ship. I had, *pro tem.*, had enough of the island, in brief I was "full" about it. I longed for some more congenial spot, where licensed watermen's boats plied, and where quays and jetties rendered embarkation and debarkation somewhat less of a harlequin and acrobatic style of business, than appeared to be the case in these intertropical paradises of coral and cocoa palms.

Captain Gourlay had told the chief mate to show a lantern at the gaff of the "Eudora," so that, if any of us came off at night, in the whale-boat, we might not miss the ship; so, believing all to be right, we got one of the Chain Island boys to to take a lamp in his outrigger and pilot us through the deep channel, for it was now dark, and there we were, Mr. Irwin and myself, with Captain Gourlay and a couple of hands, out at sea and making for the old barque once more. Poor Irwin groaned sadly as the rolling, and pitching, of the boat made his tender skin sensible of the ravages the sun had made on it, and then, to our disgust, the Captain said he could not see the ship's light, and the other light, carried by the island boy pilot, we had long since left behind us; and so, here we were, out at sea, out of sight of the island and ship as well; in an open boat, at night, and with neither food, nor water, chart nor compass, in the boat.

I began to debate, with myself, if this little difficulty were not worse even than the island itself, and was rapidly coming to the conclusion that we had, so to speak, quitted the frying pan for a tour into the fire, when lo! the skipper "spotted" for a brief second, a light, far away on the horizon, and he, sailor-like, rapidly noting the star, which sailed just above it, in the sky, steered us for that star, and the result was that, after a long pull, we found ourselves right under the beam of the "Eudora," which had just "put about" to stand in for the island again.

The light, we had seen, was Mrs. Guthrie's candle in the starboard stern cabin (mine was the larboard one). She had left the window open, as the night was warm, and but for this fact, it is doubtful if we five in the whale-boat, would ever have seen island or ship again, and our fate, in a bare empty open boat in that lonely ocean, and at that time of year, is not pleasant to speculate upon; for, be it known, that the mate neglected to hang the lantern at the gaff, thoughtless of the lives his disobedience of orders might have cost, and it was only Mrs. Guthrie's sperm candle illuminating a cabin, that lit us across the deep.

I don't know what the Captain said to the mate on the subject, for I seized a rope that hung over the ship's side, pulled myself on deck, took a breakfast cup off a hook in the steward's pantry, filled it at the claret tap in the Tahiti hogshead, and in response to jocose enquiries after my general health, I replied that I should not care to do it all again under five pounds. I slept soundly, away from mosquitos and land crabs *that* night, but it was a long time before Irwin and others were healed of their blisters. Next morning, our boats went ashore and came off to us again, laden with the piled up spoils of the island, in pigs and pumpkins, which were bartered cheap in that market, where they seldom get any customers.

A Marquesan Maiden.

The whole affair made such an impression on me, that when, later in the year, and on the return voyage from California, we sighted the beautiful natural paradise of Norfolk Island, a flowery open park, with pine covered hills, and where, as a great favour—for it was in the days of Price (afterwards of Pentridge) and the convicted of all the convicts—we, being bound to Launceston and offering to carry letters thither, were actually invited to come ashore, when all other ships were warned off the island prison with its garrison of soldiers - then I felt inclined to resist the temptation to view its beauties, and its forests, and its dripstone rocks more closely, and to remember a vow I had made a few months before, about licensed watermen's boats, and duly constituted wharves, and quays, fit for Christians to land on, and to content myself with a glance at the monkey-like eagerness of the longing mute appealing look, which the prisoner crew of the shore boat, which brought Mr. Price on board our ship, cast up at our sailors along the bulwarks, for the convict's *one* solace, tobacco—a look which our Tasmanian tars well interpreted ; and while Price drank a glass of wine, to keep off the sea sickness, in our cabin, they threw figs of Barrett's twist into the huge surf boat rocking alongside, which treasures were caught by the Norfolk Island crew, as starving tigers might catch legs of mutton, and were swiftly hidden away in the blue serge recesses of their shirts, by these scarce human faced wearers of leather caps. Poor creatures! *I* was no smoker, and I reflected how they might have looked long at me before I should have divined what they wanted, and so earnestly asked for, in that indescribable monkey-like look and working of the facial muscles. On the whole I concluded not to land on Norfolk Island, though the rest of us in the " Harriet Rockwell " did ; but I bought a dripstone, and some birds, and paid for them with a little of the gold dust, of which, with doubloons, I brought nearly twenty pounds weight back from the North Pacific, in barter for the Hobart Town "notions," named at the commencement of this true story, which I must now bring to a close with a hope that all readers who may at times, find themselves, like me, " in a tight place," will get the same deliverance that I did.

At any rate, I can recommend the dietary scale of Caroline Island, on the side where *we* landed, as a sovereign specific for plethoric or gouty subjects, whose only complaint is, too much to eat.

INDEX.

A

	PAGE
Adsett, Moses	209
Agars, Thomas	5
Allwood, Rev. R.	2
Appel, George	211
Armitage J. T.	2
Atkins, J. B.	180
Australian Club	3
"Australia Felix"	32
Australia in 1842	1
Australian Newspapers	13
Australia, Proper names of	349

B

Bank of N.S.W.	12, 53, 55, 57
Bank of Australia	12
Banks and Banking (Sydney)	55
Banking Statistics	57
Bank in Brisbane, First	205
Barker, Thomas	16
Barton, William	18
Bartley, N.	256
Baynes, Joseph	211
Beard, Elizabeth	54
Beck and Brown	101, 171, 176, 177, 181-187
Bell, Sir Joshua P.	171, 181, 216
Berry, Alex. (biography)	156
Bigge, Frederick	212, 216
Bingham, Rens	175
Biographies, Sydney	66-165
Blood for Blood	206
Blythe, J. A.	173
Bourne, R.	3, 13
Bowler, Chas. E.	171
Bowen to Thompson, From	197
Bousfield, Pilot	211
Bowen, Sir George	256
Bracker, Fred	171
Bramston, J.	256
Brisbane	240
Brisbane, Early Survey of	243
Brooks, Tom	211
Brooks, William	211
Brown, W. A.	256
Broadhurst, E.	10, 57
Broughton, Mrs. (Dr.)	10
Burne, F. N.	23
Burnett Pioneer, A	205
Bullock Drivers, About	338

C

Cadell, Capt.	31
Campbell, R. & Co.	3
Campbell, John	167
Camperdown, Old	7
Cannan, Dr. K.	256
Cape, Fred	27
Caste Superiority	17
Chambers, Capt.	2
Chadwick's Station	25
Chauvel, Major	173
Chess at Victoria Club	27
Child, W. Knox	5
Christie, Major	57
Clarence, Early Settlers	40
Clyres, Paddy	177
Cook, Capt.	15, 166
Cohen, J. G.	38, 57
Coley, Capt. R. J.	205
Collins, J. R.	211

	PAGE
Compigné, A. W.	211
Convict System, The	17, 18
Condamine, Settlers on	171
Cooper and Holl	3
Cowper, Chas. (biography)	148
Coveny, R. and T.	3
Cox, William (biography)	148
Coxen, Chas.	169, 172, 175
Coxen, H. W.	175, 211
Crisis of 1893	61
Cribb, R.	212, 232
Criminals, Blackfellow	335
Crisis of 1866, The	257
Crowther, John	171, 173, 176
Cunningham, Allan	167
Cricket	351

D

	PAGE
Dacre, Ranalph	2
Daisy, M.	171
Dangar, Henry (biography)	150
Darling Point	15
Darling Downs, Pioneers of	168
Davie, C. F.	263
Dean, W. & Co.	4
Dennis, Henry	168
Deuchar, John	171
Dick, Alec.	27
Dinners at Tooths'	17
Dobie, Discoveries of Dr.	41
Dockrill, W.	182
Domain, The	14
Donaldson, Stuart	15
Douglas, Robert	212, 223, 256
Dowse, Tom	263
Dowling, Judge	13
Dulacca Country	173
Droughts	274
Drought of 1866	183
Dye, Tilmouth J.	17

E

	PAGE
Egan, Dan	27
Eldridge, Ambrose	3
Elsworth, E. S.	256
Emma, The Brig	2
Ewar, J. G.	172
Expedition, A Run Hunting	189

F

	PAGE
Ferritter, John	172, 211
Fitzgerald, Bob	57
Flemming, Joseph	173
Flinders	166, 275
Floods in the Brisbane	270
Foss and Lloyd	5
Forster, W. (biography)	70
Forbes, Sir Francis (biography)	121
Forbes, F. A.	181
Fox, H. P.	229
Frith and Payten	4

G

	PAGE
Gammie, John	171, 185
"Gazette," Sydney	13
Gill, R.	211
Glennie, Canon	211
Gilchrist, John	16
Goggs, Matthew	171
Gold Discovery (N.S.W.)	60
Gordon, W. P.	175
Gorman, Major	201
Gorry, C.	211
Gray, Walter	3, 179

H

	PAGE
Haly, C. R. and W. D. G.	54, 211
Harrison, Capt. George	16
Handcock, W.	181
Hardgrave, John	211
Harris, George	212, 230
Harvey, Capt. W. W.	10
Hay, Sir John (biography)	133
Hebblewhite, George	5
Hely, Hovenden	57

INDEX.

	PAGE
Herbert, R. G. W.	256
Hodgson, A.	168, 211
Hodgson, Cecil	168
Hobbs, Dr.	205, 263
Holt, W. Harvey	205
Hook, James	176
Hovell, W. H. (biography)	133
Howe, Sir J. E.	9
Hughes, H.	168, 171
Hunt, R. A.	57
Hunter River Coy.	2
Hunter River S. N. Coy.	17

I

Inflation, First Australian	1
Iredale, Launcelot	54
Isaac, F.	168, 171
Islands, The	278-302

J

Jackson, J. W.	256
Jenkins, R. L. (biography)	144
Johnston, Capt. Robt. (biography)	102
Jolly, W.	27
Jones, David	3
" " (biography)	155
Jones, Richard	12, 57
Jordan, Henry	233
Jovial Evenings	244

K

Kemp and Fairfax	7
Kendall, Henry, Memorial Lines to	305
Kent Brewery	17, 20
Kingsford, R. A.	211
King and Sibley	168
Kite, Tom	54
Knowles, A. L.	205
Knull, E.	38, 57

L

	PAGE
Labour, Dearth of	178
Lachlan, Pioneers on the	22-32
Lade, Thomas	231
Laidley, James	13
Lang, Dr. (biography)	136
Lang, Gideon	177, 181, 185
Law Courts, Sydney, 1842	4
Leckie, John	211
Legislative Council, 1842	4
Lee, Ted	27
Leslie, Patrick	167, 202
Leslies, The	169
Leslie, Walter	201
Lester, L. E.	172
Lilley, Sir Chas.	211
Little, John	211, 256
Little, Robert	211, 256
Limestone Old	213
Lord, Simeon	224
Love, On	346
Lyons, Samuel	5

M

Macadam, George	170
Mackay, Discovery of	322
Mackay, Capt. John	322
Mackay, Old	328
Mackenzie, R. R.	13, 15, 171, 208
Macgregor, S.	32, 168
Macquaries' Chair	14
Macleays, The	16
McLean, J. D.	16, 176, 181
Macquarie, Govr. (biography)	66
McIntyre, Settlers on	171
McConnell, D. C.	202
McDougall, J. F.	211, 256
McCabe's Hotel	249
Mallard, Capt.	171
Manning, Sir William	16
Mann, Father	57
Mansfield, Rev. Ralph	2, 13, 57
Martin, Sir James (biography)	97

	PAGE
May, A. A.	256
Melbourne, Recollections of	34–39
Melhado, D.	27
Merchants, Early Sydney	3
Metcalf, J. B.	2
Miles, William	177, 182
Millar, John	177
Ministries, N.S.W.	66, 165
Mitchell, Sir T. L.	8, 13, 167, 201
Mitchell, J. S.	226
Miracles, On	347
Moffatt, T. de Lacy	171, 184
Monitor, The	13
Morehead, B. A. A.	54
Moreton Bay in 1840	201
Morey, E.	32, 212
Mort, Thomas S.	13, 15, 54
,, ,, (biography)	107
Mort, Henry... 13 (biography)	163
Munce, W. J.	230
Murray, Navigation of the	29
Murray, Sir T. A. (biography)	95
Murray-Prior, T. L.	208, 212, 216
Murrumbidgee, Pioneers on	22–32
Murphy, Peter	169
Myall Creek Settlement	171

N

Nelson, Dr.	182
New England, Settlement of	41–47
New England, First Settlers	43
Norris, Edwin	221

O

Ocean Travelling in the Fifties	253
O'Connell, Sir Maurice	8
O'Connell, Capt. Bligh	13
Old Hands of '42, Brisbane	211
Oliver, R.	211
O'Sullivan, P.	211
Overlanding	22
Overlanding Exploits	189

P

	PAGE
Palmer, Sir A. H.	212
Parramatta, The Old	340
Paterson, James	17
Pettigrew, John	182
Petrie John	210
Petrie, Walter	211
Peterson, Daniel	249
Phelps, J. L.	25, 29, 30
Phelan, R. F.	227
Picking, W.	256
Pike and Preston	3
Pinnock, P.	211
Pockley, Capt.	2
Pollett and Cardew	211
Pott's Point	16
Prince, Henry	16
Prout, Cornelius	5
Purkiss and Lambert	4
Pye and Co., James	3

Q

Queensland, Early Days of	166
Queensland	276
Queensland North, Legends of	188
Queensland Club	255
Queensland, Pastoral Occupation of	166
Queensland, Sugar Industry of	248
Queensland, Yellowstone of	313

R

Raff, A.	211
Raine, Capt. Thomas	10
Rawlins, W.	256
Remedy for Financial Trouble	64
Reeve, H. M.	211
Richardson, W.	205
Riding, Thorpe	209
Richardson & Wrench	4
Robins, George	5
Robertson, R. B. C.	54

INDEX.

	PAGE		PAGE
Robertson's, Sir John, Act	52	Sugar Industry (Queensland)	248
,, (biography)	128	Suttor, George (biography)	113
Roberts, D. F.	256	Swinnerton, George	54
Rogers, Richard	3	Sydney in 1838	15
Roley, R. M.	57	Sydney Men and Matters	
Roll-Call, The (Queensland)	211		1, 16, 66 165
Roma, Founding of	181	Sydney, Scenes of Olden	53-66
Ross, Donald	182	Sydney Streets and Suburbs	19
Run Hunting Expedition	191	Sydney Morning Herald	7, 13
Russell, H. S.	211	Squatter, The Australian	246
Ruther, J. Y.	54	Squatter, First on the Brisbane	346

S

Salwey, H.	54
Sands, John	3
Sandeman, Gordon	211
Sandgate, Early	262
Scongall, R.	168
Scott, John	212
Scott, W. R.	54, 228
Sellheim, P.	212
Settlers, Brisbane and Burnett	211
Sexes, The	343
Simmonds, Isaac	2
Smith, John	54
Smith, Shepherd	256
Smith, "Red"	211
Smythes, S. H.	16
Sneyd, Constable	244
Southerden, E. B.	211
Southerden, W.	211
South Brisbane in 1854	249
Sproule, Capt.	2
Stephens, F. B.	57
Stephens, T. B.	236
Stuart, Capt.	32
St. Stephen's Church (Sydney)	8
St. John's ,, ,,	13
St. Phillip's ,, ,,	13
Steam, Brisbane to Sydney	244
Sugar Growing in N.S.W.	47-53

T

Tait, John	254
Taylor, James	168, 171, 176
Tillman, W.	211
Thorn, George	212
Thornton, W.	256
Thornton, G.	27
Thomson, E. Deas 57 (biography)	77
Thompson A.	27
Thompson, Joseph	3
Threlkeld, L. E.	3
Tooth, R. and E.	3, 16, 54
Towns, Robt. (biography)	105
Traders, Early N.Z. and Islands	2
Trundle, C. J.	211
Tucker, William	2
Turner, J. S.	211
Turtling on the Barrier Reef	306
Tyson Bros.	33

U

Uthar, Reuben	54

V

Vigers, P. D.	246
Vignolles, Capt.	171
Vowles, W	211

W

	PAGE
Warner, James	212, 222
Warry, R. S.	229
Weather, The	272
Weir, Settlers on the	171
Wentworth, W. C.	54
,, ,, (biography)	79
Weinholt, A.	211
Western Notable, A.	174
White, W. D.	259
White, James (biography)	153
Winship, Taylor	212, 225
Wight, Rev. G.	
Wickham, Capt.	
Wilkie, P. J.	
Wilkin, Robt.	
Woolley, T. and M.	

Y

Yaldwyn, A. H.
Yarnton, G. S.
Young, William

www.ingramcontent.com/pod-product-compliance
Lightning Source LLC
Chambersburg PA
CBHW051854300426
44117CB00006B/389